Not of th

Not of the Living Dead

*The Non-Zombie Films
of George A. Romero*

Noah Simon Jampol,
Cain Miller,
Leah Richards *and*
John R. Ziegler

McFarland & Company, Inc., Publishers
Jefferson, North Carolina

This book has undergone peer review.

ISBN (print) 978-1-4766-8568-7
ISBN (ebook) 978-1-4766-4835-4

Library of Congress and British Library
Cataloguing data are available

Library of Congress Control Number 2022059064

Front cover image: director George A. Romero
during production of *Knightriders*, 1981 (Photofest)

Printed in the United States of America

*McFarland & Company, Inc., Publishers
Box 611, Jefferson, North Carolina 28640
www.mcfarlandpub.com*

Acknowledgments

The authors collectively would like to extend their thanks to the chairs, panelists and audiences in the Mid-Atlantic Popular and American Culture Association's Horror Studies area who responded to early versions of some of the chapters in this volume, as well as the anonymous readers of this manuscript, all of whom shaped its direction and details in valuable ways.

Leah and John would like to thank Renfield, Trey, Benny and Fionna for their invaluable additions to the manuscript, generated by walking and/or sleeping on their humans' keyboards, and the COVID-19 pandemic for the unbroken 16 months at those computers.

Noah would like to thank Helen and, to a lesser extent, Mabel Phillips for their unwavering support throughout this process.

Table of Contents

ACKNOWLEDGMENTS   v

PREFACE   1

INTRODUCTION   5

1. "Isn't that cheating?": Extradiegetic Narrative Control
   in *There's Always Vanilla*
   LEAH RICHARDS   17

2. "You've really got to get with it, Mrs. Mitchell":
   Freud, Friedan and *Jack's Wife*
   LEAH RICHARDS   30

3. *L'Univers Concentrationnaire* of *The Crazies*
   NOAH SIMON JAMPOL   47

4. Draining the Blood of the Patriarch: Challenging
   Hegemonic Masculinity in *Martin*
   CAIN MILLER   58

5. The King Is Dead; Long Live the King: Capitalism
   and Nostalgia in *Knightriders*
   LEAH RICHARDS   74

6. *Creepshow* and Patriarchal Horror(s)
   JOHN R. ZIEGLER   87

7. Race and Murder in *Creepshow 2*
   JOHN R. ZIEGLER   111

8. "The Monkey Ruled the Man": Phallocentrism,
   Able-Bodiedness and AIDS Anxieties in *Monkey Shines*
   CAIN MILLER   132

9. Animating Politics, Reanimating Genres in "Cat from Hell" and "The Facts in the Case of Mr. Valdemar"
NOAH SIMON JAMPOL *and* JOHN R. ZIEGLER   148

10. Queer Reproduction and the Family in *The Dark Half*
JOHN R. ZIEGLER   170

11. "The New (White) Face of Terror": White Male Victimization in *Bruiser*
CAIN MILLER   186

Conclusion: From Amusement *to* Evil   203

Chapter Notes   215

Works Cited   231

Index   241

Preface

For many, the name George A. Romero immediately conjures a man teasing his sister in a cemetery ("They're coming to get you, Barbara!") or images of zombies wandering the halls of a shopping mall. The legacy and continued influence of his zombie films cannot be denied; for example, *Dead Rising 4*, the latest in Capcom and Capcom Vancouver's zombie-in-a-mall video game series, debuted in 2016, close to 40 years after the film whose central conceit it replicates. However, what Tony Williams describes as "the critical nature" of Romero's "achievements in American cinema" is far from limited to movies involving the creatures (which the filmmaker originally termed *ghouls*) against which modern incarnations of the zombie are measured (*Cinema* 19). Of the 19 released films in which Romero had a part as either a writer or director, only the seven that comprise the *Dead* series can unhesitatingly be called zombie films, and one of those is a remake of the original *Night of the Living Dead*.[1] This book examines the other 12, beginning with 1971's *There's Always Vanilla* and extending through 2000's *Bruiser*, along with a brief consideration of the short work *The Amusement Park*, produced in the early 1970s for a chapter of the Lutheran Society, and the never-produced script for *Resident Evil*.[2]

This is not to say that the undead make no appearance in the films addressed in this volume. The rotting father who emerges from the grave in *Creepshow* provides one obvious example, but he is not entirely a zombie as defined by Romero's own *Dead* series, belonging instead to the variety of walking corpses inhabiting 1950s comics, whose "quintessential drive and function ... is vengeance" (Hand 216). These undead, which preceded Romero's landmark spin on zombies and which some scholars have identified as providing points of inspiration for movies such as *Jack's Wife* (T. Williams, *Cinema* 18–19), can be linked, according to Richard J. Hand, to a wider tradition including European folk tales, Greek tragedy and early modern English drama (216). In the same

1

way, Romero's non-zombie films remold or repurpose not only various revenants and other monsters but everything from Arthurian legend and Renaissance Faire culture to a murderous helper monkey as cinematic tools to critically engage with wider social, cultural, political and representational questions.

This co-authored volume evolved from a linked set of papers written for the 2019 Mid–Atlantic Popular and American Culture Association conference in Pittsburgh. The impetus for the papers was the recognition that Romero's zombie films, particularly the first three *Dead* films—and, to a lesser degree, *Land of the Dead*, with its racially inflected proletarian uprising—continue to receive most of the critical attention directed to his work, as well as the existence of relatively few book-length studies of Romero's oeuvre. Tom Fallows' *George A. Romero's Independent Cinema*, published as this volume neared completion, represents and points to some of the new directions that studies of Romero's work might take. Fallows explicitly positions his study as a corrective to "text-centric readings" and "the classical auteur model" in order to take into account the "industrial conditions" that are inseparable from filmmaking (*George* 11). While acknowledging the clear value of this media industry studies lens, we suggest that there is also value in a text-centered scholarly reexamination of Romero's body of work outside of the zombie genre that pays close attention to his nearly forgotten films, such as *There's Always Vanilla*, alongside his more commonly explored works, such as *Martin*. This study covers films that Romero wrote, directed or both. (Thus, for example, we include a chapter on *Creepshow 2*, for which Romero only wrote the script.) But it does not discuss portions of anthology films for which he did neither. (Thus, for example, it does not include discussion of Dario Argento's half of *Two Evil Eyes*, although the two stories could certainly be analyzed as a whole.) It also does not extend to Romero's work in television, print or other media, or his on-screen appearances, although all of these are themselves worthy of study.

This volume considers the movies in question from the perspective of current scholarly conversations in film, horror and pop culture studies, among other approaches. Analyzing these texts in a long-form study allows us to probe how Romero modulated repeated motifs and concerns across his career as a writer-director. Through the juxtaposition of variously focused readings of individual films or film segments, patterns emerge that demonstrate repeated engagement with issues of capitalism, gender and race, among others. The result is a body of work that performs a sustained intersectional critique of American culture and society.

Romero's interrogation of capitalism and consumerism is well-known to anyone with even a passing familiarity with those mall zombies, and these concerns intersect with his repeated use of Pittsburgh, "an example of post-capitalist decline in American society" (T. Williams, *Cinema* 11), as a shooting location and his primarily, though not exclusively, working as an indie filmmaker who owed more to the "radical potentials" and "promised revitalisation" of Hollywood film in the 1960s and 1970s than to a mainstream industry that instead "deteriorated into a complicit alliance of corporate conglomerates" (4). Considerations of gender, familial, sexual, reproductive and racial constructs—all present from early in Romero's career (despite his famous denials of any intentional subtext about race relations in *Night of the Living Dead*)—and even posthumanism often work in tandem with those related to capitalism, as well as with one another (and with the *Dead* films), in producing Romero's cinema of critique. The chapters herein also touch on the ways that Romero employs or reacts against elements not only of the horror genre but also genres such as the Western and the mainstream action movie. The variously focused chapters produce an overall picture with particular points of emphasis, which necessarily leaves room for future research, but we hope that the interplay among them enriches that picture as a whole in a way that is useful for scholars and students who are already familiar with the range of Romero's work as well as for those zombie scholars and fans who are about to press PLAY on something called *Jack's Wife* for the first time.

Finally, and coming, in a way, full circle, while zombies continue to be ubiquitous, perhaps returning to Romero's non-zombie films can disrupt some of the more rote aspects of our consumption of the genre, and maybe even of Romero's zombie films themselves.

Introduction

George A. Romero's influential career as a writer-director spanned just over four decades in the film and television industries. He is most widely known for his genre-redefining 1968 film *Night of the Living Dead*, in which he mixed influences including existing representations of the zombie rooted in Caribbean mythologies and Richard Matheson's 1954 novel *I Am Legend* to create the "ghouls" that would revolutionize the zombie film. Owing to this pervasive influence, Romero's zombie films, particularly the initial trilogy comprising *Night* and its sequels *Dawn of the Dead* (1978) and *Day of the Dead* (1985), have attracted the decisive majority of scholarly attention. In one example of such attention, Tony Williams enthused, "*Night of the Living Dead* is one of American cinema's most important cultural achievements" (*Hearths* 137).[1] Asked about his place in film history in a 1992 interview, Romero responded: "I'll be in the chapter about Earl Owensby and John Waters, if there is ever a definitive Britannica on this. At least I've earned that much. [*Pauses*] I hope that someday one of my other films may buy me another inch of space in that book, and it doesn't just continue to remain to be for *Night of the Living Dead*" (Wiater 119). Indeed, while Romero films such as "Cat from Hell" and *The Dark Half* may not figure among "American cinema's most important cultural achievements," that does not render them undeserving of scholarly attention—in some cases renewed, and in other cases for almost the first time.

The explosion of scholarly interest in zombies has meant that Romero's zombie films, even the later, less iconic ones, have continued to garner sustained scholarly engagement. This has not been the case with Romero's non-zombie films, even with a film like *Knightriders*, which was the object of academic analysis—much of it focused on the film's Arthurian elements—closer to the time of its release. Films such as *There's Always Vanilla* and *Creepshow 2*, meanwhile, received little analysis in the first place. The present volume, although it may not

5

be "a definitive Britannica," aims nonetheless to go some way towards redressing this neglect.

The films with which Romero was involved throughout his career as a writer and/or director provide a rich body of cinematic texts for thinking about, for example, capitalism, gender (including or in relation to masculinity, patriarchy, family, sexuality and reproduction), race, spectatorship, the body and non- and posthuman Others. Stacey Abbott, writing of the indie vampire film *Nadja*, observed, "[T]he choice to make independent rather than mainstream films enabled the filmmakers to undermine the established conventions of the genre" ("Taking" loc. 810),[2] and Romero enjoyed that privilege as well. Tom Fallows—while also noting the way in which the positioning of Romero as an *auteur*, to which critics and public engagement contributed, obscures collaborative work in his filmmaking career—highlights the attempts with which Romero was involved "to cultivate real-world alternatives to the mainstream industry" as "exciting transgressions in and of themselves" ("Independent" 53–54, 48).

Romero's remaining an independent filmmaker may not have been entirely by choice. While he may have been telling interviewers as early as 1972 that "Hollywood is dead" ("but," he added, "the distributor ain't!") and complaining "[Y]ou cannot get the most basic filmic understanding from any one commercial distributor" (Bloc 15), 1993's *The Dark Half* represents an abortive move into mainstream filmmaking. Whatever his intentions at any given point in his career, however, Romero's indie status allowed him the same freedom that Abbott describes to revise, subvert and reimagine genre conventions in concert with the freedom to turn at least some of those conventions, in whatever form, towards ethical engagement with the social, political and ideological contexts of their time.[3]

Romero defended the ability of genre film to address what one interviewer termed "serious concerns": "We have to speak in terms that are recognizable and understandable. And I don't think that it has to be realistic or contemporary in order to do that" (Hanner and Kloman 100). Regarding horror specifically, he argued, "It's much harder to take a parable and squeeze it into a real-life story. Whereas with supernatural material, you can make anything happen so as to fit the notion that you want to fit between the lines. You can go back and forth between the text and subtext much more freely! It's a bonus in this genre, which I rather freely have done over the years" (Wiater 115). According to Romero, "those supernatural monsters that are part of our literary tradition are, in essence, expurgations of ourselves. They are beasts we've created in order to exorcise the monster from within us." Since we all have the potential for evil and guilt-bearing moments of dissatisfaction with our own behavior, "We can then punish ourselves by punishing the monster, allowing our good side to prevail" (Seligson 78–79). In part resulting from such subtexts, the richness of Romero's corpus of non-zombie films invites multifarious critical examination. We will turn now to a brief discussion of some of this volume's major areas of analysis.

Focal Points

The varied approaches of the chapters in this book echo the varied concerns and the polyvocality both of any given individual film (a text produced by numerous contributors) and of these films considered as a whole. Nonetheless, certain areas of analysis recur, and we highlight these here. We often do so in the context of the horror or Gothic genres, since the majority of the works discussed herein contain elements of these genres if they don't conform to them entirely, with *There's Always Vanilla* and *Knightriders* being the only real outliers in this regard.

One of the most discussed aspects of *Dawn of the Dead*, and perhaps one of the reasons that *Dawn of the Dead* is so often discussed, is its use of zombies to "represent, on the metaphorical level, the whole dead weight of patriarchal consumer capitalism, from whose habits of behavior and desire not even Zen Buddhists and nuns are exempt" (Wood, "Apocalypse" 167). Variations on this vision of capitalism consistently appear, albeit not as apocalyptically, in Romero's non-zombie films as well. The destructive functioning of capitalism and its manifestation in socioeconomic class come under scrutiny in, for instance, the obvious greed and excessive wealth of *Creepshow*'s Upson Pratt and "Cat from Hell"'s Drogan, ruthless business owners who get their comeuppance, as well as the title character in "The Facts in the Case of Mr. Valdemar," who is murdered for the wealth of which he is jealous. The murderous men of *Creepshow*'s "Father's Day" and "Something to Tide You Over" are linked to wealth as well, while the same film's Jordy Verrill suffers from a sympathetic poverty, similar to the small business owners in *Creepshow 2*'s opening segment and *Martin*'s title character, and the traveling band of performers in *Knightriders* attempts (unsuccessfully but with the respective film's sympathy) to carve out an alternative, non-commercial way of living. More subtle but nevertheless significant are the bourgeois ennui of Joan in *Jack's Wife*, the bourgeois fears of Annie in *Creepshow 2*'s "The Hitch-hiker," and the bourgeois male rage of *Bruiser*'s Henry Creedlow. Perhaps one reason for this recurrence in films that are largely horror or horror-adjacent is the unsettling nature of capitalism itself. In defining the eerie, Mark Fisher writes that it

> is fundamentally tied up with questions of agency. What kind of agent is acting here? Is there an agent at all? These questions can be posed in a psychoanalytic register—but they also apply to the forces governing capitalist society. Capital is at every level an eerie entity: Conjured out of nothing, capital nevertheless exerts more influence than any allegedly substantial entity [11; see also 64].

This invisible, diffuse, hegemonic force, a force whose characteristics have affinities with the supernatural, pervades Romero's non-zombie films. Sometimes this force manifests explicitly, through direct, observable negative effects or the association of capitalist ideology with villainous or unethical characters, and sometimes it takes the less explicit form of a framework, primarily or entirely implied or assumed, within which or against which characters react. (In this last case, in addition to characters such as Joan and Annie, we might think of the class- and commercialism-related inflections of Thad Beaumont's discomfort with his artistic and domestic lives in *The Dark Half.*) Capitalism is also intimately linked to and dependent upon forms of identity-based oppression. It is, "as a social-economic system, ... necessarily committed to racism and sexism" (Federici, *Caliban* 30), issues that also recur in Romero's work. This commitment obtains because "capitalism must justify and mystify the contradictions built into its social relations—the promise of freedom vs. the reality of widespread coercion, and the promise of prosperity vs. the reality of widespread penury—by denigrating the 'nature' of those it exploits" (30). This dynamic too recurs in the body of films under consideration here, with wives, often housewives, whose relationships are defined by their husbands' wealth, sometimes with violent results, and non-white characters who are defined by their lack of wealth or who occupy service positions.

Apart from its intersections with capitalism (and race), gender normativity forms its own nexus of concerns throughout Romero's work. These concerns encompass issues not only of gender roles and expectations for women but also for men, including constructions of masculinity, as well as (and relatedly) anxieties around family, reproduction and the body. Most, if not all, of these issues involve hierarchy (including hierarchies generated and reinforced by capitalism), and most, if not all, of these hierarchies arguably derive from patriarchy (including the traditional patriarchal family). As a means to avoid loss and accrue status, "[t]he sacrifice of love is the thumbprint of patriarchy. It clears the way for establishing and maintaining hierarchy. Patriarchy is an order of living that privileges some men over other men (straight over gay, rich over poor, white over black, fathers over sons...) and all men over women" (Gilligan and Snider 33). In the films discussed here, such privilege is embodied in a range of domineering (white) fathers and husbands, although single (white) men such as Joan's condescending lover Gregg in *Jack's Wife* and Thad Beaumont's hyper-masculine alter ego George Stark in *The Dark Half* manifest it as well. As these films repeatedly reflect, "[t]he politics of patriarchy is the politics of domination—a politics that rationalizes inequality and turns a blind eye to what from a democratic vantage-point looks like oppression" (33). Chris, the would-be bohemian protagonist of the relationship drama *There's Always Vanilla*, is pushed inexorably into conformity with traditional capitalist heteronormativity; and the *faux*-medieval social organization of the traveling troupe of motorcycle jousters in Romero's dramatic tragedy *Knightriders* obviously raises questions around gender roles.

The rest of the films examined here, again, fall into or employ elements of the horror genre; Barry Keith Grant underscores "the genre's marked emphasis on gender" and includes *Jack's Wife* in a list of examples in which "the politics of sexual difference is immediately signaled as an issue by the title" (1, 2). He also observes the tendency of horror to displace "the possibility of male inadequacy" onto the female Other (3). We might think here of emasculating wife Billie in *Creepshow*'s "The Crate" or even female monkey Ella in *Monkey Shines*, though of course Romero's films displace anxieties of male inadequacy onto threatening non-female figures as well. Grant finds that "gender is central to the horror film in large part because it inevitably involves other ideological issues as well" (11).

A final such issue to point to here is queerness. Queerness emerges in these films in a range of forms (a range that mirrors its elastic usage by scholars), from, for instance, a literal expression of sexuality between two characters, such as Pippin and Punch in *Knightriders*, to an anti-normative enactment of gendered roles, behaviors and practices, such as Aunt Bedelia acting as the patriarch of the Grantham family in "Father's Day" or Thad symbolically giving birth to George in *The Dark Half*.

In thinking about gender's role in horror, Grant writes that "the experience of horror in the cinema is almost always grounded in the visual representation of bodily difference" (6). Horror's reliance on observable physical difference extends beyond gender to walking corpses (e.g., Ernest Valdemar and Robert Hoffman in "Valdemar"; several characters in *Creepshow*). The corpse, according to Julia Kristeva, "is the utmost of abjection. It is death infecting life" (97). An animated corpse then (and zombies are of course included in this category as well) troubles the boundaries between life and death that much more. The horrific representation of bodily difference extends as well to non-human Others (e.g., the Others in "Valdemar"; the avenging cat in "Cat from Hell," who is also a variation of the undead; the monster in "The Crate"; Ella in *Monkey Shines*). *Bruiser*'s Henry, meanwhile, with his face metamorphosed into a blank mask, might be seen as in the tradition of the freak, a socially marginalized person whose visible ambiguity elicits "simultaneous horror and fascination" by defying our fundamental, binary "modes of self-definition" (Grosz 274). Disability too falls into this category of representations. In representing disability, horror films often continue the long tradition of "convey[ing] spiritual or moral weakness through physical difference," which has persisted in the arts for centuries (Sutton 76). The unethical, wheelchair-bound Drogan in "Cat from Hell" certainly follows this convention.[4] Allan, who becomes a quadriplegic in *Monkey Shines*, "presents a more thoughtful and complicated take on issues of ability" in his complexity, "inner conflicts" and "emotional range" (80).

Travis Sutton argues that horror films also link disability and sexuality, working "to reinscribe (or much more rarely critique) the allegedly heteronormative and able-bodied nature of human beings and human cultures" (80). "Compulsory heterosexuality and compulsory able-bodiedness work in tandem," meaning that the disabled body is commonly conceived as non-sexual, with the result that expressions of sexuality by disabled bodies are "generally marginalized as perhaps curious or gratuitous but most certainly unusual/queer" (76). Sutton views Allan's sex scene with scientist Melanie as a "rare" exception to this marginalization (80).[5] Although this is true, it is also true that Ella's jealousy of human women *vis-à-vis* Allan suggests a love triangle with "unusual" implications.

A less prominent category of bodily difference in the films examined in this book is race in the figure of the non-white Other (as opposed to a default whiteness that goes uncommented upon). Annalee Newitz writes, "White people are the closest thing the United States has to a colonizing group" (258). As one effect of this hierarchy, horror has offered in its treatment of black characters "plenty of lessons ... about stereotypes and oppressions" but also plenty about "subversion" and "resistance," an observation that one can extend to other groups viewed as non-white groups (Coleman 215). In some modern horror films, Newitz argues, "The oppressed remain monstrous" but are presented as more sympathetic than their human opponents (Newitz 261); and this claim certainly applies to the monstrous indigenous and black characters in *Creepshow 2*. Using *Night of the Living Dead* as one example, she also elucidates the impact of class position on how we evaluate black heroes and monsters in horror (258–63). This intersection also applies to *Creepshow 2*'s indigenous and black monsters; the latter suffers from a lack of resources and the former avenges theft from his impoverished community. In *Bruiser*, while Henry's housekeeper is not a monster as such, the white protagonist feels justified in killing this working-class Latinx woman for theft.

Bodies and their perceived differences also provide points of projection and identification for spectators. Additionally, various potential spectatorial identifications intersect with other categories of difference. What are the implications, for instance, of seeing an invitation in *Bruiser* for the viewer to identify with the middle-class white male protagonist? Can we interpret the viewer's "consumption" of a film and its characters as compounding critiques of how capitalism defines relationships and the relationship of that process to violence, such as in "The Hitch-hiker," "Valdemar," or *Knightriders*? Romero's films also sometimes present figures of fans, such as George Stark fan Fred Clawson in *The Dark Half* and horror comic fan Billy in *Creepshow*—the latter a much more appealing point of identification for spectators than the former—as vehicles not only for identification but also for metacommentary on the creation and consumption of horrific texts.

What Lies Ahead

This book's individual chapters employ a range of critical lenses through which they offer different emphases; taken together, they trace the recurrence of many of the themes and concerns outlined above throughout Romero's non-zombie films. They proceed for the most part through the films considered in chronological order. The exceptions are only "Cat from Hell" and "The Facts in the Case of Mr. Valdemar," which are segments in multi-director films, and deferring until the conclusion a brief discussion of the PSA–*cum*–short film *The Amusement Park* and the first draft of Romero's rejected *Resident Evil* script.

Chapter 1 investigates the means by which masculine control over female-centered narratives is exerted in *There's Always Vanilla*. Protagonist Chris' direct-to-camera commentary both accords him a privileged position of hindsight about his relationship with Lynn and resonates with the twin figurative and literal male gazes—those of the camera and a leering creative, respectively—on the set of a beer commercial in which she appears. Chris, his father and Lynn's (male) director attempt to control the story and the women within it, but Romero's

script and camera are objective rather than objectifying, undermin-
ing both the camera's male gaze and male fantasies of control over
women and their own narratives. Chapter 2 focuses on women's agency
as well, examining *Jack's Wife* (also titled *Hungry Wives* and *Season of
the Witch*) as a critique of the patriarchy and the suburbs that feed it,
a representation of the nightmares of being a housewife in 1970s suburban America that ends on a note that encompasses both the patriarchy's nightmare view of women with agency and a female fantasy of that
agency. Bored suburban housewife Joan dreams in Freudian and eventually begins to cast spells and seduce men, and the film ends with a
confident and independent Joan identifying herself as a witch even as
another woman, speaking from off-camera, identifies her as "You know,
Jack's wife." This chapter argues that Joan—who has resolved Betty Friedan's "problem that has no name," exacerbated by Catholicism and bad
psychotherapy, with matriarchy and witchcraft—has gotten away with
murder, and as a response to the patriarchy as represented by the movie,
that is a triumph.

The third chapter shifts its focus from gender to post–Holocaust
ontology, focusing on how, within the universe of *The Crazies*, the
clear categories of them and us, them vs. us, and infected and uninfected inherent to Romero's *Dead* oeuvre are blurred, and the ability
to distinguish perpetrator from victim among government officials,
the uninfected citizenry, and the Crazies themselves is thus radically
undermined. The elimination of difference creates—per Primo Levi—a
Gray Zone: a blurred space between victims and victimizers which ultimately facilitates behavior that begets total and mutual destruction.
The Crazies is particularly postmodern insofar as the epistemological
question of who is "us" and who is "them" is ultimately meaningless.
We cannot tell, and it does not matter. Rather, the meaningful question is ontological: What is a victim, and what is a perpetrator? This film
presents, then, the autonomous and poisoned universe apart: *L'Univers concentrationnaire* of "the crazies" is not only marked by imagery
that implies the Shoah (uniforms, fires, the discourse of "just following orders") but also fashions a world of all-encompassing gray death, of
collaboration and cinders.

Chapter 4 turns to a different type of ontological crisis, analyzing
how *Martin* deconstructs the typical patriarchal "Van Helsing" character common to vampire narratives in order to represent how hegemonic masculinity was challenged throughout the 1970s. While horror
scholars such as Robin Wood and Tony Williams have analyzed *Martin* in relation to its themes of sexuality and socioeconomic class, less
attention has been given to the text's portrayal of masculine anxieties

that emerged throughout this decade. The decade's masculine anxieties are manifested in *Martin*'s Tateh Cuda, a patriarch who attempts to eradicate Martin's supposed vampirism with the aid of Christianity. Yet unlike the conventional Van Helsing character, Cuda's actions are largely unsuccessful, which indicates his loss of masculine authority, and his patriarchal status is threatened by his nephew's metaphorical homosexuality and his granddaughter's emerging sense of independence.

The fifth chapter brings us to the 1980s and *Knightriders*, a modern-day take on King Arthur and his knights. King Billy and his motorcycle jousters struggle to live outside modern America and capitalism, having created a mobile Camelot. Despite functioning at the edges of society, the troupe members are not the outsiders that they think they are, occupying a space that is neither ye olde nor 1980s America and is subsidized by capitalism even without corporate sponsorship. While it is not the same nostalgia that got Ronald Reagan elected in 1980, the kingdom similarly embodies a desire for (and makes way for the commodification of) an older, simpler, more honorable—and completely made up—time. Nostalgia figures as well in the subject of the sixth chapter: *Creepshow*, Romero and Stephen King's cinematic homage to EC comics. While *Creepshow* primarily adheres to the trend by which 1970s American horror cinema moved its threats inside the traditional nuclear family, which is inseparable from patriarchal heteronormativity, these anxieties over the family occur in tension with an anxiety over the lack of family or patriarchal norms. This anthology film's stories feature the abusive father of an audience surrogate horror comics fan, a murderous husband, and a couple of murderous fathers, as well as a pair of characters at opposite ends of the socioeconomic spectrum who lack a spouse or family and who come to equally bad ends. If heteronormative institutions' norms act as loci of horror, then their absence, as an alternative, figures as equally threatening.

If *Creepshow*'s relationship to patriarchy and its traditional norms is one of tension, the same might be said of its sequel's relationship to race. Chapter 7's examination of *Creepshow 2* centers on this relationship, particularly in regard to racial privilege and representation. In the segment "Old Chief Wood'nhead," only one of the three significant indigenous characters is played by an indigenous actor, and one of these characters is a wooden cigar store Indian[6] come to life, the story's avenger but also a white capitalist stereotype of an indigenous person. "The Hitch-hiker" presents a well-off white woman who accidentally strikes and kills a black hitchhiker with her car and flees the scene. His continued, undead reappearance and her increasing violence in reaction presents a perverse echo of systemic racism. In "The Raft," the default subject, the straight, white, cisgender, seemingly middle-class male, proves to be the segment's secondary monster. In contrast, the animated wraparound segments offer Billy, a white suburban child, as the avatar of the *Creepshow* reader/audience member and culminate in a power fantasy in which the comics provide him an avenue to exact revenge on a set of (also white) bullies.

The eighth chapter's analysis of *Monkey Shines* focuses on privilege as well, that of able-bodied normative masculinity. *Monkey Shines* serves as a representation of physical emasculation relevant to the 1980s—a decade that heavily defined hegemonic masculinity through a newfound objectification of the male body and in which a lack of able-bodiedness was often represented as a site of fear, as best displayed in the trend of body horror texts which presented images that correlated with the decade's AIDS crisis. *Monkey Shines* is a significant contrast to these able-bodied hegemonic images, presenting a multitude of emasculation anxieties. Allan, a former collegiate athlete, is emasculated through his loss of bodily control, an interruption to his higher education—which, as Robert W. Connell and James W. Messerschmidt argue, is the most conventional path to achieving financial success—and the loss of his girlfriend shortly after his accident.

Chapter 9 pairs the next work chronologically, the 1990 anthology film segment "The Facts in the Case of Mr. Valdemar," with the 1997 anthology film segment "Cat from Hell," both of which filter inspiration from Edgar Allan Poe stories through reimaginings of their own antecedents to introduce or modify critiques of capitalism. "Cat from Hell" renders capitalism as the "perverse"—that which undermines the industrialist, Drogan, and hitman, Halston, from within and leads to their respective deaths, and the reanimation-*manqué* of the cat draws the segment more closely into the domain of Romero's anti-capitalist undead humans. In "The Facts in the Case of Mr. Valdemar," Valdemar's reanimated corpse and the doctor who hypnotizes him to seize his assets resemble but function differently from the zombies for which Romero is most well-known, instead reanimating pre–*Night of the Living Dead* conceptions of zombiism that are rooted in the Caribbean tradition.

Chapter 10 engages with material adapted from closer to home, considering the ways in which family, reproduction and masculinity both threaten and are threatened in Romero's film of Stephen King's *The Dark Half*. In *The Dark Half*, George Stark, who functions simultaneously as the alter ego and the doppelgänger of protagonist Thad Beaumont, represents a threat to the heteronormative nuclear family that is both physical and ideological, the latter extending to the normative primacy of family itself.[7] By creating an embodied Stark, the generative force of Beaumont's writing works as a type of asexual (and thus, queer) reproduction, and Stark's connection to Beaumont's parasitic twin reinforces the image of queer birth. While Stark is ultimately killed and literally spirited away, this containment of dangerous queerness plays out in tension with the fact that the family and domestic life itself pose a threat to unfettered creativity and perhaps to fully realized masculinity, even as the existence of the hyper-masculine alter ego depends entirely on the seemingly compromised creativity of the family man.

Chapter 11 picks up the thread of masculinity in its analysis of Romero's sole non–*Dead* film of the new millennium, *Bruiser*. While released in 2000, *Bruiser* embodies the "masculinity in crisis" concerns of the 1990s, a decade heavily defined by white men's feelings of victimization, including in the cinema. Lauren Berlant argues, "[O]ptimistic attachment is invested in one's own or the world's continuity, but might feel any number of ways, from the romantic to the fatalistic to the numb to the nothing" (13). Here, that attachment is to the world of hegemonic white masculinity, and that way is anger. *Bruiser* is a slasher film about Henry Creedlow, a middle-aged man who has his hegemonic masculinity threatened by his unfaithful wife, sleazy boss and money-laundering best friend. After waking up to find that his face has transformed into an expressionless white mask, Henry utilizes his newfound anonymity to take violent vengeance against those who emasculated him. As with the slasher films, "white male as victim" movies invite some degree of sympathy for and identification with the antagonistic killer, making *Bruiser* particularly noteworthy in its connections to masculine spectatorship.

The volume concludes by looking at a pair of anomalous works in Romero's oeuvre. The 1973 short work *The Amusement Park*, commissioned by a Lutheran group to highlight the problem of ageism, provides an early example of the blending of sociopolitical and socioeconomic commentary with elements of the horror genre, anticipating how that commentary would be delivered throughout Romero's career. A quarter of a century later, in 1998, Romero wrote a script for a film adaptation of the video game *Resident Evil*. The available draft of this script engages with themes that recur throughout his work, such as critiques of gender inequality and capitalist exploitation, as well as with genre traditions, including the zombie tradition that he helped to define.

These two works again highlight the concern with and often the challenge of boundaries and social constructs that appear throughout Romero's films, including, of course (but far from limited to), the

Dead series. While the particulars of the films' social contexts shifted over time, one constant is what we might term their revolutionary consciousness. In Sara Ahmed's formulation, while bourgeois society veils its own nature and the reproduction of its own order, a revolutionary consciousness recognizes and draws attention to the veil and to "the interested nature of social belief" (*Promise* 165–66). Romero's films, we argue, perform just such recognition and revelation. The films and their characters display the ways in which a revolutionary consciousness "means feeling at odds with the world, or feeling that the world is odd," as well as being or becoming "estranged from the world of good habits and manners, which promises your comfort in return for obedience and good will" (168). In such estrangement can be found the possibility for alternative ways of being. So while *Night of the Living Dead* may have revolutionized both zombie cinema and American cinema more broadly, the entirety of Romero's film corpus is revolutionary.

1

"Isn't that cheating?"

Extradiegetic Narrative Control in There's Always Vanilla

Leah Richards

In a 1969 interview, George A. Romero described his current project as "a film looking at quote 'the American hippie' four or five years from now and where he is going to be and where the people are going to be around him and what happens to their whole communication" (Ork and Abagnalo 6). When he was asked by a different interviewer from the same publication in 1973 if he'd ever made the "movie about ... hippies and what they would be like in a few years," Romero only eventually realized that that was how he had once described his second movie, 1971's *There's Always Vanilla* (Lebowitz, Hackett and Cutrone 36–37), his gesture toward "something commercial that was trying to be a little bit intelligent too," like *The Graduate* and *Goodbye, Columbus* (Nicotero 32). In a 2000 interview, Romero replied to the question of why he "allowed" the movie to be released on home media by saying, "I have no objection to anyone seeing it. But I didn't think it would be worth anyone's while to watch it" (T. Williams, "An Interview" 137).

"Positioned," Tom Fallows claims, "as a counterculture romantic comedy" ("'More'" 90), *There's Always Vanilla* (like the films with which Romero classified it) is more precisely an anatomy of a relationship. It isn't a relationship that is doomed from the start, but it is a relationship that ends with good reason. Rather than romance, it is a story about illusions and storytelling. Although its points aren't very clear, it *is* a Romero movie, a display of the tensions between the creative and the commercial that uses its counterculture "sellouts" to articulate objections to patriarchal hegemony, and its ultimately separated couple faced with an ill-timed unintended pregnancy anticipates plot points in *Dawn of the Dead* (1978).[1]

17

Three narratives run in parallel through the opening minutes of *There's Always Vanilla*. One is largely a first-person monologue, a direct-to-camera address delivered in hindsight by the male main character. The second is a scene of the female protagonist at work filming a beer commercial and navigating sexual objectification. In these scenes, both Chris (Ray Laine) and Lynn (Judith Streiner) make statements, to the camera and to other characters respectively, that provide an overview, thematic as well as narrative, of the movie that will follow. The third narrative, which opens the film and plays beneath the opening credits, is what looks like news footage, accompanied by man-on-the-street voiceover interviews about the value and meaning of a piece of student-made kinetic modern art, "The Ultimate Machine," on display in downtown Pittsburgh. Clarifying the role of the art installation within the opening narrative, Chris' first statement to the camera is that "the whole thing was kind of like that machine," and he goes on to explain not what "the whole thing" is but how it is like the Ultimate Machine: "Everything's so confusing. Everything's going round and round. And you know, we have to have caused that. And then we can't understand it." This sort of existential stoner deep thought, something that sounds like it's saying more than it is, is a throughline in the movie, which isn't very good and features absolutely abhorrent male characters. Quality and engagement aside, however, the narrative devices and reflections on narrative employed in *There's Always Vanilla* are rich and worthy of exploration.

The three intertwined scenes opening the movie both represent and comment on masculine control over narratives and thus over the meanings that narratives create. This chapter will explore these three scenes and their relation to the overarching idea of where "the hippies" will be in a few years. Through Lynn's experience, I will examine the cultural moment at which *There's Always Vanilla* takes place as illustrated by the antagonistic relationship between advertising and counterculture; I will then assess the Ultimate Machine as a real-world cultural artifact and as a symbol within the movie. Finally, I will look at Chris' addresses to the camera throughout the film, which were added to the script late in production to pad out the movie to just over 90 minutes and were perhaps suggested by Jean-Luc Godard's use of similar documentary-style "interviews" to deconstruct the romantic relationships in *Masculin Féminin* (1966). Through these addresses, Chris functions as a narrator—a device traditionally used in prose that, having largely disappeared after the silent film era, becomes a modernist or even postmodern device in drama, film and television—and attempts to exert control over the story of his relationship with Lynn and how that story is perceived. Indeed, textual clues raise the possibility—although contradictory evidence also exists—that the movie itself is Chris' version of things, not just his commentary. This chapter will close with the evidence for and against that reading and what it might mean if Chris is the source of the story, not just a participant.

Since few people have seen *There's Always Vanilla*, let's start with a quick plot summary to provide context for this chapter's arguments: Chris returns to Pittsburgh after bumming around for the three years since he got out of the army. He's at least partly bankrolled by his wealthy parents. After a drunken, debauched night out with his father, he meets Lynn, a model and actress and daughter of a local talk radio personality, at a train station; he first pretends that she injured him and then pretends that she is unattractive to get her attention. They spend a contrivedly whimsical day together and picnic on the grass while asking each other getting-to-know-you questions. Notably, "What's your name?" is asked well into the conversation, shortly before they end up at Lynn's home, having sex on her living room floor, establishing them just as much as their clothing does as members of the late '60s–early '70s countercultural "great American sex party," when abstinence became "distinctly unfashionable" (Skal 288).[2] Chris immediately moves in, and for a brief period everything is great. By what dialogue marks as two months into their relationship, however, they're arguing about fundamental differences in their characters. Assuring her that she isn't making him do something he does not want to do, he applies for and gets, but then almost immediately quits, a job as an advertising copywriter. Unbeknownst to Chris, Lynn is pregnant, but having no illusions about their relationship, she arranges to have an abortion. It is unclear if she intends to continue the relationship afterwards.

Not knowing where she is, Chris angrily leaves their apartment; within the traditions of horror *and* films that punish women for their sexuality, it is surprising that she does not die having the abortion but less surprising that she changes her mind and, the next time we see her—in the final scene of the movie—she is very pregnant and married to another man, living in a large, pleasant suburban home. In the penultimate scene, Chris has gone to his parents to ask for money and is willing to accept a stern talking-to from his father in exchange. Early events in the film established the father as powerful and superficially respectable—but *only* superficially. He enables Chris and paradoxically envies his lifestyle but not how it positions him outside of mainstream society; he tells Chris that he understands his reluctance to join mainstream culture and likens it to being at an ice cream place, confronted with "all sorts of wild, exotic flavors" and not being able to choose between them.

"[S]omehow," he says, no matter how tempting the other flavors, "you always end up with vanilla," that is, the plain, maybe a little boring, and omnipresent. Chris asks, "What about the poor bastard who gets hung up on butter pecan?" and his father replies, "He's disappointed when he can't get it" because the only flavor one can count on is vanilla: "There's always vanilla, Chris. Always vanilla."

Advertising as the Oldest Profession

Previous to and while making of *Night of the Living Dead* and *There's Always Vanilla*, Romero and his Latent Image team were making highly regarded commercials; there was little filmmaking in Pittsburgh at the time, although it was a nexus for advertising agencies, "largely thanks to its thriving steel industry and status and the nation's third largest corporate headquarters" (Fallows, *George* 29). According to Romero, "[R]ight around the time when television commercials were becoming good in the sense of the craft that was being used to produce them, we got a rep there as a commercial house, and then that really started to accelerate and the company got pretty big ... and then we started to make some money" (Lebowitz, Hackett and Cutrone 40). Romero uses his own experience to shape Lynn's work as a commercial actress in the opening scene and at points later in the movie; Lynn's experience in turn influences her shift toward the counterculture even as she continues to participate in work that she acknowledges exploits both the vulnerability of the women who participate and the susceptibility of the audience.

There's Always Vanilla "engages in an ironic depiction of the deceptive media practices designed to sell products" and lifestyles and explores how everything has "become hopelessly corrupt and tarnished as a result of the manipulations practiced upon viewers by the dominant media" (T. Williams, *Cinema* 33). In the opening moments of the movie, we see a beer commercial being made; the finished product is featured near the end, on the television that a very pregnant Lynn, with her new husband, are watching at a point in the future. This juxtaposition is a reminder that, in addition to a product, advertisements, like all mass media, are selling a way of life. Commercials take place in a world that is constructed from the ideals of dominant culture. The limits of capitalism "are so strong and pervasive that the chance to pursue qualitatively different forms of life is severely restricted" (Fraser and Jaeggi 187) and, in addition to a particular beer, cleaning product, processed food, car or whatever, ads are selling the status quo.

Part of the status quo, particularly at this time, was traditional roles for women; Lynn's Bold Gold beer commercial[3] is marketing what they identify as "the beer for the man who thinks bold and acts bold," and Lynn's role is as the reward in this masculine narrative: the beautiful woman whom the man boldly kisses after taking a drink of Bold Gold. During a break in filming—while assistants wet glasses so that they sparkle when filled with soap suds and beer-colored water— Michael Dorian (Richard Ricci), the lead creative on the shoot, makes a move on Lynn. She responds by asking him if "making the beer look better than it actually looks" is cheating. The defense of advertising seems to be the one thing that can distract Michael from sexual harassment, and he identifies the incomes that depend on the beer looking as good as possible before looking her up and down and, using her language, saying, "Isn't *that* cheating?" implying that she is, perhaps, looking more sexually available than she is. (Shortly after, as the main narrative commences with Chris and Lynn's first meeting, Chris also takes commenting on Lynn's appearance as his right, first criticizing the pictures in her portfolio and then telling her that she'll never make it as an actress because her butt is too big. Only once he feels that he has sufficiently undermined her self-confidence does he begin to woo her.) Lynn maintains her critical attitude toward advertising, challenging Michael later as he pontificates about advertising as the means of "building bridges— bridges between people." She says, "I'm trying awfully hard to justify the fact that I'm contributing. If I'm going to interrupt millions of people's evenings by standing around grinning and eating potato chips...." He interrupts her to explain that advertising is selling illusions as well as commodities and that a beautiful woman in their living room telling them to eat a particular kind of chip is a moment of brightness in the gloom of the daily grind and world events.

Sex sells, audiences are frequently reminded, but it is not selling itself; instead, commercials use the illusion of sexual availability to sell products, implicitly making an empty promise that the commodity being marketed is the way to access the world of the commercial and the life of one's dreams.[4] While most people don't take that promise at face value, they are still impacted by the illusory world in which the "promise" is being made.

Over the course of the movie, the line between sex and marketing becomes less distinct. At one point, Lynn tells Chris that one of the things she likes best about him is that he is "honest. About everything," and in her experience, "[p]eople just aren't like that"; they then engage in the most explicit sex scene in the movie. During that scene, the movie jumps back and forth between Lynn and Chris and Lynn at a commercial shoot that initially, especially in the brief flashes that are first shown—a second at most of dark, obstructed shots that slowly become clearer—looks more like a softcore porn shoot. Lynn is naked in a bathtub full of bubbles that a makeup artist and Michael keep strategically relocating, and the clip ends as filming presumably begins. It is possible that the shoot is a dream rather than a memory, but its status is not particularly important: Reality or dream, Lynn knows that sex sells, and the scene that immediately follows has her complaining to her mother about her growing disillusionment with "trying to get excited by a lousy glass of beer" and wondering if perhaps she is "just cut out to be a wife and mother." Lynn's arc transitions from being part of the marketing to being the consumer; she may or may not consume the products, but by movie's end, she has bought into dominant culture.

It is no accident that Chris' foray into an office job is also in advertising, working as a copywriter. Showing up for his interview and then for work in a dark suit and glasses—very much dressing a part—and brimming with the confidence of a narcissist, he explains that his qualifications for the job lie in his experience as a writer and as a pimp: he can write, but more importantly, he sold things, he is selling himself to them, and he can "apply this approach to whatever [they're] selling." Advertising and pimping, he says, "deal with the public in the same way. Offering a release. A solution to frustrations. A fulfillment of desires," whether with "a quick piece of ass" or "a new deodorant." His strategy is successful: Pierce, Burns and Manspeaker (yes, really) are hoping to "communicate with the 'Pepsi generation'"—which makes him angry. On the one hand, he knows that advertising is selling more than a product and that his youth and audacity may have been what sold him to his employers, but on the other, he sees being offered something mainstream based on his countercultural status as selling out rather than changing the system, or at least claims to believe it so that he can continue positioning himself as an outsider.

The Ultimate Machine: "Oh, it's beautiful—but what does it do?"

The footage of the Ultimate Machine establishes the precise cultural moment in which *There's Always Vanilla* takes place, and in fact, precisely dates the events if they are taking place in the "real" world. Shot in mid–1970 (*"There's Always"*) and released in late 1971, the film itself appears to be set in 1969.[5] The Ultimate Machine was a real work of art created by members of a fraternity at Carnegie Mellon University, exhibited as a part of the 1969 Three Rivers Arts Festival and not a permanent installation.[6] The exhibit placard, shown in the footage, explains: "Carnegie-Mellon [sic] University's contribution to the Three Rivers Arts Festival was originally created for CMU's Spring Carnival. It was designed and constructed entirely by members of the ΣAE [Sigma Alpha Epsilon] fraternity." The creators describe the work of art as a "serious bit of Kenetic [sic] Art, involving light, movement and sound[, that] is also a happy spoof aimed at our machine-oriented society," and Tony Williams describes it as "a bizarre Heath Robinson type contraption" (*Cinema* 35). The footage, perhaps deliberately, does not provide unobstructed shots of the whole piece, instead showing parts of it in quick cuts. A later scene seems to provide an aerial view of the piece. Although the entire piece is shown between these scenes, one still does not have a clear sense of what it actually looks like.

Pittsburgh Post-Gazette writer Geoffrey Tomb described the Three Rivers Arts Festival, in its tenth year in 1969, as "[t]he yearly head shaking ... in Gateway Center" that workers from the area meet with "wonderment on their faces as they return to the office" ("Heads" 27). Although it was not explicitly a contemporary arts event, the conclusion to be drawn from references to head-shaking and "many perplexed looks" (27) is that the Ultimate Machine was not the only avant-garde piece. The 4000-pound "huge moving sculpture," "designed to show what a Victorian computer would have looked like" (27), included "whirling gears, spinning rollers, flashing lights and a waterfall" (Tomb, "Arts" 13) made of "an old thresher, ... parts of a wine press, a sod roller, a mill wheel and a 1912 fire engine" as well as a means to play recorded music. Fifty years later, the piece was described in retrospect as "a silver painted Rube Goldberg–like contraption with colorful wheels that spun on a motor" (Paul 1).

Like most works of art, the Ultimate Machine does not actually do anything, unless of course one considers how it makes people react. Observers at the start of the movie respond with either inchoate optimism and a sincerely held belief in coming change or resentful anger that takes Geoffrey Tomb's bemused response to the piece and to the Festival as a whole several steps further. When asked if they think it means anything, one respondent says, "Of course," but does not elaborate, while another person says, "I think basically it's camp." A fourth person, asked if it is "essentially purposeless," says, "No, because you got something happening. If anything has something happening, it has a purpose to it," even if that purpose isn't immediately clear. (The same could be said of *There's Always Vanilla* as a whole.) Another viewer says, "I really think that it's more or less what this country needs."

Conversely, of course, there are viewers who "think they're try-ing to make fun of us ... and they're trying to say that our society is screwed up," representatives of the more traditional values at odds with counterculture. The opposing viewpoints illustrate the divide between Chris, Lynn and the counterculture that they represent and the more traditional world in which they were both raised and in which they are declining to participate. Additionally, the ratio of positive to neg-ative responses anticipates the cultural shift within dominant culture over the course of the late 1960s and early '70s, the shift that allows for the reincorporation of the Chrises and Lynns of America back into the mainstream. Although Romero felt that the finished product was unsuccessful, this point of reincorporation was his initial goal in mak-ing the film.

Before resigning from the mainstream job for which he was under-qualified but talked his way into, Chris looks out his office win-dow at the Ultimate Machine and responds not to the piece itself but to others' reactions: There is additional footage of the installation, this time accompanied by viewers' facial expressions rather than ver-bal commentary, and they are followed by Chris' equally puzzled but also angrily supercilious response. He takes the interest in the piece as an offense, perhaps a symbol of selling out and commodifying the avant-garde, surrounded by "[a]ll these goddamn people, all these god-damned gray flannel, briefcases, afternoon shoppers, staring at the silly-ass collection of gears and pulleys" looking for meaning. He does not claim to understand the piece, calling it a "[s]illy-ass piece of junk," but does seem to resent having something (seemingly) counterculture "out there where [anyone] can get a good look at it." It is notable that he chooses the Ultimate Machine as the simile with which he sums up the events of the movie in his opening address to the camera.

Masculine Narrative Control: "The man who thinks bold and acts bold"

Despite their significant presence within the film, as mentioned, Chris' direct-to-camera addresses weren't part of the original, unfin-ished script and were largely improvised scenes filmed late in pro-duction. Chris functions as a modified prose narrator, specifically a participatory, narcissistic first-person narrator telling a story that has already ended. Williams says that Chris, "like several of his literary pre-decessors and many key characters in naturalist fiction, ... is an 'unre-liable narrator' in more ways than one ... and the developing narrative will ... undermine any claims Chris has either in regard to intellectual and moral superiority" (*Cinema* 37). Although I agree that Chris is a largely unreliable, and certainly unlikable, narrator, I argue that, through the use of techniques more frequently aligned with written narratives, his addresses to the camera are ultimately revelatory, even when he is not aware of what he is revealing about himself.

Rather than advancing the plot, Chris provides commentary on the events as they unfold on screen and, as the only commenter, can manipulate and interpret events to represent his own actions in the most positive light. That he fails is not for lack of trying; particularly in early scenes, he maintains a persona that is equal parts ironically detached observer and stoned philosopher. However, there are distinct phases to this sequence of addresses to the camera; the unsentimental commentary delivered as though from a distance becomes an act of narration as Chris begins interrogating his actions and motivations, eventually breaking into some scenes to link events together, and becoming less confident in his portrayal of himself and the relationship. As such, his narration aligns with distinct acts of literary confession.

First, in the opening minutes of the movie, he delivers a lengthy monologue that essentially outlines the film: There was a "chick," and their relationship has since ended; he says that "the whole thing was kind of like" the Ultimate Machine and that he "tried to make the chick understand that" but "could never get the chick to appreciate anything like that"; while what he means by "the whole thing" is the movie that follows, the whole thing "will be a disclosure which reflects negatively on him" (T. Williams, *Cinema* 36). This early part of his narrative functions as a dramatic monologue in the style of Victorian poets Alfred, Lord Tennyson, Christina Rossetti and, most famously, Robert Browning. While a dramatic monologue in a play is simply a character speaking at length, uninterrupted, to other characters, in poetry, a dramatic monologue is a poem entirely in the voice of a persona speaking, under specific circumstances, to an auditor whose presence is inferred but whose voice is not heard. What is fundamental to the poetic dramatic monologue is that the speaker reveals something about themself to their auditor and to the reader, something that they are not aware that they are revealing. For example, Browning's Duke of Ferrara is showing his art collection to a representative of the family into which he hopes to marry as evidence of his wealth and taste but, in discussing a portrait of his late first wife, reveals that he had her killed ("My Last Duchess," published 1842). In Browning's "Porphyria's Lover" (published 1836), a man tells of how he strangled his beloved with her own hair, at her wish, so that they could be together forever, but the language that he uses to tell the story shows that he is delusional and controlling. Similarly, Chris reveals a great deal about himself while explaining how he was not looking for anything and got caught up with Lynn. Although his intention (as a character, not as a mouthpiece for the creators) is to charm the audience with his honesty, he instead presents himself as a narcissistic, controlling manchild, a sexist pseudo-intellectual who likes to think that he's rejecting social norms when he simply wants things to go his way with no effort. Shortly after, his defensiveness about why and how the relationship with Lynn happened, his claim that it wasn't important to him and that really, he had nothing to do with it, and his continued assertion that things happen that we simply cannot understand indicate his discomfort with self-examination and his place within patriarchy, which associates "masculinity with pseudo-independence" and an ingrained denial "of relational desires and sensitivities" (Gilligan and Snider 22). Additionally, his assertions are contradicted by the events unfolding within the film.

Moving from general commentary and preemptive justification into a more narrative role by mid-movie, Chris begins to consider possible motivations and to question his actions, and starts to reveal a deeper emotional investment in the relationship than he initially claimed. When Lynn asks him why he wants her, his direct address actually shifts into a "he said, she said" prose-style narrative before the line between his commentary and the story becomes more fluid:

> [*To camera*] "All I could come up with..." [In-story] "You're a hell of a beautiful lady." [*To camera*] "She was a hell of a beautiful lady but that's not enough to ... well, I dug her. I mean, there was something. There was a certain part of Lynn that always got to me. I could never really understand it. I [*stammers a bit*] could never figure it out. I couldn't tell her. I still don't have it clear. I still can't figure out how the whole thing happened."

Notably, this is the first time that he calls her Lynn in his commentary. In his next address, he begins to acknowledge uncertainty and attempt to explain the end of the relationship, saying over a scene of them smoking marijuana, "Maybe this will explain it. I don't know if Lynn was really into it or if she was just behaving the way she thought I wanted her to behave, or what. I don't know." As he continues to interject throughout the next few minutes of the film, it is possible to see this next stage, beginning with his commentary on the idyllic, "honeymoon" stage of their relationship, as confessional in the sense of *Confessions of an English Opium Eater* (1821), the Newgate Calendars, or *Penthouse Forum* letters as well as, to a lesser degree, in the sense of the mid–20th-century poetry movement exemplified by Sylvia Plath and Robert Lowell. These forms are written in the first person and are rooted in the religious concept of confession, that is, acknowledgment of one's guilt in committing sins and injuries to others, but move beyond acts of contrition or penance to a secular consideration of motivations and internal states. Rather than saying "I did this thing and will repent," confessional writing, which may be pure fiction, autobiography or something falling in between, says, "I did this for these reasons," seeking to rationalize as well as acknowledge guilt. Confessional poetry is deeply personal and takes its subject from "beyond customary bounds of reticence or personal embarrassment" (critic Mack Rosenthal in 1959, qtd. in Patterson), moving further to establish the deeper or hidden psychological influences, the motivations that it may be challenging to examine.

After acknowledging his role in their relationship, Chris spends a portion of his commentary resisting further self-examination and reflection: "Who the hell knows what they want? You know, who knows what they want, who knows what's right or wrong? ... A lot of it is wrapped up inside [my head], but why do I have to keep spending time trying to figure out why, and telling people why? And why do I have to have a reason for the whole thing all the time? I don't *know* why it happened." And neither does the audience: the movie skips forward two months and they have begun fighting; for the next portion of the film, details are missing from both Chris' commentary and from the movie itself, suggesting that his own need to repress has manifested as control over, a silencing of, the story, an example of the power that a narrator can have over events. Most significantly, when he tells Lynn about the young child whom he has been told is his, most of what he says is replaced by the sound of a train in the background. This means that we do not know what he said to Lynn nor how she reacted; when he says to the camera with a nod, "If Lynn and I had a kid, I would have married her. Yeah," the question is raised of whether he ever said that to her. When he says to Lynn, "Jesus, I wish I could talk to you," the last thing he says to her in the movie, that sets up the final portion of his commentary, which falls at the end of the relationship rather than at the end of the film.

While he is waiting at home, Lynn is traveling to her scheduled abortion, but he does not know that. His commentary suggests that she never told him:

> I waited there until 10:30. And I guess I even had my mind made up before that and I welcomed the chance.... I don't know, she could have been with some other guy, I don't know. I don't know where she was, and I think right at that point, I didn't even really care. I think I was happy that she wasn't

there, and I think I was happy that I was angry with her, and I think I was happy to just get the hell out of it.

In his anger, the deepest emotion he has thus far admitted to having, he leaves and ends up at his parents' house, at which point the possibility is raised that this is Chris' story rather than a story that he is in. He is wearing the denim jacket and blue shirt that he wore when he arrived in Pittsburgh, before he met Lynn, and this is also what he is wearing in his direct-to-camera addresses (see Fig. 1). While this can be seen as a symbol of the lack of change that his character has undergone throughout the film or a negation of everything that fell between, it also raises the suggestion that he is telling his version of events to his father, with whom he has an off-camera conversation in an outdoor setting that resembles the background for his addresses. It is clear that he told his father some story about his romantic life, since that is what leads to their ice cream conversation; additionally, referring to Lynn as "the chick" seems in character with both his and his father's sexism and, given that his performance of counterculture has been shown to be an easy way to get a reaction out of his father, his early monologues, full of slang and rejections of the mainstream, as well as his continued

Figure 1. Chris (Ray Laine) delivers a direct-to-camera address in *There's Always Vanilla* (1971, The Latent Image).

assertions about the pointlessness of understanding why things happen, make sense. While, of course, there are parts to the movie that he did not experience and even things that he did not know occurred, it is possible that, for example, Lynn told him about her initial encounters with Michael Dorian and the Michael Dorian in the movie—leather pants, perpetual seduction and so on—is an imagined version of the man. Additionally, it is possible that Lynn's abortion adventure was in some way imagined, given its theatricality.

There is no lack of evidence that Chris is seeking to control the narrative in a way that is similar to the means by which the "male gaze" controls film narratives more generally; the "gift" of two helium balloons in a whimsically decorated box that he sends to the very pregnant and married Lynn at the movie's end, seemingly just to re-insert himself into her story, is a closing example.[7] He explained to Lynn at one point that he was writing a novel about "nothing ... and everything. It isn't *about* anything; it *is* something." Recalling what one commentator said about the Ultimate Machine, it's not purposeless "because you got something happening. If anything has something happening, it has a purpose to it." Through this story of something happening, the storyteller creates something with purpose, which may be contrary to Chris' countercultural persona but reflects the redirecting and mainstreaming of the counterculture that in many ways defined the era and that, his father suggests, Chris will eventually accept. Although he shows little growth or introspection during the events of the film, there seems to be an awareness within Chris' narrative that, until he finds a purpose, he is "the poor bastard hung up on butter pecan."

"You've really got to get with it, Mrs. Mitchell"

Freud, Friedan and Jack's Wife

LEAH RICHARDS

"Witches have always been women who dared to be: groovy, courageous, aggressive, intelligent, nonconformist, explorative, curious, independent, sexually liberated, revolutionary," proclaimed the Women's International Terrorist Conspiracy from Hell (W.I.T.C.H.) Manifesto in 1968; the radical feminist group went on to identify the witch as "the free part of each of us, beneath ... the acquiescence to absurd male domination." It concluded, "You are a Witch by being female, untamed, angry, [and] joyous" (465–66).

Five tempestuous years later, just a month before George A. Romero's more well-known *The Crazies* was released in 1973, his film *Jack's Wife* was released.[1] *Jack's Wife* is the story of Joan Mitchell (Jan White), a wife and mother in her early 40s, living in the suburbs. She takes up witchcraft to address her dissatisfaction with her life and her place in the world; although the film borrows from the horror tradition, it does not fit within the continuum of witch and occult films of the 1960s and '70s. Romero intentionally made what Sady Doyle calls a "sexy witch thriller as second-wave feminist manifesto" (230), a film that is aligned with the work of Betty Friedan—and the alienated heroines of novels like Sylvia Plath's *The Bell Jar* (1963) and Shirley Jackson's *Hangsaman* (1951)—rather than with the witch films of the era that "concentrated on the witch hunt or the presence of the Devil" (Russell 71), with "male control ... as a central theme" and the emphasis on "the hunting and burning of witches rather than the power inherent in the figure" (67). Tropes of the horror genre are employed to present the nightmare—literal and metaphorical—of being a housewife in 1970s suburban America.

Jack's Wife is one of many pieces of popular media participating in "a revival of esoteric occultism the likes of which hadn't been witnessed in the West since the fin-de-siècle" (Owens 17–18) that "translated into big collective business, particularly in the entertainment industry" (18) and "quickly ascended to the heights of 1960s counterculture" (18), the sexual revolution, and the women's movement. While it is deliberately sympathetic to Joan and gives her a relatively happy ending, it is perhaps more a film about feminism, about one woman living under patriarchy and her personalized engagement with concepts of women's liberation, than a feminist film, a film that challenges the patriarchy itself and viewers' complicity in it. Regardless of where it is most successful, however—and that's definitely not the box office—*Jack's Wife* makes a significant (albeit trippy and low-budget) contribution to the second-wave (white, middle-class) feminist movement, ending with Joan's ultimate victory-through-witchcraft over her family's patriarch and the patriarchy and her assertion of her own identity as a witch, not as "Jack's wife."

The Opening Scenes

It is not my intention to walk through the film scene by scene, but the first 12 minutes of the theatrical release version are a series of dream sequences, with what follows illustrating the reality that Joan's dreams represent and her eventual rejection of that reality. The extended-release version—the closest thing we have to Romero's original vision for the film, since the distributor's edits were made to the original negative—restores about 14 minutes to the film, but apart from added and expanded scenes, it re-orders a few incidents as well, most notably within these opening episodes. Again, I will not catalogue each of these changes but will discuss some significant elements of the opening scenes in the extended release.

The film opens surreally, with the tolling of a bell and Joan Mitchell blankly following her husband Jack (Bill Thunhurst) through a leafless grove of trees in what seems to be early spring. He is completely indifferent to her, reading a newspaper and possibly having breakfast; a cup of coffee and a hard-boiled egg variously demand his attention where his wife cannot. As he walks, he lets go of branches that smack, cut and entangle Joan. What is eventually revealed to be a three-minute-plus dream sequence seems to end, as Joan wakes up in bed while her husband dresses for work, but she then finds herself in the car with Jack outside a suburban home. When he gets out and comes to her side, she initially locks the door, and when it unlocks, he first smacks her with a newspaper and then attaches a leash to the collar she is suddenly wearing and leads her to a kennel where she is locked in by another man. "A cage," Sady Doyle reminds us, "has two purposes. Of course it serves to keep women confined," unable to access the things that give the patriarchy its power, "[b]ut the second purpose of a cage—the more interesting one—is to protect the world from what's inside it" (xvi); "the cage of patriarchy is flimsier than it looks, and it is only a matter of time until we find our way out" (xxi). While Joan is, at the start of the film, confined within "the cage of patriarchy," witchcraft provides her with the means to escape.

Once again, Joan wakes up in bed. Her first act of the day is to check her face in the mirror for wrinkles; her nightmares sometimes take the form of seeing herself as an old woman, and her almost child-like pleasure when her daughter Nikki tells her she looks great and has a great figure underscores Friedan's arguments about the attractive, feminine appearance that the feminine mystique demands of women. It seems that aging is, at the start of the film, her worst nightmare, and it is notable that she quits having visions of her elderly self as she enters into witchcraft. In the session with her psychiatrist (Neil Fisher, who resembles but whom I cannot confirm to be the other man in the kennel dream) that follows, he tells her that, while dreams are repressed truth, dreamers are the least qualified people to understand their own dreams. (Joan's dreams don't, it should be said, seem particularly challenging to interpret.) He first reminds her of how superfluous she is now that her daughter is an adult and her husband is immersed in work before acknowledging that her dreams represent her sense of feeling "imprisoned, trapped," but then says that she, not the patriarchy the suburbs, or early 1970s America, is the cause of her sense of imprisonment.

Tony Williams notes, "[I]t is often difficult to distinguish the fantasy sequences in *Jack's Wife* from the world of everyday reality ... [but] the fantastic levels of meaning complement, rather than contradict, the realistic aspects of the narrative" (*Cinema* 48–49). Joan's dreams are intercut with scenes of reality early in the theatrical release; after the session with her psychiatrist, Joan is at a cocktail party, where the first words spoken (by another housewife) are "She's a witch!" and Joan learns that a neighbor, Marion (Virginia Greenwald), is "an honest to God witch." She listens as her friends rattle off a string of stereotypes about witches, establishing that, within the film, the community's understanding of witchcraft and the occult is rooted in clichés and stereotypes even as it is acknowledged that "[i]t's like a religion with them," setting up a passing comparison of witchcraft with Joan's Catholicism to which the film returns.

The discussion of what Marion's practices might be is interrupted by a drunken game of Mad Libs in which "Jack Mitchell works at the dog pound" and "brings Catholicism to evildoers." Given the surreal nature of early scenes set both in dreams and in reality, as well as a re-ordering of these scenes in the extended release, it is not clear whether Joan's dreams have taken place before this scene or if the chronology is non-linear; scenes like the game of Mad Libs could clarify the origins of her dreams' symbols, with this small interaction giving form to her dream of the dog kennel that night or shortly after, or represent a memory of her dreams and the disquiet that they caused. The cocktail party, then, introduces essential elements of plot, characterization and the themes of the film, while also showing Joan as more a silent auditor than a participant in the suburban shenanigans.

This is followed by another sequence that is eventually revealed to be a dream: Joan is being shown around her own home by a male realtor, played by the actor (Ken Peters) who plays John Fuller, the Mad Libs–reading neighbor,[2] who is also marketing her life to her. While John was collecting words for the game, he took Joan's unconscious exclamation of "Oh, God" as her response, "the first [noun] that pops into [her] mind," and the realtor, a more youthful-looking version of John, also seems able to speak with her unconscious. In addition to jewelry and checkbooks (financial comfort), the neighboring housewives (social interaction) and a medicine cabinet full of tranquilizers (escape), he tells her that there are three televisions "with special programming to give you ideas ... in case you should run out of ideas."

Everything that the realtor says has a dual meaning (much like Mad Libs), most of it sexual (again, like Mad Libs), suggesting that Joan's unconscious is as discontented as she is. He also introduces her to a handyman who provides a range of services, including the "et cetera, et cetera" that the realtor notes Joan has never wanted. "Maybe this time" she will be interested in the "et cetera," he says: "You've really got to get with it, Mrs. Mitchell. It's later than you think, and all that." As, throughout these scenes and afterwards, Joan is seeing herself as an old woman in mirrors around the house—just as Lincoln Maazel's old man encounters his unhappy double in *The Amusement Park* (1973)—she seems fully aware of how "late" it is, and the ticking of a clock wound by the realtor continues through the rest of the dream. This scene clarifies that Joan-the-housewife is as much married to her home as to her husband and raises the eventually fulfilled suggestion of an affair, which a later scene reveals Joan has already considered in the abstract but feels guilty even thinking about, because the combination of Catholicism and the feminine mystique, the socially constructed and internalized expectation that women would find absolute fulfillment in housework and child-rearing, ensures that women will always feel guilty about something.

Reinforcing the Nightmare

The theatrical release of *Jack's Wife* was deliberate in its attempts to undermine Romero's intentions, and the attempts at reconfiguring Romero's ideas are immediately evident. The theatrical release begins with white text on a black screen reading "Jan White in ... *Hungry Wives*" before the opening shots of the film, while the extended release reads "Jan White **as** ... *Jack's Wife*" over the opening scene. In addition to being a part of the film in a way that the plain text is not, reminding the viewer that what follows is the filmmaker's work, the extended release's use of the word "as" emphasizes the tensions of the film: The lead actor plays a character who is identified by her relationship to a named figure rather than by her own name. This version of the credits includes a symbol, a stylized ankh-like shape with the lower bar split into two "legs," that is animated to flip into position as the C-K in "Jack" (see Fig. 2 and 3). Presumably, this symbol is included to suggest the esoteric and occult[3]—albeit neopagan—practices rather than historical, more traditional witchcraft (which is a distinction that it is unlikely most audience members would make: It looks arcane and mystical).

While the opening scene in the woods and at the kennel remains the same, it is followed by the realtor scene, keeping the three dream

Figure 2. Frame grabs from the opening credits of *Jack's Wife* (1973, The Latent Image): theatrical release on top, extended release below.

sequences together before Joan's visit to her psychiatrist to discuss them. The visit is followed by a series of mundane errands—grocery store, dry cleaner, car wash—that are cut from the theatrical version but repeated later in the extended release, showing the monotony of Joan's life. Additionally, there is a scene of Joan talking with her college-aged daughter Nikki (Joedda McClain), who asks about a child that Joan lost before Nikki was born; the suggestion is that this is a discussion they've had before, so one must assume that the conversation is an expository introduction to the film's feminist themes, as Joan says that she wasn't sure she would be able to

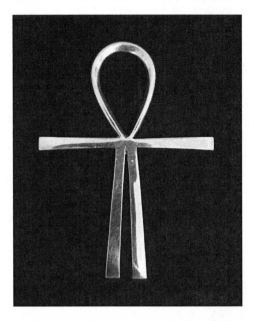

Figure 3. An Atlantean Cross, from eme raldinnovations.co.uk (available to "harmonise negative energies" in several sizes, brass or silver, and starting at just £4.95).

have a child, and "mother" is an essential part of Joan's identity both in what Friedan identifies as "the era of 'Occupation: housewife'" (47)[4] and within her Catholic faith. Additionally, the conversation shows the difference, besides 20 years or so, between the bored, repressed housewife and the frank, sexually liberated female college student in the early 1970s. The inability of either the wife or the daughter to satisfy the patriarch(y) is demonstrated by Jack's first appearance outside of a dream in the film: He comes into the house, interrupting the conversation to snap at Joan about the garage door and being late to "Larry's" (not Larry and his wife Shirley's) cocktail party, and to snidely tell Nikki to "try to stay a virgin."

The cocktail party is a more elaborate affair in the extended release, with waiters serving canapes and several pieces of information that reinforce Romero's feminist argument that were cut from the theatrical release. There's a brief shot of a woman having her ass deliberately grabbed by a man who plays it off as accidental, and Joan's therapist is in attendance, establishing that he is a neighbor, has more than one wife as a client, and is paid by their husbands, raising questions about his

objectivity. Before the witch conversation, one snippet of barely over-
heard conversation is a woman critiquing an action or desire of other
women who "have empty houses or they're menopausal or they have
too much money and don't know what else to do, and that's ridiculous."
After the cocktail party scene (and before the realtor dream sequence in
the theatrical release), a post-dream, next-morning scene of Joan awakening, disconcerted and then startled by Jack, foreshadows the film's
climax, while Jack's remarks further establish him as the distant but
controlling patriarch(y): After speculating about Nikki's sex life in
terms of the "trouble" she'll get in, he says, twice in the largely one-sided
30-second conversation, that Joan should "just get back to sleep," that is,
quit thinking about her dreams or her life, maybe take the tranquilizers
that the realtor mentioned (and which she is shown almost taking and
then throwing away shortly after this scene in the extended release), and
fill the role created for her by society and by Friedan's "feminine mystique." As "Jack's wife," she is a woman whose life is lived through her
performance of femininity and entirely for her husband, her child and
her home, and whose value correlates to her successes in these areas.

In her book on the suburban Gothic, Bernice M. Murphy interro-
gates "the paradoxical comforts and perils of conformity" to ask if the
suburbs are "a particularly dangerous place for wives and mothers left at
home all day" (4). The older "first-generation" suburban mothers were,
when Friedan was researching *The Feminine Mystique*, well-educated
women living lives as full-time housewives (Friedan 289), who saw "lim-
itless challenge" for their energies and intellect in the suburbs. They
"seized the opportunity and were leaders and innovators in these new
communities" and "used [their] strength to resist the pressures to conform, resist the time-filling busywork of suburban house and community" (291). The "next generation," however, the women who succumbed
to the feminine mystique before or as their reason for attending college,
who married and started families in their late teens or early 20s, "were
looking for sanctuary; they were perfectly willing to accept the suburban community as they found it (their only problem was 'how to fit in');
they were perfectly willing to fill their days with the trivia of housewif-
ery" (291). Joan is likely of this generation, of an age with the younger
housewives with young children whom Friedan interviewed in the early
1960s, living in a split-level house where "they almost *have* to live the
feminine mystique" (291), a woman who, when her child is grown, has
no self to have interests.

For this latter group, the answer to Murphy's question is pretty
definitely *yes*, although who is under threat varies between suburban
texts. In Ira Levin's novel *The Stepford Wives*,[5] for example, the threat

is to housewives who dare to be bored by homemaking and childrearing, whereas in *Jack's Wife,* the boredom is a source of a threat to those in power. Unlike sociological studies of the era that "generally refuted the suggestion that suburbia was an inherently damaging locale for women" (Murphy 61) or that suburbia itself was a "breeding ground for discontent and [or because of?] mindless conventionality" (4), Romero recognizes "the soul-destroying tedious reality of life as a middle-aged woman in 1970s suburbia" (61) and "that even well-behaved, well-off suburban women can have much bigger and more painful problems than you might expect" (Doyle 89). *Jack's Wife* is a horror movie, but the monster is the product of patriarchal oppression and the norms that it constructs, "the problem that has no name, a vague, undefined wish for 'something more'" (Friedan 58). Even those, like Joan, who went along with social expectations for decades—who "were taking tranquilizers like cough drops" (20), reading magazines that told them what they should be and that what they were probably wasn't yet enough, accepting the feminine mystique as a guide and goal rather than as normalized oppression and abuse—even those women might, in the 1970s, push back, with whatever weapons were available.

Friedan identifies the "jumping-off point at 40" as one of the "crucial points in [a woman's] life cycle." Denied the ability to construct a self or "see themselves after twenty-one" and "answer[ing] the question of 'Who am I?' by saying 'Tom's [or Jack's] wife'" (70), the middle-aged suburban housewife is a source of "the most damning indictment of the feminine mystique" (loc. 166). In middle age, facing an identity crisis, Joan declines to be "Jack's wife" any longer and turns to an age-old source of female power: witchcraft.

Enter the Witch

Beginning in the 1920s, anthropologist Margaret Murray argued that witchcraft was the residue of a matriarchal pagan religion and witch hunts a tool of the Christian patriarchy to destroy that bastion of female power. By the late 1960s and early 1970s, Murray's work had been thoroughly debunked within academic circles,[6] but her ideas retained popular currency and in fact gained greater symbolic value to many feminists. Furthermore, she authored the entry on "witchcraft" that appeared in subsequent editions of the *Encyclopædia Britannica* between 1929 and 1969, and her work influenced developments in Wiccan and other neopagan practices and beliefs. It is entirely reasonable that, despite absolute academic rejection, her theories retained cultural capital and have continued to contribute to explicit connections between witchcraft and feminism, not just witchcraft and women. It isn't necessary that her conclusions be true as long as they contribute to the larger conversations.

Myths are often used in media to create figures that may be inaccurate but that in turn are used to present social constructions as natural, to provide meanings that suit the needs of those in power, and thus, to shape reality in the sense of lived experience. A movie like *Black Sunday* (1960) may employ the myth of wanton, vengeful witches who, like Snow White's stepmother or folklore's version of Erzsébet Báthori, use their power to remain young and beautiful, but the truth behind that myth is that women's value lies in their beauty, youth and virtue and thus, women are pitted against one another, a divide-and-conquer strategy that protects the patriarchy. In *Bell, Book and Candle*[7] (1958), the heroine uses a love spell to bewitch the man of her dreams although, the mythology says, she is unable to "have it all," romantic love and her powers; in the movie, this creates just enough tension to fill about 100 minutes of screen time, but the comedic hijinks and romantic ending justify masculine suspicions about women's dishonesty, necessitate a women suffering to ensure (and show) that her partner has all of the power in their relationship, and demonstrate the incompatibility of women's careers with marriage as well as the expectation that a woman will, and should, give up her own interests for her husband and, eventually, children. Both of these examples employ a "myth of the witch [that] is essentially a male creation, a product of male fears ... diluted by the addition of woman as temptress leading men to their doom" (Russell 71). Despite being a product of the patriarchy, one that dabbles, as always, in woman as sexualized object, though, this figure of the witch has powerful symbolic value because "[s]he embodies fears that men would rather forget" and "the ultimate expressions of male fears of castration" (71) and loss of agency.

Sharon Russell explores the mythic figure of the cinematic witch (pre–1984, when her article was written) as distinct from witches in other media of the time, and the films that she discusses seem to have shaped the perceptions of Joan and her female friends as well: They make jokes about chalky mousse and dancing naked in the woods; the power of the moon; and Marion, the neighbor who acknowledges that she is a witch, as "weird." While on the surface, the women seem to share the perception of witches that Russell ascribes to men, it becomes apparent that, at least for some of the women, expressing this dominant view is merely a gesture of conformity. Their discussions, despite some catty remarks, suggest a genuine, albeit kind of forbidden, interest in

Marion and her practices, and Marion represents the feminist potential of witchcraft in many ways.

It is not clear if Marion is a wife—there is no reference to a husband, but then, all of her scenes would pass the contemporary Bechdel Test with flying colors. But she lives in the same kind of middle-class suburban neighborhood as the women whom we see with their husbands. She says that her mother was a witch but that her father "belonged," presumably to what she has clarified is the religion that she practices, a linguistic manipulation that puts her father in a subordinate position, and then acknowledges how things have changed: Where once she was "sworn to secrecy" about "recipes and incantations," "in today's age, with 'anything goes,' a lot of people are beginning to take it seriously," and "the tools of the trade" are much easier to get.

More explicitly aligning witchcraft with feminism than her general statement that "anything goes" in "today's age," though, is the card-reading that Marion gives Joan's neighbor Shirley (Ann Muffly). Although Marion identifies the rather bleak reading (which is more detailed though no less depressing in the extended release) as specific to one all-consuming element of Shirley's life, the reading, to which Joan is a silent observer, could be taken from the pages of *The Feminine Mystique*: Hope will exist but will not be fulfilled, and "[r]omantic love has failed. ... Strength and hope keep you armed through all this, while not changing things for the better, making things bearable." The reading acknowledges Shirley's unhappiness, unhappiness that is described in ambiguous enough terms that it could be that of any number of the suburban housewives whom Friedan interviewed. Shirley is unhappily married as well as older than Joan, and Marion's reading emphasizes that, in Shirley's life and for women like her, nothing will change. "Bearable" is as good as it will get. Joan is apprehensive and listens in on Shirley's tarot reading and the subsequent discussion rather than participating, looking up in surprise when Marion pointedly mentions prophetic dreams.

Romero's film is very much a product of "today's age, with 'anything goes,'" although its dominant culture is more conservative. The visit to Marion clarifies the witchcraft as practiced within the movie and its relationship to what Friedan learned from her research and Joan is on the verge of discovering. As Shirley says in the extended release after reading aloud that "[t]he religion often served as a retreat for emotional women, repressed women, masculine women, and those suffering from personal disappointment or from nervous maladjustment,'" "Christ, what other kind of women are there? No wonder this stuff's getting so damn popular!" While her statement could be read as critical (it sounds like Freud's categories of women), it clarifies that witchcraft is a way to counter the discontent caused by the feminine mystique. Joan identifies witchcraft in the hands of complacent suburban wives as "another socially fashionable path rather than a radical alternative designed to question programmed behavioural patterns, both past and present" (T. Williams, *Cinema* 53), and says that "it becoming the in-thing for the WASP set, something kicky" is "not the way to get anything out of it." She then admits, "I *could* get with it, I really could. Curiosity or whatever, I'm nutty enough to believe there's something to it." She is talking about witchcraft, but her statement can also apply to the white suburban move toward feminism. Joan does not want the rest of her life to be merely "bearable."

It may be too soon for "the WASP set," the other women in their community, but not for Joan: The W.I.T.C.H. Manifesto makes it clear, "If you are a woman and dare to look within yourself, you are a Witch. Your power comes from your own self as a woman, and it is activated by working in concert with your sisters. ... You are a Witch by saying aloud, 'I am a Witch' three times, and thinking about that" (465–66). However, the entire conversation on the drive from Marion's home to Joan's is cut from the theatrical release (as is a subsequent discussion that both further critiques the majority of the community's housewives and expands the discussion of witchcraft in the next scene), again undercutting the film's examination of a woman's journey from "occupation: housewife" to "I'm a witch."

Joan's first step toward witchcraft and the empowerment it offers is a defense of religious magic or miracles. In a conversation that makes a great deal more sense with the cut scenes included, Nikki's occasional sexual partner Gregg (Ray Laine) attributes the apparent success of curses (or prayers) to the power of suggestion rather than traditional Christianity or "that crystal ball mumbo-jumbo." Joan uses a hypothetical, saying for the first time "I'm a witch" to challenge him. In an example of how men will use women for their purposes and the particular contempt that men have for older women, Gregg then uses Shirley's drunkenness (as Joan says, she's going through a "bad time," and the tarot reading made her vulnerable) to "prove" his point, telling her that she has smoked marijuana. This leads to a rambling outburst from Shirley about her age and her knowledge of what that means for her as a woman. She says that being past her prime doesn't bother her but instead makes her angry "[b]ecause I'm not finished yet. I'm not finished with ... things. I want to do things. I want to do something besides—" When she is pushed to complete the statement, she curses at Gregg and breaks down. When Joan angrily shuts down the conversation, Gregg suggests that he knows why she's reacting the way that she is, and it's not because she's angry on Shirley's behalf: She is angry because she too is not finished yet but, as far as society is concerned, she's washed up. Furthermore, he suggests that she sees her future in Shirley and wants something different.

As Joan drives Shirley home, Shirley self-deprecatingly makes reference to "recognition of self" and the "poor cat she's become in her old age," before reiterating what Gregg said, that Joan is not far behind her. Joan has seen into Shirley's inner life, the reality behind the fun, gossipy cocktail party hostess who teased Joan about even thinking about having an affair, and this seems to be a catalyst. Returning home, she first seems to be trying to shut everything out: the sounds of Nikki and Gregg having sex, the things that she has learned, and the storm that seems an appropriate end to such a chaotic day. But she quickly becomes turned on, writhing on her bed (while still wearing her very proper suit and chunky jewelry) and seeming to orgasm before knocking her copy of *To Be a Witch: A Primer*[8] onto the floor.[9]

Becoming a Witch

In a series of short scenes, Nikki catches her mother listening in and runs away, and Joan visits her therapist, ostensibly because she is worried about Nikki but admitting, in tears, that she is worried about herself and what is happening to her. Her therapist sees this as a breakthrough, but the scene cuts immediately to Jack shaking Joan and yelling that she is both a bad mother and "sick"; it appears that she has told him why Nikki left (without mentioning her own response, one assumes), and he seems more angry at Joan for not knowing how to respond and not "kick[ing] some ass" than worried about his daughter (presumably because now he knows that she is not a virgin). It is here that we see evidence of physical violence, as Jack hits her in the face twice while berating her. There are bruises, covered with makeup, evident in the next scene as Jack poses as the "concerned father" to the police whom he has called in. As Joan says later, his only real concern is Nikki getting pregnant.

In the extended release, this is followed by a short scene with Jan telling her cleaning woman[10] to take a paid vacation since Jack and Nikki will be gone; this is significant in that it shows both that Joan's actions are premeditated and that she has help with the house, meaning that there is less to occupy her than many other suburban housewives.[11] This excised clip also includes the cleaning woman's comments on Joan's outfit (of the type that women use to criticize one another indirectly:

"I could never wear that" and "Watch you don't get picked up in that outfit"), which calls attention to the perhaps-youthful, stylish outfit she wears to go ask Gregg if he knows where Nikki is, a very different outfit from the gray checked suit she wore the last time they met. During their conversation, he speaks frankly, to Joan's discomfort, about the sexual revolution, birth control and casual sex and calls her Mrs. Robinson, a reference to the older woman who seduces a young man who also has a relationship with her daughter in *The Graduate* (1967). Given Mrs. Robinson's predatory and manipulative behavior toward her own daughter and Benjamin, the comparison is not particularly flattering, much like Marion being compared to the witches in *Rosemary's Baby*.

That night, Joan has what turns out to be her first nightmare about home invasion; significantly, her first thought on being woken up (in the dream) by a noise is to ask if it is Jack, anticipating the film's conclusion. Going downstairs, she finds a masked figure, sometimes trying to break in but at a few points seeming to already be in the house. This first nightmare sequence, not yet clearly a dream, is probably the most traditional horror scene in the movie: Joan tries to call for help as the figure breaks in and picks up the knife that she had dropped in fear. Joan tries to get out another door, but it is chained and otherwise secured, reminding the viewer that the house, however large, is a cage. The figure eventually gets into her bedroom and is revealed to be masked, wearing something that almost looks like a "Green Man" mask, but in grays and reds, and that gives the suggestion of horns in silhouette. He attempts to sexually assault her and, as she fights back and attempts to unmask him, Jack wakes her up, as she has been flailing and hitting him in her sleep. He again tells her to "just go to sleep."

The next day, she drives into "the city," presumably Pittsburgh, to buy supplies with her credit card.[12] She visits a counterculture market to buy several ingredients including musk incense, Roman vitriol, fennel seeds and camphor, and then a junk or antique store to buy a "chalice, thurible, knives ... witches' tools," as the clerk remarks before asking if she is a witch. Joan is not ready to identify herself as such yet and says (twice) that she's just interested, but immediately goes home to complete an exercise identified as preliminary from Chapter Two of *To Be a Witch*[13] through which she will learn or determine her witch name and then complete at least one more ritual that seems to place some sort of protective aura around her.

It is after this first ritual, with candles, incense, a plate, and a cup that the film provides evidence that Joan is more than just interested in witchcraft. Despite being a Catholic, to the extent that it is commented on earlier in the film, she has conducted these rituals on Ash

Wednesday and rubs soot on her forehead to pretend to Jack that she went to church to receive the penitential ashes to mark the start of Lent (and to avoid going with him after dinner). Since the ashes used in Catholic services are blessed, Joan's action may compound the blasphemy of performing witchcraft, and doing so on a holy day may also compound the venial sin of lying. By choosing to become a practicing witch on a holy day, at the start of Lent, Joan has turned her back on her Catholic faith deliberately.[14]

Once Jack leaves town, we see Joan again interacting with the neighboring women, discussing, as is so often the case in movies, their husbands and having them around. This cross section—a bridge foursome made up of an older married woman, a much younger married woman, an unmarried woman (who, given that it is the 1970s, is presumably unmarried because she is overweight) and Joan, who married young but now has an adult child—shows a range of perspectives on marriage. This scene could be taken directly from Friedan's book: The older wife says that she would love to have her husband out of the house and that she married because "it got a little more difficult each day to get makeup on in the morning," that is, she was getting older. The younger wife says that she doesn't know how she'd feel about having her husband travel as much as Jack does, but acknowledges that her thoughts about marriage and being a housewife might change when her small children get older. And the unmarried woman asserts that if she were married, she would definitely not want her husband to be gone. They then discuss (while day drinking and playing cards) "taking some courses at the Y[MCA] this spring." The ensuing conversation illustrates what Friedan writes, that

> the education a woman can get at forty is permeated, contaminated, diluted by the feminine mystique. Courses in golf, bridge, rug-hooking, gourmet cooking, sewing are intended, I suppose, for real use, by women who stay in the housewife trap. The so-called intellectual courses offered in the usual adult education centers—art appreciation, ceramics, short-story writing, conversational French, Great Books, astronomy in the Space Age—are intended only as "self-enrichment." The study, the effort, even the homework that imply a long-term commitment are not expected of the housewife. ... [M]any adult education courses are unsatisfactory simply because they are not serious. The dimension of reality essential even to "self-enrichment" is barred, almost by definition, in a course specifically designed for "housewives" ... [of] thirty-five or forty, whose children are all at school [436].

As this scene is followed by Joan's next ritual, clear connections are made between Joan's study of witchcraft, learning, enrichment and exploring the self. Friedan notes that a return to degree-granting college has many challenges for older women, but says that, given the nature of other programs, such a return may be the only option for those seeking "a new life plan ... for serious use in society" (437). *Jack's Wife* shows a different possibility: When Joan visits Marion to talk about becoming a member, Marion acknowledges that Joan's fear and hesitance are necessary for belief but that there is more to it: "We'll have to see if you can learn. It's a long process. We'll have to see if the interest is as great after all the study," she says, also reminding Joan that the power is not one to be overused or used without care.

In this final portion of the movie, Joan uses witchcraft (plus a phone call) to summon Gregg to her, unaware or disbelieving (because society has told her so) that she doesn't need to make any additional effort to seduce him. When she has the intruder nightmare again, she becomes fearful of the power, perhaps in light of Marion's warnings. She tells Gregg that she made him come to her using witchcraft, but he refuses to humor her, seeing her panic as a way to shift agency for something that she wanted onto something else. Gregg is consistently awful, but he does have insights into the power that society has over women. While she does not agree with his dismissal of her power, Joan seems to accept Gregg's interpretation of her actions and performs a ritual to summon "Virago," a woman hero. While the word *virago* is now used almost exclusively in a pejorative sense to describe aggressive women acting in traditionally masculine ways, Joan has joined the ranks of second-wave feminists and unhappy housewives who do not see rejections or transgressions of traditional gender roles as negative traits. As the film never commits to the supernatural vs. the non-supernatural, the cat who comes in an open window as Joan finishes the ritual may or may not be Virago or a witch's familiar, but Joan does confidently tell Gregg she does not want to see him again.

Leading up to the film's climax, Joan engages in a series of domestic tasks—gardening and laundry—which, like the mundane actions in the opening scenes, turn out to be, at least in part, another manifestation of her home invasion nightmare. This time, empowered, she does not just attempt to hide; she grabs and loads Jack's duck-hunting shotgun. The figure is able to get the gun away from her, and she wakes up screaming in bed. Although the film is ambivalent about precisely what causes her actions, she is then at the top of the stairs with the gun and shoots and kills Jack, who has returned unexpectedly and late at night, as he tries to enter the house.

The final moments of the film feature the aftermath of Jack's death and a discussion between two police officers, whose dialogue explicitly states the ingrained misogyny and "the deeply held suspicions as to the true nature of women" (Russell 63). Debating whether it was an accident or not, they abandon the idea of looking into insurance or other motives because "it doesn't really matter if she's lying or not, she'll get away with it ... goddamn women, they get it all in the end, they get it all from us, they wind up with everything." This is intercut with Joan's initiation into Marion's all-women coven, with the coven's incantations about the power of the female body, loyalty and self-knowledge alternating with the cops' discussion. Doyle notes that "the circle of dangerous women in a suburban living room look[s] more than a little like a demonic feminist consciousness-raising group" (231), but Joan returns to "the soul-destroying tedious reality of life as a middle-aged woman in 1970s suburbia" (Murphy 61) for what one hopes may be the last time. The film closes with a boozy neighborhood women's get-together, Joan's first party since Jack's death. One wife says that, although "we were all terribly distressed at the time ... now I must admit, I'm just a bit envious" of what some of the women recognize as Joan's absolute freedom. Speaking with another woman, Joan very simply states, "I'm a witch."

Debate exists over the nature of the film's ending, in no small part because, despite Joan's identification of herself, the film ends with another woman identifying her as "you know, Jack's wife." Murphy says that this moment undermines "the possibility that her immersion in witchcraft provides a successful escape from the sterility of her previous life" (60) and asks if it is "possible that her new life as a witch is in its own way as hollow as her previous existence as a housewife and mother" (61). I would argue that this represents not a tragic ending for Joan but a final reminder of what she no longer has to be a part of: She can sell the house with the groovy wallpaper and move somewhere interesting! Williams agrees with Murphy, writing that Romero's "early version of the woman's nightmare will never end. It will continue well beyond the film's actual conclusion[,] trapping her in a type of psychic-repetition compulsive situation due to the fact that she is not really as liberated as she believes" (*Cinema* 50), but he also says that Joan is "one of Romero's most sophisticated attempts to analyse the personal dilemmas affecting individuals in contemporary society who are often faced with different choices but who end up choosing *the wrong path*" (48, emphasis added), so I don't think that he and I are watching the same movie. Sharon Russell concludes that the witch "leading men to their doom ... may be a way to achieve tragedy or revenge, but it is not the road to liberation" (71). Again, I would disagree. Whether it was witchcraft or not, as with seducing Gregg, the rituals gave her the power to do what she wanted to do; the film is ambivalent about if that is to protect herself or kill Jack, but Sady Doyle reads Joan's act as deliberate, because witches "kill men who harm women" (231).

Joan needs the promises of witchcraft whether she plans to use it to kill her husband or not; when she attempts self-reflection, literally looking into mirrors around her home, she increasingly sees herself as an old woman, a crone, no longer sexual and therefore no longer useful by society's terms, a confrontation with the self and aging that plays out in Romero's 1973 short film *The Amusement Park*, featuring a different socioeconomic class of elderly people also pushed aside and perceived as useless. At the film's end, Joan's body is still that of an aging woman, but after the initiation ritual, which pays tribute to each part of her body as it is, it is a sacred thing rather than something that will inevitably be discarded. The film, which began with Freudian nightmares, ends with a Freudian fantasy of "meeting violent male power with violent female resistance, taking patriarchy down man by man by man" (Doyle 231).

3

L'Univers Concentrationnaire of *The Crazies*

Noah Simon Jampol

Released in 1973, *The Crazies* was both written and directed by George A. Romero.[1] A broad outline: Due to a downed plane, a government-made bio-weapon (code-named Trixie) makes its way into the water supply of an exurban Pennsylvania community. An attempted government clean-up (quarantine; martial law) is botched and—in true Romero style of the era—death, destruction and mayhem ensue, as does a searing critique of humans and humanism.

The film was shot on location in Evans City and Zelienople, Pennsylvania, hill towns not far outside of Romero's native Pittsburgh.[2] The film, though since enshrined as a cult classic and deemed marketable enough a concept to warrant a remake, received quite poor initial critical evaluations. Vincent Canby, writing for the *New York Times* was particularly unreceptive to the film's conceit:

> The symptoms of the illness: uncontrollable giggles followed by madness and probably death. Thus begins *The Crazies*, an inept science-fiction film from George A. Romero, the Pittsburgh man who established himself as the Grandma Moses of exurban horror films with *The Night of the Living Dead*, a movie whose stark, primitive style has made it into a classic of low camp.

Ignoring the classist and anti-genre elements of Canby's analysis, he does helpfully note: "The film's real subject is not bacteriological weaponry, or the idiocies of the military, but the collapse of community presented as a spectacle, prompted when the Army moves to quarantine Evans City without explaining what is wrong." This introduces an avenue for potentially productive analysis of what makes the film compelling: why rely on "spectacle" (a noun suited well to horror films) to dramatize the collapse of civic life?

Sight and Sound magazine's James Blackford asked interviewee Romero:

> There is a sort of naturalism to the performances in many of your films. I'm thinking about films like *Hungry Wives* and *The Crazies*, where the performances give the films a realism that horror hadn't had before. Details too: in *The Crazies*, the extras in the white radiation suits. In most films they would be background characters, but you make them human. You show them getting frightened. And there is that great shot where one steals a fishing rod. That sort of naturalistic detail seems to me to be a real Romero trait.

Romero responded:

> It's hard for me to talk about that specifically because so much of that is spontaneous. I'm just always looking for things, you know? Like, this guy is going to walk through here, he might think, "Oh, look at those fishing rods. Why don't I just grab 'em?" Or the scenes of them going through [dead people's] pockets. Maybe that recalls the Holocaust.... I wasn't thinking so much about that at that moment, it's just these guys would probably be doing that kind of thing. So, I always throw that in.

The Crazies is not a film explicitly about the Holocaust. And yet Holocaust imagery abounds. Romero mentions soldiers looting the bodies of the deceased—an apt observation—though the effort here was, if we take his word for it, something nearly subconscious. But the images pile up: round-ups, burning bodies, medical exploitation, etc. Again, while *The Crazies* is not explicitly a Holocaust film, the potency of these specific images demands, even unconsciously, a consideration of Romero's film and Holocaust representation.[3]

Previous pathbreaking work by William Graebner has examined the significance of the Holocaust within Romero's *Dead* films, connecting the consciousness- and emotion-devoid zombies to the *Musselmänner* (those concentration camp inhabitants rendered "living dead" within the camps) and the treatment of these bodies.[4] But the clear categories of them and us (them-vs.-us; infected and uninfected) inherent to Romero's *Dead* oeuvre are blurred within the universe of *The Crazies*, wherein the ability to distinguish perpetrator from victim—government officials, uninfected citizenry, the "crazies" themselves—is no easy matter, as their mutual survival instinct-driven violence varies little across groups. As these lines blur, differences are reduced to what Derrida identifies as *différance*, a difference smaller than how we might traditionally define "difference, and potential espacement is undermined."[5] The elimination of difference creates what Primo Levi has called a gray zone: a blurred space between victims and victimizers which ultimately facilitates behavior that begets total and mutual destruction; a space of moral ambiguity within the world of the Holocaust in which the roles of perpetuator and victim are blurred. This blurring moves the film into the domain of the postmodern as defined by David Roskies and Naomi Diamant. If indeed, as these critics postulate, "[t]he 'postmodern' world began in Auschwitz" (26), then a potentially productive analysis of *The Crazies* might begin at the junction of the Holocaust and the postmodern. *The Crazies* is a particularly postmodern film insofar as the epistemological, how-can-you-tell business is meaningless; we cannot, and it doesn't matter. Rather, the questions in play are ontological: What is a victim, what is a perpetrator? What is a civilization?

This undermined humanism is the autonomous fully functioning and poisoned universe apart—*l'univers concentrationnaire*—of *The Crazies*.[6] This universe is not only marked by imagery that implies the Holocaust (looted bodies, burning bodies, the discourse of "just following orders"), but fashions a world of all-encompassing gray death, of collaborationists and cinders. The result is a film which extends the cynicism of *Night of the Living Dead* to a larger argument for post–Holocaust posthumanism and perhaps a prayer for its practical expediency in a world of mushrooming poison.

The Holocaust, Representation and Genre

As opposed to Daniel Goldhagen's infamous study, Hitler's *Willing Executioners* (1996), in which he theorizes hatred (specifically the cultural hatred of Germany for its Jewish denizens) as the primary motivator for the Holocaust, Christopher Browning suggests that the cause and subsequent legacy of the Holocaust is more ambiguous.[7] In *Ordinary Men* (1993), he contends that the group that formed Reserve Police Battalion (*Ordnungspolizei* or *Orpo*) 101—not the SS, but Hamburg-based civilian, working- and middle-class perpetrators of mass violence and death during the Holocaust—were transformed from initially ambivalent to ultimately effective killers of Jews. Browning's study leaves us with an unsettling question: If these unlikely killers of Reserve Battalion 101 could become such, what does this say of all men—and the sorts of men typically assumed to be murderers? The question simultaneously implies the dehumanizing effects of the Holocaust and anticipates a critical shift towards posthumanism, an understanding of humanity as something more ruthless and prone to brutality than humanism would have us ascribe to people's condition and their potential behaviors. The liminal and uncertain space created by the Holocaust and those who perpetuated its cruelty echoes Levi's notion of the gray zone.

While Lawrence Langer contrasts the views of Browning and Levi, positing that Browning's theoretical approach to the Holocaust would frustrate Levi's efforts to bear witness to the camps, Browning and Levi's approaches to the Holocaust have a problematizing effect on simplistic or binary notions of who did what to whom and why. Browning and Levi's interpretations challenge the notion of a dichotomous Holocaust, one that can be interpreted along traditional lines and narratives of good vs. evil, victim vs. violator.

Such a reading of the Holocaust frustrates traditional modes of representation and interpretation. We may approach texts asking if there is a lesson to be learned from the camps and other horrors of the Holocaust. Is there a lesson for humanity that can be abstracted out of the ash per Tzvetan Todorov (or, in more mass-culture-self-help-friendly spheres, Viktor Frankl)? If such a lesson exists, can it be expressed or represented by the writer?[8] The frustration of redemptive readings of the Holocaust is compounded by the impossibility of true verisimilitude in Holocaust representation.

The effects of the Holocaust have the capacity to fracture individual consciousness as understood before the trauma, the sense of an integrated or whole personhood as known before the Holocaust. Charlotte Delbo speaks of this "deep memory" associated with Auschwitz:

> Unlike those whose life came to a halt as they crossed the threshold of return, who since that time survive as ghosts, I feel that the one who was in the camp is not me, is not the person who is here, facing you. No, it is all too incredible. And everything that happened to that other, the Auschwitz one, now has no bearing upon me, does not concern me, so separate from one another are this deep-lying memory and ordinary memory. I live within a twofold being. The Auschwitz double doesn't bother me, doesn't interfere with my life. As though it weren't I at all. Without this split I would not have been able to revive.[9]

Fracture is hereby a necessity of survival, a way of achieving an integrated and whole sense of self following the Holocaust. Delbo thereby calls the capacity for authorial integrity into question, echoing Judith Lewis Herman's notion of trauma as potentially disrupting the relationship between the memory and emotions of a survivor.

If the Holocaust could fracture a human or require human fissure as a survival mechanism, the effects of this trauma move beyond implications for an individual's sense of self. German Jewish writer and Holocaust survivor Jean Améry spent the war years as a resistance fighter and then prisoner in the concentration camp system. While a prisoner in Breendonk in occupied Belgium, Améry was tortured. His reflections on this experience, published more than two decades after his liberation from Bergen-Belsen, explore the impossibilities of representation, specifically that the pain of torture defies representational expression in any traditional sense of a rhetorical author-text-audience relationship. Améry argues that such experiences cannot be understood by those who have not experienced them firsthand. Further, for the victim, the experience of torture is a permanent shattering of faith in the self, others and language. These reflections are echoed and extended by Giorgio Agamben as "not even the survivor can bear witness completely, can speak his own lacuna. This means that testimony is the disjunction between two impossibilities of bearing witness; it means that language, in order to bear witness, must give way to a non-language in order to show the impossibility of bearing witness" (39). A person's relationship to the world and self as structured by language is hence denaturalized, and post-war writing thusly inherits a shattered world; we can piece it together, but it is forever broken. If in fact Améry is right and torture, or torture as extended to the Holocaust at large, cannot be understood by those who have not experienced it and simultaneously is unpresentable, what are writers who are further removed from the events of the Holocaust who wish to explore the subject to do? If we accept that the event is unknowable to those who did not experience it and recalcitrant to representation, is the writer now free from the conventional limitations imposed on writing by traditional realistic modes of expression? The question hence returns: How does one begin to represent the events of the Holocaust? And by extension, what does it look like when the cultural consciousness of the Holocaust as understood by American filmmakers as its unrelenting force comes to bear on their oeuvre?

Though the specific relationship between fantastic genres and Holocaust narrative is seldom examined, several studies have examined the relationship between genre writings more generally and the Holocaust. *The Fantastic in Holocaust Literature and Film* contains a number of essays exploring the titular topic. In this collection, Judith B. Kerman identifies the potential challenge that the Holocaust poses to comprehension or interpretation: "[A]lthough we know these events took place, it is difficult to understand the relationship between events like the Holocaust and the realities of everyday life" (13). The cognitive rift between the events of the Holocaust and our current universe is, at times, incomprehensible, and Kerman pointedly asks (when visiting Dachau and observing the physical reality of the camp as well as the rather plain suburbs that now form its environs): "Which is real, the concentration camp or comfortable middle-class life? Is it only a question of 45 years, or a different universe?" (13). The physical encounter with the remnants of the Holocaust and the understanding that the events occurred in our world, in plain, common places that can be found on maps and in which one can buy a cup of coffee, creates a cognitive fissure; the individual encountering the world of the Holocaust faces a lacuna occupied by both and neither of these worlds.

The question of cognitive dissonance is expanded when Kerman states, "The moral questions are much more complicated than Good versus Evil. Although without any question the concentration camps and ghettos were unmitigated evil, as soon as we look at individual human beings rather than a social system, motivation becomes complicated—even Mengele, even Hitler was once an innocent child" (15). As the notion of the geography of the camps is now characterized by the banal, the Holocaust and its defiance of material cause similarly challenge the distance and sanctity of abstract evil (i.e., the progression of a child-monster to a Nazi), as clear-cut categories and monads are grayed much like the textual explorations that follow.

This breakdown of material cause as a predictable mode for anticipating not only the actions of others but our own responses challenges both the interpretation as well as artistic exploration of the Holocaust. Langer recalls hearing the horrors of witness testimony and the subsequent struggling in the search for a response of those parties who witnessed the horror of the camps or writers, historians, academics and artists attempting to do something to materially respond to these events. Such an exercise is devastatingly challenging insofar as the Holocaust has no peer—there is no event to look to for an example of how one might react to such crimes. The nature and scale of the Holocaust make it a hauntingly novel antecedent without any obvious outcome, with an according burden placed on the non-witness to find an appropriate and ethical mode of response to the event and its narratology.

The Postmodern

While the fantastic may connote the "hard" sci-fi images and scenes originating from H.G. Wells' *The Time Machine* (1895) or the popular fantastic–science fiction pulps of the early 20th century, the genre is more inclusive and further-reaching, including postmodern narratives that make use of (and often flout) the genre's tropes to explore the human psyche—what is often called "soft science fiction." If indeed, as aforementioned per Roskies and Diamant, "[t]he 'postmodern' world began in Auschwitz," the Holocaust is implicitly and inexorably correlated to the rise of postmodern literary methods of representation and exploration, inclusive of so-called "soft" science fiction—fictions less tied up with the scientific "hows" of their harder generic counterparts, instead focusing on matters more closely aligned with the concerns of the social sciences.

With the initiation of the postmodern—a function of the Holocaust—comes a shift from epistemology to ontology. Per Brian McHale:

> [...] a general thesis about modernist fiction: the dominant [component] of modernist fiction is epistemological. That is, modernist fiction deploys strategies which engage and foreground questions such as ... "How can I interpret this world of which I am a part? And what am I in it?" Other typical modernist questions might be added: What is there to be known?; Who knows it?; How do they know it and with what degree of certainty?; How is knowledge transmitted from one knower to another, and with what degree of reliability?; How does the object of knowledge change as it passes from knower to knower? And so on [8].

Modernism is concerned with epistemology and meditates on the nature of knowledge. Postmodernism is concerned with ontology, with the nature of existence. This is a pivot from questions of how we come to know something to questions of what that "something" is—a productive heuristic for evaluating *The Crazies*.

Within the universe of *The Crazies*, distinctions between "crazies" (those who have been infected) and those who haven't are not easily discernible. There is the bizarre laughter, the occasional bouts of violence. But the same can be said (and identified) in those who are not "crazies"—be they civilian or military populations. Hence, thematically, *The Crazies* is not a film which benefits from an inquiry into how we can tell *who* is a "crazy" but—*what* is a "crazy," what is the nature of the world in which these types might emerge? Challenges to the rote and, perhaps, audience-friendly distinctions between an implied them and us force the narrative to be consumed as one of ontological inquiry.[10]

The Crazies, Fantastic Genres, the Holocaust

Thematically, Romero has identified *The Crazies* as a film levied in the direction of the military. When interviewed:

> **DY:** Are you satisfied with *The Crazies*?
> **GEORGE ROMERO:** I think maybe it was a little ahead of its time. At the time I made it, we were still in Vietnam and it was a very heartfelt problem, a part of the national consciousness and I don't think anyone was ready to see that situation—even though it's not a Vietnam film, it's an anti-military film [Yakir 56].

As such, Romero's film is not a Holocaust film but an "anti-military film," born out of the specific violence of the Vietnam War. As such, reading *The Crazies* as an explicitly Holocaust film is a misguided effort, regardless of the auteur's intentionality.

As such, again, *The Crazies* stands in contrast to Romero's zombie films as critiqued by the work of William Graebner. Graebner argues that while American directors (and hence cinema) were reluctant in the post-war years to address the events and themes of the Holocaust, Romero was willing to approach this subject. As such, the films in Romero's zombie trilogy of *Night of the Living Dead* (1968), *Dawn of the Dead* (1978) and *Day of the Dead* (1985) are indeed Holocaust-inflected texts, specifically insofar as the *Muselmänner* of the camps are readily recalled by the reanimated dead of these films. Further, this reading relies on an analysis of the zombies of these films as those trapped between life and death—that "anonymous mass" of something posthuman. According to Graebner, not only are Romero's zombies dehumanized, but this dehumanization is further reinforced by their treatment as sub-human, without the dignity becoming human life; this mistreatment translates beyond the living dead to the outright dead as these zombies are disposed of their right to proper funerary practices, rituals and traditions.

It is in this disregard for human life and human death that one must begin connecting the narrative and visuals of *The Crazies* to the Holocaust and Holocaust representation. With the accidental proliferation of the Trixie virus on the unknowing population of Evans City, the government—specifically, the Department of Defense—conducts an experiment *manqué*. This unethical biological experimentation on the minds of these citizens casts the military in an unambiguously villainous role. The nuclear bombers which circle the town and are prepared (*à la* Chrome Dome) to render Evans City a crater if the virus breaks containment, speak to an escalating disregard for human and planet alike. The military is hence rendered unequivocally and unambiguously as a force—a human force—of destruction towards individuals, communities and civilization. Upon interrogation for their actions in the community during martial law, one soldier defends himself: "We're only following orders"—a discourse that quickly connotes the Holocaust in the most overt manner possible.

These military men, agents of destruction on both macro and micro scales, are presented in alternating Battle Dress Uniforms and hazmat suits. The sartorial distinction is almost humorous, as the behavior of soldiers dressed for the battlefield or to do a bit of cleaning is interchangeable. All are armed. All kill civilians. All are extensions of the

American military dropped on the citizens of Evans City. Yet the relatively anodyne anonymity of Battle Dress Uniforms is escalated when they are exchanged for full-on, fully masked hazmat suits, rendering the military now faceless. Those in hazmat suits are the ones who loot the bodies of the deceased, emptying pockets with aplomb, taking jewelry, watches (Fig. 4). This image—one which overtly recalls the Holocaust and Holocaust representation—features men without faces, without discernable individual identities. They are presented as a mass of their own: an amorphous anti-human, dehumanizing machine of death. The hazmat suits and masks facilitate an enhanced dissemination of responsibility which is anticipated by the release of Trixie (as well as its subsequent cover-up) and the initial acts of violence against the victims of the virus.

As the soldiers are paired alongside the growing number of "crazies" who look no different from the uninfected, the viewer is left with fruitless epistemological inquires piling up, one on the next.[11] Further, the conduct of the uninfected citizens, guns of their own turned on other uninfected (and recalling the climax to *Night of the Living Dead*), only further serves to ablate categorical differences between all classes affected by this virus in one way or another.[12] This inability and unproductivity is what leads the viewer from epistemological inquiries to more ontological concerns. The behavior of civilians, "non-crazies," further blurs lines. Would-be hero and Vietnam veteran Clank, while

Figure 4. Soldiers loot dead civilians in *The Crazies* (1973, Pittsburgh Films).

initially a sympathetic figure, declines in moral stature and personal
ethics well before succumbing to the actual Trixie virus. The interpersonal violence that he enacts is near-impossible to distinguish from that
of the occupying military force. Other "non-crazy" civilians banally
kill Judy, the mother of protagonist David's unborn child. The end of a
potential life and a tragic conclusion to the film's narrative are the products of the hands of uninfected, non-military townspeople. These are
David's neighbors, known, not in the least anonymous. These two vec-
tors—Clank and the death of Judy—move the theme of the film beyond
a mere critique of the military.

What, then, we arrive at is an *univers concentrationnaire*. The world
of *The Crazies* is a world apart from reality, like the separate universe of
the Holocaust. This is indeed an alternate universe—one of Levi's gray
zones and one which mushrooms outward eternally.

The virus and the response are front and center; the film closes
with Colonel Peckem being sent to Louisville as the virus seems to have
taken hold there. Trixie (gendered female by virtue of her code name),
biological destruction and the military response move the flatten-
ing and gray world of death south and west. However, the expansion
of Trixie, of military violence and the destruction of civilization also
flows back through history, returning to the Holocaust and then for-
wards again to Romero's critique of the military.

The Crazies' anti-military theme, bolstered and informed by Holocaust imagery, allows for an enhanced consideration—via what Michael
Rothberg has identified as "multidirectional memory"—of violence on a
civilization-destroying scale. These arenas—the Holocaust and military
violence—are no part of "an ugly contest of comparative victimization"
(7). Rather, simultaneous consideration of these topics and their totally
deleterious effects mutually advance understanding and perhaps even
empathy, indicating that "social conflict can only be addressed through
a discourse that weaves together past and present, public and private"
(285).

As such, there is the opportunity for a simultaneous multidirectional indictment of the military as a male-driven organ of hegemony. Kendall R. Phillips observes: "What makes *The Crazies* a particularly interesting narrative experience is that we are, in essence, invited
to root for a group of individuals that, should they succeed, will likely
spread a deadly, mind-altering virus to the entire population" (43). As
such, we are compelled to root against uniforms, patriarchy—against
the military, against irrelevant definitions of humanism. The looming
phallic violence of bombs hangs over the entire narrative universe of
The Crazies, extending well past the geography of this bit of Western

Pennsylvania and the end of Romero's film. Given the choice between death by bomb and a global Trixie pandemic, we are all voting for Trixie. This alignment places the viewer and Romero in clear opposition to the hegemonic and gendered forces of violence endemic to the military, and, by extension, the United States of America.

Draining the Blood of the Patriarch

Challenging Hegemonic Masculinity in Martin

CAIN MILLER

As the 1970s entered an era of "realist horror," thanks to influences from the likes of Michael Powell, Alfred Hitchcock and Herschell Gordon Lewis, the decade witnessed a crop of young, independent horror directors like Wes Craven, Tobe Hooper and John Carpenter who produced films that not only pushed the boundaries of on-screen violence but also produced works that exemplified the genre revision that defined the New Hollywood era. Leading the way for these radical horror filmmakers was George A. Romero, whose *Night of the Living Dead* (1968) proved to be a major commercial success and subsequently one of the most influential horror titles from this era. *Night* is significant for two primary reasons. Firstly, it further cemented the realist scares that would dominate American independent horror cinema throughout the following decade. While the *Living Dead* franchise established Romero as an auteur of zombie movies (certainly not a realist subgenre), *Night* is nonetheless marked with more subtlety than later installments. Without the elaborate makeup and prosthetics that highlight creatures' rotting flesh like in *Dawn of the Dead* (1978) and *Day of the Dead* (1985), the "ghouls" in *Night* resemble average-looking, albeit sickly pale, humans. Furthermore, while these cannibals are certainly fear-inducing, much of the film's true horror is derived from the tensions between the non-infected human characters, which grounds the narrative in realism. Secondly, *Night* serves as one of the earlier examples of revisionist horror, as exemplified in its bleak conclusion and racial subtext, the latter deconstructing the antagonistic racial Other commonly associated with classical horror. This postmodern ideological deconstruction was later exemplified in Romero's pseudo-vampire film *Martin* (1977), due to its portrayals of the decade's generational divide and the connections that it makes between masculinity and monstrosity. This chapter will analyze how *Martin* complicates the patriarchal "Van Helsing" character to represent how hegemonic masculinity was challenged throughout the 1970s in favor of more complex, albeit (in this context) unsettling, masculinities.

Masculinity in Horror from Classical to Postmodern

As Robert W. Connell and James W. Messerschmidt note, hegemonic masculinity—a term formulated in the early 1980s—is "normative" and represents the "most honored" form of manhood that is specifically signified through the subordination of women (832). As such, hegemonic masculinity can be traditionally demonstrated through the man possessing dominance within the domestic sphere or signifying his authority over Others, whether they be women, non-heteronormative individuals, people of color, etc. Classical Hollywood certainly has no shortage of hegemonic figures, as displayed in their abundance of leading men. At first glance, classical horror is no different. For example, *Dracula* (1931), the catalyst for the classic Universal horror cycle, features Prof. Van Helsing (Edward Van Sloan), the patriarchal authority figure who uses the hegemonic forces of Christianity to vanquish the titular sexually Othered vampire (Bela Lugosi). *Dracula* also serves as an apt metaphor for masculine anxieties relevant to the 1930s. Dracula is an elite aristocrat who quite literally feeds off of peasants—an image that likely resonated with Depression-era audiences. Due to the rampant unemployment in the U.S. throughout that time period, many men experienced economic emasculation. Van Helsing thus represents the "good" patriarchal protagonist who ultimately defeats the vampiric Other for having posed these threats of emasculation. In relation to Laura Mulvey's theories of male spectatorship, Van Helsing is the most readily available option on to which male viewers (or at least those who fit a similar straight, white mold) can narcissistically project themselves (8–11). This form of horror spectatorship thus potentially provided a sense of comfort for '30s male audiences because the genre promised that their real-life fears (like the Depression) would soon come to an end just as the on-screen monsters did. Likewise, the authoritative action of every patriarchal protagonist like Van Helsing likely provided reaffirmation to men that their hegemonic masculinity could also be restored.

But this reading is also reductive given horror's frequently trans-gressive portrayals of gender. Sticking with the reading of *Dracula*, while Van Helsing is the closest thing the film has to a conventional protagonist, he is far from a hegemonic figure. Although Van Hels-ing violently asserts his authority over the Other, his aging physique starkly contrasts typical Hollywood tough guys like James Cagney or John Wayne. Furthermore, Van Helsing lacks any explicit romantic partnership, and thus he does not signify his masculinity through the subordination of women. Indeed, all of *Dracula*'s male figures display impotent masculinities. While John Harker (David Manners) displays his hegemony through his romantic pairing with Mina (Helen Chan-dler), though he is also largely ineffective at preventing Dracula from seducing her. Furthermore, John and Mina's ultimate pairing is only tacked on in the closing seconds of the film, their romance (and conse-quently John's hegemonic masculinity) glossed over. Renfield (Dwight Frye) is one of the bluntest juxtapositions to hegemonic masculinity because his constant state of hypnosis under Dracula signifies his sub-ordination to his vampire master. Lastly, there is Dracula himself. On one hand, Dracula's hegemony is supported through his wealth and sub-ordination of women, considering that the count has not one but three wives. Yet Dracula's hegemony is countered by his queer love trian-gle with Mina and Renfield. Firstly, Dracula is ultimately unsuccessful in "turning" Mina into a vampire (an allegory for sexual penetration), hence his hegemonic masculinity cannot be affirmed. Secondly, Drac-ula's relationship with Renfield codes him as non-heteronormative, and consequently non-hegemonic. Lastly, Dracula eventually succumbs to subordination when Van Helsing penetrates him with a phallic wooden stake, killing him.

Perhaps the most provocative complications of hegemonic mas-culinity in classical horror can be found in James Whale's filmogra-phy. Whale, being one of the few gay filmmakers working in studio-era Hollywood, is of course known for his consistent queering of domestic familial units. In *Frankenstein* (1931), Henry Frankenstein (Colin Clive) is the film's most apparent patriarch due to his engagement to Elizabeth (Mae Clarke). Heterosexual pairing, though, is of little interest to Henry, who is far more devoted to creating life through non-heteronormative means. When Henry finally creates his Monster (Boris Karloff), his hegemony is immediately mitigated because the Monster's violent ram-page through the village signifies that Henry is no longer in power. Early in the film, Henry knows "what it feels like to be God!" but he quickly becomes a mere spectator who can do nothing but passively watch as his creation runs amok. Even by the end of the film, Henry is not the one who vanquishes the Other, as the Monster is burned in the windmill by the horde of angry villagers. Henry's subordination is also signified when he is overpowered by the Monster and thrown from the windmill. Moreover, Henry's subordination of Elizabeth is noticeably lacking from the film's conclusion. While Henry survives his fall, his final romantic pairing with Elizabeth is never shown on screen. Instead, Henry's father, Baron Frankenstein (Frederick Kerr), stands outside the couple's bedroom while Henry recovers. The baron lackadaisically expresses his hope that the two will provide him with a grandchild. His half-hearted interest in the couple's romance demonstrates that, like in the conclusion of *Dracula*, heterosexual pairing bears little importance here and that Henry, like John, never fully affirms his masculinity on screen.

The lack of patriarchal authority is even more apparent in *The Old Dark House* (1932) and *Bride of Frankenstein* (1935). In *Bride*, Henry's hegemonic masculinity is once again diminished because he cannot solidify his romance with Elizabeth (Valerie Hobson) due to his devotion to creating the Bride. Furthermore, Henry's relationship with Dr. Pretorius (Ernest Thesiger) signifies his emasculation in two ways. Firstly, Pretorius holds Elizabeth hostage, thus further delaying her marriage to Henry and consequently Henry's subordination of her. Secondly, the power dynamic between Pretorius and Henry is considerably lopsided, as Pretorius is the "master" to Henry's "servant." As Harry Benshoff argues, this master-servant relationship common in many classical horror titles serves as a metaphor for the two characters' queer relationship, with one being the "top" and the other being the "bottom" (48). Hence, Henry is subordinated; he is reduced to an inferior ranking similar to Pretorius' henchman Karl (Dwight Frye). Even the Monster (Boris Karloff) is subjected to emasculation in a number of ways. Throughout the first half of the film, the Monster is victim to various acts of mob violence which, as Elizabeth Young notes, serve as allegories for racially motivated abuses (372–74). In this context, the Monster is simply another racially-coded Other who falls victim to a white power structure. The Monster's emasculation is further signified in the film's climax when he meets his Bride (Elsa Lanchester), only for her to reject him. The Monster, like Henry, cannot obtain hegemonic masculinity because his romantic partnership is denied—the Bride refuses to be contained within the familial unit.

The Old Dark House offers a similar queering of traditional gender roles. Here, the domestic sphere, Femm Manor, is not a site of patriarchal authority and instead subverts the gender-sexual norms associated with the nuclear family. This subversion features sexually liberal characters like Roger Penderel (Melvyn Douglas) and Gladys Perkins (Lilian Bond), and various queer-coded characters like the effeminate William Porterhouse (Charles Laughton) and Horace Femm (Ernest Thesiger) as well as Horace's butch sister Rebecca (Eva Moore). The most radical subversion of patriarchal authority is present with the character Roderick Femm, the owner of the house and father to Horace and Rebecca. Roderick's patriarchal power is firstly diluted due to his age. Similar to Van Helsing, Roderick is exceptionally aged (102 years old, to be exact) and bears no physical authority over anyone. Instead, Roderick is bedridden and, similar to Henry Frankenstein, can do nothing when the horrors unfold and Penderel must fend off the Femms' crazed eldest son Saul (Brember Wills). Roderick's patriarchal status is skewed further through the casting of actress Elspeth Dudgeon in the role, a transgressive decision that blurs the lines between the male-female binary.

With the growth of postmodernism in the late 1960s and 1970s, the horror genre's depictions of gender became even more transgressive. In "Recreational Terror: Postmodern Elements of the Contemporary Horror Film," Isabel Pinedo argues that postmodern horror texts, specifically those produced after 1968, feature narratives in which "familiar categories collapse" and emphasize the "violation of boundaries" in which the good-evil binary is no longer clearly defined. As such, postmodern horror revolves around "the erosion of universal categories," "a profound loss of faith in master narratives" and "a crisis of cultural authority" in which "the master status of the universal (read: male, white, monied, heterosexual) subject deteriorates" (17–26). Indeed, in a period that witnessed numerous political assassinations, the highly publicized Manson Family murders and the Vietnam War, the horror genre could no longer offer narratives that assured the abolishment of violent Others and the subsequent restoration of normality. Postmodern horror instead offered scathing, albeit sometimes inconsistent, criticisms of various dominant ideologies. Peter Bogdanovich's *Targets* (1968) and Bob Clark's *Deathdream* (1974) provide unnerving insights into the effects that Vietnam had on its participants. Brian De Palma's *Carrie* (1976) and numerous rape-revenge titles like *I Spit on Your Grave* (1978) feature themes that correlate with second-wave feminism. Bill Gunn's *Ganja & Hess* (1973) and the surplus of Blaxploitation horror titles like *Blacula* (1972) and *Blackenstein* (1973) offer horrific insight into contemporary issues of racism, police brutality and neocolonialism, all of which were topics of focus during the decade's Black Power movement.

Pinedo's notion of the deterioration of the patriarchal white male particularly relates to the decade's changing perceptions of hegemonic masculinity. With America's defeat in the Vietnam War in 1973 and

Richard Nixon's resignation the following year, the U.S. witnessed disruptions to two once-dominant hegemonic forces: the country's military and the president. By 1979, these hardships, along with the energy crises and subsequent economic turbulence, led to President Jimmy Carter stating that the U.S. was experiencing a "crisis of confidence," a period in which American morale was seemingly at an all-time low. Elaborating on Carter's claims, David Brian Robertson stated that citizens' trust in governmental institutions was waning, arguing that "the ability of the political system to solve problems seemed to evaporate. Parties weakened. Interest groups proliferated. Public and private hierarchies lost authority. Vietnam, Watergate, and the perceived weakness of Presidents Ford and Carter undermined the belief in the strong presidency widely shared since the 1940s" (1). Indeed, during this era, authoritative figures—politicians, soldiers, etc.—who were once common examples of hegemonic masculinity were now figures of whom many Americans became more critical and distrustful. Consequently, postmodern horror's portrayal of patriarchal figures became more subversive.

Postmodern horror often portrays the patriarch as a less-than-commanding figure. In Hooper's *The Texas Chain Saw Massacre* (1974), Grandpa Sawyer (John Dugan), a once-dominant slaughterhouse worker, is now too comically decayed to bear any remnants of hegemony. The loss of Sawyer's patriarchal power is best displayed in the film's infamous dinner scene where Sawyer is unable to wield the hammer and assert his phallic dominance over Sally (Marilyn Burns). Craven's *The Last House on the Left* (1972) provides one of the few narratives that reaffirms the patriarch as an authoritative figure as the father, John Collingwood (Richard Towers), successfully exacts his revenge against the criminals who killed his daughter. Yet even *The Last House on the Left* displays anxieties regarding the patriarch's dominance given that the entire narrative revolves around Collingwood's inability to command the domestic sphere, as displayed through the disruption of his familial unit. *Last House on the Left* even displays the theme of literal loss of phallic power in a scene in which Estelle Collingwood (Eleanor Shaw) bites off the penis of one of the criminals. In fact, the masculinities present in these postmodern films are not as different from those in the forementioned classical texts as one might assume. Grandpa Sawyer and Roderick Femm mirror each other in their inability to command physical, patriarchal power over their dysfunctional families. Moreover, both characters' physical inferiorities are heightened to almost cartoonish extents through their over-the-top age makeup, with Roderick bearing layers of fake gray facial hair and Sawyer wearing layers upon layers of thick prosthetics that make him look practically mummified.

Perhaps the most provocative deconstruction of the patriarch is present in *Targets*. Here, Boris Karloff plays Byron Orlok, an aged horror star from the classical era whose Gothic films no longer frighten audiences like they did in decades prior. Being one of the last films of his career, *Targets* unabashedly reflects Karloff's real-life star status at the time and shows that old-fashioned monsters could not compete with the fears engendered by the violent actions of real people like Bobby Thompson (Tim O'Kelly), the white-collar everyman who viciously assassinates numerous people with a sniper rifle. Karloff, who once played physically domineering monsters as well as other hegemonic roles like doctors and well-educated detectives, was now an outdated figure who no longer commanded the screen like he once did. Orlok is eventually granted a brief moment in which he regains his masculine power by not only stopping Thompson's rampage but also physically overpowering the much younger former soldier. Following his physical subordination of Thompson, Orlok asks, "Is *that* what I was afraid of?" *Targets* concludes, however, with a return to the themes of fear and paranoia. Unlike the classical monsters, Thompson is not eradicated by the end of the narrative, only arrested, and he even eerily gloats how he missed very few of the people he shot at. This final statement provides a dark foreshadowing of how America's violence, and subsequent threats of hegemonic emasculation, would not come to an end any time soon.

Romero's Disruptions of Hegemonic Masculinity

George Romero is no stranger to postmodern revisions of hegemonic masculinity. As an extension of its racial subtext, *Night of the Living Dead* certainly does not portray the hegemonic law enforcement in a particularly positive light, as the police ultimately shoot and kill the protagonist Ben (Duane Jones) and burn his body. Criticism of the police's hegemony is exemplified in their unclear reasoning for killing Ben, as it is never stated if they truly thought Ben was one of the infected or if they simply shot him because he is black. Was the murder a mistake, or were the police merely another form of white terror whose intentions mimicked those of the pasty flesh-eating corpses?[1] *Night* further subverts the patriarch through, similar to *Last House on the Left*, the destruction of the familial unit, as the father Harry Cooper (Karl Hardman) is not only unable to maintain the safety of his family, but he is even ultimately consumed by his infected young daughter Karen (Kyra Schon). As discussed in Chapter 2, *Jack's Wife* also challenges hegemonic virility, as the film's antagonist is not Joan (Jan White), the woman practicing witchcraft, but is instead the amalgamation of the various oppressive men in her life.

The Crazies (1973) presents the director's most chaotic skewering of hegemonic forces. Here, the American military are not dominant patriarchal units like one would find in a 1950s creature feature. Instead, not only are the military depicted as overly violent and in some instances incompetent, but they are responsible for exposing the public to the deadly virus in the first place. Kendall Phillips provides further historical context for the film's transgressive portrayals of masculinity and the military–law enforcement, noting that much of the imagery reflects various real examples of abuse of hegemonic power during this time period, such as the violent actions of the Chicago Police Department against Vietnam protesters during the 1968 Democratic National Convention and the shooting of four Kent State students, also protesting the war, by the Ohio National Guard in 1970 (45). The film does have a male protagonist, David (Will McMillan), a firefighter and Vietnam veteran, who helps his family and friends avoid danger. David is ultimately unsuccessful in his attempted heroism, however, as his pregnant girlfriend Judy (Lane Carroll) is killed by a group of armed civilians. Because he cannot hold the husband-father role due to Judy's death, David, like the American military, has his hegemonic masculinity challenged.

The richest example of Romero's subversive approach to the collapse of hegemonic structure can be found in his downbeat horror-drama *Martin*. *Martin* revolves around its titular character (John Amplas), a young man sent to live in Braddock, Pennsylvania, after being ostracized by his family due to a series of murders he committed. Martin, believing himself to be a vampire, frequently sedates women, murders them with razor blades, drinks their blood, and engages in sex acts with their unconscious (or dead) bodies. Under the supervision of his elderly cousin Tateh Cuda (Lincoln Maazel), Martin is warned that he will meet fatal consequences if he continues his killings. Cuda, an updated version of the Van Helsing character, sincerely believes that Martin is a vampire and aims to either save Martin's soul or eradicate him. Meanwhile, Martin forms a mutually empathetic relationship with his cousin Christina (Christine Forrest), who longs to escape poverty and the authoritative Cuda.

Despite the frequent allusions to the decade's generational divide symbolized by the clashes Martin and Christina have with Cuda, the categories of "good" and "evil" in *Martin* are not clearly defined. After all, Cuda's hostility to his cousin is, in fact, valid. Whether or not Martin actually is the mythic monster that Cuda believes him to be is largely irrelevant, given that Martin's murders are real and not simply a part of a Cuda fantasy. Martin is, despite his violent actions, also sympathetic, given that he is the victim of oppressive forces in his own right, the most apparent of these being the poverty that surrounds him. However, Martin's most overt oppression stems from the bisexuality implied by his choice to "feed" on both men and women. This is showcased in a scene in which Martin sedates a man, penetrates his throat with a tree branch, removes his own shirt, and drinks the man's blood, an image suggesting oral sex as Martin's mouth becomes covered in the man's abject liquid. Martin's "vampirism" (a non-heteronormative identity) could signify why his other family members refused to raise him and further relates to Cuda's oppression of Martin because he feels as though his patriarchal, heterosexist status is threatened by Martin's sexuality.

Robin Wood notes that the repression of bisexuality is a key tactic in maintaining a dominant ideology, in this case the patriarchy. According to Wood,

> Bisexuality represents the most obvious and direct affront to the principles of monogamy and its supportive romantic myth of "the one right person"; the homosexual impulse in both men and women represents the most obvious threat to the norm of sexuality as reproductive and restricted by the ideal of the family. But more generally we confront here the whole edifice of clear-cut sexual differentiations that bourgeois-capitalist ideology erects on the flimsy and dubious foundations of biological difference: the social norms of masculinity and femininity, the social definitions of manliness and womanliness, the whole vast apparatus of oppressive male/female myths, and the systematic repression from infancy ("blue for boy") for the man's femininity and the woman's masculinity, in the interest of forming human beings for specific predetermined social roles [*Hollywood* 65].

In relation to Wood's argument, Cuda believes that his masculine hegemony is put at risk through Martin's allegorical bisexuality because it disrupts conventional straight-gay, masculine-feminine binaries.

The obscuring of binaries is a common theme throughout *Martin*, most notably through the forementioned erosion of "good" and "evil" categories. As is typical of the American New Wave era, *Martin* does not feature a clearly defined protagonist or antagonist, a characteristic also not uncommon in the horror genre, whether classical or postmodern. As Peter Hutchings argues, the horror genre's many monsters are no strangers to these blurrings of ethical classification due to the abuses that they often face, and consequently, these monsters are equal parts victim and victimizer (86). Rick Worland provides further insight into this notion, stating: "[M]any of fiction and cinema's most enduring and compelling monsters are also complex figures. In the Frankenstein Monster and King Kong, to cite two iconic examples, viewers quickly turn from fear to sympathy and regret at their deaths, reactions that indicate a recognition of the monster's dilemma as in some way our own. Even Bela Lugosi's icy Dracula, wandering through the ages, courts a moment of pathos when he wistfully allows 'To die—to be really dead. That must be glorious'" (146). This duality is a common theme with the many characters in *Martin* who abuse and exploit those around them while simultaneously being victimized by various systemic and familial hardships. For example, Mrs. Santini (Elayne Nadeau), a housewife with whom Martin has an affair, victimizes her husband through her infidelity, but she is simultaneously a victim due to her unhappy marriage, signified by her alcoholism and depression and culminating in her death via suicide.

Martin himself is the most obvious example of this victim-victimizer duality, as demonstrated not only through Martin's dual role as a murderer and a sufferer of homophobic oppression but in his mental polarity as well. As the narrative progresses, Martin becomes increasingly unsure if he should continue his killings. As Stacey Abbott argues, Martin's mental conflict is symbolized through the changing nature of his Gaze. Early in the film, Martin is granted the power of the Gaze through a narrative told solely from his perspective as he stalks and spies on his victims. Martin's Gaze eventually becomes obscured as his intimacy and human connection with Mrs. Santini leads him to question whether he can continue his killing. Martin's surveillance of his victims, enacted in his Gaze, becomes less effective, as shown in a botched home invasion in his pursuit of a victim, and consequently, Martin's Gaze becomes more focused on self-surveillance as he reflects on whether to continue his murders or perish due to his lack of blood consumption. Abbott elaborates on Martin's self-surveillance, arguing that Martin

> complains that he continues to survey his surroundings but cannot choose a victim. His relationship with Mrs. Santini does not cure Martin of his bloodlust but fragments his desires; his sexual desires are satisfied but his thirst for blood remains unquenched and this paralyzes him. ... Martin wants blood but can no longer decide upon what to base his decision [*Celluloid* 97].

Mirroring the revisionist horror trend itself, Martin has now become self-reflexive, questioning the harmful violence he once enacted. Connecting this to the decade's broader national emasculation, Abbott writes, "The reduction of Martin to a fragmented, paralyzed figure questioning his very being and seeking to find definition for himself, ...

embodies the paralysis and identity crisis that characterized America in the 1970s. Vampirism itself was undergoing an identity crisis" (*Celluloid* 97–98). Indeed, this identity crisis represents the widespread feelings of emasculation America experienced during this period—feelings that were manifested in horror cinema. Even big-budget Hollywood products like *The Exorcist* (1973) present relevant masculine anxieties, as Father Karras (Jason Miller) experiences a personal "crisis of confidence" due to his fractured faith in Catholicism and his uncertainty as to whether he can save the possessed Regan (Linda Blair).

Building off of Worland's examples of classical monsters, the duality of *Martin* is also present in its blurring of generic-historical boundaries through its constant references to classical horror cinema, specifically in Martin's various black-and-white fantasies that reference Gothic horror cinema from the '30s and '40s. In these fantasies, Martin envisions himself and others in castles and wearing Victorian clothing. These interludes always depict Martin as a conventional "beast in the boudoir" vampire attempting to feed off of entranced virgins, a fitting parallel given that Martin indulges in these fantasies whenever he is stalking and killing. For example, in the opening scene, in which Martin pursues and eventually murders a woman on a train, the sequence repeatedly cuts from reality to black-and-white images of a woman who is not a helpless victim, unaware that she is about to be preyed upon. Instead, the woman wears a sensual gown and seductively invites Martin into her room.

In these sequences, however, Martin is also frequently hunted by hegemonic figures like Catholic priests. In one instance, Martin, after killing a homeless man and drinking his blood, is chased by the police. Images of the police are intercut with black-and-white images of torch-wielding Victorian villagers chasing after Martin with the intention of eradicating him for his killings. Through this cross-cutting, Romero associates the contemporary hegemonic figures of the police with the older hegemonic vigilantes of classical horror films. But unlike in older horror cinema, these hegemonic individuals are not portrayed positively. Martin hides in a warehouse occupied by what appears to be a group of drug users, one of whom is black. As Martin hides, the police enter and shoot and kill the various inhabitants. Similar to the military in *The Crazies*, the police are not the heroic characters who save the day by vanquishing the Other; they are figures who abuse their hegemonic power to eradicate more contemporary forms of Otherness like drug addicts and the homeless.[2] White hegemony's demonizing of racial and lower-class Others is a subtle theme throughout *Martin*. Earlier in the film, Martin stalks a housewife who briskly runs past a group of black teenagers catcalling her outside a grocery store. The housewife's fear of the black teens contrasts the sympathy she expresses to Martin, who later poses as a deaf homeless person to learn where she lives. The irony here is that Martin, the white man, is a far greater threat than the black residents, as demonstrated through the housewife eventually being a victim of one of Martin's assaults.[3]

This thematic duality marks *Martin* as one of the most unsettling works in Romero's filmography. There are no "progressive" masculinities present. On one hand, Martin is the only male character who displays any form of emotional sensitivity. He listens to Christina vent her frustrations with Cuda, he carries groceries for women, and he provides emotional support for Mrs. Santini. He even displays a level of sensitivity during his murders, sedating his victims and assuring them that they won't feel any pain as he kills them. Martin's sensitivity feminizes him— he expresses an emotional vulnerability that opposes typical masculine stoicism. Moreover, Martin's status as a victimized-feminized figure is often the result of his own doing, as he frequently places himself in instances of sexual subordination. For example, when he murders the woman on the train, he first sedates her and rests her naked body on top of his, positioning himself as the "bottom," an act of self-subordination. Martin subordinates himself further when he cuts the woman's wrist with a razor blade and allows her blood to flow onto his chest, which positions him as the submissive figure passively receiving abject fluid, a status typically held—at least in the context of a heterosexual sex act such as this one—by the feminine figure. Through this sexual subordination, Martin mirrors the many housewives in his neighborhood who are expected to similarly submit within their domestic spheres, and like these women, oppressed by their husbands, Martin is also oppressed by a male figure: Cuda.

Through Cuda's constant verbal abuse and attempts to keep Martin from leaving their home (an act he enforces by attaching bells to Martin's door), Cuda serves as a common patriarch attempting to confine the feminized figure to the domestic sphere. But no matter how hard Cuda attempts to assert his masculine dominance over Martin, his actions are largely ineffective. Cuda's masculinity, like Martin's, is complex and contradictory.

The Aging Patriarch

At the beginning of the film, Cuda appears to hold strict masculine dominance. When Martin first arrives, Christina tells him that Cuda is the head of the household and, that under their roof, "things are done *his* way" because he supports them financially. Cuda is indeed symbolic of older generations; he dresses in tailored suits, sports a white beard and clings to traditional Catholic beliefs. As Tony Williams describes, Cuda is "[d]eeply immersed in reactionary patriarchal values" (*Cinema* 78). Williams further notes that Cuda is unapologetic in his inability to change because he lives in a society that, through his eyes, is held together by "traditional and stagnant values" and is in no need of evolution (*Cinema* 79). However, it is his stubborn mindset that brings about the consistent challenges to Cuda's patriarchal authority. Despite her familial respect for Cuda, Christina nonetheless quarrels with him and expresses dissatisfaction with her domestic lifestyle. Her unwillingness to be contained within their household threatens Cuda's hegemonic masculinity. This emasculation is further exemplified in Cuda's inability to maintain control over Martin. Cuda sincerely believes the prospect of Martin's vampirism, even referring to his nephew as "Nosferatu" (a signifier of his, and Martin's, devotion to the ideologies of classical horror and Otherness), and uses traditional Christian imagery in an effort to weaken the curse under which Martin's supposedly suffers. Martin, however, scoffs at his uncle, asserting that "there is no real magic," an indicator that he wants no association with Cuda's regressive beliefs.

Similar to Orlok from *Targets*, Cuda is an aging symbol of stripped hegemony in a world that is seemingly progressing beyond him. This is best showcased in Cuda's conversation with Father Howard, a younger Catholic priest played by Romero in a cameo. When Cuda asks Howard if he believes in "the old ways" through concepts like demons and satanic possessions, Father Howard responds with irreverence, claiming that the only priest he knows who holds these beliefs is considerably older, closer to Cuda's age. This dialogue is representative of the horror genre's then-shifting thematics, as the regressive views held by Cuda are challenged by the young, progressive Father Howard, just as the older conventions of the genre itself were challenged by young auteurs like Romero. In a subsequent scene, Cuda hires the older priest mentioned by Father Howard, to perform an exorcism on Martin. It fails because Christian iconography like crosses and holy water prove ineffective against the supposed vampire.

The disruption of Cuda's masculinity is best exhibited in the scene that follows. Cuda walks the city streets wearing a suit and wielding a cane, a phallic symbol that signifies his masculine ability, as copious amounts of fog smother the *mise-en-scène*—an homage to older horror texts like *Dracula* and *The Wolf Man* (1941). Cuda is initially displayed through a series of low-angle shots to indicate his patriarchal power.

However, when he enters a playground, he is met by Martin dressed as a vampiric caricature, complete with a cape, pale face makeup, and oversized plastic fangs. Startled, Cuda falls to the ground and clutches a rosary as Martin taunts him. In contrast to the prior perspective, Cuda is now displayed through high-angle shots and Martin in low-angle shots, indicating their shift in supremacy (Fig. 5). Martin's laughter and his overly theatrical costume, paired with action taking place in a literal playground, cast as childlike the fears that haunt Cuda. The scene concludes with Cuda swinging his cane at Martin in one final attempt at masculine assertion. Martin grabs Cuda's cane, negating his phallic power, before spitting out his fangs and stating, "It's just a costume," effectively pulling back the curtain on the artificiality of Cuda's anxieties. Moreover, Martin's "It's just a costume" statement refers not only to himself, but to Cuda as well, drawing attention to how Cuda's clothing relates to his own gender performativity. Cuda, with his suit, beard and cane, is signaling his masculinity through his own "costume," yet Martin proclaims that this wardrobe, like his own vampire attire, is entirely performative and an inorganic attempt to convey power to and induce fear in others.

When assessing the childish iconography present in the playground sequence, one can't help but compare it to *The Amusement Park* (1973), in which Maazel plays an unnamed elderly carnival-goer who is constantly physically and emotionally abused during his visit to the fair. These abuses range from Maazel being pickpocketed to being violently

Figure 5. Martin (John Amplas), wearing a cape and plastic fangs, looks down at Cuda (Lincoln Maazel) in *Martin* (1977, Laurel Tape and Film).

assaulted by a biker gang. Cuda and the carnival-goer have striking similarities: visually, they mirror each other, as they both dress in pristine white suits, possess trimmed goatees, and brandish canes. Thematically, the characters draw further comparisons given that they are both aging men in a rapidly changing, unpredictable world. Romero's mirroring of Maazel's two characters provides a new framework through which to interpret Cuda. On one hand, Cuda is certainly the violent oppressor who despises those whose ideas challenge him, yet Cuda, like Martin, is equal parts victim and victimizer. While Cuda seeks to physically and mentally dominate everyone in his life, Cuda is also dissatisfied with his living situation in Braddock. Like Martin, Christina and Mrs. Santini, Cuda longs to escape, in his case to a bygone era in which his male authority is not opposed. Cuda clings to dated folklore and ghost stories to appease his emasculation; it is a means of escapism comparable to Martin's vampiric identity.

Cuda's feelings of inadequacy and persecution are paralleled in Maazel's more sympathetic carnival-goer. Throughout *The Amusement Park*, Maazel is often lost in the horde of carnival attendees. His figure frequently becomes obscured by the extras who consistently swarm the *mise-en-scène*, leaving him hidden by the characters around him and concealed from the viewer. The carnival-goer's subjection to oppression is best demonstrated when he attends a freak show in which a collection of elderly people are displayed on a stage in front of a booing audience.[4] When Maazel attempts to calm the audience, the mob quickly turns on him and chases him away, an action that draws comparisons to Martin being chased by the oppressive police officers. Even the carnival-goer's attire invites sympathy, as his cane does not boast phallic power like that possessed by Cuda, but rather it is only gifted to him by the carnival's infirmary following his assault by the biker gang. *The Amusement Park* provides a more empathetic, albeit equally pessimistic, take on how older generations are often viewed as obsolete, while *Martin* focuses on the growing anxieties and national identity crises that continued throughout the 1970s. Additionally, both films' uses of childish, whimsical iconography (the playground and the carnival) indicate how both of Maazel's characters are patronized and taken advantage of by younger generations.

Nevertheless, it is Cuda who conducts the final act of masculine assertion. Towards the end of the film, Cuda's hegemonic masculinity is challenged even further when Christina moves out to escape his oppressive attitudes. Cuda's hegemony is fractured because he no longer has patriarchal authority over his family. With his patriarchal voice gone, Cuda opts to express his masculinity through other, more violent means. The film concludes with Cuda mistaking Mrs. Santini's suicide as an act of Martin's doing and consequently hammering a stake into Martin's chest, killing him. Narratively, this conclusion mirrors those of more conventional horror films: The patriarch abolishes the Other. Cuda's final hammering of the stake into Martin's chest additionally represents the impending death of the counterculture and unfortunately foreshadows the return to regressive ideologies that would characterize the 1980s. Simultaneously, however, this ending also points to how ineffective horror's patriarchs can be. Like the impotent masculinities in classical horror, Cuda's hegemony is not concretely reaffirmed. With Martin dead and Christina gone, Cuda has no one over whom he can assert patriarchal authority; his domestic space, and thus his hegemony, remains fractured. Moreover, the thematic dualism is present one last time in the final shot of Cuda burying Martin in a garden. On one hand, the garden serves as Martin's grave and signifies his physical abolishment. On the other hand, the garden also symbolizes rebirth. Although Martin will not physically come back from the dead like one would expect of a real vampire, his body will symbolically return through the greenery that will grow above him. Through this final allegory, Romero concludes with the notion that although Otherness (whether it be sexual, gendered, racial or otherwise) might be oppressed, it can never be fully eradicated.

The King Is Dead;
Long Live the King

Capitalism and Nostalgia in Knightriders

LEAH RICHARDS

As discussed in Chapter 1, George A. Romero had originally conceived 1971's *There's Always Vanilla* as a movie about what would happen to members of the 1960s hippie subculture with the passage of time, about how they would be assimilated, whether because they gave up their ideals, because the interests of mainstream society expanded to include objectives once seen as countercultural, or because of compromises on both sides. This was not the movie that he ended up with, but the idea seems to have stuck with him in a modified form. A decade later, he released *Knightriders*, another non-horror property about a group led by a man who holds ideals that are at odds with the world—a man whom many see as somewhat autobiographical, given Romero's "quixotic exuberance for tilting at the windmills of corporate power" (Bernardini 177), a characteristic shared with the film's protagonist—and about the impossibility of living those ideals in 1980s America.

Knightriders is a modern-day take on the spirit, if not the details, of the legends of King Arthur and his knights.[1] It was released in 1981, the same summer as John Boorman's *Excalibur*. Boorman's epic was an adaptation of the fifteenth-century *Le Morte d'Arthur*, the origin for most contemporary narratives of chivalrous knights and ladies fair, including T.H. White's *The Once and Future King* (1958), identified in *Knightriders* as a source[2] for the modern-day knights' ideals and ceremonies. King Billy (Ed Harris) and his motorcycle jousters imagine that they live outside, or at least at the fringes of, mainstream society as modern-day knights of the Round Table. In what seems to be a response to the depersonalization and isolation of modern America and capitalism—and, given the diverse makeup of the troupe, sexism, racism, ageism and homophobia as well—they have created a mobile Camelot, one that adheres to the feudal power structures of the Middle Ages, with everyone swearing fealty to King Billy and his romanticized vision of a medieval utopia. Their collective fantasy of an imagined past participates in the projection of an edited history, using artifice to stage a sanitized and family-friendly, counterculture-friendly version of the age of chivalry. *Knightriders* is about the death of the king and the encroachment of 1980s American neoliberalism and Reagan-era nostalgia—itself a longing for an imagined past—on his kingdom.

King Billy and his troupe have spent what is eventually revealed to have been two years relocating to fields outside various towns in Western Pennsylvania to stage their tourneys to crowds who are largely presented as boorish yokels; that they are, with a few exceptions, "[c]ynical, disdainful, often lusting for blood and belittling the efforts of performers" (T. Williams, *Cinema* 105) makes the decision to live outside of society completely reasonable.[3] In addition to Billy, his queen Linet (Amy Ingersoll), and several knights of varying importance to the plot, their group includes crew members who maintain a Camelot made of painted wood and, one character says, tin foil—as well as merchants selling food, drinks and artisanal wares. Although, as Ed Sikov explains, they all "openly admit their association to be a reaction against the plasticity of a decidedly unheroic America" (31), the motivations for choosing this life varies from person to person. The Black Knight, Sir Morgan (Tom Savini), "was never into this King Arthur crap anyway; I was into the bikes" (which another character explains is how he ended up naming himself after the sorceress Morgan le Fay). Other characters have a much deeper commitment to the community and Billy.

Like the carnivals and freak shows of the earlier 20th century, outcasts find their place in this Camelot: Billy welcomes "every damn long-hair that knows how to make a pair of sandals" and assumes responsibility for them. In return, however, he demands belief in his ideals, "his ethos of personal honor" (Pugh and Weisl 96), which he identifies as the community's Code, not just his own. Attributes including "martial valor, fellowship and fidelity" to their king (Blanch 62) are the basis of their Code, "chivalric trappings" that Susan Aronstein expands to include "violence" as well as "vague ideas of self-sacrifice and community" (qtd. in Pugh and Weisl 96). "[L]ionizing purportedly anachronistic values of honor and chivalry" (96), Billy attributes the absence of these virtues to materialism and demands that his subjects[4] do the same. The alternative to adhering to this Code, and to Billy's sometimes arbitrary and always absolute rule, is, he warns, exile: "[a]nybody who wants to live more for themselves, he doesn't belong with us."

Tison Pugh and Angela Jane Weisl argue that, in *Knightriders*, "even an undefined and anachronistic code is superior to prevailing American mores, as Billy's kingship and moral example allow others to be *true to themselves*" (96, emphasis added). But that is only true as long as what they want aligns with what Billy wants. Given the "difficult[y] to establish appropriate ethical standards" in resisting capitalism, it is "all too easy to lapse into romantic communitarian thinking that airbrushes domination from precapitalist society" (Fraser and Jaeggi 129), as Billy does. This works out for members of the troupe who are not yet "aware of the devastating contradiction between their need to find a place for their fantasy and the absurdity of the fantasy they need to create" or the escapism offered by modern knighthood as "inadequate therapy for the social ills that drive them to it" (Sikov 32). But others challenge the "most disturbing assumption" that underlies their society, "the question of monarchy and its ability to sustain ... an autocracy based on wish-fulfillment and the ridiculous subjugation of an entire group" (32). As another classic piece of Arthurian cinema noted a few years earlier, neither "hanging on to outdated imperialist dogma which perpetuates the economic and social differences in our society" nor "strange women lying in ponds distributing swords" is a "basis for a system of government: supreme executive power derives from a mandate from the masses" (*Monty Python*).

The Divine Right of King Billy

While Billy gestures toward a more egalitarian rule, serving with the knights on a council, the merchants, identified by other characters as the serfs within their hierarchy, and crew have no representation and ultimately, the role of the council is purely advisory: "The King makes the final decision," the troupe's master of ceremonies, Pippen (Warner Shook), says in response to Morgan's assertion of the knights' role in policy-making, and everyone is to do as Billy says without fail. Furthermore, he expects others to follow his instructions in his absence and even if they put the group at risk. When Billy is arrested, preferring to join one of his knights in jail as a witness to any violence rather than come to an "informal bail arrangement," he orders everyone to stay where they are, leaving them within the jurisdiction of an extremely hostile and corrupt sheriff's department and delaying their arrival at their next site: "The rest of you stay here 'til we get out," he orders, repeating the command as he is taken away. Queen Linet countermands his orders and gets the group out of town almost immediately, for their safety and financial security. When Billy hears that they've gone ahead, he repeats several times that he told them to wait, never offering a reason but focusing on what he sees as insubordination: "Nobody goes anywhere in this outfit without my permission."

Sikov places emphasis on what he identifies as the "progressive and bizarre insanity ... of a demented king" and exceptionally incompetent administrator who is "morally and psychologically unfit to play his own role in his own myth" (32) and argues that Billy is an "internal corruption," the real threat to the troupe's future. While I was initially skeptical of this characterization—other critics and scholars uniformly cast Billy as naive and idealistic, sometimes to the point of simple-mindedness, but noble in his adherence to asceticism and anti-capitalism, and my personal objections are to the fundamental presence of a hierarchy—it is fully supported by Billy's rigid inflexibility as well as by his including self-flagellation in his morning routine. His refusal to acknowledge that his personal feelings about capitalism and materialism do not change the fact that they exist or just how close to financial ruin and therefore dissolution they are. While Morgan, possessed of an "aggressive narcissis[m]" (T. Williams, *Cinema* 102), is firmly cast as the antagonist when he expresses a wish for stability and money, he is not alone; another character acknowledges that the fight for "truth and justice and the American way of life[5] and all that, that's gotta take a back seat to the one for staying alive" and argues, "We gotta stay together. We gotta keep this troupe together. And if keeping the troupe going means that we have to take some of this promoter's money, well, then I say let's take it." While Billy equates financial stability with materialism and puts tremendous energy into resisting "the materialistic values of the real world [that] gradually creep into Camelot" (Blanch 64), their financial and legal advisor Steve[6] (Ken Hixon) reminds him, "Money makes the world go round, even your world."

"Despite the threat of economic ruin stemming from increased overhead expenses, Billy rejects the lure of the commercial world" (Blanch 62), refusing to consider working with a promoter and increasing profits, responding only with a reminder of their Code. While he is right that a Vegas-style promoter like Joe Bontempi (Martin Ferraro) probably isn't the right fit for their group, people are hurt by his unyielding antimaterialism. The system may be wrong, several knights argue when a cop shows up in search of a payoff, but it costs less in the long run to treat the bribe as part of their overhead than to antagonize a small-town deputy sheriff on the make. While no one argues with Billy's statement "It's wrong to pay this guy off," Billy's refusal, along with the deliberate provocation and contempt that he displays toward the deputy, leads to the severe beating of one of the men whom they arrest. Billy may not like commercial celebrity, which he aligns with materialism, Linet says, but to refuse to sign a photograph in a magazine for a small child who looks up to him, "reject[ing] the child's adulation as inherently complicit in degrading his personal integrity" (Pugh and Weisl 96) because he doesn't personally like a publication that places motorcycle jousts on the same footing as Evel Knievel, is unnecessarily cruel and controlling.

Attempting to maintain absolute control over his slowly degenerating kingdom, Billy acknowledges that outsiders may see him as a Jim Jones or a Charles Manson but fails to understand that the only thing keeping him from becoming the next notorious cult leader is the resistance of his subjects. Insisting that he is not a hero, he says that he is "fighting the dragon" without seeming to be aware that that is what heroes do. He positions himself as a figure of sacrifice, sometimes Christ-like, other times as a saint or martyr, but always as a chosen one whose ideology is the only path to a terrestrial paradise. Billy argues that everyone made a conscious adult decision to join his community (and chose their roles within it) and uses this to make a virtue of their stagnation, but he is unable to compromise the beliefs on which he becomes increasingly fixated. While he recognizes "the differences between fantasy and reality," he "wishes to avoid" them, "stubbornly adher[ing] to the values he personally holds until denial becomes impossible" (T. Williams, *Cinema* 104). It becomes necessary that he relinquish some of his control to the community members, whose principles include financial solvency as well as honor, loyalty and skill in battle, construction, marketing, pageantry or whatever role they fill.

Hierarchy and Dominance in Camelot

When Billy rejoins the troupe after his release from jail, he interrupts a discussion that serves as exposition, explaining the power structure and emerging dissent as well as the (extremely precarious) financial arrangements of the group, and provides him with an opportunity to reiterate his absolute power over his subjects. He joins the conversation immediately after a question apparently about the distribution of resources; the audience learns that all food and supplies are provided according to each person's need based on their role within the community, along with an equal amount of spending money for each person;

that the most significant outlays seem to be for motorcycle parts and weapons; and that some of the merchants and crew members aren't happy:

> "We could all take in a little more cash if we didn't spend so much on weapons."
> "Yeah, and a lot less on parts, too."
> "Oh, yeah, the goddamned knights have it the cushiest. ... They don't care what they smash up. We blow five bikes a week, parts cost a fortune, and those lances! Then they let the townies ride with the stuff!"[7]

Billy overhears the end of this airing of grievances and interprets the exchange as a challenge to his authority and a council meeting held without his permission. First belittling the work of the artisans and merchants as well as misinterpreting what he interrupted, he then insists that they cannot have a council meeting without all members of the community. Given that members are absent, the discussion is clearly not a council meeting, and his response is completely out of proportion, underscoring not his authority but his fundamental inability to lead with anything less than absolute power. Occurring at the midpoint of the film, his unhinged rant marks a turning point and is a catalyst for a rift in the community. Some of the merchants leave immediately, and Morgan and his faction of knights begin to plan their departure with the promoter who is "offering ... the world," while former colleagues insist that only their troupe can be the Camelot that they need.

Morgan has been challenging Billy for the throne and believes that he has won those challenges. "I've been beating him regularly," he says, and Billy does not disagree, acknowledging, "Morgan proved he could kick my ass." But he retains the throne because of a faction of knights led by Sir Alan (Gary Lahti), who has a deeper investment in both their Code and Billy as their king than Morgan and some of the others. Alan explains to an audience stand-in, "If the king goes down, we have to be ready for rescue. ... We have to get to Morgan before he can make the king yield. If Billy surrenders, he loses the crown." Thus, Billy retains the power ostensibly awarded on the basis of strength and prowess; the audience does not align with Morgan only because riding to the king's rescue is the equivalent of voting, of expressing a preference for one leader over another.

It is difficult not to see Billy's refusal to give up the throne or allow one of his champions to fight in his stead as an issue of specifically masculine power and power struggles. As a Romero movie, the gender politics are better than one might expect in 1981, but there is a lot of emphasis on the jousters' lifestyle, and thus their Code, as evidence of masculinity. There is repeated mockery of less fit or older men and calls of "May the better man win," even though one of the "knights" is a woman, Rocky (Cynthia Adler). During one event, as the animosity between factions grows, the jousts become more aggressive, and the elimination rounds turn into a melee as the knights resolve "two years' worth of gripes" that are no different from those that would accumulate in any small, insular community but with violence and motorcycles raising the stakes and the negative masculine energy.

Machismo, as evidenced by both martial skills and sexual prowess, is clearly a motivation for Morgan, and while Billy is less conspicuously macho, he chooses to ride against Morgan more than once to reassert dominance (or, Tony Williams suggests, to fulfill "unconscious masochistic desires" [*Cinema* 108]); as the king, he is not expected to participate, and as a man who is dealing with cumulative injuries sustained before the start of the film, he should not. However, early in the movie, he enters into a tourney when Morgan is positioned to be the champion. Later, an unknown knight (Albert Amerson) identified as only the Indian (and serving a muddled allegorical role through the remainder of the movie) challenges Billy, whose injuries have gotten worse. Alan pleads with Billy to let him be his champion and fight in his place. Billy's response seems to be in part driven by masculine pride, as he sees fighting this figure as his destiny. However, his decision to ride against Alan, knowing that his most loyal knight will do little to defend himself, injures both his body and his pride and drives him away as well. One could attribute a refusal to back down from physical challenges, particularly on the part of a character who refuses to concede as what seems like a matter of course, to motives other than hypermasculinity, but it certainly seems to be a factor in "the temporary collapse of the perfect society" (Blanch 65).

Morgan and his faction have left to start their own kingdom and are in Washington, D.C., partying poolside and experiencing "Washington D.C. decadence," but Morgan is the first to see how corporatization turns hobbies and vocations into jobs, finally understanding, on some level, the Code: In Billy's Camelot, they "are not merely engaged in a spectacular performance for viewer pleasure but are professionally involved in something they regard as a vocation rather than a day's entertainment" (T. Williams, *Cinema* 106). Realizing that it is better to be a big fish in a small pond with friends than to be a fish who belongs to someone else, Morgan also "realizes that, in contrast to the masculine puissance available to modern-day knights who practice Billy's code, consumerism emasculates him" (Pugh and Weisl 97). Intriguingly, it is the elevation of his masculinity—culminating in a hilarious

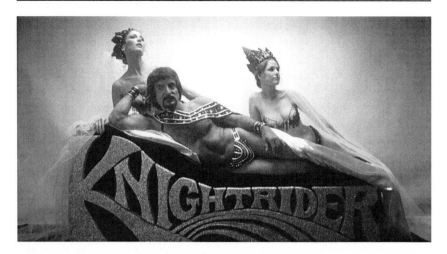

Figure 6. Morgan (Tom Savini) "think[ing] medieval sex" in *Knightriders* (1981, Laurel Entertainment); actresses are unidentified.

photo shoot (Fig. 6) showcasing his sexual and physical strengths—that brings about his reevaluation of himself and the troupe and the realization that, under modern American capitalism, "manhood suffers, and Arthurian virtue thus provides an anachronistic template against which to measure modern masculinity" (96–97).

The Once and Future Kings

When Morgan encounters Alan, also ready to return, on the side of a road, the two are able to bring their perspectives—Alan's adherence to the Code manifesting as blind allegiance to Billy and Morgan's challenges to its execution—together and return. Alan says, "There can be only one king, Morgan. You can't just split off and start over again"— the result is a troupe that has the fighting skills but none of the purpose that holds Billy's Camelot together: "hooligans without honor" (Pugh and Weisl 97). The Code and "Billy's exemplary lifestyle of truth and honor saves his followers from degrading themselves" (97), and while, as Alan repeats, there can be only one king, his first words to Billy on their return are: "My king. If you'll allow me, I will fight for you in defense of the crown. These others will challenge ... shit, I can't talk like that. Morgan's agreed to fight and if you promise to sit on your ass and stay out of the way, there's still some of us that'll fight for you." That is, give up control and let people fight for what *they be*lieve in; acknowledge that you do not have the strength to hold the crown. Alan and the others know that Morgan is the most skilled of the knights and that they aren't favored to win—and Billy knows that too—but the entire community comes together to prepare for the battle and the likely transition of power, with the understanding that the outcome will be fair. More important than who is king is that Camelot remains Camelot.

On their return—Billy and others, having faith that Morgan would realize that it wasn't only the bikes that drew him to the troupe, haven't broken down camp yet—they are welcomed back into the fold, and we get to see Ed Harris cry (but only a little). Morgan has "learned a moral lesson through his encounters with big-time bike promoters" (Sikov 32), while Billy has begun to acknowledge that he has not been a good leader, at least not recently, in a conversation with one of the musicians:

> **BILLY:** I got nothing left to give. I take you all for granted. I don't give you anything.
> **MUSICIAN:** Man, you give us everything, man. You give us, you know, a chance.
> **BILLY:** Yeah, but I don't pay you any attention. I'm sorry about that.

"Billy's anachronistic lifestyle inspires those around him to surpass the ordinary and achieve the extraordinary feat of adhering to antiquated values" (Pugh and Weisl 97), but while he provided the spark and sustained Camelot thus far, with his strict control and inflexible adherence to the Code as a necessary element of its development, his ideals are not those of the group: "It is the king himself—not the Black Knight or commercialism—who most severely threatens this Camelot" (Sikov 32).

To represent their new direction, the knights' council meets to establish the new rules for the challenge: "No boundaries. ... Nobody's gonna surrender, and I don't think it's necessary for anybody to get hurt bad" or go through the humiliation of being forced to performatively yield to the victor, so, they collectively agree, "any knight separated from his machine is out," and the faction with the last knight standing is the victor. While not everyone understands why Billy has agreed to the challenge, Merlin explains,

> Billy the King turned around one day and seen how many of us was looking to him. He say, "What's all this noise? And what's all these folks looking to me for?" They think you're trying to look bad, trying to get your ass whooped. They think you're ... trying to prove you don't deserve to be king. You're saying, "In you, look past the mist, see what you be, your own majesty, don't try to find yourself in me. I ain't that great, no-how."

The movie does not show its hand; the battle is long (the day progressing from foggy early morning to bright midday shows that the lengthy scene in the movie—one of many lengthy battle scenes—is only a fraction of the actual scene), and the two sides are evenly matched. Ultimately, Morgan "wins his lord's crown honorably" (Pugh and Weisl 97), and there is a peaceful transition of power. Billy abdicates and, like many a former king, enters into what stands for the monastic life in the modern world, riding out of the camp with only the ambiguously symbolic— but gesturing, at least in part, toward a romanticized past—Indian by his side, so that "the Black Knight [can be] elevated to the role of king ... [and] a new reign of pragmatism and sanity ... [can] rule while the outside world remains as greedy and corrupt as ever" (Sikov 32), fulfilling Morgan's version of Billy's "dream of keeping Camelot intact" (Blanch 65). We do not see much of this promise manifesting because this is the modern King Arthur's story, and Arthurian stories end with the death of the king; "the impossibility of the Arthurian myth in twentieth century America is the defining concept of the film" (32), and Billy's death takes place very much in the 20th century. Like too many motorcyclists, he is killed in an accident, in his case a head-on collision with a semi, and the film ends with his funeral and his former subjects paying final tribute before riding off in formation.

Artifice and Nostalgia

The denizens of Camelot follow all of the pageantry that is part of their performances for the final battle "without any intrusive and uncomprehending audience present to demean the nature of their personal ritual battles" (T. Williams, *Cinema* 112). This emphasizes, and indeed shows the whole troupe's alignment with, what Billy said earlier. Despite the anachronisms and the fantasy, they are "not an act"; this is their real life. However, the movie engages in critique of the era as "the materialistic values of the real world gradually creep into Camelot" (Blanch 65) through an emphasis on both deliberate and malicious artifice. It is made clear that the "thrones" that Billy and Linet sit on are wooden, and the music ostensibly played by three heralds is actually recorded and is being piped in through the same system that amplifies Pippen's explanations and introductions for the audience. One knight reminds Morgan, who is using a very real mace, "Some of us are wearing tinfoil" armor, and even jousting itself is a simulation of a battle.

King Billy's, later King Morgan's, subjects aren't trying to deceive anyone, though: they're people dressed up as heralds, friars, wenches, alewives, blacksmiths and any number of other figures representing hundreds of years of history and culminating in knights riding motorcycles. Their reality lies in the space where feathered helmets and 1000cc engines overlap, a space that exists only when it is in use. However, their audiences (and thus, the outside world) project dishonest artifice onto them. During the first tourney, "Hoagie Man" (Stephen King in a brief role) insists, "It's all a fake," "like the wrestlers on TV," and that it is staged to "try to make it look tough" and "dangerous." At the tourney following Hoagie Man's verbal assault on King Billy's subjects, the expertise behind their performance is challenged by "all these local guys [who] came in all duded up," some in homemade armor; it is these "townies" who ride in after the melee between factions and wage an attack, turning a display of skill by itinerant performers into a "turf war."

In the outside world, Morgan and his cohort must fight or yield to "the morally corrupted business ethics of the twentieth century, a modern-day dragon" (Blanch 65), but Morgan is the first to see that "D.C. decadence" and everything they are being promised "represent an unreal world" (65). "[T]he glitter of commercialism" (65) is represented by the glitter on their new outfits, including a black-and-silver armor-inspired mankini for Morgan to wear for an "everybody think medieval sex" photo shoot. When someone asks why the (would-be) documentary photographer who has largely aligned herself with them can't do the shoot, Bontempi (a fake name or a serendipitous one, it means "good times" in Italian) replies that she could, but that there would be no point: "Well, look at it. It's porn. That's ... look, see, they're set-up shots. That's just ... that's controlling the environment. That's not real life." Equating the photo shoot, that is, promotional material, with pornography is a means of telegraphing performance and artifice of what many audiences would consider to be the lowest form: sexual encounters, some simulated and all staged, that lonely men use to feel less lonely. Bontempi wants it to be fake, from the actual performances to the brotherhood between knights.

A catch-all term that I have avoided using to discuss *Knightriders* is a Renaissance Faire, and this has been deliberate, in part because Billy's troupe is a motorcycle jousting group at its core, with the "Ren Faire" style booths, bells and whistles subordinate to the martial displays, whereas the jousts are just part of a Renaissance Faire. The other reason is that Renaissance Faires are commercial undertakings and always were, exactly what Billy was trying to keep his kingdom from becoming.[8] Even in their earliest days, in 1960s California, they were conceived as a way to make money although they were also "a locus for challenging the staid suburban ideal" (Rubin 5). There are similarities, and the differences are individually minor, but my distinction is based on Billy's Code as an idealized reimagining of the chivalric codes of the Middle

Ages as recorded in medieval romances and his attempts *not* to fit his ideals into the world but to use force to shape a world that will fit his ideals.

Rachel Rubin writes about the roots of the Renaissance Faire in California's 1960s counterculture as well as the shift to a higher degree of historicity in *Well Met: Renaissance Faires and the American Counterculture.* In her brief discussion of *Knightriders*, she identifies it as an "under-the-radar movie about *a version* of the faire" (295, emphasis added), one that, through its "exclusive focus on jousting ... represents the faire as a literal battlefield" (297). On the other hand, the Renaissance Faire, which struggled early in its history with its "relationship to Renaissance history," "began by organizing around a specific historical precedent: the Old Woodbury Hill Fair in Dorset, England," a pleasure faire (33). One could certainly see Billy's subjects as former Renaissance Faire participants, but to join Billy means committing to the Code, whereas the Renaissance Faire "became a place to experiment with the new—new sexual arrangements, new ways of understanding and enacting gender roles, legal and illegal drugs ..., communal living, and ideals of art taken directly to the people" (5). Billy's subjects explore drugs, gender, sexuality and communal modes of coupling while taking their tourneys "directly to the people," but they were doing that before they joined with Billy, as is emphasized by every character who utters a variation on Alan's statement: "We're all in this because of the lifestyle. And we got our own place, and you did that. You set that up. And you know what it's about. And what it's about is having things we can count on." They're more aligned with the faction of Faire attendees for whom "authenticity meant the countercultural ideal of 'being real' as opposed to fake—which had a lot to do with emotional truths or anticonsumerism and almost nothing to do with historical exactitude" (Rubin 35).

Ultimately, there is a nostalgia to Billy's Camelot that Renaissance Faires do not possess, a longing for an imagined past, a past that never existed, a past that misrepresents the age of not only chivalry but the Black Death and feudalism.[9] It isn't the same nostalgia that got Ronald Reagan elected in 1980 (and 1984), and Billy is no Ronald Reagan; his intentions are pure even though his overdeveloped notions of honor do not accommodate human desires and behaviors. But there is a common embracing of a past that was "better" than the present, with *better* meaning "better aligned with his personal ideals." Instead of such longing, Renaissance Faires embody a "'functional paradox,' in which attempts at historical authenticity act as commentary not on the past but on the present" (Rubin 34) or what Pugh and Weisl identify as *tragic anachronism* in their discussion of *Knightriders*, "engage[ment] with the decline of the present moment in relationship to the past" (84). George A. Romero may be using functional paradox or tragic anachronism, but his characters are not. Through Billy's struggles against "the materialistic values of the real world gradually creep[ing] into Camelot" (Blanch 65), Romero highlights "the failures of the present in light of the glories of the past" and uses "modern-day Arthuriana [to create a] cinematic critique of American consumer society" (96). It's like *Dawn of the Dead*, but with motorcycles instead of zombies.

6

Creepshow and
Patriarchal Horror(s)

JOHN R. ZIEGLER

Violence, Silvia Federici tells us, has always been a "subtext, a possibility, in the nuclear family" because of the power accorded to men in patriarchal capitalism (*Witches* loc. 692). The George A. Romero-directed anthology *Creepshow* (1982) was not Romero's only Stephen King adaptation but the only time when Romero directed a script by King (S. Brown 8); the film repeatedly positions violence and death in the context of patriarchal marriage and family (or its lack). According to Robin Wood, in the 1970s horror film, the family itself, innocently or not, produces the monster in its various forms (*Hollywood* 75). In the 1980s, however, Wood sees horror's "reactionary inflection" emerge as dominant (169–70).[1] One result, in Tony Williams' estimation, is that "[m]ost 1980s horror films represent patriarchy's last stand" (*Hearths* 217). *Creepshow*, arriving early in the 1980s, straddles these eras and exhibits the tensions of this transition. Wood famously refers to the film as "the worst of Romero with the worst of Stephen King, ... a series of empty anecdotes in which nasty people do nasty things to other nasty people, the nastiness being the entire point and purpose" (*Hollywood* 169). But are the reasons for the nastiness as utterly empty as his oft-quoted assessment asserts, or do they deserve more consideration? While *Creepshow* primarily adheres to the trend in which 1970s American horror cinema moved its threats inside the traditional nuclear family,[2] which is inseparable from patriarchal heteronormativity, these anxieties over the family occur in tension with an anxiety over the lack of family or patriarchal norms. *Creepshow* may indeed not be what Wood calls elsewhere a "message movie" (*Hollywood* 116); but if happiness is the reward for "being a certain kind of being," and that being is "recognizable as bourgeois" (Ahmed, *Promise* 12), then the parade of unhappy marriages and families

displayed in *Creepshow* can be seen to resist, if uneasily, bourgeois patriarchal norms. If these norms act as loci of horror, then their absence, as
an alternative, figures as equally threatening.

Kimberly Jackson suggests that horror's focus has always been the
nuclear family (1). Williams terms "family horror" a "fundamental structure" in Hollywood cinema (*Hearths* 11–12); and Wood traces its beginnings primarily and more specifically to 1960's *Psycho*, positing in the
decades prior the movement of horror's associations from the foreign to
the American and finally to "its true milieu, the family" (*Hollywood* 76).
Vivian Sobchack points to "the crisis experienced by American bourgeois patriarchy since the late 1960s," the same period in which Wood
sees family horror gaining momentum and relates this crisis to the
nuclear family's "disintegration and transfiguration" while underscoring
the family's role in the reproduction and naturalization of heteropatriarchal, capitalist norms (Sobchack 172). By the early 1980s, masculinity,
gender roles and the patriarchal family were all in the midst of profound
destabilization (Jackson 66; T. Williams, *Hearths* 18). Horror's engagement with such destabilization is rarely entirely unitary; the genre is, as
Jackson highlights, quite comfortable with contradiction in its relationship to the structures that it critiques (20).[3] Mark Browning points to
this comfort when he says of a group of Stephen King–related anthology
films (including *Creepshow*) that they "offer a ritualistic view of genre,
in which the audience can invest significance and meaning in a shared
act of imaginative, transgressive play but also, arguably, they are being
duped here into accepting overtly conforming forms of behaviour as a
means to be happy in society" (81). The latter part of Browning's evaluation could serve as a description of the functions of the traditional family, which helps to perpetuate heteropatriarchal normativity through
what Sara Ahmed calls the happiness duty, the obligation to "promote
what causes happiness" according to such norms (*Promise* 6). In terms of
a description of *Creepshow*, however, I would argue that the unresolved
tension in *Creepshow* between creating spaces of transgressive potential
and duping the audience into internalizing normativity renders the duping the less dominant part of that tension.

Internalizing patriarchy's explanation of its own continued existence, which is that patriarchy "persists because it gives us rewards we
desire" (including, for men, "power and privilege"), similarly dupes us,
argue Carol Gilligan and Naomi Snider, into viewing patriarchy according to its own values and accepting its inevitability (35). In its ambivalence towards patriarchy, *Creepshow* unsettles this self-perpetuating
narrative and tells a divergent story, one that might be seen as an indi-
rect method of the kind of protest that patriarchy seeks to eliminate.

Patriarchy works to disrupt and limit protest, empathy and "the capacity to repair" because they threaten the division of people "into the superior and inferior" based on "race, gender, class, caste, religion, sexuality" and so on[4]; and upon these divisions depend the "hierarchies of power and status" that structure patriarchy (12). Gilligan and Snider distinguish between relationship ("the experience of connecting") and relationships ("the appearance of connection") and argue that giving up the former is "adaptive, culturally sanctioned and socially rewarded" (18). We, in other words, sacrifice the former for the latter because the latter constitutes "a place within the patriarchal order" (14). *Creepshow*, oscillating between 1970s horror's critiques of "bankrupt systems of meaning" and 1980s horror's "attempt to assert patriarchal power" (T. Williams, *Hearths* 213), oscillates too between anxieties about having and not having a place in that order, and so also about losing and maintaining relationship.

In addition to the horror film tradition, *Creepshow* also draws on the EC comics published in the 1950s, which had their own tradition of critiquing the "institutions of American society" (S. Brown 40).[5] EC itself balanced joyous indulgence in "horrific imagery" with a focus on retributive morality and poetic, often undead, justice. But as Simon Brown points out, *Creepshow* is, unsurprisingly given the tensions discussed so far, more morally complex and ambiguous (38, 43). He notes, for example, that the patriarch in the segment "Father's Day" is, in the EC mold, the revenger from beyond the grave, but he is far from, as many of EC's avengers represent, "a wronged innocent" (38).[6]

"Father's Day" is one of three original stories ("Something to Tide You Over" and "They're Creeping Up on You" are the others) featured in *Creepshow*, along with adaptations of two lesser-known King stories, "The Lonesome Death of Jordy Verrill" and "The Crate," that appeared in magazines and still have yet to be anthologized (12).[7] "Father's Day" is preceded by the first portion of the film's wraparound, which also concerns a less than stellar patriarch, although here the father is not the avenger but the object of revenge by his son, Billy, a reader of EC-esque comics. Billy's revenge can be read as a defense not only of himself but also of audiences of horror comics and, by extension, films, including their critiques of patriarchy and the nuclear family. The bad father of "Father's Day" takes revenge on his own relatives, presenting the family as dangerous and (self-)destructive, failing in its duty to guarantee the social future.

"Something to Tide You Over" narrows the focus to patriarchal marriage, with vengeance deployed both by and against a husband whose possessiveness and investment in surveillance suggests an exaggerated form of heteronormative romantic relationships. A troubled marriage occupies the center of "The Crate" as well, with a husband using a monster to dispose of a wife whom he regards as monstrous herself for her outspokenness and lack of deference—in other words, her failure to be a woman properly. In "The Lonesome Death of Jordy Verrill," however, it is not marriage or family but the lack of marriage and family that contributes to the title character's demise. Upson Pratt in "They're Creeping Up on You" also lacks a wife and family, but at the same time, his isolation might be read as an extreme form of patriarchy's sacrifice of relationship for power and privilege. His rejection of marriage and, by extension, the reproductive family unit is ultimately punished when he symbolically births innumerable roaches. Patriarchal structures are dangerous, but so is their absence. It's a tough world out there for a horror anthology protagonist.

Monster Fans and Monstrous Fathers: Billy and "Father's Day"

In Wood's view, 1980s horror film invites identification not with the monster (representing the repressed) but with "punishment" (*Hollywood* 173). However, *Creepshow*'s wraparound segments and its opening story, "Father's Day," conform to this pattern only partially. In the wraparound, the punishing father, representative of an abusive patriarchal system, becomes the final recipient of punishment.[8] That his son delivers this punishment reverses the "natural" flow of authority. That the father is anti-horror as well locates horror on the side of such subversion. In "Father's Day," the father doles out punishment for his own murder, but that murder seems at the same time to be, in the EC-style moral code established by the wraparound, justified. Both, then, depict the patriarchal family as dysfunctional and dangerous.

The film's wraparound segments feature an angry, abusive father, Stan (Tom Atkins), whose son Billy (Joe Hill, credited as Joe King) functions as an audience surrogate. Billy's revenge on his father is framed as justice not only because of Stan's abuses but also because of his denigration of horror (and so, by extension, the audience for the film), a genre that, as here, often critiques the traditional family unit (as in, for instance, *Night of the Living Dead*). Gilligan and Snider argue that patriarchy requires "a sacrifice of love for the sake of hierarchy" and thereby "steels us against the vulnerability of loving," becoming "a defense against loss" (9). This dynamic certainly obtains in Billy's family, in which hierarchy is paramount and love is not expressed between father and son (or, if we are being generous, is expressed through verbal and physical violence), while the mother (Iva Jean Saraceni) reins in expressions of love (and of her own will) in deference to the patriarchal hierarchy in her relationships to both her son and husband. The fact that Stephen King's son Joe Hill makes his screen debut as Billy (M. Browning 64) adds a metatextual layer in which a father creating (or perhaps bequeathing) a place for his son within the horror community contrasts the father who attempts to bar his son from participating in that community. It is significant to this contrast that Billy ultimately assumes a position of power *vis-à-vis* his father, upsetting the patriarchal hierarchy, by means of his horror fandom.

The film opens with a medium shot of the exterior of a suburban single-family home, the stereotypically imagined location of the traditional nuclear family, and its first lines establish the hostility of Billy's father to his son reading EC-style *Creepshow* comics. "I told you before I didn't want you to read this crap," he pronounces. "I never saw such rotten crap in my life. Where do you get this shit? Who sells it to you? ... You remember who puts the friggin' bread on the table around here, don't ya?" In this reaction, Stan exemplifies how, for "anti-fans," horror exists less in its actual texts than in those "audiences' moralizing discourses" (Hills 206). In addition to attempting to impose his moral-aesthetic perspective on his child, Stan explicitly connects his power within the family hierarchy to his power as its wage earner, the one who "puts the friggin' bread on the table." The traditional division of unwaged labor as female and waged labor as male afforded the patriarch the power of "discipline" over those economically dependent upon him, but the decade leading up to *Creepshow* saw this power being eroded by greater numbers of women becoming waged laborers (Federici, *Revolution* loc. 1076).[9] Billy's mother does in fact resist her husband's discipline, albeit briefly and ineffectually, telling him not to be too hard on their son because "[a]ll the kids read them."[10] Billy himself resists much more strongly. When Stan replies, "My boy isn't 'all the kids'" and announces that the comics are going into the garbage,[11] Billy counters that he doesn't see how they are any worse than the books that his father keeps in his dresser, "those ones under your underwear, those sex books."[12]

Billy's resistance to his father's patriarchal power is linked to Billy's horror fandom and thereby to horror's own history of critiquing the traditional family. *Creepshow* as a whole "represents a defence of the pleasures of ... 'trash culture' in the face of parental (and by extension, critical and academic) opposition" (M. Browning 67); and Billy's pointing out his father's own enjoyment of a different type of low-culture commodity constructs anti-horror moralizing as mere hypocrisy. In these oppositions, *Creepshow*'s Billy recalls *Knightriders'* two Billys, one the child Billy carrying a fan magazine and the other, King Billy, who similarly champions a mode of low-culture entertainment in the face of mainstream disapproval. This parallel is underscored not only by the characters' shared names but also by Ed Harris' presence in *Creepshow*. *Creepshow* Billy's resistance, by positing an equivalence between father and son, works to level the patriarchal hierarchy. The film further establishes Billy as an audience surrogate as it cuts to shots of Billy's monster toys during the heated exchange that follows his father slapping him in the face hard enough to leave a handprint. Through the juxtapositions that these cuts create, the toys simultaneously function as tokens of Billy's fandom and identify his father as another monster. Later, after his father has tossed what we see is a *Creepshow* comic in a curbside garbage can, he fumes to his wife, "You see that crap? That horror crap? Things coming out of crates and eating people, dead people coming back to life, people turning into weeds, for Christ's sake." These references to the film's own segments identify Billy not just with horror fans in general but with audience members for Romero's film in particular. Billy makes an especially fitting audience surrogate because, as Hills observes, the "'obsession/fascination'" that horror fans use to explain becoming horror fans is typically, across the range of horror fan cultures, displaced onto the "child-self" in order to discursively preserve the adult, "rational" self (77–78).[13] Even teenagers, as a part of constructing their fan identity, often locate their first experiences of horror fandom in the distant past (Hills 82–83). At the same time that the film positions Billy as the audience stand-in, it also, with its knowing invocations of the EC tradition, echoes the (masculinized) adult fan posture of connoisseurship rather than fear (Hills 78). The film openly gestures to this tension in the self-construction of fans when in the final wraparound segment, one garbage collector (Marty Schiff) says of a discarded *Creepshow* comic, "My kids love these things," while the other, played by Tom Savini in a metadiegetic moment that is exactly the type of connoisseur-friendly inclusion that lends authorization to adult fans, says, "I do too."[14]

If Billy acts as an audience surrogate, however, he also becomes a kind of monster, and this happens both because he has access to *Creepshow* comics and because his father attempts to deny him that access. Billy's father assumes that he has successfully deployed his authority as patriarch, assuring his wife, who now expresses agreement with his anti–*Creepshow* stance, that he has taken care of the problem: "That's why God made fathers, babe. That's why God made fathers" (a statement that recalls the traditional equivalency of father-family, king-kingdom and God-world and, as Williams remarks, authorizes his violent dominance of the family by invoking religion [*Cinema* 116]). As he speaks, the markers of his position in the patriarchal hierarchy—his alcoholic drink and padded wingback chair with ottoman—contrast with his wife's wicker-back rocking chair and sewing. But his authority is not as absolute as this suggests or as he believes: We soon see Billy smiling and rubbing his hands in anticipation at the Creep, *Creepshow*'s decaying undead mascot (and Billy's alternative father figure?), who floats outside his bedroom window.

In the final wraparound segment, Billy transforms his anger at his father into vengeance, attacking him via a voodoo doll for which an advertisement is visible in the *Creepshow* comic in the animated transition between "The Lonesome Death of Jordy Verrill" and "Something to Tide You Over" and again in the final wraparound segment, when one garbage collectors notes that someone has already sent for the doll. The punning references, in the style of the comics as Billy, upstairs, repeatedly stabs the voodoo doll, further tie his violent acts to their horror media inspiration: Stan complains of a "stiff neck" (which also points to his inflexibility, as well as his puritanical attitude to Billy's comics), and Billy taunts, in a put-on voice, "Ready for another shot, Dad?"[15] Indeed, immediately upon his Creep imitation, "[r]ed light and a zig-zag background blurs the comic book/reality border once more" (M. Browning 66). Billy, then, seems actually to play into the idea held by people such as his father that horror media is detrimental to children and that they will mimic its violence. EC, of course, was famously a target of a Congressional investigation into juvenile delinquency (S. Brown 38–41), and Billy seemingly plays out the worst fears of its critics. Not least among such fears is the shift in power and inversion of patriarchal authority symbolized and enacted through the displaced penetration of Billy's father via Billy's stabbing the voodoo doll. At the same time, however, the film presents Billy's violence not only as justified but, ironically, as justified to protect himself from a parent in his nuclear family, one who acts as a protector in the anti–EC, anti-horror worldview.

As retribution for abuse, Billy's horror-inspired and facilitated supernatural violence empowers him, as it does again in *Creepshow 2* (see Chapter 7). With *Creepshow* a transitional text between 1970s and 1980s horror, it is fitting that audience surrogate Billy also straddles the transition that Sobchack identifies from children in horror films acting as "terrors" in the 1970s and being "terrorized" in the 1980s (177–78). Billy terrorizes his terrorizer, and only becomes a terror *because* he is terrorized, much in the way that Sobchack describes Carrie, another transitional murderous child, as harmed by the very "bourgeois family structure" responsible for protecting and nurturing her (179).[16] On the one hand, Billy's being terrorized reflects the way that the figure of the terrorized child shifts responsibility for the breakdown of "traditional family relations" away from the child (who lacks the apocalyptic powers of his filmic antecedents) and instead often "single[s] out Dad as the primary negative force in the middle-class family" (Sobchack 180). On the other hand, however, as a terror, he evokes Andrew Scahill's category of "The Destroyer," the imaginative horror film child who dislocates "play from the register of creation to that of death and destruction" (18).

The pattern that Billy sets of the child as simultaneously victim and aggressor is echoed with Bedelia Grantham (Viveca Lindfors), or Aunt Bedelia, in "Father's Day." Bedelia is an adult rather than a young child like Billy, however, when she kills her abusive father, Nathan Grantham (Jon Lormer), and her revenge is balanced by the murdered patriarch's own fatal vengeance against his relations, which occupies center stage in this segment. Grantham is not only abusive, like Billy's father, but also a murderous criminal, and Bedelia dies for having killed him after her drinking, presented as another ethical lapse, leads to her awakening a rotting, reanimated Grantham—all of which locates justice outside of the family unit and sees it destroy rather than protect its progeny, a function that Lee Edelman notes is "widely (if inaccurately) presented as extrapolitical" (loc. 46). The nuclear family is central to a politics that is "conservative insofar as it works to affirm a structure, to authenticate social order, which it then intends to transmit to the future in the form of its inner Child" (loc. 68). In failing to protect its children, the Grantham family thereby fails to fulfill the paramount heteronormative function of reproduction as a (putative) guarantee of and vehicle for the social future.

Williams asserts that "[b]oth *Creepshow* and the EC comic traditions utilise the horror tradition of the 'return of the repressed' whereby signifiers of the injustices perpetuated by the world of normality return in a distorted, corrupt and decaying form to avenge themselves upon the representatives of a normal, but corrupt, world" (*Cinema* 117). The private world of the Grantham family can certainly be read as corrupt, or at least decadent: the first live shot in the segment shows family members Cass Blaine (Elizabeth Regan) and Richard Grantham (Warner Shook) drinking alcohol and smoking while their aunt, Sylvia Grantham (Carrie Nye), calls Cass a "hog" and says she has always had "extremely healthy appetites." Hank Blaine (Ed Harris), who has married into this family, sticks to tea. Harris' casting here functions similarly to Joe Hill's in introducing an extratextual contrast, here between

Harris' recent role as the increasingly authoritarian father-figure King Billy in *Knightriders* and the victim of an authoritarian father here. King Billy, though, recognizes his failings and leaves his position as head of his "family" (and passes his sword onto the child who shares his name) while Nathan Grantham unrelentingly exercises his patriarchal power even from beyond the grave. No matter the indulgence and insults on display, however, it remains very difficult to see Nathan as a signifier of injustice, certainly not in the vein of the dispensers of revenge in "Something to Tide You Over," "They're Creeping Up on You" and even the wraparound. If anything, he represents the change in 1980s horror that set, albeit with significant exceptions, "the patriarchal father" as the monster (T. Williams, *Hearths* 214).

Nathan, who is buried under a gravestone whose epitaph reads merely **Father**, offers a very literal example of the patriarch as "the synchronic repressed who, first powerfully absenting himself, returns to terrify the family" in horror films of the period (Sobchack 180). Before his death, he had always been, in Richard's words, "hysterically jealous" of Bedelia in a "Freudian" way, behavior that marks him as a monstrous father not only in relation to the incest taboo but also through hysteria's association with femininity and the uterus. Bedelia evokes the former while addressing Nathan's grave: "You stupid bastard, you screwed it all up. You screwed up my mother. *You screwed me* [emphasis added]."[17] Additionally, "bastard" here injects a further undertone of illicit sexuality in connection with the family. Nathan can also be seen as infantilized by his tantrum demanding cake (Hofmann), all of which gives particular weight to Bedelia's declaration to her father that her much older beloved, Peter Yarbro (Peter Messer), was a "man, a real man."[18] Nathan, of course, has this love object and alternative father figure murdered, eliminating his "Freudian" competitor in what is made to look like a hunting accident. We can link this masculine-coded murder with the recurrence in the segment of jump cuts to animal heads, which Williams labels "characteristic" of Romero (*Cinema* 118). As they occur during Bedelia's murder of her father, they suggest an inverted repetition of Yarbro's murder, in which Bedelia usurps the role of "hunter" from the patriarch. These cuts also both recall and perform the same symbolic function as the animal heads in Billy's home, marking the domestic space of the family as unsafe and threatening rather than protective and nurturing. Such spaces demonstrate that when patriarchy and paternity compete in the home to "constitute" the child, they cannot both "end happily" (Sobchack 184). And compounding the fearfulness of the family is that it transmits its "psychopathological" behaviors while naturalizing them (T. Williams, *Cinema* 118).[19] In an extreme example of such transmission, Nathan's family was able to cover up his murder because they followed his own criminal example: As Bedelia says to Nathan's grave, "You taught us all."[20]

Not all of the adult children's learned behaviors rise to the level of murder, but they nonetheless signify the patriarchal family's malign influence. Undead Nathan, after he kills Hank, demands, "Where's my cake? I want it. It's mine." This repetition of his cries on the last day of his life evoke the infantilized elderly father through the powerful, murderous undead monster and so provide an embodied instance of horror film's representation by the early 1980s of patriarchy as "simultaneously terrified and terrorizing in the face of its increasing impotence" (Sobchack 181). Shortly after this moment, Cass sounds very like Nathan when she says of Hank, whose whereabouts are obviously unknown, "Well, I want him. And I want my dinner." Her statement, with its equivalency between her husband and her meal, demonstrates that part of what Nathan has "taught" his family is the same self-centered acquisitiveness that led him not only to demand his Father's Day cake but to view his family merely as "vultures" waiting to get his money.[21] Richard shows even less concern for Hank; he just wants another bottle of wine. In the disconnection of the members of this family group from one another, we see one manifestation of the way in which patriarchy persists by causing, in the face of ineffective protest, a movement into despair and then detachment as a self-defensive withdrawal from relationship (Gilligan and Snider 14).

Bedelia may indeed have made such moves herself, but she also threateningly appropriates patriarchy and its signifiers of masculinity. In advance of her arrival, Richard calls Bedelia both "dotty" and "the patriarch of our clan," the former pointing to the transgressiveness of the latter. The audience's first view of Bedelia reveals her speeding along in a car and smoking a "phallic cigar" (T. Williams, *Cinema* 117). When she kills her father, resisting his authority and opening the way to her becoming clan patriarch, she does so with a marble ashtray, associating the murder with the appropriation of the phallus suggested by her cigar.[22] Nathan himself is introduced with his own phallic implement, the cane with which he bangs on the arms of his chair. The banging of the cane, which asserts the claim of the patriarch(y) to be heard, is emphasized by reverb and echo as Nathan demands his cake, asserts his position as Bedelia's father, and reprimands her that she is "supposed to be taking care of" him. His reprimand crystallizes the structuring of patriarchy under which "men have selves, whereas women ideally are selfless" and have relationships that "surreptitiously serve men's needs" (Gilligan and Snider 6). Bedelia, obviously, violates this binary, and her avowal "I don't need you!" can be interpreted as a rejection not only of her father but of the system of gender hierarchy that he represents.

Ultimately, however, Nathan would appear to overcome Bedelia's usurpation of masculine-coded signifiers and power. Bedelia, drinking Jim Beam at Nathan's grave, drops the bottle, and Nathan's hand shoots out of the ground shortly after, almost as if her loss of the masculine-coded drink causes his re-emergence. When he crawls from the grave, she tries to fend him off by putting her (phallic) stick between them. He chokes her, a method of murder that silences her voice even before death.[23] Nathan later kills the servant Mrs. Danvers in the kitchen, a domestic space coded as female, and in the segment's climax, brings out Sylvia's head on a platter, decorated with candles and frosting.[24] Williams sees the deaths as connected by the framing of Mrs. Danvers' head in a window, linking it to Sylvia's severed head as well as Sylvia's status as "nominal head" of the family (*Cinema* 119). He further sees Sylvia's decorated head as resembling the Statue of Liberty, linking "a pathological living dead family unit" to America's "bankrupt" conception of itself (120). In the end, transformed into an object to be devoured, Sylvia indeed serves men's needs. When Nathan says, "I got my cake," it marks the reassertion of his prerogatives under patriarchy: Bedelia is no longer the clan patriarch, Sylvia is no longer its "nominal head," and Nathan has overcome the female-initiated frustration of his desires. Gwen Hofmann contends that Cass and Richard are still alive when the segment ends because the former abides by traditional gender roles and the latter is "effeminate," and so they do not threaten Nathan's white male privilege. But there's also no reason to assume that they won't be next to die, the heteropatriarchal family having entirely destroyed not only its transgressors but also itself.

I Used to (Not) Love Her, But I Had to Kill Her: "Something to Tide You Over" and "The Crate"

While the wraparound and "Father's Day" reflect their ambivalence about patriarchy through the prism of familial relationships between parents and children, the segments "Something to Tide You Over" and "The Crate" pivot more particularly around the proprietary dynamics of heteronormative couplehood. Both segments, in their own conflicted engagement with patriarchal norms, demonstrate how some men, as part of the psychological self-defense concomitant with the withdrawal from relationship that patriarchy impels, participate in "the conspiracy of violence," which includes making objects of women and lashing out if they feel that their "manhood is shamed or their vulnerability exposed" (Gilligan and Snider 43). In "Something to Tide You Over," Richard Vickers (Leslie Nielsen) murders his wife Becky (Gaylen Ross) and her lover, Harry Wentworth (Ted Danson), while monitoring their deaths via closed-circuit cameras, a method that suggests surveillance as both a means of control over romantic partners and a form of voyeurism that negates sexuality. Richard's aggressive enforcement of patriarchal monogamy leads to his own death at the hands of the undead lovers. The monster within "The Crate," meanwhile, provides its professorial protagonist, Henry Northrup (Hal Holbrook), the consequence-free means to murder a wife, Wilma (Adrienne Barbeau), who impugns and embarrasses him, equating her mockery with the more serious fatherly abuse that occurs elsewhere in the film.

Simon Brown posits that Richard views his wife as a "thing" in the same way that he views his collection of AV equipment as things (47). While this is true, we should make sure to see this view not merely as a personal failing but as indicative of the conception of women as possessions inherent to heteronormative monogamy itself as an ideology and practice. If a woman's sexuality is the object of a competition between men over exclusivity, then that woman becomes conceived of as an object herself. And if the family is a microcosm of the state, then the monogamous patriarchal family-marriage, in its concern with controlling female sexuality, is a dystopian, if not totalitarian, surveillance state, unceasingly on the lookout for disobedience or disloyalty.[25]

The "domestic possessive motif," Richard's regard of "family as his own personal property," both echoes Nathan's perspective in "Father's Day" and marks this segment as "an explicit patriarchal revenge fantasy" (T. Williams, *Cinema* 122–23). "Tide" wastes no time in establishing heteronormative marriage as a site of confinement and of male competition. The first shot is of a goldfish in a very small, suspended enclosure, evoking the restriction and scrutiny that are Becky's lot as a wife.[26] As the camera pans away from the fish, Richard knocks on Harry Wentworth's door, and immediately upon opening the door on the chain, Harry says that he can "bench press 300 pounds" and that Richard will lose his foot if he doesn't remove it from the door. Harry's masculine posturing and threats of physical violence exemplify the construction of romantic and family relationships as venues for male competition over hierarchy and ownership that patriarchal norms engender.

Richard quickly frames marriage as fundamentally a system of exclusive possession and not a way of being, as Gilligan and Snider would say, in relationship. Harry proposes that his rival ought to be grateful to him: "I mean, if you ever loved her, you don't now." In doing so, he also emphasizes the masculine disdain for sharing: "There won't be any alimony, *none of that community property shit* [emphasis added]." Richard strips heteronormative monogamy of its veneer of romantic affection to expose the underlying dynamics of proprietary ownership by which it operates: "Well, I don't know whether I ever loved her or not, Harry. That doesn't matter. The point is, I keep what is mine. No exception to that rule, ever." His assertion that his relationship with his wife has nothing to do with love and everything to do with possessiveness (and thus with power and control) subverts at least one form of the happiness script attached to the practice, "that marriage causes happiness and thus that we have a moral obligation to promote marriage" (Ahmed, *Promise* 199). Richard does acknowledge that he takes his possessiveness further than is typical, admitting, "On the subject of what is mine, for example, I am not sane, at all"; but this does not negate its centrality, in attenuated or less overt form, to heteropatriarchal romantic relationships.

During this scene, Richard pokes around Harry's television and VCR setup, linking Harry too with the segment's network of male-associated screens and cameras, as well as with the "social and financial benefits that patriarchy bestows on some people" (Gilligan and Snider 15). After all, it is Richard's wealth—he mentions that he owns all of Comfort Point, the beachfront area where he will act out his revenge—that permits him to maintain his elaborate surveillance apparatus. Richard here plays some audio of his wife on a portable tape recorder, but we later see that he both monitors his entire house with cameras and owns the equipment to remotely monitor the beach where he drowns Harry and Becky.[27] Richard's cameras, tapes, recorders and screens all function as technological prostheses that allow him to "capture" and so control, possess and dominate others. This audio-visual capture doubles and is doubled by the physical capture of Becky and Harry being buried up to their necks in sand, an immobilization that constitutes an ideal state for surveillance (as well as physical control).

When Richard shows Harry the buried Becky, he lets him know that he is taping the ordeal on a VCR, and that she and Harry will both become part of Richard's "home movies." This phrase points to the collapse of the roles of family man–patriarch, surveillant and spectator.[28] With his personal horror movies, Richard stands simultaneously as the horror filmmaker and, like Billy, the "pathological" horror fan of mainstream imagination, which leaves Harry, who calls Richard "insane," in the censorious role occupied by Billy's father and associates Richard's homemade horrors with the comics condemned by Billy's father but celebrated by *Creepshow* itself.[29] As a creator of horrific spectacle,

Richard occupies the same ranks not only as the creators of *Creepshow*'s (and EC's) comics but also as King Billy and his knights in their creation of violent popular spectacle and the amateur filmmakers of *Diary of the Dead*, whose ambivalently presented filming of diegetically real horror most directly parallels Richard's. *Martin*'s alignment with its titular character's perspective, which joins surveillance with horrific spectacle, offers another, similarly ambivalent analog. Unlike Richard or Harry, Becky, as a woman, does not get to be a spectator at all, censorious or otherwise.[30] In addition to his personal snuff films, Richard also watches the 1932 W.C. Fields comedy *The Dentist* in bed. We hear the title character remark, "That kid's so dumb, he doesn't know what time it is." When the dentist is asked in response, "What time is it?" he cannot say: His bullying masculine authority is revealed to be empty posturing.

If the comedic dentist fails to back up his projection of patriarchal authority, then Richard attempts to back his authority up with violence. As we have seen, "Tide" offers an exemplary instance of the theme that Raechel Dumas neatly sums up in discussing another, later horror film as "the incompatibility of male authority and female desire" (109). A wife's adultery as "a man's worst nightmare" is a "script" that works to suppress certain voices and feelings that would be incompatible with the perpetuation of patriarchy (Gilligan and Snider 115). Women themselves come to act as "containers and concealers" of some of these disavowed male feelings and needs, which causes men to threaten or enact violence if these women try to leave them (Gilligan and Snider 71). Such disavowal, in combination with Richard's denial of love for his wife, might be reflected in his insistence to the buried Harry that the only way for him to survive is to "hold your breath" and his own, segment-ending boast while himself buried up to his neck: "I can hold my breath for a *long* time!" Richard first threatens violence against his wife in order to gain entry to Harry's home. At another point when, gun in hand, he admonishes Harry (whose potential weapon is a shovel): "Now, if you're thinking of becoming a hero, I suggest that you remember the lady fair." This time, Richard frames the threats of violence that he uses to control his rival in terms of extremely traditional gender roles. And much as Harry is associated to a lesser degree than Richard with screens, so too is he symbolically implicated, in a milder way than Richard, in patriarchal violence. Richard declares that a crab near the buried Harry's head is "just getting revenge, Harry, for all the relatives of his that you ate, baked and stuffed at Ma Maison." While "Ma Maison" most probably refers to a restaurant, it carries the additional sense of Richard's rival encroaching on his home, and, either way, it links domesticity to violent acts in a humorous analogue to Richard literally killing his relative.

Richard's fate partly reverses this mapping of gendered violence.[31] The drowned Harry and Becky return, reborn into undeath from the primordial womb of the sea. Accompanied by gaze-obscuring mist, they penetrate Richard's home, catching him in the private domestic space of his bedroom. Before this, we see Richard showering, unaware of the approaching supernatural danger, a position commonly assigned to female characters in horror films. When he confronts his reanimated victims, his phallic gun proves ineffective. Richard ends the segment stripped of his power and mobility, defiant of the waves that will nevertheless overcome him in the end.

"The Crate" ends with another killer being disposed of in another body of water, but in this case, rather than marking the revenge of a wife and her extramarital lover, it marks the end of a husband's successfully covered-up murder of his wife. College professor Henry Northrup rids himself of his wife Wilma, who, significantly, goes by Billie, by arranging for her to be attacked by the creature inhabiting the titular crate. Williams perceives the suggestion that the creature will ultimately break out of its confines as promising that Henry's "moral punishment" is forthcoming (*Cinema* 125). Brown writes, somewhat less assertively, that the creature's likely breakout "suggests that retribution may be coming" (S. Brown 50). I see little support for this position. The creature displays no particular degree of abstract thought in the segment. Its behavior, whether caused by hunger, instinct or both, is quite simple: Someone gets close to the crate; the creature kills and eats that person. There is no particular reason to believe that it is aware of or cares about Henry as an individual (although its failure to instantly kill Billie might be read symbolically, on which more below) or that it would want to or be able to track him down once it escapes from the crate and the quarry into which Henry dumped it. Henry's arrest after the creature's escape is equally unlikely, since there is nothing to link the two except for the involvement of his colleague Dexter Stanley (Fritz Weaver), who has agreed to silence and who would himself be implicated in covering up multiple deaths. Henry's murder of Billie, then, represents a violent reestablishment of patriarchal supremacy over an unruly woman that is without consequences but not without the ambivalence towards patriarchy that characterizes the film as a whole.

Williams calls Wilma a "vulgar, lower-class wife," although "lower-class" seems to function here as a synonym for classless, and a "human monster," although he does clarify that despite being annoying, she is still a person, and "average" audience members may themselves act monstrously by laughing at her fate without thinking about its "wider implications" (*Cinema* 123–24). Tom Fallows and Curtis Owen, rather more colorfully, term her "a booze-sodden bitch" who talks "like a hyena on crack," and argue that we "sort of understand" her husband wishing to murder her (70). These descriptions suggest, though, that the audience's view of her (and the film's subtexts) aligns relatively unproblematically with Henry's. The mere fact that she prefers to be called Billie, a direct echo of the wraparound's audience surrogate Billy, as well as of *Knightriders'* outsider King Billy, implies that there are more favorable ways to perceive her (as does the casting of Barbeau against her usually likable type), even as that doubling might simultaneously be seen as a threatening encroachment by a woman who inappropriately arrogates a signifier of masculinity.[32] Her name is only one area in which Billie violates "the feminine taboo on having a voice of one's own" (Gilligan and Snider 35), violations for which her husband plans her death.

Patriarchy rewards women for not being too loud, angry or honest (Gilligan and Snider 33), but Billie displays little hesitation to be all three. At the outdoor faculty party where we first meet her, she literally speaks louder than the others (at least partly, we assume, due to alcohol), but she is also "loud" in the sense of not ceding the conversational reins to Henry when he clearly expects it. He looks unhappy at Billie's use of words such as "friggin'" as she gossips and gives unfiltered voice to her thoughts, including informing a male guest that he just needs to "get laid." With this framing, her red dress too reads as undesirably "loud," the lowest cut at the gathering and almost the only piece of clothing that isn't beige, white or gray. Meanwhile, Henry's colleague Dexter hits on one of the female guests, but, unlike with Billie, no one says that they don't understand why they keep inviting him—perhaps because his behavior conforms to rather than contravenes gender expectations.

If Billie recommends sexual attention for one man, the ministrations that she believes most men to be in need of are more maternal. Her very first lines call Dexter "such a child," and she continues, "You and Henry both, you're such children. At least Henry has me to take care of him, don't you, dear?"[33] Further, she expands this dependence to all men: "I just take care of Henry. Believe me, he needs it. Did you ever meet a man who didn't?" While she would seem to be espousing the selfless serving of men's needs that Gilligan and Snider identify as a patriarchal ideal, she does so in an infantilizing manner that undermines rather than caters to Henry's sense of his masculinity. "Oh, Henry, can't you do anything right?" she chides. This infantilization (a different form of which we see with Jordy Verrill) contributes to a gendered conflict over hierarchy, authority and control. Although the segment does not present Billie as a feminist, her comportment aligns with Ahmed's description of the feminist refusal to maintain the happiness of others by "erasing the very signs of not getting along" (*Promise* 66). Faculty wife Tabitha (Christine Forrest) chastises, "Your husband's *calling* you, Billie," implying a failure to properly obey male authority, and Billie's total lack of deference to her husband means that while she gives Henry orders to refill drinks or to (like a child) stay put, he fantasizes about shooting her in the head, a reassertion of control that he imagines met with the social approval of applause. At their home, Billie's telling Henry to scrub and put away the pots and wipe the stove (addressing him like a woman) and to have his friend (Dexter) gone before she gets back from her classes (addressing him like a child) prompts another murder fantasy: this time of strangling Billie, silencing her unwelcome, unruly voice.

In a way, the monster in the crate acts for Henry as Billie's inverse: While unruly in its own way, it possesses no real voice, it fulfills his wishes, and it allows him to occupy a position of power in his marriage. We might go so far as to see the creature, which, from what we see of it resembles an ape with copious sharp teeth, as at least partly a symbolic embodiment of Henry's male rage. The crate is marked shipped "via Julia Carpenter," suggesting an echo in its confinement and disempowerment by a woman of how Henry perceives his treatment by Billie. Its retreat back under the stairs "where it felt safe for so long" after it eats the janitor also parallels the childishness and weakness ascribed to Henry by his wife. Further, the crate's dating from 1834 links it with an era of strongly held traditional gender roles, roles to which Henry would doubtless like a return in his own life.

This is not to say that Billie herself, despite much of her behavior, entirely escapes the ideological influence of these roles. Henry uses Dexter's stereotypically masculine foibles to help lure Billie to her death, leaving her a letter saying that Dexter has had trouble "coping" with young female graduate students since his wife died (the actor portraying him would have been in his mid–50s when the film debuted). The letter claims that Dexter lured a young woman to a college campus building "under false pretenses" and then "attacked her," and it asks Billie for help. Although these are what at least today would be considered fairly serious offenses, Billie seems to find this all rather amusing, even managing a "poor Dex." While she shows some consideration of the victim when her expression changes briefly to disgust as she drives to the college and when, at the scene, she asks if the young woman has been beaten unconscious, even then she still refers to Dexter getting "in a scrape with a girl." Boys will, after all, be boys, even when they are middle-aged men.

As with Billie, however, Dexter does not display an entirely uncomplicated relation to normative gender roles. When the creature claims its first victim, Dexter panics in what could be perceived as a less-than-masculine way, grabbing hold of a colleague in the corridor and babbling at him in a high-pitched voice. After the creature kills this colleague, Dexter shows up at Henry's house, clutching a bloody shoe and crying.[34] While Dexter evinces what is implied to be feminine behavior—his thanking God for Henry at the end of the scene puts him in the weak position of being cared for that Billie ascribes to both men— Henry sees his chance to reclaim his rightful position as a man by getting rid of his wife, a plan that both exploits Dexter and differentiates Henry from him. By the end of the segment, this reclamation seems to have succeeded: With Billie gone, Henry projects calm and confidence as he sits across an overtly symbolic chessboard from a disheveled Dexter.

This Henry presents a clear contrast with the Henry who sends Billie to her death in a confrontation that foregrounds anxieties around gender. Just before Billie arrives at the college, Henry has been cleaning blood in a rubber apron and gloves, like a monstrous housewife. When he laughs in response to her inquiry about the non-existent co-ed, she calls him "hysterical," which she "would've expected."[35] Henry links a gendered insult of his own to his wife's use of a masculine name (with all that that implies) when he pushes her further under the stairs that shelter the crate, yelling, "Just tell him to call you Billie, you bitch!" As they struggle, Henry repeatedly cries out to the creature—figuring his caged, repressed male anger—"Wake up!"[36] When Billie counters his attack, asking if he wants to "see some real punching," she pummels him with her purse. That this female-coded object holds the "real" power reinforces the inverted gender hierarchy. After striking Henry, Billie "begins attacking his impotence on every conceivable level" (T. Williams, *Cinema* 124):

> Same old Henry—afraid of your own shadow. ... No good at departmental politics, no good at makin' money, no good at makin' an impression on anybody! And no good at all in bed! When was the last time you got it up, Henry? Huh? When was the last time you were a man in our bed? Now get outta my way, Henry, or I swear to God, you'll be wearing your balls for earrings. And I swear to God, if you ever touch me again...

His wife's impugning of his career and sexual prowess (the things men "should" be good at) ends with a castration threat, which seems to be what finally wakes the creature.[37] We see anger on Henry's face as the monster bites his wife and he repeats, "Oh, just tell it ... tell it to call you Billie." Once Billie and the creature are out of the way, Henry is free to displace his own patriarchal monstrosity onto Billie, telling Dexter that he has disposed of the remains of "two human beings and Wilma."

The Perils of Men Without Family in "The Lonesome Death of Jordy Verrill" and "They're Creeping Up on You"

If the segments discussed so far foreground, however ambivalently, the dangers of patriarchal marriage and family, then the remaining pair present the absence of those institutions as equally dangerous. In "The Lonesome Death of Jordy Verrill," the lack of an intimate partner or family, perhaps related to his rural poverty, intensifies the danger that Jordy (Stephen King) faces: He unsuccessfully confronts the extraterrestrial infection alone, and his failure to heed the advice of his father's ghost leads directly to unfortunate consequences. Upson Pratt (E.G. Marshall) in "They're Creeping Up on You" occupies the opposite end of the socioeconomic spectrum from Verrill, but he too suffers due to his solitude, here not only an absence of but also a hostility towards family or marriage. While clearly one can read the segment's roaches as the masses that Pratt disdains, they also represent unchecked, overwhelming reproduction as he symbolically births them when they erupt from his body in his sterile, solitary penthouse.

Ahmed includes "the family, marriage, class mobility [and] whiteness" among social forms promoted as "happiness-causes" (*Promise* 112). Impoverished Jordy, living alone on a farm, possesses only the last of these. The opening shot establishes that the family homestead is in disrepair, and the interior of the home where Jordy spends his time in solitary television watching and drinking is cluttered and messy. As he puts it, imagining his socioeconomic position as a family inheritance, "Verrill luck" is "always in" and spelled "B-A-D." Jordy's attribution of his difficulties to luck, including the luck of being born into a particular family, suggests a rejection of capitalist culture's "fantasy of meritocracy" (Berlant 167). While the host of one of the shows that appears on his TV, *Let There Be Light with Father Martin Burdee*, exhorts viewers to have faith that they "will succeed," the implied promises of this "Father" are hollow: state, religion and family have all failed Jordy, just as they overwhelmingly fail those in similar situations. *A Star Is*

Born (1937) also briefly appears on Jordy's TV, with Grandmother Lettie Blodgett (May Robson) telling upwardly mobile protagonist Esther Blodgett (Janet Gaynor), "They said this country would always be a wilderness. ... We were going to make a new country. Besides, we wanted to see our dreams come true." Grandmother Lettie here invokes the secular version of the ideology espoused by Father Martin, the national self-mythologizing of the American frontier as an instantiation of the American Dream. Contrary, however, to this mythologizing of American industriousness, within late capitalism, "the lower you are on economic scales, and the less formal your relation to the economy, the more alone you are in the project of maintaining and reproducing life"—in other words, enacting the "affective" and "instrumental" transactions of living on (Berlant 167). It is no surprise then that, affectively, Jordy interacts only with his television and the ghost of his father, and instrumentally, his first thought upon finding a meteor that has impacted on his land is how much "they would pay for it."

The segment arguably links money and excrement via Jordy calling the contents of the meteor "meteor shit" (T. Williams, *Cinema* 120). This shit, however, holds out, in Jordy's mind, the potential for what Lauren Berlant describes as "living the *proper* life that capitalism offers as a route to the *good* life" (164). He fantasizes about bargaining with a scientist (Bingo O'Malley) in the "Department of Meteors" while clad in a suit and invoking the good influence of his mother: "Anita Verrill didn't raise no idiots" (a contrast to Nathan Grantham, the father, as bad influence, in the preceding segment). He imagines the power of being able to say, "My meteor, my price," but neither in his fantasy nor in his real life does his modest dream to pay off a bank loan with profits from the meteor come to pass.

Jordy's socioeconomic status is connected to anxieties about his masculinity and his father(lessness). Although Jordy in a way fathers the alien weeds—kick-starting their reproduction by pouring water over the meteor, which cracks it and activates its contents, and pouring those contents into the soil—he is primarily depicted as a childlike figure. Aside from a generally childish affect, when he first finds the meteor, for example, he reaches slowly towards it and touches it only to draw back in pain and suck on his fingers, evoking the proverbial child touching a hot stove. He later imagines a doctor (Bingo O'Malley again) telling him that those same fingers will have to be chopped off, a clear "castration fantasy" (T. Williams, *Cinema* 121). Jordy drinking in a chair in front of a TV that shows not only Father Burdee but also the successful, hypermasculine men of professional wrestling, may also suggest his playing, in the absence of his own father, at the behaviors exhibited by other patriarchal figures in the film, such as Billy's father.

Jordy's observation "I'm growin'" (spoken to the Father Burdee program) can be taken, then, in multiple senses. It is followed by shots of vegetation overtaking the house and surrounding area, and when we next see Jordy, the vegetal growth on his face resembles a large, masculine beard (Fig. 7). When he goes into the bathroom and removes his clothes, however, he sees that the green growth has overtaken his genitals, returning to his castration anxiety, significantly, at the same moment that his three years-dead father appears in the bathroom mirror. Also significant is that Jordy's father is played by the same actor who plays the scientist who refuses to pay for a broken meteor and the castrating doctor: For Jordy, all authority figures are not just father figures but figures of his actual father. His father warns him against getting into the bathtub: "It's the water that it wants, Jordy. Don't ya know that?" Jordy replies, correctly, that he is a goner anyway, and when he turns back to the mirror, "Daddy," whether ghostly or imagined, has disappeared. Williams sees here another "punitive and threatening" father and says that his warning is in effect trying to stop Jordy decontaminating himself (*Cinema* 121). Again, though, we have little reason to think that Jordy is wrong about being a goner no matter what he does. Hofmann views this scene as another example in the film of "father knows best. The outcome is the same, when you don't listen to your father; you unleash doom upon the world." However, by this point, as the outdoor shots preceding this scene demonstrate, the doom is already unleashed.

Figure 7. Jordy Verrill (Stephen King) with beard-like vegetation in *Creepshow* (1982, Warner Brothers).

The real problem is not that the father is punitive or correct, but that he is absent, his advice only having value before Jordy first touches and waters the meteor. In the end, reflecting his non-existent domestic relations, Jordy's domestic space ceases to exist as a separate, protective space, the boundaries between it and the (alien) nature outside erased. In all of this, Jordy stands out as a victim of circumstance rather than of poetic justice. As Mark Browning points out, all of the other segments focus on someone who has committed a crime, and even his calling Jordy only a "slight exception … who is seeking to exploit something" seems rather too harsh (66). As someone on the fringes of the socioeconomic and patriarchal orders, Jordy's only piece of luck, the only way to escape circumstances alien, social or familial, comes from successfully completing suicide as updates on commodity prices drone from the radio.

Federici pointedly observes that only a "capitalist viewpoint" considers *productive* to be "a moral virtue, if not a moral imperative" (*Revolution* loc. 705). However, in this system, "if one has only surplus amounts" of money (and the power to which it equates), the "infinite" sovereignty that it confers becomes "a nightmarish burden, a psychotic loneliness" (Berlant 42–43). If Upson Pratt represents Jordy's opposite in terms of capitalist productivity, he is yet quite similar in his isolation and the negative effects that it incurs. While Pratt's embrace of the capitalist imperative to the exclusion of relation aligns him with and thereby critiques patriarchy, his rejection of patriarchy's institutions also represents a site of anxiety and danger.

Measured against the model of ruthless businessman, Pratt is certainly successful as a man. He asserts in his first stretch of dialogue that he "own[s] this goddamn building," and his $3200-a-month penthouse apartment boasts cutting-edge technology for the time (even his phone beeps futuristically). However, the blank white sterility of his living space, while a practical choice for the special effects involving roaches, also resonates symbolically with his solitude and antipathy towards marriage and the reproductive family (we in fact first see Pratt wearing a surgical mask and gloves in his quest to keep his apartment free from the bugs that represent both the lower classes and their prolific reproduction). Wood notes the psychoanalytic connection between "the bourgeois obsessions with cleanliness" and "sexual repression," with their "inverse reflections in the myths of working-class squalor and sexuality" (*Hollywood* 67). Pratt's investment in these myths is apparent not only in his pathological hatred of bugs but also in his threat to fire one of the building's employees, Carl Reynolds (Mark Tierno), who is currently at Disney World with his wife and kids. Although Disney World presents something of an opposite to Billy's *Creepshow* comics—and although Disney is, ironically, a ruthless practitioner of capitalism comparable to Pratt—the trip nonetheless marks Reynolds as a "good" father. In threatening to remove Reynolds' ability to continue as such, Pratt also makes clear his contempt for fatherhood by telling Reynolds that he can try taking his family to Disney again next year on a welfare check. Further, Pratt not only disdains the reproductive family but also expresses a distaste for sexuality in general. He tells one of the men involved in his company's corporate takeover of Pacific Aerodyne, "You did well. Go out and fuck somebody. But wear a damn rubber. Everybody's got the damn herpes these days." Women are a reward but also a source of disease, and Pratt's seeming condemnation of promiscuity dovetails with a view of the masses as excessively sexual.

Pratt's isolation from these masses (who, to him, encompass pretty much everyone), as well as from relationships, links his behavior with at least one aspect of patriarchy. Often, "detachment is mistaken for maturity ... because it mirrors the pseudo-independence of manhood, which in patriarchy is synonymous with being fully human" and reflects the ideal of "the emotionally stoic man more concerned with the accumulation of power and the provision of material security than with emotional intimacy of human connection" (Gilligan and Snider 55). Pratt has been trained towards this ideal, and away from empathy, since learning as a child to kill bugs, and its perhaps most important expression comes in his phone call with Lenore Castonmeyer (Ann Muffly), wife of a man who has shot himself as a result of Pratt International's recent takeover. Pratt has earlier called the news "wonderful" since he won't have to offer the dead man a seat on the board of directors. While Lenore, who says he "murdered" her husband, is on the line, he cheerfully asks how she is, plays an imaginary violin as she talks, and puts on a record. Asserting his attachment only to (masculine) competition and accumulation, he avers that he has only (metaphorically) killed men who "fucked up" and held the knife for their offered throats.

Lenore, a woman and a wife, is specifically connected with Pratt's punishment for his practices. Within the bounds of the segment, he threatens other families, but he actually destroys her marriage. She wishes him dead, and two scenes later, it happens, with her voice heard over the invasion of multitudinous roaches into the small room in which Pratt has sealed himself. The failure of what is promised to make us happy (such as foregoing relationships for capitalist accumulation) can translate into rage (Ahmed, *Promise* 42); and Pratt rages at both humans and roaches as bastards. His penalty is to become what he rages against, father to roaches and a site of excessive reproduction, as his dying body gives "birth" to innumerable bugs that flood his once-exclusive space.[38]

Conclusion: Patriarchy: Can't Live with It; Can't Live Without It

Brown points to greed as the moral infraction that connects all five *Creepshow* stories (see S. Brown 43–52). We might point to the crimes of patriarchy as an equally strong connective thread. Marriage and family and their associated gender expectations serve throughout as sites of horror. Hofmann contends that any subversion of patriarchy is consistently contained in the film, but I would argue that its treatment remains more inconclusively in tension. *Creepshow* offers strong critiques of patriarchal dynamics and institutions. Its murderous, selfish and jealous husbands and fathers undercut the equation of adherence to certain norms with happiness, a linkage that "make[s] certain forms of personhood valuable" (Ahmed, *Promise* 11). The film illustrates that, both for men and those around them, "hegemonic masculinity does not necessarily translate into a satisfying experience of life" (Connell and Messerschmidt 852). It throws into question the myth of the happy family, which also functions as a "powerful legislative device" that, like patriarchy, demands the reproduction of its own form (Ahmed, *Promise* 45). And if part of being feminist is being a "troublemaker" and "refusing to make others happy" (Ahmed, *Promise* 60), then we might even view Bedelia, Becky and Billie, who do what they want rather than what their respective fathers or husbands want, as resisting patriarchal control. However, as most clearly shown in the bad ends to which Jordy Verrill and Upson Pratt come as men outside the institutions of marriage and family, *Creepshow* is not finally comfortable with entirely abandoning patriarchy, nor does it offer an alternative vision.

Among patriarchy's many other corrosive effects, its hierarchies enable racism (Gilligan and Snider 101), as demonstrated in Upson Pratt's interactions with Mr. White, a black building superintendent. Pratt tells him that he notices that "people like you, people of color" often go far in service jobs and later refers to him as a "black bastard." He also only speaks to White through the visually and aurally distorting peephole in the door, which dehumanizes him. Once Pratt ceases to have (economic) power, White, symbolically stuck in the elevator and unable to move up to Pratt's level, calls Pratt a "honky bastard" and mocks him. Race and racial privilege play only this relatively brief part in *Creepshow*, but *Creepshow 2* engages these themes much more extensively.

Race and Murder in *Creepshow 2*

John R. Ziegler

As recounted by Simon Brown, the failure of 1983's *Twilight Zone: The Movie* likely contributed to Warner Brothers dropping out of the proposed film sequel to the previous year's *Creepshow* (92–93). *Creepshow 2* (1987) was originally intended to have five stories (including "Cat from Hell," which would find a home in *Tales from the Darkside: The Movie* [1990], see Chapter 9); it eventually emerged under the aegis of a new film company with three of the five planned segments (plus the wraparound sections) and a lower budget. What little critical attention that the George A. Romero–authored *Creepshow 2* has received is largely dismissive. Brown affirms that the movie "bears little relation either stylistically or thematically" (S. Brown 95) to EC comics themselves and "lacks the considered attempt to adapt the look and tone of EC that underpinned the original" (98). Tony Williams, whose brief discussion of *Creepshow 2* in his book on Romero's oeuvre appears in an appendix dedicated to films that Romero had a hand in but did not direct, grants this sequel a bit more connection to the series' printed inspiration, writing that while its stories "formally reflect EC moral codes, their individual renditions are often glib and perfunctory" (*Cinema* 178), and he sums it up as an "empty Hollywood 'sequelitis' product" with "little, if any, redeeming value" (178). Beyond the question of the extent of *Creepshow 2*'s reflection of either *Creepshow* or EC comics, Williams asserts that while certain of Romero's favored themes appear in this second installment, they fail to achieve a "satisfactory degree" of development that would put them into true creative conversation with the films that Romero directed (*Cinema* 178).

Creepshow 2 may not provide nuanced social critique, but racial privilege, an issue that Romero engaged with throughout his career, functions as an important subtext throughout. In the first segment, "Old Chief Wood'nhead," the politics of race hold acute significance, both in its inversions of historical traumas suffered by indigenous North American cultures and particularly in its fraught indigenous representation.[1] In "The Hitch-hiker," the dynamic between the well-off white woman and the black male hitchhiker whom she strikes with her car is similarly fraught, evoking anxieties linked with structural racism and perceived black poverty and criminality in a decade in which Ronald Reagan had succeeded in making the term "welfare queen" a commonplace of the national lexicon. The middle segment, "The Raft," perhaps related to its being a substitution for one of the stories originally intended for inclusion (S. Brown 94), lacks the more overt engagement with issues of race evident in the other segments, but the sexual assault perpetrated by one character can be read as a critique of middle-class white masculinity. The wraparound segments position the assumed reader of the fictitious *Creepshow* comics (and so perhaps the default viewer of the film) as white and suburban and associate the status of (white) reader-viewer with the ability to take revenge on one's enemies, making a gratifyingly powerful point of identification more easily available for some audience members than for others.

Admittedly, the discussion that follows includes extensive consideration of elements of the finished film that are external to Romero's script. However, director Michael Gornick's repeated collaboration with Romero prior to *Creepshow 2*, as cinematographer for *Martin*, *Dawn of the Dead*, *Knightriders*, *Creepshow* and *Day of the Dead*, provides some rationale for examining *Creepshow 2*'s casting and directorial choices in juxtaposition to the films that Romero directed. Further, and more significantly, such analysis allows us to see not only the continuities with Romero's work as a director but also, as in "Old Chief Wood'nhead," some of the tensions between the critiques in his script and their on-screen realization.

HollyWooden Indians: "Old Chief Wood'nhead"

"Old Chief Wood'nhead" emphasizes greed (and narcissism, which can perhaps be read as a type of greed) rather than race as its central conflict and appears to aim for at least some measure of positive indigenous representation. Of its three significant indigenous characters, one, Ben Whitemoon (Frank Salsedo) is introduced giving a good-faith deposit of collateral from his "people" to white general store owner

Ray Spruce (George Kennedy): being, in other words, a good capitalist, despite his collateral consisting of things that his presumably impoverished people "hold precious"; and a second, Old Chief Wood'nhead himself, is the tale's moral avenger. The attitude of Ray's wife Martha (Dorothy Lamour) towards Ben and the local indigenous population is clearly intended to be contrasted negatively to Ray's own, with her claim that "these people" don't care about Ray and will take his charity until it dries up, invoking the stereotype of the lazy minority.[2] Additionally, the fact that the antagonist who robs the store and kills the couple is Ben's nephew, accompanied by two non-indigenous accomplices, sidesteps a straightforward white against indigenous narrative of the kind found in many classic Westerns. The result is interpretations such as Brown's that "race is not the issue" and that "the conflict is generational" (S. Brown 95).

Nonetheless, indigeneity occupies a more complex position in "Old Chief Wood'nhead" than such readings would suggest, one that raises questions of indigenous representational and historical narrative erasure and appropriation by the cinema of United States settler culture. The character of Sam Whitemoon, Ben Whitemoon's nephew, acts as one significant figure through which these dynamics play out. While Ben is played by an indigenous actor, Sam is played by white actor Holt McCallany, and Sam's ambition to be a movie star, his defining character trait, thus (re)enacts on a meta level the erasure of indigenous actors from cinema. Michelle H. Raheja observes that indigenous actors have long been radically underrepresented in film roles and absent from leading roles in film and TV (loc. 1030), due in part to casting practices in which "most Indian characters in Hollywood films have been played by non–Indians" (loc. 1613).[3] In Ted Jojola's view, "The absurdity of casting non–Indians reached its pinnacle in the mid–1980s," a timeframe that includes the release of *Creepshow 2* (15). From the time of early Hollywood, indigenous people were constructed on film as lighter-skinned Plains Indians with the "standard war bonnet and buckskin fringe costume" (meaning, for example, that many indigenous people were considered too dark to play indigenous people) (loc. 558). Sam's apparent belief that Hollywood provides not only wealth but also a space for indigenous people to act authentically is thus multivalently ironic. As he fires his shotgun at Ray's store, he proclaims, "No more eatin' dust for a livin'. There ain't no dust in Hollywood, man. And there ain't no fuckin' tribe of Tommin', wimpy-ass red men neither." What Sam calls "Tommin'," Raheja includes under her term "redfacing," "the complex performances of the Hollywood Indian both on-screen and off-screen," and makes a similar racial analogy, comparing redfacing to the "ambivalent cultural and political work" of black minstrelsy (loc. 487).[4] Sam delivers his line about Tom-min' while staring at Old Chief Wood'nhead. He then shoots the chief, and the film cuts to a close-up of red paint spilling from an overturned paint can: a representation of blood for a representation of a represen-tation of an indigenous person. Such "tension between and overlapping of the discourse-generated representations of Native Americans"—again, both on- and off-screen—means that "the representations have come to serve as the markers of indigenous identity and identifications for both non–Natives and some Native American people" (Raheja loc. 681). While Sam does not wear the marker of the stereotypical Plains Indian costume (that is reserved for Old Chief Wood'nhead himself), he is certainly light-skinned, and his indigeneity is signified by his long, black, flowing hair and his shirtlessness, a sartorial state that evokes the bare-chested warrior and that he shares with the chief. Sam's combina-tion of shirtlessness and a denim jacket when he is introduced perhaps simultaneously aligns him with the rocker-motorcycle gang villains so beloved of 1980s genre films, a modernized form of the hordes of enemy savages of the Western.

By framing Sam both in juxtaposition with the traditional Western and through his dreams of movie stardom, the segment draws atten-tion to its own tangled representational dynamics and to its relation to such dynamics within dominant culture's cinematic history. Kers-tin Knopf traces the evolution of indigenous representation from early Hollywood's tendency to categorize indigenous people within a binary of "docile and submissive" and ready to cooperate with whites or "fierce, ready to attack, take hostages, and kill (and, of course, take scalps)" (9) to a current binary that shifts between "either the notion of the 'dumb, drunken, lecherous, and lazy Indian' or the 'nature-loving spiritual traditionalist' and 'exotic lover'" (she marks the "'drunken, poor, and degraded Indian'" as a possible third category) (11). Ben and Sam might be seen as occupying the two halves of that older binary (with the chief, who does scalp someone, falling in between), but in resorting to armed robbery, Sam also fits the more contemporary clichés of indigenous laziness and poverty (he doesn't want to expend the time or effort to acquire the money that he lacks by means of sanctioned labor) as well as the image of the fierce, murderous Indian (he accidentally shoots Mar-tha but then deliberately and unnecessarily shoots Ray). Ray invokes these binaries when he calls Sam a disgrace to his people and claims that it's "hard to believe the same blood flows in your veins" as in the veins of Ben, whom he considers one of the best people he knows.

Sam's character additionally suggests the stereotype of the strongly sexual indigenous man, which may feed into the type of the exotic lover but also imagines indigenous people tending towards the bestial (Knopf 12). As Sam inserts a coin into the photo booth in Ray's store, he contemplates himself aloud: "They gotta make me a movie star. Hey, as soon as they see this hair, they're gonna say, 'Sam, get over here. Get in front of these cameras. There's 100 million women out there just waitin' to run that hair between their legs.'" He continues to make the connection between the hair that represents the clearest signifier of his indigeneity and his overpowering sexual desirability, adding after he steps out of the booth, "Nine years it took me to grow this hair, man. I'm not just fuckin' around here. I'm going to Hollywood, man. And this hair is gonna get me paid and laid." His metaphor for sex with likely non-indigenous women (running that hair between their legs) not only renders his hair a perhaps exoticized synecdochic fetish but also suggests that these women will want to overlay the hair between their own legs with his indigenous hair, like a strange, overtly sexualized variation of playing Indian. Further, Sam asks for agreement that he is better-looking than a particular movie character with "like, these superpowers and shit because of his hair," whose hair then gets cut off by "this bitch," which makes him an "ordinary guy." Sam is most likely referring to director Cecil B. DeMille's *Samson and Delilah* (1949), which extends the parallels beyond the equivalence of his power with his hair: he is comparing himself to lead actor Victor Mature, a white actor playing Samson in a film full of white actors playing Philistines and Hebrews (the latter of whom are never referred to as Hebrew or Jewish).

Sam's self-image is inarguably bound up with his imagination of himself in and on film, and it is significant that his imagination of stardom centers on the part of his appearance that most closely reproduces a bodily signifier of Indian-ness that occurs across Hollywood cinema. Sam assumes that his hair, to which he calls attention at the end of his pronouncement about getting "paid and laid" by sweeping it back over his shoulders, confers not only sexual but mass-market cinematic (and, by extension, capitalistic) desirability. On a metatextual level, this desire as a diegetically indigenous character to be a Hollywood star is extradiegetically undercut by the fact that he is not played by an indigenous person: The indigenous actor playing Ben and the white actor playing Sam do not (to use Ray's phrase and in terms of common constructions of race) have the same "blood" in their veins. Sam's conviction that he is "movie star" material is further undercut by his consistent association with the traditional Western, a genre that employed the same type of casting practices as *Creepshow 2* and offered little space for indigenous leading men.

Sam conducts the robbery of Ray's store with two white companions, Fatso Gribbens (David Holbrook) and Andy Cavanaugh (Don Harvey). Sam's status as leader would seem to invert Western tropes, but
at the same time, deviations from such tropes remain in nostalgic tension with them. Fatso, for example, gets the group's first line, and it is
"How," delivered with one hand upraised, a word that Barbra A. Meek
includes in a subcategory of words within "Hollywood Injun English"
(94) that have been "borrowed from American Indian languages," angli-
cized and incorporated into common English usage, allowing them to
"be readily identified and reduced to indexes of Indianness" (113) and
to serve as part of "racialized, and often pejorative, images" (118).[5] The
raised hand gesture in combination with "How" also hails from "pre-
existing 'Hollywood Indian' racial characterizations" (94). Andy, meanwhile, directly invokes the Western by donning a white cowboy hat
at a jaunty angle and taunting Ray, "Yeah, why don't you run us out of
town, sheriff?" If Andy's hat figures him as an outlaw cowboy, though,
his sleeveless denim vest associates him with Sam: the smaller patches
on the front may suggest, again, a rocker villain,[6] but the large patch
on the back depicts the logo of the Pontiac Firebird automobile that
he owns (Fig. 8). Both "Pontiac," taken from an 18th-century Odawa
leader, and "Firebird," taken from a creature in indigenous folklore,[7] are
dominant-culture commodifications of indigenous culture. (Sam plays
on this when he says that the car will "fly" them to Hollywood.) On the
one hand, then, the fact that, after killing Andy, Old Chief Wood'nhead
places Andy's corpse on the hood of his Firebird, which the chief has
smashed up with his tomahawk, hints at resistance by the chief to such
commodification. On the other hand, however, the chief himself represents the same type of commodification, leaving us with one appropriation smashing another, two instances of the replacement of "the Indian
as a material object" by "an endlessly reproducible ... image" (Raheja
loc. 1930) clashing with one another. A similar abstraction occurs in
the additional linkage of Fatso and Andy with what in a Western would
be further (and differently hierarchized) categories of racialized Others, Andy through his Irish last name and Fatso through Sam's explanation of why he would not leave Fatso behind: "Shit, man, I gotta have my
slave with me wherever I go."

All three members of Sam's criminal trio are also linked to the tra-
ditional Western via the TV show that plays in each of their homes, *The
Cisco Kid* (1950–1956), which followed a pair of Mexican Robin Hood–
esque outlaws, Cisco and his sidekick Pancho (played respectively by
Romanian native Duncan Renaldo and actor of Castilian ancestry Leo
Carrillo). That the show is being watched, presumably three decades after

Figure 8. A shirtless, long-haired Sam Whitemoon (Holt McCallany), Martha Spruce (Dorothy Lamour) and Andy Cavanaugh (Don Harvey) with his Firebird patch and cowboy hat in *Creepshow 2* **(1987, Laurel Entertainment).**

it ended production, both by Fatso on a small black-and-white TV in his trailer and by Andy's muscle car–gifting parents on a color TV in their living room, emphasizes the centrality of the Western to a broad spectrum of consumers of American culture, avowing its appeal to young or old, rich or poor, and even white or, like Sam, non-white.[8] The dynamic between the non-white Cisco and Pancho reproduces a binary similar to those that we see with screen Indians. "Indian enemies or sidekicks were presented as innately less intelligent than their Euro-American counterparts" (Knopf 12), and sidekick Pancho, in contrast to the heroic (though non–Euro-American) Cisco, is similarly portrayed. His broken English echoes one common mode of on-screen representation of indigenous speech, and both are "part of a larger national U.S. imaginary that routinely portrays minority (and immigrant) speech styles in a dysfluent, 'Othered' fashion" (Meek 95).[9] Further, the small amount of *The Cisco Kid* integrated into *Creepshow 2* includes Cisco comparing Pancho unfavorably to his own horse, saying, "Loco has more sense than you have." It is the TV suddenly being cut off as Sam is watching the show (again brushing his hair back over his shoulders) that announces the arrival of Old Chief Wood'nhead and thus Sam's impending death. This moment of collision among the chief, *The Cisco Kid* and Sam provides a useful image of the tensions and contradictions inherent in the way that the film segment both modernizes and remains beholden to nostalgic forms of the elements of the Western that circulate within it.

In this moment, the chief, it must be noted, replaces—or perhaps extends into the diegetic real world—the nostalgia of the TV Western and puts an end to the updated Indian savage in Sam.[10] His climactic victory enacts a return to and dominance of one model of familiar Hollywood Indian stereotypes, accomplished through the stereotypical action of scalping, which also removes the most explicit marker of Sam's indigeneity.[11] Extradiegetically, Old Chief Wood'nhead, like Sam, is played by a white actor (Dan Kamin), and, as a wooden cigar store Indian that comes to life, he is a commodification of a stereotype of an indigenous person, a simulacrum at several removes.[12] As such, the chief forms part of an extended tradition of continuously "resurrecting the mythic Indian" in order to sell the image in a wide range of "objectionable souvenirs of Indian stereotypes and Indian icons" (Büken 50). This profitable commercial exploitation dates back far enough that Gülri Büken identifies "a vogue for decorative mementos of the old-time 'wooden Indian'" at the turn of the 19th century (50). Since the chief *is* a wooden Indian, Ray literally owns him, and it remains unclear if the chief intends to avenge Ray's death or if that is merely a side effect of avenging Sam's theft of the collateral that Ben Whitemoon gave Ray, an act that Brown terms a betrayal of Sam's "heritage" and what makes him "bad" (S. Brown 95).

The heritage that the chief embodies largely reproduces the Indian of dominant culture mythology. His literal woodenness accords with the "'wooden' Indian that mainstream culture commodifies and admires as noble, but silent" (Magoulick 100), like the Indian in *Knightriders*. In Mary Magoulick's examination of the Potchikoo stories in Louise Erdrich's volume of poetry *Jacklight*, she discusses a tale in which Potchikoo marries a female cigar store Indian whom he finds in Minneapolis and who comes to life after he throws her in a lake (he accidentally set her on fire while flirting with her). In Erdrich, the cigar store Indian woman coming to life makes the "woman *real*, vibrant, and talkative, affirming her humanity (and thus that of all Natives)" (100). The cigar store Indian of *Creepshow 2*, in contrast, gains little humanity in gaining life, instead hewing close to Magoulick's description of Potchikoo's wife in her lifeless form: "While in her wooden guise, the cigar-store Indian is inherently stoic, static, and silent, as Indians were considered and expected to be by many non–Natives" (101). Old Chief Wood'nhead begins the segment static and silent, becomes violent and silent, and returns to silence and stasis at the segment's end.[13] The chief's lack of voice, in both senses of the word, mirrors the same lack in a media tradition that frequently represents indigenous people as silent warriors (Meek 94). The chief's voicelessness further links him with the by-then established slasher villain, most popularly exemplified in Michael Myers of the *Halloween* series and Jason Voorhees of the *Friday the 13th* series, silently stalking and murdering a series of victims. However, insofar as we see the chief's murders as justified, he simultaneously recalls the protagonist of the thriller or action movie who exacts violent retribution, often for wrongs done to his loved ones. This doubling might be seen as overlaying the Hollywood binary of the noble Indian warrior and the bloodthirsty Indian savage, with the chief occupying both positions at once. In this dualism, along with the further duality of white actor and indigenous character, we can glimpse the ambivalence of white "desires to play Indian" that connects indigenous people with an ennobling American national mythology that simultaneously "discursively deprive[s] them of land and life" (Raheja loc. 1157). When Sam says, then, to the chief, "You're not alive man. You can't be alive," he speaks as much to the continued reproduction of the white-constructed, white-(en)acted Indian stereotype, whatever its seemingly noble or heroic qualities, as he does to the literal fact of the chief's supernatural animation.

Finally, the relationship of these characters to place in "Old Chief Wood'nhead" demonstrates a similar uneasy mixture of stereotype and revisionism, as do the characters themselves. First, by locating Ray's store in a dying, depopulated town, the segment appropriates signifiers of indigenous historical trauma for white characters. I do not claim that the western United States is not home to any decaying small towns, but in this context, the segment's emphasis on its setting cannot help but suggest the displacement and dispossession of indigenous North Americans. Ray's store resembles the typical general store in a Western, complete with dirt road out front. As a site of capitalist critique, the store occupies a more ambivalent position than, for example, the mall in *Dawn of the Dead* or the magazine publisher's offices in *Bruiser*. The store stands as a symbol of settler colonial expansion, but its failing state does not directly indict such expansion—in fact, it appears to function as an important, if last-resort, financial resource for the indigenous community. The store's robbery by the indigenous Sam might be viewed as an act of poetic justice, but it acts as a catalyst and justification for indigenous vengeance against Sam and his companions for transgressions against white life and property. At the opening of the segment, Ray refreshes the chief's paintwork, beginning with his "war paint," as Martha makes explicit the analogy between her husband and this avatar of the (Hollywood) Indian:

> **RAY:** Big chief without war paint is like … is like….
> **MARTHA:** Like a storekeeper without a town to sell his goods to?

Ray furthers the analogy by pointing out that he and the chief share a long-standing attachment to this particular place, having been "standing on this porch for more than 30 years," and that he has no intention to leave. Martha's argument for Ray closing the store places the white proprietors in the role normally occupied by indigenous characters in the Western, "situated in the past with no viable future" (Raheja loc. 76). She says, "This store, Ray, at one time, sat in the middle of a thriving young town that seemed to have a future to it. Look at it now. The town of Dead River is finally living up to its name. It's dead, Ray."

In addition to the cinematic trope of the vanishing Indian, Martha's characterization of their position also evokes the historical destruction of indigenous communities and stereotypical images of contemporary life on reservations. Lack of a future here also means a loss of heritage, a failure to share with future generations the past in and through which the (vanishing) Indian is predominantly imagined. Martha scolds, "If you keep supporting these people, we won't have anything to leave to the grandchildren"; and Ray's response expands the scope of the conversation to national history: "Well, there's worse things to inherit than good intentions. Good intentions built this country."

Ray's focus on "good intentions" as a personal and national heritage, his initial reluctance to accept the "treasures" offered by Ben on behalf of his "people" as collateral for their debts, and Ray's stated desire to give back after having taken "a lot of healthy profits out of this town" contrast the predominant national heritage of theft and exploitation of land and resources and its attendant environmental devastation. This contrast casts Ray as the genially paternalistic white man, willing to lend a hand to indigenous people both wooden and flesh, at the same time that his character faces the threat of displacement and dispossession that marks indigenous history in North America.[14]

Ray's contradictory position reaches its point of crisis in the robbery. The invasion of the space of the store, the destruction of some goods and theft of others, and the murders of Martha and Ray gesture at once to the cinematic trope of the Indian attack on a white settlement and the large-scale campaigns against indigenous people of murder and theft by North American nation-states, especially because the attack is carried out by a mixed group of white men with an indigenous leader. Relatedly, Sam's description of the stolen items as "the keys to the city of Los Angeles" implies a type of (westward) territorial expansion. Brown reads Sam as symbolizing the "1980s fixation on ... fame and material wealth" (S. Brown 96), but we might equally read this greed in the context of North American settler culture on a much longer historical scale. If Sam's murdering and stealing from Ray and Martha is a

partial, somewhat muddied reversal of the dynamics of colonial expro-
priation and violence against indigenous people, then the chief's vengeance inverts these dynamics more straightforwardly. He invades two
white spaces of differing class status to kill their occupants and a third
space to eliminate Sam, the bad, savage Indian, and ultimately return
the indigenous "treasures" stolen by Sam and his white acolytes to Ben
Whitemoon, the good and honorable Indian. In this revenge might
also be seen an ironic parallel to Nathan Grantham's revenge in the
first *Creepshow*'s "Father's Day," including his pursuit of what he feels
he is owed (cake rather than treasure). In both cases, younger characters—Bedelia in the former and Sam in the latter—commit murder in
the pursuit of independence, for which they and those around them
are murdered in turn. Nathan, however, is never less than corrupt and
villainous himself, while "Old Chief Wood'nhead" splits the authority figure in two, neither of whom are presented as overtly villainous:
the paternal(istic) Ray and the chief, who enforces morality through
violence.

Before Ray's good intentions prove to be a failure and are replaced,
successfully, by that violence, Martha emphasizes her skepticism of
assisting their indigenous customers. "Good intentions tore this country down, Ray," she says, deriding Ben's dusty, smoking, decades-old car
as a "chauffeur-driven limousine," and warning Ray not to let Ben "take
too much advantage." Her assertion that Ray is "too good to these people" and her view of them as untrustworthy, lazy and living beyond their
means fits with stereotypes of the impoverished Indian but also, as mentioned above, with broader discourses of the lazy minority who lives off
of white generosity. In this, Martha's remarks anticipate the recurrence
of this discourse as central to the later segment "The Hitch-hiker."

Black Skin, White Mercedes: "The Hitch-hiker"

While racial representation in "The Hitch-hiker" segment is less
tangled than that in "Old Chief Wood'nhead" (it helps that the actor
portraying the titular hitchhiker is not in blackface), it is no less shot
through with sociocultural anxieties. "The Hitch-hiker" centers on
Annie Lansing (Lois Chiles), a well-off white woman who accidentally
strikes and kills an unnamed black male hitchhiker (Tom Wright) with
her car and flees the scene. In other words, she harms him, uninten-
tionally, as he seeks help, and then seeks to avoid any responsibility.
When he reappears multiple times in undead form, always invoking his
request for assistance (thanking her ironically for a ride), she continues,

unsuccessfully, to try to escape her responsibility, becoming angry and violent. Brown characterizes theirs as "a conflict between callous white privilege and a poor black underclass that won't stay down" (S. Brown 95), but Williams claims that "significant implications within the plot remain unrealised" (*Cinema* 179). However, while it may be true that the segment does not construct any overt argument about race, it does, I would suggest, realize some of the "significant implications" at a subtextual level. The dynamic that plays out between Annie and the hitchhiker presents a perverse echo of systemic racism. In his repeated attempts to enter her vehicle, the hitchhiker can be seen as threatening not only her bodily integrity but also her spatial boundaries, and his persistence despite increasingly grievous physical harm recalls stereotypes about dangerously strong black male bodies and black insensibility to pain. These representations unite the perceived excesses of the black (supernatural) body with the perceived excesses of black reliance on aid, most commonly represented as a supposed dependence on welfare.

The characters and their relationships in "The Hitch-hiker" are from the beginning conceptualized in terms of socioeconomic status and capitalist exchange. Annie's introduction involves her having overslept because her male escort's (David Beecroft) digital alarm clock lost power. She immediately introduces the inequality of their economic relationship when she calls the digital alarm clock junk and offers to buy him a wind-up replacement, an offer that also makes oblique reference to a nostalgia that aligns with her affluent white suburban life.[15] The car that will kill the hitchhiker is also quickly connected to Annie's class status, with her escort complaining that she already has "her Mercedes" but isn't paying him enough for him to ever be able to afford his own. The framing of their relationship in emphatically capitalist terms—he points to her six or more orgasms as evidence that he deserves remuneration commensurate with the performance of his labor—looks forward to the framing of Annie's conflict with the hitchhiker in the same terms. Her marriage too is conceptualized through economics and, ironically, a kind of marital welfare: Annie does not want to arrive home late because she does not want to "lose" her attorney husband George (Richard Parks), which would in turn mean, she says to the escort, "you'd never get your Mercedes."[16]

Interpersonal relationships here operate largely as a network of monetary exchanges, and while Annie's weekly purchase of sexual-romantic companionship could be seen as an exercise of feminist agency, at the same time, capitalism in the United States operates in ways that are inextricable from patriarchy and institutionalized racism. Ibram X. Kendi reverses the cause-and-effect commonplace that ignorance and hate lead to racist ideas and thereby to discrimination and points out that "[r]acially discriminatory policies have usually sprung from economic, political, and cultural self-interests. ... Capitalists seeking to increase profit margins have primarily created and defended discriminatory policies out of economic self-interest—not racist ideas" (9–10). As Annie speeds towards home wearing a white top and cardigan listening to classical music, the segment continues to emphasize her class (and, relatedly, racial) status, and when she drops the lighted cigarette that causes her to swerve wildly and ultimately strike the hitchhiker, her first reaction is to mention how much it will cost to repair real leather seats.

Annie does not purposely harm the hitchhiker, but when she kills him with the automotive symbol of her privilege and then leaves the scene as soon as she hears another vehicle—the arrival of which might impose responsibility for her actions, however inadvertent—without even stepping completely out of her Mercedes, she reproduces some of the ways that systemic racism functions and perpetuates itself. The popular focus on individual ignorance or hate that Kendi critiques obfuscates the institutionalized character and workings of racism and thus allows those who consider themselves not to be racist to deny culpability for racialized inequities.[17] Annie evinces this sort of denial while she contemplates whether she can "live with this": She first asserts that she can't know for certain that the man is dead and then says, "Legitimate accident. So why should I fuck up my life, right?" The second of these attempts at self-absolution echoes common arguments against social assistance, such as welfare: If what happens to someone else (the harm of being hit by a Mercedes or the harm of inequality) is an accident, why is providing assistance my problem?

The fact that any hitchhiker is defined by his or her request for assistance, and the fact that this particular hitchhiker in his undead form speaks only in variations of the phrase "Thanks for the ride, lady"—ironic not only because of the manner of his death but also because of its phrasing as if Annie actually did use her privilege and resources to assist him—allow us to read him through the lens of racialized stereotypes around social assistance, particularly welfare. The "racialization of public images of the poor occurred fairly suddenly and dramatically between 1965 and 1967" (Gilens 104), partly as a result of the increased black population in the northern United States and a new emphasis on economic equality in the Civil Rights movement, along with repeated instances of urban unrest from 1964 through 1968 (106). Daniel P. Moynihan's 1965 report *The Negro Family* contributed to this racialization with its claim that moral failure in black communities was driving uncontrolled "welfare dependency among single-parent African American families" (198), and the "Right campaigned on this theme for three decades" (198–99).

The career of Ronald Reagan, president during the release of both *Creepshow* films, took consistent advantage of this strategy. He campaigned against "welfare bums" in a 1966 bid for the governorship of California; as a presidential candidate in 1976, "he had advanced his fictional welfare problem enough to attract Nixon's undercover racists"; and he invoked black so-called welfare queen Linda Taylor in both his 1976 and 1980 presidential campaigns as a method of "feeding the White backlash to Black power" (Kendi 424). Black poverty in America had reached its lowest rate in history in 1973, but in "Reagan's first year in office, the median incomes of Black families declined by 5.2 percent, and the number of poor Americans in general increased by 2.2 million" (424, 431). The Anti-Drug Abuse Act of 1986 began America's period of mass incarceration. The CBS news special *The Vanishing Family: Crisis in Black America* (1986) presented stereotypical images including "Black male laziness," typifying media representations of black communities at the time of *Creepshow 2*'s release (435, 438). Martin Gilens observes that in newsmagazines between 1950 and 1992, "pictures of African Americans are disproportionately used to illustrate the most negative aspects of poverty and the least sympathetic subgroups of the poor" and finds the same trends in television news (121–22). While we don't know much about *Creepshow 2*'s hitchhiker beyond his need for a lift, that need at least makes available a reading of him as impoverished or falling within one of the decade's dominant depictions of blackness. Annie herself certainly seems to see him this way: Her final lines, as the undead hitchhiker attacks her inside her vehicle, are, "How much do you—how much do you want? Fifty [dollars]?"

The hitchhiker's intrusion into Annie's vehicle is significant not only or primarily because the Mercedes represents, as discussed, a class marker, but also and more importantly because its interior both stands in for and provides access to bounded, white-dominated suburban space. In the 1980s, black characters were absent from horror films (and mainstream films, the "'buddy' subgenre" excepted) set outside urban locations, which resulted in "an affirmative construction of Whiteness through racial segregation or exclusion" (Coleman 146–47). Exclusion of the black hitchhiker from the space of her car as she tries to reach the perceived safety of her large suburban house is Annie's primary concern throughout the segment, while his repeated attempts to breach those boundaries collapse the threat to her bodily integrity with the integrity of her spatial boundaries. As the hitchhiker continues to reappear—an instance of Robin Wood's return of "the repressed/the other, in the figure of the monster" (79), here, to use his categories, of the proletarian and ethnic Other ("Introduction" 78), as well as of Annie's guilt *vis-à-vis* the hitchhiker-as-these-Others—he incrementally encroaches on Annie's space.[18] When he first reappears, he knocks on her car window; subsequently, he reaches inside the car through the open sunroof; still later, he opens the car door and reaches inside; and finally, he ends up inside her car inside her garage. Annie uses the privilege of her mobility to reenact the "White flight away from the urban black and poor" to the assumed order and safety of the suburbs (Coleman 148, 147), but the assumption that the suburbs will provide protection from the hitchhiker, whose lack of a vehicle may mark him as urban, proves unfounded, as he penetrates that zone of exclusion and kills her in a sexualized manner (first wagging his protruding tongue and then appearing to lick her) that evokes the stereotype of the violent "Black Buck" who "could not refrain from raping white women" due to his hypersexuality (B. Robinson). It is noteworthy that the man is trying to reach another white-dominated space when Annie runs him down. He holds a sign for Dover, and road signs, including for Interstate 396 and Hampden, suggest that the segment takes place near Bangor, Maine, home to Stephen King. If the Dover of the hitchhiker's sign is Dover-Foxcroft, Maine, then the man's destination is a location that recorded three black and 4592 white out of 4657 residents in the 1990 census (*1990 Census*). His attempted movement into new spaces may, then, be seen as potentially disruptive from the first.[19] Perhaps this explains why the truck driver (Stephen King) who stops at the site of the hit-and-run feels it necessary to point out, "Looks like a black guy, huh?"

These dynamics of space and race can be revealingly juxtaposed with those found in *Night of the Living Dead*. Through the character of Ben (Duane Jones), who enters and exerts control over an otherwise white-occupied domestic space, *Night of the Living Dead* engages the anxieties and "race-based expectations" of the late 1960s without providing "the panacea" either of an unimpeachable black hero or "readily identifiable and, therefore, containable black stereotypes" (Bruce loc. 1186), breaking "new ground" in its refusal of easy answers to the "complex issues" of race and gender that it raises (loc. 1326). Ben, unlike the hitchhiker, is coded as middle class (loc. 1233); but like the hitchhiker, he, in Kyle William Bishop's view, "becomes something of a monster himself," including striking Barbara (Judith O'Dea), a white woman (119). Bishop calls Ben "almost as violent and irrational as the zombies themselves" but also "the closest thing the movie has to a real hero" (119), again paralleling the hitchhiker, who is violent and a literal monster but also exacts the sort of revenge that the *Creepshow* films present as morally justified. If Ben, however, reflects Civil Rights–era fears "that black men would become socially impertinent and come to threaten the safety of white women" (119), in addressing the racial anxieties of its own era, "The Hitch-hiker" renders this fear more openly a vehicle for critique. And although Big Daddy (Eugene Clark), the black monster-hero of *Land of the Dead*, lacks a central conflict with any white women, his penetration of the boundaries of the white-run enclave Fiddler's Green places him in the same lineage as Ben and the hitchhiker.

As Annie attempts to evade her responsibility and preserve her own physical boundaries, she turns to violence against the undead hitchhiker, compounding the violation of bodily integrity that she committed when she first struck the man. If the car acts as a self-contained synecdoche of the space of her suburban home, then this violence is not surprising. Private property, after all, "does not merely describe a relation between an owner and thing. It is a social relation—the right to exclude—shot through with violence," and, crucially, "[P]roperty has always been a racialized category" (Correia and Wall loc. 1428, 1465). The perceptual disjunction within this relation is made obvious when, after yelling about the irrepressible hitchhiker, "Who is he?" Annie turns her attention back to the impact on her property of her own violence, saying to herself: "Look at this car. Three thousand [dollars], maybe four. Four thousand, Mrs. Lansing, and the car will look like you just drove it out of the showroom." Shortly afterwards, the hitchhiker climbs up from somewhere beneath the moving car onto the hood and holds up a new cardboard sign: "You killed me!!!" If the collateral damage of policing property and its boundaries is acceptable from Annie's point of view, the hitchhiker resists this naturalization of violence in his refusal to stay dead and to disappear.

Annie at one point hopes that such a disappearance has indeed been effected. Having repeatedly rammed the hitchhiker against a tree with her car and then pinned him there, she passes out. After she awakens, in what Williams calls "a characteristic Romero act of denial" (*Cinema* 179), she tells herself, "There was no hitchhiker. There was nobody at all." While this denial of the man's existence—and by extension, personhood—would conveniently excuse her actions (the lack of physical evidence in the form of the man's corpse allows her to assert that nothing happened after all and drive away), conceptualizing him as "a dream," a figment of her mind, alludes to the way that both she and the nation imagine the poor, threatening, invasive black man. Annie's worry that she may have had a concussion ironically contrasts the fact that she has recently smashed the hitchhiker into unrecognizability.[20] That even this physical violence will not be enough to stop him evokes the related stereotype of black bodies, especially black male bodies, as unnaturally strong and resistant to pain. This stereotype has a long history: Thomas Jefferson, for example, wrote in *Notes on the State of Virginia*, first completed in 1781, that Africans did not feel pain to the same degree as others (Kendi 109); and Benjamin Rush presented a paper in 1797 that discussed, in Kendi's summation, blacks' "laziness, their hypersexuality, and their insensitivity to pain," which Rush proposed were effects of the leprosy that made them black in the first place. Relatedly, the increase in black rights and power after the end of the Civil War "was met with a shift from Black people being viewed as compliant and submissive servants to savages and brute monsters" who "were naturally more prone to violence and other aggressive behaviors" (Smiley and Fakunle 353). In the capacity of the hitchhiker's body to absorb physical punishment, even as his reactions tend to suggest that he can feel it to at least some extent, he embodies the limit case of this brute monstrosity and invites increased levels violence against him. Annie drives through woods to knock him off her car with branches, shoots him five times with a gun from her glovebox, drives over him twice, and drives again into the woods and hits him four times with her car while he is slumped against a tree. Again, one may observe a parallel to the violence done to the body of Ben at the end of *Night of the Living Dead*; but Ben, unlike the hitchhiker (and, of course, almost every other character in *Night*), does not have the opportunity to return from the dead.

In the end, the perceived excesses of the hitchhiker's need for aid (invoked with the phrase "Thanks for the ride, lady") form part of the same Othering imaginary as the excesses of the hitchhiker's monstrous black body (in blood and fluids as much as in strength and resilience). When Annie rams her undead pursuer, though, she is thinking not about the violence done to black bodies but about the violence done to her automotive property: "That'll cost you, Mrs. Lansing," she quips before passing out. Annie's own actions represent an analog to *Night of the Living Dead*'s "despair that Americans are not capable of pulling together to solve their ... problems" (Bruce loc. 1415). Not everyone follows Annie's pattern, however. She still manages to arrive home before her husband because, unbeknownst to her, he stopped at the scene of the hit-and-run, along with the truck driver mentioned previously and another couple. With her husband making a call on his car phone and the trucker lighting a road flare, the segment provides a picture of people coming together to help one another; this picture starkly contrasts Annie's behavior (and perhaps thereby reimagines wider systemic problems as individual anomalies). While her husband is delayed, Annie is killed alone in her garage, and, according to the avenger-friendly morality of EC Comics, her death enacts justice. From this perspective, Annie is not the monster, but she is the villain. The segment "The Raft" makes a similar division.

That (White) Boy Ain't Right: "The Raft" and Billy's Revenge

Brown sees the EC-style mode of supernatural retributive justice, present in "Old Chief Wood'nhead" and "The Hitch-hiker" (plus, arguably, the wraparound segments involving Billy) as absent from "The Raft," which he says displays "no sense of divine retribution or social commentary" (S. Brown 96). "The Raft" also seems at first glance to lack the engagement with race and racial representation of these other two segments, aside from Deke (Paul Satterfield) and Randy's (Daniel Beer) habit of referring to each other as Cisco and Pancho, an appropriative act that Deke uses to position Randy as his sidekick and that mirrors the privilege-enabled practice of playing Indian. But this impression of the absence of race from the segment would hold true only if one did not recognize that whiteness in American society occupies the privileged position of the default, aracial subject. Whiteness constitutes an "unmarked marker" that constructs one as "'neutral' and creates what is called the 'norm'" while it "remains unnamed in its processes to construct racialized 'other/s'" (al-Samarai and Piesche). Within "the U.S. context, white, heterosexual males ... have, historically, been considered as representative of the 'norm'" and "have, typically, been privileged over" those of other races or ethnicities, genders or sexualities (Asher 65). In "The Raft," Randy is one of these "unmarked" subjects, a straight, white (and blonde), cisgendered, able-bodied, apparently middle-class male. He exhibits, to a greater degree than Annie in "The Hitch-hiker," monstrous behavior even though he is not the story's monster. That monster may be read as symbolizing white fear of being consumed by a faceless, unknowable, undifferentiated black mass, which could be a stand-in for blackness itself, and perhaps the stereotyped black masses of which Annie views the hitchhiker as an avatar. However, diegetically, this monster is only acting naturally in devouring the quartet of youthful swimmers, whereas Randy makes a conscious decision to act monstrously. With these decisions, Randy mirrors the trend identified by Robin R. Means Coleman in 1980s film horror of its monsters being "White, male, and suburban," meaning "that their evil-ness was not immediately identifiable due to their lack of color-coding" (167). *Bruiser* would later overtly highlight its violent protagonist's whiteness, and thereby whiteness-as-race, via the white mask that man-ifests on his face, and "The Raft," though more subtly, ultimately pro-vides the same emphasis, a resistance to unmarked whiteness that also serves as a critique.

Until the aptly named Randy opts to commit sexual assault against Laverne (Jeremy Green), "The Raft" hits many of the typical beats of the 1980s teens-in-jeopardy horror film. While the narrative does subvert expectations a bit by having Rachel (Page Hannah), the one who declines to smoke pot, be the first to fall victim to the not-an-oil-slick monster, the rest of the group is introduced smoking pot, and friends are going somewhere isolated that they aren't supposed to be with the intention of smoking more pot and having sex. These planned good times are inter-rupted when they start getting murdered one by one. The segment does suggest the group's (bourgeois) privilege without explicitly signifying it as white. Deke drives a muscle car, and Randy studies pre-med. Deke feels insulated enough from the effects of environmental degradation to say that he doesn't "believe in" oil slicks. Laverne's Horlicks Univer-sity shirt also connects the group to a system of higher education that remains plagued by institutional racism and inequality and to a par-ticular institution that, in *Creepshow*'s "The Crate," boasts at least one murderer among its faculty. In a more openly racialized moment, Deke responds to Randy and Rachel's account of cleaning oil off of birds in the surf with the racist "Oh, mucho ecological, Poncho. Mucho ecological." The men also reveal their sexism both when Randy admits that saying to the women that they will acclimate to the cold water once they jump in is "bullshit" and he is "playing Deke's game … to get laid out here," and when Deke threatens and excludes a panicking Laverne after Rachel's death so that he can consult with the other man present about what to do.

Once Rachel and Deke are dead, however, Randy's character takes an unexpected turn when he sexually assaults Laverne and exploits her death in order to swim for safety. Randy, who had had to be restrained from jumping into the water to help Rachel and vomited after her death, and "who appears at first glance to be a quiet, decent nerd, proves to be the most reprehensible character" (S. Brown 96). Laverne asks Randy that they hold each other for warmth while they stand guard against the creature, and when he wakes before her the next day, they are still clasp-ing one another. Randy seems to take this physical contact and the lack of witnesses as cues to commit sexual assault against the woman whose survival he is ostensibly helping to ensure. He proceeds to kiss her temple and then lowers her into a prone position on the raft, despite knowing quite well that the creature can attack through the spaces between the boards.

Abandoning any pretense of keeping watch, he devotes his attention instead to assaulting Laverne, claiming privilege over her body: He pulls up her sweatshirt and t-shirt, exposing her breasts, and kisses and gropes her breasts and stomach. When she reacts in her sleep, he briefly removes his hand, and when she reacts more strongly as he is putting his face between her breasts, he stops what he is doing and pulls her clothing back into place, demonstrating that he is worried about being caught, even with no further witnesses, at something that he knows is wrong. The creature has indeed come through the gaps during the assault, and Randy merely stares as she screams to him for help, her face symbolically stained by the not-oil, and then takes advantage of her being consumed to swim for safety.[21] Having directly contributed to and then exploited Laverne's death, both for self-serving ends, he yells at the monster from what he thinks is the safety of the beach, "I beat you. Whatever you are, I beat you." His taunt, read uncharitably, points to the same self-centeredness displayed by Annie and Sam in their respective segments, but his triumph is short-lived as the creature flings itself wave-like upon him. Brown may be correct that, strictly speaking, "the thing in the water is not an agent of vengeance" (S. Brown 96), but one can argue that Randy does experience deserved if not purposeful retribution. There may be an "absence of any kind of moral message" (98), but there is certainly one of anxiety about what might lurk underneath any given wholesome white pre-med student exterior.

Like "The Raft," the primarily animated wraparound segments are entirely white. Their protagonist, Billy (Domenick John), a white suburban child, returns us to the realm of violence that the film presents as justified, as Billy takes revenge on his bullies. Whether murdering four other children by means of giant, carnivorous Venus flytraps purchased from the in-film *Creepshow* comics constitutes a proportionate response to bullying is, however, debatable. From one perspective, Billy embodies another version of the monster-in-plain-sight of 1980s suburban horror, his murderousness rising up from out of sight in the same way that his flytraps are depicted as doing. Disturbingly, the child killer is not only one of white suburbia's own but also himself a child.[22] The sinister way that Billy's smiles are drawn at several points and the equally sinister way that he says "They eat *meat*" do not exactly militate against such an interpretation.

Billy's class status does figure in this revenge: The shopkeeper notes that his package is "quite expensive for a toy ordered out of a funny paper," and the mobility afforded him by his bike allows him to lure bullies to a location where he can cause their deaths unobserved. The bullies too have bicycles, and the lead bully's spurs, along with a shot of Billy through his legs evoking a cinematic gunslingers' duel, cast the bikes as horses and the conflict in terms of the Western.[23] The animated sections conform to the Western too in an emphasis on masculinity: There are no female characters, the bullies taunt Billy by saying he will cry or tattle to his mother and calling him a pansy, and their leader is shown sharpening a stick held at crotch level, suggesting a phallic weapon/phallus as weapon. Billy, then, enacts a power fantasy that draws on the nostalgic fantasy of the Western, is enabled by the nostalgic fantasy of the *Creepshow* comics, and, in pint-sized shades of the later *Bruiser*, provides an aggrieved bourgeois white male an avenue to violently assert his masculinity.[24]

If Billy, like the chief, successfully solves his problems through masculine violence, Randy and Deke's masculinity does them no good in the end. Their normative, and in Deke's case, chiseled male bodies are merely broken and dissolved. While *Monkey Shines*, appearing the year after *Creepshow 2*, lacks the latter's knotty representations of race, except insofar as we can read its white, suburban protagonist and almost exclusively white cast through this lens, concerns about bodies and masculinity do recur, especially in the form of anxieties about emasculation and disability.

8

"The Monkey Ruled the Man"

Phallocentrism, Able-Bodiedness
and AIDS Anxieties in Monkey Shines

CAIN MILLER

It is not uncommon to read 1980s cinema as a mirror image of America's reactionary politics throughout that decade. In contrast to the New Hollywood's anti-authority, anti-establishment films, 1980s cinema returned to the safer themes and narrative structures of the classical Hollywood era—films that promoted values, held by the Moral Majority, like traditional gender roles and heterosexual coupling. This return to conventional sex-gender norms corresponded with Hollywood's reinstatement of on-screen hegemonic masculinity as images of men were often hypermasculinized through their muscled frames, violent actions and obtainment of women as sex objects. Andrew Britton argues that this "Reaganite entertainment" offers an "unabashed apology for patriarchy," given that many '80s films feature a father figure as the protagonist and often conclude with the restoration of the familial unit (128–29). While these hypermasculinized images coincide with the decade's attempt to reaffirm patriarchal power, the blunt emphasis on the domineering, able-bodied male physique also correlates with the decade's AIDS anxieties. These silver screen protagonists were strong specimens who were impervious to physical harm or disease; they were antithetical to the sexually "Othered" AIDS victim.

Never one to follow generic trends, George A. Romero unsurprisingly offered more complex approaches to these reactionary themes throughout his 1980s output. One of Romero's more transgressive subversions of the decade's gender-sex norms can be found in *Monkey Shines: An Experiment in Fear* (1988), a film about a man with quadriplegia whose service monkey violently manifests his feelings of bodily emasculation and sexual jealousy. This chapter will analyze how

Monkey Shines presents anxieties of emasculation through its depictions of disability, queer identity and the loss of one's phallocentric power, and will further assess how these subjects relate to the film's implicit themes of AIDS paranoia.

Body Anxieties and 1980s Horror

The return to reactionary narratives in 1980s Hollywood corresponds with America's growth in neoconservative ideologies. Much of Ronald Reagan's appeal stemmed from the nostalgia he represented as a former classical Hollywood actor; thus, much of his campaign promoted the concept of returning the nation to the "good old days," specifically to a time before the social progressions of the '60s and '70s. Reagan himself was the poster child of this patriarchal agenda, naturally representing the stoic masculinity of the cowboys, soldiers and athletes he previously portrayed on screen. Reagan was perceived as a masculine force who could fix the country's "crisis of confidence" and undo the counterculture's supposed wrongdoings.[1]

One of the decade's defining symbols of masculinity was the strong, active male body. This newfound objectification of the male physique could be traced to Reagan himself, as his physical stoicism (something demonstrated in his survival and recovery from a 1981 assassination attempt) was a key reason that so many Americans felt secure under his leadership. Susan Jeffords provides substantial insight into the decade's fascination with bodies, arguing that it "constituted the imaginary of the Reagan agenda and the site of its materialization," whether it be through muscled movie stars, the aerobics fad, the pushback on women's rights to abortion, or AIDS paranoia (24). Jeffords further notes how '80s bodies were categorized as either "normative/ hard bodies" or "errant/soft bodies," the former representing strength and durability and the latter representing disease and idleness. In correlation with other social binaries, hard bodies are linked to white men (as a mirroring of Reagan's persona) while errant bodies are linked to women and people of color (24–25). Accordingly, '80s body politics promoted a strict masculine-feminine binary in which able-bodied hegemony opposed the weak-diseased Other (whether it be a woman, person of color, HIV-positive person, etc.).

While these hard bodies are most apparent in the numerous action blockbusters like *The Terminator* (1984), *Predator* (1987) and *Bloodsport* (1988), this bodily dichotomy is also present in '80s horror. On the surface, slasher villains Jason Voorhees and Freddy Krueger represent the errant body because their decaying flesh is far from normative. However, much emphasis is conversely placed on the killers' physical durability; these men can be shot, impaled and bludgeoned, yet never conclusively destroyed. Even originally "realist" figures like Michael Myers and Leatherface become more superhuman as their respective franchises progressed.

These body politics are more directly displayed in the decade's other dominant horror trend: body horror. Prior analysis of this subgenre has primarily focused on its connections to anxieties about AIDS, for example by Edward Guerrero in his readings of *The Thing* (1982) and *The Fly* (1986) as allegories for how HIV infiltrates men's bodies. Guerrero further argues that these films consequently uphold the "sanctity of the monogamous, traditional family" due to their connections of AIDS imagery with hypersexual and implicitly homosexual characters (89–92).[2] Along with these AIDS allegories, body horror also presents fears of emasculation and castration anxiety brought on by the sight of decaying, deformed male bodies. In contrast to slasher films' focus on the punishment of women, body horror instead places greater emphasis on male suffering. Texts like *Altered States* (1980), *Scanners* (1981), *The Thing*, *Videodrome* (1983), *Re-Animator* (1985), *The Stuff* (1985), *The Fly*, *From Beyond* (1986), *Hellraiser* (1987), *Hellbound: Hellraiser II* (1988), *Brain Damage* (1988), *Society* (1989), *Bride of Re-Animator* (1989) and *Spontaneous Combustion* (1990) all feature male victims who undergo some form of bodily transformation. This errant body, then, presents fears of emasculation because it represents a male body antithetical to the stoic, hegemonic body.

In her analysis of masculinity in David Cronenberg's filmography, Linda Williams argues that the body horror auteur consistently showcases masculinity in crisis through his frequent depictions of deteriorating male bodies.[3] Specifically, Williams notes how these bodies become feminized through their transformations ("Inside-Out" 32). Examples of this include Max's (James Woods) vaginal slit in *Videodrome* and Seth's (Jeff Goldblum) genitals falling off in *The Fly*. Williams further notes that the grotesque body in Cronenberg's films is thus "naturally" male, a direct contrast to horror's typical themes of monstrous femininity (35–36). As such, body horror presents apparent fears of castration anxiety because it depicts male figures becoming feminine, often through the literal loss of phallic power. While it is not conventional body horror per se, these themes of bodily deterioration and loss of the phallus are certainly apparent in Romero's final film of the decade, *Monkey Shines*.

Given that Romero consistently produced films that challenge dominant ideologies, it is unsurprising that he countered widely accepted notions of masculinity present in the '80s. *Knightriders* (1981) pokes fun at male chauvinism as its characters theatrically battle for phallic dominance by jousting on armored motorcycles. A blunter critique of stoic masculinity is present in *Day of the Dead* (1985), in which the antagonists are not the zombies but the impulsively violent, pigheaded white male soldiers. Even in *Creepshow* (1982), the ultimate villain is the suburban father who confiscates his son's comic books during the prologue. And as discussed in Chapter 7, *Creepshow 2* (1987) features male characters worthy of criticism, most notably in "The Raft," when the threat of the lake monster is almost secondary to the sexually predatory white male Randy (Daniel Beer). However, Romero's most unmistakable attack on the decade's masculine anxieties is in his first major studio project.

Adapted from Michael Stewart's 1983 same-name novel, *Monkey Shines* tells the story of Allan Mann (Jason Beghe), a law student and track star who becomes quadriplegic after being hit by a truck. He is gifted a capuchin monkey named Ella from his scientist friend Geoffrey Fisher (John Pankow); Ella becomes increasingly hostile due to Geoffrey constantly injecting her with a chemical concoction designed to increase her intelligence. Past analyses of *Monkey Shines* have largely focused on its complex portrayal of a character with a disability,[4] but far less attention has been given to the film's connections between disability and masculinity, specifically in how Allan's disabled body contrasts the era's hard-bodied leading men. *Monkey Shines* indeed presents one of the decade's more provocative portrayals of disability and hard-bodied phallic power, particularly in how it relates these themes to AIDS anxieties.

Monkey Shines *and the Hard Body*

The attention to the male physique is immediately apparent in *Monkey Shines* within the opening scene. Set in an upper-middle-class suburban neighborhood, the film begins in Allan's bedroom, where he lies naked with his girlfriend, Linda (Janine Turner), after a presumed night of intercourse. In a medium shot, Allan nuzzles Linda while concurrently taking the "top" position over her. This action signifies Allan's phallic power through his sexual subordination of Linda. Allan then begins a ritualistic exercise routine, starting with a series of nude stretches (Fig. 9). In another medium shot, Allan does the splits while in the "Monkey Pose" position with his back to the camera. This shot

Figure 9. The camera emphasizes Allan Mann's (Jason Beghe) muscular naked body through his exercise routine in *Monkey Shines* (1988, Orion Pictures).

emphasizes Allan's muscular back, legs and buttocks, as his naked body is packed tightly within the frame.

In correlation with Laura Mulvey's Male Gaze theory, this opening sequence invites the male spectator to narcissistically project himself into Allan because he possesses both sexual prowess and the hard body (8–11). Allan then jogs through his neighborhood while carrying a backpack of bricks. As he runs, the camera cuts to various close-ups of his feet. These close-ups objectify Allan because they reduce him to a body part, but in contrast to conventional fetishistic scopophilia, these fragmented shots instead emphasize Allan's virility and athleticism. Moreover, the previous shot of Allan stretching displays his body as a whole rather than a fragmented sex object, ergo the attention to his physique— along with his established sexual dominance and upper-class financial status—is meant to signify his hegemonic masculinity.[5] Allan, however, is then hit by a truck. As he flies through the air, the bricks from his backpack fall to the ground. In a close-up shot, one brick shatters as it hits the concrete, symbolizing the destruction of Allan's hard body.

A sedated Allan lies face down in a hospital bed as various doctors prepare to perform surgery. Dr. John Wiseman (Stanley Tucci) pierces

Allan's back with a scalpel. This action contrasts the opening scene in which Allan displayed phallic dominance through his "top" position over Linda. Here, Allan is now the "bottom"—rendered subordinate due to his unconsciousness—as he is penetrated by Dr. Wiseman, who holds the "top" position. This further symbolizes Allan being stripped of his hegemonic masculinity, as the injury renders Allan quadriplegic and no longer in possession of the idealized male body.

Allan's emasculation is underscored in the succeeding scene in which he arrives home. His mother Dorothy (Joyce Van Patten) has thrown him a party consisting of Allan's friends and family, as well as Dr. Wiseman. Before Allan's arrival, Wiseman is approached by Esther Fry (Tudi Wiggins), Allan's law professor, who asks if Allan can continue his studies. Wiseman explains that Allan could certainly *physically* continue as a student, though the larger question is whether he is mentally prepared to do so. Wiseman's assessment of Allan's fragile mental state implies a more psychological emasculation, as Allan's mental well-being is yet another bodily component over which he has no control. When Allan arrives, now in a motorized wheelchair, his emasculation continues. This is most apparent when Allan's nurse, Maryanne (Christine Forrest), serves him watered-down Scotch from a sippy cup. Here, Scotch, a common symbol of hegemonic masculinity, is diluted, representative of Allan's own loss of power, while the sippy cup signifies Allan's symbolic regression to a childlike figure, one who has lost his independence. In the context of Sigmund Freud's psychosexual stages of development, Allan has reverted to a pre-phallic, pre-superego stage. Due to his evident impotence, Allan is unable to enter the phallic stage or the succeeding latency stage and eventual genital stage, in which he would assert his phallic-masculine power through sexual intercourse.[6] Furthermore, given that there is never any mention of Allan's father, Allan does not have a figure to model his masculinity after; thus, he remains emasculated. This loss of phallic power is best articulated in a conversation between Allan and Geoffrey. When Allan speculates that Linda will likely dump him, Geoffrey responds with a bitter "Fuck her," to which Allan dryly replies, "I can't." Allan's emasculation is complete when his prediction comes true: Linda leaves him for Dr. Wiseman, a figure who epitomizes hegemonic masculinity through his profession, wealth and, now, sexual subordination of her.

The filmic narrative up to this point is more or less the same as it is in Stewart's original novel, aside from the setting unsurprisingly changing from England to Pittsburgh. Nevertheless, Stewart's narrative includes a few noteworthy differences that further highlight Allan's emasculation. Firstly, Stewart draws even more attention to Allan's hard body, devoting two entire chapters to his athleticism, the first discussing his morning exercise and the second detailing him winning a track race. One of the starker differences in the novel is how Allan becomes paralyzed. Allan is instead injured in a motorcycle accident after a heated argument with Linda, during which she revealed that she was previously pregnant with Allan's child and opted to have an abortion. This detail signifies Allan's first experience with emasculation, as the termination of Linda's pregnancy hinders Allan's ability to attain the role of patriarch. Upon hearing this news, Allan furiously leaves on his motorcycle; the implication is that Allan's rage distracts him and causes him to hit an oncoming truck and further situates Linda as the cause of Allan's paralysis and bodily emasculation.

While the film never mentions Allan's father Jock, he plays a substantial role in the early portions of the novel. Jock is openly loving of his son, as he makes an effort to emotionally support Allan after his accident, indicating that Allan was never denied paternal affection. Yet it is Jock's seemingly healthy masculinity that leads Allan to resent him, as he believes that his father is "unambitious" and possesses a "second-best" attitude (18). This resentment of Jock is what drives Allan to pursue hegemonic masculinity, as showcased in his athleticism, higher education and subordination of Linda: He strives to be everything that he believes his father is not. Allan's dislike of his father becomes more important later when Jock suddenly dies of cancer, emasculated as a result of not being in control of his own body. In the same chapter as Jock's death, Allan attempts suicide. While the grief of Jock's death itself could have led to Allan's suicide attempt, it is also possible that Allan's action was the result of him seeing parallels between himself and his father. Just as Jock died of bodily deterioration (thus labeling him with the errant body), Allan experiences similar physical decline through his paralysis. As a result, Allan compares himself to his father and views suicide as a more viable option than living a life without hard-bodied masculinity.

In Romero's film, Allan also attempts suicide early in the narrative, although in this context he is motivated by depression. After he survives his suicide attempt, Dorothy opts to move in with Allan and care for him. This reliance on his mother further signifies Allan's regression to the pre–Oedipal stage, unable to fulfill the "head of the household" role. Allan's patriarchal inadequacies are exemplified in a scene in which Allan struggles to operate an environmental control unit designed to aid with basic household operations like opening and closing doors and turning lights on and off. Allan cannot effectively operate the technology: He quite literally does not have control of his own household.

To help his friend, Geoffrey gifts Allan with Ella, a service monkey trained to assist with household tasks. Although Allan and Ella's relationship begins positively, Geoffrey frequently injects her with human brain tissue, which drastically alters Ella's psychological state, causing her to form a psychic bond with Allan—a connection that culminates in Ella enacting Allan's violent fantasies that stem from his emasculation. The first of these instances occurs when Bogey, Maryanne's pet bird, pesters Allan by continuously pecking at his face. Given that the bird is named after Humphrey Bogart, a recognizable example of classical Hollywood-era stoic masculinity, this action showcases Allan being taunted by the masculinity that he no longer possesses. Sensing Allan's feelings toward the bird, Ella kills Bogey, prompting Maryanne to quit. As this series of events demonstrates, Ella represents Allan's id: She is the embodiment of Allan's immoral desires, which revolve around harming those who emasculate him. Because Allan has symbolically regressed to a pre-phallic stage, his superego is no longer intact, and consequently, Allan's id (Ella) roams unpoliced.

A notable example of how Ella represents Allan's id is her murder of Linda and Dr. Wiseman. When Allan learns that Linda left him for Wiseman, his feelings of emasculation are manifested into Ella, who then travels to Linda and Wiseman's isolated cabin and burns it down with them inside. Wiseman's hegemonic masculinity is on full display prior to his murder. Firstly, Wiseman stands half-naked next to Linda, indicating his recent (or nearing) sexual subordination of her. Secondly, the situating of Wiseman's bare chest in the middle of the frame stresses his hard body. Importantly, due to their psychological bond, Allan frequently enters a dream-like trance in which he views Ella's actions through her eyes, and the scene of Linda and Wiseman's murder is primarily portrayed from Ella's point of view, a choice similar to many of the decade's slashers situating the camera to capture the killer's perspective. Kendall Phillips provides further insight into Allan's mental bond with Ella:

> At the narrative level, Ella's actions are driven by Allan's unconscious impulses, and these actions propel the plot towards its eventual resolution. At a cinematic level, it is interesting the way that Romero utilizes the point-of-view shot to implicate us in the connection between Allan and Ella. Thus, it is not only Allan who sees through the eyes of his surrogate—and unconstrained—body but also the audience, who, having experienced the wrongs visited upon Allan, also sees through the eyes of the body that seeks violent redress for these wrongs [49].

In relation to Phillips' point, Allan is not a character whom the male viewer can narcissistically identify with due to his possession of the errant body. Consequently, the male viewer is expected to project himself into Ella, the able-bodied figure, whose violent acts of retribution against those who pose threats of emasculation appease both Allan and the viewer's castration anxiety. As a result, while Ella symbolizes Allan's id, she also serves as a superego, similar to the slasher antagonists, because she abolishes those deemed immoral. However, this spectatorship is complicated in that Ella is female and possesses the errant body. Furthermore, Allan's projection of himself into Ella indicates a layer of queerness in their relationship: Ella's physical female body bears Allan's male psyche and, consequently, his castration anxieties. The duality of Ella's body and Allan's mind being present in one figure transcends the male-female binary and presents the bodily transgression common to the body horror subgenre.

As his relationship with Ella develops, Allan's emasculation is somewhat reduced thanks to his budding romance with Geoffrey's colleague Melanie (Kate McNeil), who trains service animals. In contrast to Linda, who is both passive and sexually liberal, Melanie is portrayed as active and maternal, as showcased in her first scene, in which she teaches a female monkey to care for a baby doll. Given that she lives on a rural farm, dresses in rustic clothing like blue jeans and flannel, and participates in outdoor activities like fishing, Melanie's femininity is closely associated with American frontier iconography; she is independent though she does not embody the threatening "radical feminist" persona that was debased by many of the decade's reactionary pundits. In short, Linda is the stereotypical "whore" who is punished for her sexual deviances, while Melanie is an unthreatening "Madonna" figure who serves as a safer love interest for Allan. And yet Melanie's independence and stoicism simultaneously further Allan's emasculation because Melanie is not subordinate within their relationship. Because Melanie feeds Allan, drives him around, and assists him with household activities, she seemingly "wears the pants" in the relationship. Moreover, Allan cannot sexually subordinate Melanie because he cannot penetrate her. When Allan and Melanie eventually have sex, Melanie takes the top position and Allan is only able to suck on her breast.[7] Although Allan regains some of his masculinity through heterosexual coupling, he is nonetheless still a "bottom" who does not bear phallocentric power.

Allan's hegemonic masculinity is not fully restored until the final act, where Ella, having become increasingly violent, kills Dorothy and Geoffrey and attempts to keep Allan hostage in his own home, confining him to the household in a similar fashion to a subordinate housewife. Following the murders, Ella feeds Allan some of her own food pellets and urinates on him, signifying her power over him. When Melanie arrives, she is knocked unconscious by Ella. Before Ella can kill

Melanie, Allan miraculously leaps from his wheelchair and bites Ella's neck, graphically killing her. This final action demonstrates how the narrative ultimately reaffirms patriarchal power, as it is Allan, the man with quadriplegia, who saves the day instead of Melanie, the able-bodied woman, who is rendered a passive damsel in distress.

Patriarchal authority is further restored in the following scene, where Allan undergoes a miracle surgery that fully cures his paralysis. During this scene, the film provides one last cheap jump scare through a nightmare sequence: As a doctor penetrates Allan's back with a scalpel, a blood-soaked Ella tears through Allan's skin and lets out a shriek before Allan suddenly wakes up in his hospital bed post-surgery.[8] This scene, which mimics the chestburster from *Alien* (1979), presents one final impression of emasculation. Since Allan symbolically births Ella, he possesses the errant body, and similarly to other body horror films, this bodily transformation marks Allan as feminine. These emasculation anxieties are quickly subdued in the following scene, in which Allan leaves the hospital. When Melanie arrives to pick him up, she excitedly says, "Let's go fishing!" Allan, having regained his able-bodiedness, triumphantly stands up and enters Melanie's car, proud that his hegemony has been restored and he can now physically partake in a masculine activity.

The Intersection of Emasculation and AIDS

While the proliferation of images of hard bodies in 1980s media certainly shaped the American public's expectations for how men should look and behave, another crucial factor that affected the era's cultural perceptions of gender and sexuality was the AIDS crisis. The AIDS epidemic undeniably launched a new wave of homophobia which aligned with the decade's rise in neoconservatism; however, a less-studied component of AIDS hysteria is its connection to emasculation and body anxieties. Specifically, AIDS signifies emasculation due to its presumed connections to both homosexuality (which contrasts hegemonic masculinity's reliance on the male's heterosexual subordination of women) and drug use (which denotes a lower socioeconomic standing). Furthermore, the rapid decline in one's physical health which results from contracting AIDS also brings forth associations with the errant body that opposes hard-bodied hegemony.

In her 1996 book *AIDS and the Body Politic: Biomedicine and Sexual Difference*, Catherine Waldby provides a wealth of insight into the social implications of the AIDS crisis, particularly how HIV/AIDS is interpreted within heterosexual-homosexual and masculine-feminine binaries. Waldby first notes how the inherent phallocentric power granted to heterosexual men naturally disassociates them from AIDS:

> By remaining the only unmarked category within the terminologies of sexual risk, heterosexual men effectively occupy the position at the top of the hierarchy. As the only group exempted from direct address by public health discourse, they are freed from internalising the idea of their bodies as dangerous or infectious, relying instead on the willingness of heterosexual women to undertake such internalisations. Heterosexual men are thus allowed to maintain the (imaginary) position of the clean who are threatened by infection from below and elsewhere, and are not required to consider themselves as possibly infectious for another [9–10].

This ultimately creates a dichotomy between the active-masculine-hard body, assumed to be free of disease, and the passive-feminine-errant body that is more vulnerable to AIDS and bodily deterioration.

Building on this concept, Waldby argues how, in correlation with the era's rise in homophobia, male homosexuals were so stigmatized by the relationship between their sexuality and AIDS that gay male masculinity was often equated to the virus itself. Gay men, like heterosexual women, were expected to "bear the burden" of AIDS, an obligation not faced by heterosexual men (11). With regard to how these gender and sexual assumptions relate to body politics, Waldby argues,

> To the extent that aspiration to a phallic status organises the heterosexual masculine body, it must suppress its capacities for passivity and anal and oral receptivity, capacities which are then projected onto the bodies of women and gay men. In other words, the permeability of the heterosexual male body is suppressed in dominant forms of cultural representation, and this general suppression enables the confusion in AIDS discourse between the normative ideal and particular heterosexual masculine bodies [12].

In short, AIDS signifies sexual passivity through the act of being penetrated, which is itself a representation of emasculation. Lastly, in relation to the gendering of bodies diagnosed with AIDS, Waldby states,

> In the case of AIDS ... codification as feminine is not restricted to the designation of the body of woman, but also marks certain non-phallic masculine bodies, that is gay male bodies or male bodies that engage in sexual relations with other men. Under conditions of epidemic the association between nature and the feminine is readily conjured into an agentic alliance, where the feminine becomes the ally of the virus. Bodies coded as feminine are understood to lend themselves to viral hybridisation because they are already on the side of the natural [19].

Based on Waldby's analysis, not only are the bodies of those with AIDS often perceived as feminine due to their passivity, but feminine bodies in general (even those that are healthy and able-bodied) are linked to AIDS due to their lack of phallocentric power.

Waldby's rhetoric helps to explain why '80s body horror revolves around images of male bodies (which are symbolically suffering from AIDS) becoming feminized, as discussed earlier in this chapter. In his analysis of the intersection of AIDS, masculinity and horror cinema, Peter Redman argues that it is the erosion of boundaries as a result of AIDS which makes it so ideologically threatening. Through the lens of venereology, AIDS seeks to disrupt the nuclear family due to its associations with sexual promiscuity and homosexuality. In short, AIDS is simply another form of Otherness that opposes the dominant structure (105–06).

Redman further notes how horror films often feature a symbolic "AIDS carrier" who is "inextricably bound up with the fear, anxieties and secret desires of hegemonic forms of heterosexual masculinity, articulated through the figure of the 'AIDS carrier' as monster" (99–100). Horror's inclusion of a symbolic AIDS carrier is often presented in the form of a "hyper-penetrative gay man" who manifests the heterosexual male character's–viewer's fears of being penetrated.[9] Furthermore, Redman notes how many cinematic AIDS allegories revolve around characters being "taken over" by the monstrous-venereal Other (112). This dynamic is prevalent in body horror, given that virtually every text within this subgenre revolves around a male character being taken over by a metaphorical version of AIDS and consequently emasculated through this bodily submission. *Monkey Shines* presents AIDS anxieties through Ella, who is the symbolic AIDS carrier, as well as through the subtextual queer relationship between Allan and Geoffrey.

In an effort to be more productive with his lab work, Geoffrey frequently uses a syringe to inject himself with a chemical that keeps him awake for prolonged periods, suggesting the intravenous drug user. As the narrative progresses, his physical appearance becomes more disheveled, as his bloodshot eyes, five o'clock shadow and unkempt hair paint him as a stereotypical junkie. Additionally, Geoffrey's repeated use of a syringe to inject Ella, which in turn makes her violent, further situates this drug iconography as the catalyst for the narrative's conflict. This allusion to drug use is best showcased in a scene in which Geoffrey attempts to solve the mystery of Ella's violent behavior. In his lab, Geoffrey injects himself with Ella's chemical concoction, which causes him to go into the same trance that Allan experiences. As Geoffrey does so, his body becomes limp, he gapes, and his eyes roll into the back of his head as he symbolically enters a drug high.[10]

More overt themes of AIDS are present in the implicit queerness of Allan and Geoffrey's relationship. The bond between them displays queer subtext given that the line between homosociality and homosexuality is often obscured—an applicable detail here given that Allan and Geoffrey once lived together. Yet the pair's implicit queerness becomes more apparent when one considers how Allan and Geoffrey represent older stereotypes associated with queer horror, specifically the homoerotic mad scientist and henchman archetypes. Harry Benshoff traces the histories of these character types all the way back to the 1930s, beginning with

> the mad scientist, who, with the frequent aid of a male assistant, sets out to create life homosexually—without the benefit of heterosexual intercourse (*Frankenstein, Island of Lost Souls* [1933], and *Bride of Frankenstein*). Together the mad scientist and his sidekick become a major generic convention that is easily read as queer: the secret experiments they conduct together are chronicled in private diaries and kept locked away in closed cupboards and closets [48].

Given the horror genre's frequent hybridization with science fiction in 1980s media, it is unsurprising that the mad scientist archetype appears in many texts throughout the decade. Body horror was specifically prone to mad scientist characters. *Altered States, Re-Animator, Bride of Re-Animator, From Beyond* and *The Fly* all feature male scientists engaging in secretive experiments that lead to their, or others', bodily transformations. The re-emergence of these characters is partially due to the decade's various remakes of, and homages to, 1950s science fiction cinema. With this in mind, these mad scientist characters also tap into the decade's scientific-medical anxieties as a result of the AIDS crisis. Furthermore, the scientist characters' bodily transformations are often intertwined with overt, occasionally grotesque sexual themes. In *The Fly*, after Seth's DNA is infused with that of a housefly, he immediately experiences sexual virility, only for his body to begin deteriorating shortly after. *Re-Animator* perhaps has the most notorious example of sex and bodily transformation intersecting in a scene in which the severed head of Dr. Carl Hill (David Gale) performs lewd sex acts upon the restrained Megan (Barbara Crampton). In body horror, the AIDS paranoia is apparent: sex and bodily degradation are intrinsically connected.

In *Monkey Shines*, Geoffrey is a replica of past mad scientists like Colin Clive's Henry Frankenstein (1931) and Charles Laughton's Dr. Moreau (in *Island of Lost Souls*, 1932) because he devotes himself to controversial lab experiments, at one point even referring to his beakers as a bubbling cauldron. In Geoffrey's case, he forces his lab animals like Ella to behave against their natural instincts, much to the displeasure of his employers as well as various animal rights protesters who frequently vandalize his testing facility. The "unnatural" essence of Geoffrey's work causes him to be oppressed and harassed by disapproving outside forces, thus signifying a layer of queerness with his character.

Furthermore, Geoffrey's gifting of Ella to Allan is done without the knowledge of his employers, indicating the secretive nature of both Geoffrey's work and his relationship with Allan. The queerness of Allan and Geoffrey's relationship becomes apparent due to how their power dynamic mirrors the forementioned scientist-henchman duo. As mentioned in Chapter 4, Benshoff notes that these queer couples often revolve around hierarchies in which one figure holds power over the other to adhere to conventional masculine-feminine binaries: The mad scientist typically holds power over his henchman and thus, the pair have a "dominant-submissive, master-servant, top-bottom" relationship (48). This power hierarchy is also displayed through the sheer physicality of these characters, as the scientist is commonly able-bodied while the henchman bears some form of physical abnormality such as a hunched back or a limp.[11] This hierarchy is present in Allan and Geoffrey's relationship, as Geoffrey is the able-bodied scientist while Allan is his subordinate sidekick who has a disability. Lastly, Allan and Geoffrey's queer relationship is stressed through their symbolic creation of Ella. Similar to Frankenstein's Monster (Boris Karloff) or Island of Lost Souls' Lota, the Panther Woman (Kathleen Burke), Ella is the product of non-heteronormative procreation. As such, Ella serves as the "monster queer"—the antagonist whose threat lies within her sexual Otherness (Benshoff 4–16).

As the narrative becomes increasingly violent, *Monkey Shines* makes more connections between AIDS, queerness and monstrosity—a popular trend throughout this decade. In Benshoff's analysis of how AIDS was often associated with horror themes and iconography, he notes how individuals with AIDS were often compared to silver screen monsters, as displayed in various tabloid headlines like "Gay Vampire Catches AIDS," "AIDS-Wary Vampires Pull in Their Fangs" and "The AIDS Monster." These titles not only depict people with AIDS as predatory, but they also specifically sensationalize the threat of AIDS against "normal" society, as the latter headline was used for a story about a man who allegedly infected a woman on purpose (242). David J. Skal also notes how '80s media represented AIDS anxieties through "monster-vampire" figures who embodied America's paranoia of "blood taboos" (349). These images are most apparent in *Monkey Shines* when Allan develops ape-like (or vampiric) fangs due to his physiological connection with Ella.

When Allan first transforms into this symbolic AIDS monster-vampire, he accidentally bites his lip, which prompts Ella to lick his blood—a transgressive portrayal of body fluid transmission that embodies Skal's rhetoric on blood taboo paranoia. These anxieties surrounding bodily fluids are present in a later scene where Allan, after the murders of Linda and Wiseman, claims that his relationship with Ella is "sinful" and that their bond is built on the "desire to sin." Geoffrey responds by saying that if he ran experiments on Ella, he would not "expect to find sin in a urine sample." This dialogue exchange signifies the supposed sinful-unnatural circumstances of Allan, Geoffrey and Ella's queer relationship, and also reinforces Skal's point about how themes of rotten-sinful blood and bodily fluids in media boosted fears of AIDS.

Monkey Shines concludes in the same fashion as any reactionary horror film: with the destruction of the sexual Other. During the climax, Geoffrey is killed by Ella, who penetrates him with a syringe filled with pentobarbital. Geoffrey then enters one final drug high before dying. He is killed by the very thing that caused the overarching conflict with Ella: the syringe, the icon associated with AIDS and drug use.

A commercial flop, *Monkey Shines* failed to break even despite a modest $7 million budget. Critical responses were lukewarm, with many taking issue with the film's cramped narrative structure and clichéd ending, both of which were the fault of the studio, not Romero. Orion Pictures forced Romero to cut the film down to two hours after realizing that his rough cut was nearly double that length. Romero also originally shot a different, much darker ending that was more comparable to the source material. In Stewart's novel, Allan does not receive a miracle surgery that brings back his able-bodiedness. Rather, he remains paralyzed, though he somewhat regains his masculinity through his coupling with Melanie, who makes him "begin to feel a complete man," indicating that Allan bears some power of sexual subordination over Melanie, even if it is not in the form of traditional phallocentrism (255). The novel's conclusion is ultimately foreboding, however, as it is revealed that one of the university's scientists continues the experiments even after Geoffrey's death, indicating that cases similar to Ella's will follow. Romero's original ending was much closer to Stewart's story. Here, Allan indeed regains his mobility, though the story concludes with Harold Burbage (Stephen Root), Geoffrey's colleague, injecting the remaining lab monkeys with Ella's formula; Burbage forms a psychological bond with them, just as Allan did. This original ending embodies the darker narratives of 1960s–1970s apocalyptic horror that Romero was rooted in, while simultaneously furthering the film's themes of AIDS paranoia because it indicates that this deadly problem would not end any time soon.

On the one hand, *Monkey Shines* deserves praise for its depictions of taboo subject matter, particularly its inclusion of a sex scene involving a character with a disability, something that is so rarely shown in Hollywood products. On the other hand, *Monkey Shines* also boasts regressive themes that align with the decade's trend of reactionary horror, such as its connections between queerness and antagonism, as well as how Allan arguably exemplifies the "Obsessive Avenger," a stereotype coined by Martin F. Norden to describe a character with a disability who becomes irrationally violent due to their lack of able-bodiedness (128). *Monkey Shines* ultimately remains a complex portrayal of masculinity due to its surplus of images that so heavily contrast the popular hard bodies of that era.

9

Animating Politics, Reanimating Genres in "Cat from Hell" and "The Facts in the Case of Mr. Valdemar"

NOAH SIMON JAMPOL *and* JOHN R. ZIEGLER

George A. Romero's anthology film segments "Cat from Hell" (as writer) and "The Facts in the Case of Mr. Valdemar" (as writer-director) filter inspiration from Edgar Allan Poe stories through reimaginings of their own antecedents in the horror genre to introduce or modify critiques of capitalism. "Cat from Hell," the second segment in *Tales from the Darkside: The Movie* (1990), is Romero's adaptation of Stephen King's 1977 short story "The Cat from Hell." By placing this story within the context of Poe's "The Black Cat" (1843), one can see Romero working through the perverse of Poe's darkly humorous tale and extending the inherent anti-capitalism of King's short story. In each case, the segment introduces a variation on its generic antecedents that produces a "shock" that invites contemplation of real-world issues with which the segments engage, comparable to the function of Darko Suvin's concept of the *novum* in science fiction. Whereas Poe's cat functions as a symbol of guilt and retribution from beyond the grave, an index of the perversion of human nature, King and Romero use the same trope to render capitalism as the "perverse"—that which undermines the industrialist, Drogan, and hitman, Halston, from within and leads to their respective deaths. Romero's inclusion of a reanimation *manqué* of the cat extends the political content of King's story and draws it more closely into the domain of Romero's anti-capitalist undead humans.

"The Facts in the Case of Mr. Valdemar," the first half of the two-segment anthology film *Two Evil Eyes* (1990), adapts Poe's "The Facts in the Case of M. Valdemar" (1845), in which mesmerism arrests decay and

148

allows communication after death. In Romero's imagining, the reanimated corpses of Valdemar and the doctor who hypnotizes him resemble but function differently from the zombies for which Romero is most well-known. Rather than reduce the individual solely to his embodiment, these walking corpses controlled by others destabilize the relationship between the subject and his embodiment. To make this film's anti-capitalist critique, Romero, credited with inventing the modern zombie, instead reanimates pre–*Night of the Living Dead* conceptions of zombiism that are rooted in the Caribbean tradition.

Everything Undead Is New Again: Shocking Estrangements in Horror

Suvin's notion of the *novum* in science fiction offers one way into thinking about the way that Romero's reworking of sources and genre facilitates social critique in "Cat from Hell" and "Valdemar." For Suvin, science fiction's mirroring of our world includes some "strange newness" that pushes audiences to consider their world through cognitive estrangement, the rupture with their world that this novel element creates (4). In discussing the utopian genre and texts that include a "Utopian impulse," Fredric Jameson has argued that Suvin's "principle of 'cognitive estrangement'—an aesthetic which ... characterizes SF in terms of an essentially epistemological function (thereby excluding the more oneiric flights of generic fantasy)—... posits one specific subset of this generic category specifically devoted to the imagination of alternative social and economic forms" (xiv). While the utopian or utopian-inflected text invites such imagination by depicting those alternatives as accomplished, horror texts such as the short films considered in this chapter depict instead the continued existence of social and economic forms that cry out for alternatives by way of their destructive effects. In doing so, they enact, mirroring science fiction's utopian impulse, what we might call a dystopian impulse. Utopia and dystopia "are structurally the same genre," one in which "[v]iolence and horror are inextricably connected with hope and desire" (Gomel 225). The dystopian, like the utopian, has "a function of mobilising political affects" but, like some horror, is "more likely to rouse fear and anxiety than hope or desire" (Firth loc. 6763). Unlike in science fiction, much horror does not displace the dystopian into the future or onto other worlds. In Romero's "Cat from Hell" and "Valdemar," for example, the monsters themselves function as the nova that cause a cognitive estrangement that asks us to see our existing capitalist society as *already* a dystopia.

Cognitive estrangement, then, works within these films in a similarly epistemological manner to Jameson's utopian texts, removing Romero's works from the realm of the merely "oneiric" and imbuing them with the capacity to level critiques of modern American socio-economic forms. These critiques reside not in reimagining our socio-economic forms so much as in imagining our own socio-economic forms wholly or partially accelerated or exaggerated. The cognitive estrangement produced by a supernatural cat as the end result of profit-oriented pharmaceutical research or a walking corpse as the consequence of a murder for inheritance money arise from and provoke contemplation of our existing capitalist system. In taking these effects to their illogical conclusions, "Cat from Hell" and "Valdemar" recall the literary dystopias that emerged in the post-war 20th century and "extrapolate[d] features of an intensified and illiberal capitalism" (loc. 6757–6763)[1] and share the status of dystopia (and much of the rest of Romero's oeuvre) as "a kind of satire" (K. Robinson loc. 7747). Simultaneously, they enact horror film's manifestation of the repressed or objectionable "via fantasized worlds of total meaning where horrific events/acts/monsters are converted into symbolic equations (or allegories/hypersignifications)" (Hills 65).

While creators can of course enact socio-economic critiques in a more realist mode (see, for example, the opening of Romero's *There's Always Vanilla*, as discussed in Chapter 1), in some ways, horror may be particularly suited to the task. Horror's relatively marginal status and the affinity of its tropes with mechanisms of estrangement render it well suited to highlighting the inherently dystopian nature of a capitalist civilization. Writing on Karl Marx's own use in *Capital* of a discourse beyond realism, David McNally posits, "Because capitalism constitutes an alienated, topsy-turvy world, one in which phenomena regularly appear upside-down, the theoretical discourse that maps it needs to mimic the wild movement of things so as to better expose it" (116). Horror's worlds, their ontological stability upended by monsters, the apparently inexplicable and the unexpected, might be described in the same way that McNally describes the capitalist world. He adds "that capitalist inversions become normalised for everyday thought and action. As a result, like Brecht, Marx seeks to estrange us from the familiar so that we might actually see it for what it is" (116). Again, estrangement is key to the denaturalization required for critical appraisal, and here it is located in the very DNA of the anti-capitalist tradition.

The monsters of horror can further be viewed as markedly suited to this tradition owing to the monstrousness of capitalism itself:

[T]he very insidiousness of the capitalist grotesque has to do with its invisibility with, in other words, the ways in which monstrosity becomes normalised and naturalised via its colonisation of the essential fabric of everyday-life, beginning with the very texture of corporeal experience in the modern world. What is most striking about capitalist monstrosity, in other words, is its elusive everydayness, its apparently seamless integration into the banal and mundane rhythms of quotidian existence. This is why the most salient representations of the capitalist grotesque tend to occur in environments in which bourgeois relations are still experienced as strange and horrifying. In such circumstances, images of vampires and zombies frequently dramatise the profound senses of corporeal vulnerability that pervade modern society, most manifestly when commodification invades new spheres of social life [McNally 2].

The collision of the everyday and the fantastic or horrific thus yields a cognitive estrangement that can demystify and make jarringly visible the monstrosity of capitalist relations.[2]

We can see Matt Hills' concept of ontological shock in horror film as another, related way of producing cognitive estrangement. For Hills, "'ontological shock' provokes an extreme awareness of the horror text as a constructed artifact" (43). This shock entails the realization that "the text has withheld information and tricked us. Hence the ideal audience—text relation here is not one of cognitive or epistemological mastery. Quite the reverse; such texts inspire a sense of their artful ability to act on (and deceive) the audience, whose beliefs in the conventions of realist film are played upon" (43–44). Romero's works, by playing on realist conventions and audience expectations of realism, as well as, perhaps, horror's partly undeserved reputation as an apolitical or socially disengaged genre, induce this shock, their monsters shockingly irrupting into a largely realist setting.

However, and perhaps more germane here, "Cat from Hell" and "Valdemar," in reimagining elements of the genres in which they partake, also produce what we might call, after Hills, "generic shock." Hills identifies ""[u]ncanniness as a pleasure of repetition" as a discourse "of horror's pleasures" and notes horror's "immense textual and intertextual machineries of repetition" (68). In relation to these machineries, "reading horror intertextually" can involve "pleasures of knowledgeable recognition *rather than* pleasures of being scared" (170–71). But such recognition inherently involves recognition of difference, and that recognition can engineer not only pleasure but also the cognitive estrangement that makes space for social critique. "Texts seek to link themselves to preceding traditions/movements in the cultural history of the horror genre, and distinguish themselves relationally from other generic productions" (163); and "Black Cat" and "Valdemar" not only distinguish themselves by the changes that they make in repeating Poe or King, but also, and more significantly, in how they deviate from the traditions of the Gothic perverse, the crime thriller and the zombie. These deviations, rooted in intertextuality, from generic expectations potentially trigger a generic shock that allies with horror's ontological shock to draw attention to the horrific character of the objects of its critique, including consumer capitalism.

Three Lives of a Cat: Poe's "The Black Cat" (1843)

While not a tale of zombies, Poe's "The Black Cat" is a story of things that remain undead, albeit complicated by way of an unreliable narrator: Perhaps, in the eponymous feline, we have a zombie *manqué*. The trajectory of Poe's unnamed protagonist, however humorously presented, certainly would surprise no reader of Gothic tales. "Gothic," writes Fred Botting, "condenses ... threats associated with supernatural and natural forces, imaginative excesses and delusions, religious and human evil, social transgression, mental disintegration and spiritual corruption" (2). The "spirit of perverseness" that characterizes human nature leads the narrator further and further down a spiral of violence, first against his beloved black-and-white cat and then against his wife before outing himself to the law—this last as an effect of the zombie-*manqué* cat's unrelenting cries from within the walls, which conveniently or not so conveniently also contain the remains of the narrator's wife, walled up as Poe's killers are wont to do (Poe, "The Black Cat" 839).

The gradual degradation of character yoked to a narrative of violence is akin to the heuristics of William Hogarth's series of engravings "The Four Stages of Cruelty" (1751) that depict animal abuse (here a canine, rather than cat, and then a horse) undertaken by the character Tom Nero, leading to an increasingly degraded character, murder of a human, and punishment under the law. Hogarth's engravings, printed for a broad audience, are meant to be morally didactic: Tom Nero is an uncared-for orphan who, receiving no social support or services (a failure of capitalist social organization?), begins, uncorrected, to engage in violence against animals on a trajectory that leads to murder and his own execution and evisceration. The third print in the series, depicting the discovery of Tom's murder victim, might be seen as prefiguring the atmosphere of the Gothic, with its revelation of a corpse by lantern under moonlight and with an owl and bat both in mid-flight. The fourth and final print offers up an executed Tom mid-dissection in a surgeon's theater. As the doctors proceed with the dissection, a dog eats the killer's heart, very much akin to the end of "The Black Cat" as a bookend to the narrative and a bit of uncanny revenge. The cat provides the focal point for the narrator's claims that "perverseness is one of the primitive impulses of the human heart" and the mechanism for the punishment of that perverseness, that fundamental will to death, which together offer a commentary on the horrors of human nature more than a social critique (839).

Three Lives of a Cat: King's "The Cat from Hell" (1977)

In his study of Poe's influence on Stephen King, Burton R. Pollin calls King's story "The Cat from Hell" "clearly reminiscent" of Poe's "The Black Cat" (6).[3] King describes the cat of his story as "one with such unusual markings" and "with the queer black-and-white markings" ("Cat from Hell" 353, 360). This clearly recalls Poe's description of his titular antagonist: Initially, the cat, named Pluto, is entirely black, but upon seemingly returning from the grave (or being reincarnated), his coat has altered: "Pluto had not a white hair upon any portion of his body; but this cat had a large, although indefinite splotch of white, covering nearly the whole region of the breast" ("The Black Cat" 841).[4] In King's hands, however, the cat (evoking his unseen, deceased compatriots) becomes the vehicle not only for a narrative of individual guilt and punishment but also for a critique of capitalist exploitation.

Published in its initial form in two parts (the first just 500 words) in the men's magazine *Cavalier*, "The Cat from Hell" helped to sustain a young King during his own economic struggles, when the financially strapped schoolteacher and emerging horror writer and his wife were happy to see the money come in when these sorts of short works sold (King, Introduction 2–3). Republished as the oldest story in the 2008 collection *Just After Sunset*, "The Cat from Hell" was described as being in "delirious bad taste" by *New York Times* reviewer Charles Taylor, who complimented the story for taking "revenge for every fictional house pet ever perfunctorily slaughtered in the name of thrills." Given the ubiquity of the murdered pet trope in horror, this revenge might constitute its own form of generic shock, but the story's critique of the exploitation of living beings does not confine itself to the realm of horror media.

To summarize King's story briefly, a hitman named Halston is to be paid to kill a cat. His standard rate applies: $12,000, half up front and half paid upon the job's completion. The target of this hit is bent on revenge because of the source of the wealth amassed by his owner, Drogan. Drogan's company, Drogan Pharmaceuticals, conducts testing on animals, and "[i]n the four-year testing period which led to the FDA approval of Tri-Dormal-G, about fifteen thousand cats ... uh, expired" (King, "The Cat from Hell" 355). Having effectively killed off the rest of this clan of cat killers, the feline avenger now has only Drogan left, the last of those responsible for those 15,000 "uh, expired" cats. In the story's generic reworking of the Gothic perverse of Poe, as well as of the crime story, it highlights that "[c]apitalism is the reciprocal trans-mutation of life into death and death into capital" and "feeds on live and dead nature the same; it seeks to render them indistinguishable" (McBrien loc. 2438, 2440). The punchline of King's set-up is in the jux-taposition of the $12,000 payment to the 15,000 dead cats, members of non-human nature.[5] As Christian Parenti puts it, "[C]apital does not *have* a relationship to nature but rather *is* a relationship to nature" (loc. 3359). In linking capital to life and death, and in particular to the "law of Cheap Nature" in what capitalism "prioritizes in the web of life" (Moore, "Introduction" loc. 306), Drogan creates a correspondence between the two and, essentially, a reification of one by way of the other, that reflects their indistinguishability as forms of capital. Within this nexus of life, death and profit, the capitalism embodied by Drogan and his corpora-tion, Halston, and Drogan and Halston's compact is enshrined as the central locus of tension in King's tale.

And despite the potential for the story's climax to come across as comic, even as quite silly, it reinforces the anti-capitalist theme. After the cat dives down Halston's throat, the avenging feline works its way out through the hitman's belly: "Above Halston's navel, a ragged hole had been clawed in his flesh. Looking out was the gore-streaked black and white face of a cat, its eyes huge and glaring" (374).[6] This blood-wet cat's violent imitation of a mammalian birth elides the separation between human and non-human nature and emblematizes both the reproductive capacity of capitalism (a birth of that which is dead and that causes death) and a reckoning with the effects of its unsustainable exploitation. Here, perverseness and the relations of (re)production col-lapse into one another. As the cat will continue on—it has "unfinished business" (374), presumably to kill Drogan—so goes the undying leg-acy of capitalism. The discourse of "business," picked up in describing the cat's retributive mission, and the equation of business with life and death and, through the hitman, with crime, only further foregrounds the anti-capitalist critique. At the end, the capitalist bubble—here the belly of the would-be assassin, itself a site of resource consumption—literally bursts.

Three Lives of a Cat: Romero's "Cat from Hell" (1990)

Romero's adaptation of King's story, which Tony Williams calls "a horror version of *The Magnificent Ambersons* meets *The Chimes at Midnight*" (*Cinema* 180), joins two other segments and a wraparound story, all directed by John Harrison, to make up the 1990 anthology film *Tales from the Darkside: The Movie*. Upon its debut, the film garnered few critical accolades. Richard Harrington, writing for *The Washington Post*, compares the film to other entries in the horror anthology sub-genre and labels it "another miss along the lines of 'Creepshow.'" Owen Gleiberman, writing for *Entertainment Weekly*, offers scant praise for *Tales* as a whole, but calls the Romero-penned "Cat" the only segment that has "real power as a story" and enthuses, "William Hickey is in full ghoulish splendor as an old geezer whose kitty is trying to murder him. And pop star David Johansen, who plays the hit man Hickey hires to kill the cat, proves he's a terrific straight actor." Michael Wilmington at the *Los Angeles Times*, however, focuses on the film's social critique, connecting it to the Gothic and identifying it as a set of "cautionary tales about evil modern life: the greed, the lies, villainy and killing rage lurking just below polished exteriors. Rich, dumb college students take advantage of their poor competitors and get paid in kind, a sleazy old pharmaceuticals king is plagued by a murderous cat-vendetta, and a SoHo artist achieves dubious happiness by making a pact with a monster." Wilmington's reading of the film as an indictment of the stupidity, meanness and excess of the trickle-down years underscores the thematic links that run through the privileged cruelty of the wealthy students from the first segment, the "sleaze" of big pharma in the second, and the relationship between commercial success and tragedy for the third segment's artist protagonist.

Wilmington identifies the Gothic DNA that *Tales* repurposes in producing its generic and ontological shocks, noting that "the Gothic devices of the past—hellcats, murderous mummies, winged, gargoyle-devils—descend on malefactors of the present, tumbling right out of the old E.T.A. Hoffman [sic]-Edgar Allen [sic] Poe fantasy bag."[7] These classical Gothic tropes are fitting and fitted for a specific and contemporary critique of the dark heart of 1990 America.[8] This particular refitting echoes the union in *Monkey Shines* of tropes from horror and mad-scientist cinematic traditions for an exploration of normative masculinity focused through another vengeful animal connected to unethical experimentation and (re)located primarily behind the closed doors of the American suburbs. "Cat from Hell" adds to its Gothic-inflected zombie-tale-*manqué* a dash of the crime thriller as well: a hitman hired to take revenge for compatriots and family members themselves murdered in revenge might sound like the plot of a mafia movie, were not the warring factions cats and capitalists.

Capitalist critique is certainly nothing new in Romero's work—a decade before *Tales from the Darkside: The Movie*, Robin Wood had written, in an essay evaluating his perception of Romero, that *Night of the Living Dead, Dawn of the Dead*, and *The Crazies* connect the "theme of consumerism to the major relationship structures of capitalist society" and *Jack's Wife* and *Martin* present the "constricting and demoralizing" "structures and values of high and low bourgeoisie (respectively)," the realistic counterparts of the society presented parodically in the zombie films ("Neglected" 199). Romero's screenplay for "Cat" elevates the anti-capitalist strain in King's story with aplomb, even as it makes some modifications to the original. Romero adjusts the numbers if not the exact equations for rendering "life into death and death into capital": five thousand cat lives and a one hundred-thousand-dollar fee for the hit. While the cats gain more relative value here, they still embody non-human nature under a capitalist "symbolic-knowledge regime premised on separation" that enables "putting the whole of nature to work for capital" (Moore, "Rise" loc. 1844). As a result, the cats still fall victim to the way in which "capitalism's political economy" depends upon making Nature "'cheap' in a double sense: to make Nature's elements 'cheap' in price; and also to *cheapen*, to degrade or to render inferior in an ethico-political sense, the better to make Nature cheap in price" (Moore, Introduction loc. 144).[9] In addition to Romero's adjustment of the specific cheapness of nature, while King's cat, upon having killed Halston, heads off to complete his unfinished business, Romero provides the closure of Drogan (William Hickey) dying at the conclusion. (Of course, insofar as Drogan is merely one face of an entrenched and powerful hydra-headed system, it is a partial closure.)

Williams observes that Drogan and Halston (David Johansen) "are mirror images of a deadly capitalist economy" (T. Williams, *Cinema* 180), and the segment characterizes the hegemony of Drogan's wealth through the visual presentation of his large, moldering mansion, with a single man left in charge of a corporate and family fortune won by immoral gains—home, he says, to the "rich and unhappy." This wealth has been generated not only by exploiting thousands of cats (their lives and their free labor) as Cheap Nature but also by exploiting the consumer base for the drug for which the cats served as test subjects, as Drogan knows that it is a subpar and highly addictive product. As the hit goes awry, the material trappings of wealth in the house, *objets d'art* and worse, are destroyed. The symbols of Drogan's financial legacy are undone via the violence levied against and by the cat.

Drogan's death is compelling here, the stuff of the witness. For Kelly Oliver, "witnessing ethics ... can take us beyond human centrism" and "maintains that even in the face of our lack of understanding, the impossibility of mastery, and inherent unpredictability, we have a responsibility to act in ways that open up the possibility of response from our fellow earthlings and from the earth itself" and all of its creatures (489–90). Drogan sees the bubble burst, the cat exit Halston's body (albeit here from the hitman's mouth, not his guts). This sight—the sight of his crimes come home to roost as well as the undying power of capitalism to destroy bodies—witnessed firsthand gives the old man a heart attack, an ironic comment, perhaps, on his and capitalism's heartlessness. Death for Halston, a capitalist in his own right although, it should be noted, a contingent laborer, requires the physical destruction of his body, while for the capitalist mastermind, the boss and owner, it requires only recognition.

Importantly, in King's story, the relationship between cat and killer is one of greater sympathy than in Romero's screenplay. King writes Halston as a killer, but a killer with feeling: "He felt a kinship, but no urge to renege on the hit. He would do it the courtesy of killing it quickly and well. He would park off the road beside one of these November-barren fields and take it out of the bag and stroke it and then snap its neck and sever its tail with his pocket knife" ("Cat from Hell" 365). This Halston is no Hogarthian animal killer: He is by his own word opposed to the needless torture of animals. Further, in identifying with his non-human target, Halston engages in something akin to posthumanism and an empathy that both elides capitalism's divide between humanity and nature and resists the degradation of nature as cheap. Such sympathy or even identification with the victim is removed from Romero's telling. Romero's Halston is a cold and calculating killer by contract, a capitalist totem whose veneer never shows the slightest crack.

Nonetheless, some optimism, albeit a dark optimism, infuses Romero's adaptation. That capitalism may be undone, if only in the breaking of this one specific cycle, by way of its effects being made apparent to its administrators is enough to point to a way out. This cycle of abuse against man and animal alike for the sake of financial gain may be broken when those most guilty are forced to bear witness to the (undying) ramifications of their gains exacted on living flesh. At his death, Drogan bears such witness, but the final speech act of the segment belongs not to him but to the avatar of his non-human victims in the call of the undying cat. This is the wordless final word on the legacy of capitalism: The movement beyond this cycle is marked by a movement beyond human speech and, by extension, human ways of organizing the world. In place of the image of perverse birth in King's story, the film adaptation presents an image of the reversal of consumption, a reversal of capitalism's devouring of non-human nature. As a supernatural avatar of non-human nature, the cat also anticipates the image of the supernatural sparrows in *The Dark Half*, another King adaptation, unmaking George Stark, albeit for crimes against a perceived natural order rather than against non-human nature.

Further, the zombie-adjacent cat, a remainder and reminder of the violence of capitalism, gestures towards late-stage capitalism's supposition of its own eternality and, as such, embodies a specific critique of the assumption that capitalism as a system cannot and will not die, that capitalism's "commitment to endless accumulation" (Moore, "Rise" loc. 1980) is anything but phantasmatic. Here, it is not, or not merely, the system that is undying, but the punishment of those who would perpetuate such a system against their fellow animal and man. In this resolution, we might see a rejection of the would-be transformative and reformative powers of neoliberalism, for in humanity's destruction of non-human nature and "the conditions for human-friendly life in pursuit of economic growth," capitalism offers only the false premise "that humanity can resolve problems by applying the same methods that caused them" (Altvater loc. 2880–83).[10]

Reanimation and (Capitalist) Subjectivity in "Valdemar"

The debt of Romero's zombies to Richard Matheson's novel *I Am Legend* (1954) has been widely discussed (see, for example, Bishop 95ff., Luckhurst 137ff. and Yakir 47ff). In molding this inspiration, Romero also repurposed its critical schema. If Romero's zombies are in effect an index of the undying cruelty of capitalism, then in Matheson, the protagonist, not the antagonists, anchor this critique. Matheson's protagonist Robert Neville embodies a pastiche of solipsistic masculinity as he scavenges for supplies in a world where the ephemera of a capitalist economy have survived a pandemic and the subsequent proliferation of the walking undead. Upon initiating his suicide at the novel's conclusion, Neville fantasizes that he might become Legend, the stuff of tales to be told amongst this new civilization of the undead. As such, his wish is one for his life as a metonym for the world of commerce that was. His fantasy is for an afterlife of the world that was, one of commerce, and in this dream lies the implied wish that the memory of market economies will survive because, in Frederic Jameson's oft-quoted formulation, "it has become easier to imagine the end of the world than the end of capitalism" (199).

In Romero's reinvention of the zombie in *Night of the Living Dead*, the Matheson-inspired ghouls themselves become what Wood terms, in reference to *Night* and *Dawn*, "the logical end result, the reductio ad absurdum and ad nauseam, of capitalism" ("Neglected" 198). Romero's "The Facts in the Case of Mr. Valdemar" is not a zombie film, but it again reinvents the undead as part of a capitalist critique, in this case drawing on the Afro-Caribbean zombie tradition that Romero himself is credited with reimagining.[11] As in Romero's *Dead* films, in "Valdemar," reanimated corpses—a human form of Cheap Nature—provide the ontological shock, the horror novum in the dystopian landscape of late-stage-capitalist society, but the generic shock arises from Romero's simultaneous invocation and refiguring of his own zombie tradition by way of the similarly anti-capitalist (for imperialism is a mechanism of capitalist relations) Afro-Caribbean zombie tradition. Sarah Juliet Lauro highlights this nexus in her claim that if the cinematic zombie "can be said to be 'about' capitalism, this is only because the much longer-lived zombie myth that the film industry attempts to absorb is 'about' colonialism" (loc. 200). As Romero said, alluding to 1932's *White Zombie*, "[Bela] Lugosi always lived in a castle while the zombies went out to pick the sugar cane" (Yakir 47).

"The Facts in the Case of Mr. Valdemar" centers on a struggle over who gets to live in the "castle." It adapts Poe's 1845 short story "The Facts in the Case of M. Valdemar," in which the narrator's use of mesmerism as the titular Valdemar is dying arrests the decay of his body and allows communication with the subject for seven months after death. After this time, the mesmerist narrator "wakes" Valdemar, whose body famously dissolves into "a nearly liquid mass" (Poe, "Valdemar" 1072).[12] While, again, it is not a zombie film, Romero's adaptation reanimates rather than merely preserves the body of Valdemar (Bingo O'Malley), and his walking corpse visually recalls the director's living dead, as does the reanimated corpse of a second character, Dr. Robert Hoffman (Ramy Zada).

These walking dead, however, are controlled by purgatorial or interdimensional beings referred to as "Others," and they remain tethered in some way to the still-operative consciousness of the deceased. "Valdemar," then, sees Romero, credited with inventing the modern zombie, instead employing pre–*Night of the Living Dead* ideas of zombiism, those rooted in Afro-Caribbean traditions, which included seeing zombies as a form of ghost.[13] These undead can also be seen as precursors to what Kevin Alexander Boon classifies as a "'zombie channel'—a corpse deprived of his/her essential self that has had that vacated space filled by some other consciousness"—and which he claims do not appear until 2001 in literature and 2005 on-screen (23–24). In "Valdemar," the essential self and the alien consciousnesses synchronously rather than sequentially occupy the body. Consequently, rather than reduce the individual subject solely to his or her embodiment, as do typical zombies in the Romero tradition, or maintain a one-to-one relationship between self and body, as do zombie channels, "Valdemar"'s walking corpses radically destabilize the relationship between the (capitalist) subject and its embodiment. Jason W. Moore observes that "capitalism was the first civilization to organize itself" on the basis of the split between "body and spirit" ("Rise" loc. 1808), and "Valdemar" renders that split discomfitingly total.

In Poe's story, the narrator selects his friend Ernest Valdemar, a scholar and author, for an experiment to determine whether mesmerism can arrest the process of death based on Valdemar's lack of relatives and calm acceptance of his impending demise. Valdemar eagerly agrees to the proposition, which the narrator performs in the presence of a medical student and two doctors. Eventually, Valdemar, who only responds to the narrator, communicates that he has died, after which, physically immobile and unchanging, he is monitored daily for months by the narrator and his associates until it is decided to wake him from his trance. Valdemar asks to be either quickly awakened or put back to sleep as the process begins, and when he is awakened, rots away within a minute.

Romero's reimagining, set, of course, in Pittsburgh, replaces Poe's dispassionate medical experimentation with a criminal love triangle. Valdemar becomes a fatally ill rich man married to Jessica Valdemar (Adrienne Barbeau), a much-younger former flight attendant. Robert Hoffman, the doctor attending the bedridden Valdemar in his home, had been in a relationship with Jessica before she married Valdemar, and they are enacting a scheme to secure Valdemar's fortune and assets, which Valdemar wishes to withhold from his wife, and be together again. Valdemar's wealth functions as a means of maintaining possession of and control over Jessica, a situation that exemplifies the pressure exerted on women by capitalism's linking of economics and intimacy "to stay in abusive, unfulfilling, or otherwise unhealthy relationships" (Ghodsee 25). Jessica summarizes her relationship to her husband in purely transactional terms: "I let him use me—for pleasure and for show. Now I'm going to let him pay me for my services." Hoffman reinforces this portrait when he describes Valdemar as "a ruthless old man who treats people as if they were possessions." Jessica rebuffs Hoffman's suggestion of a sexual encounter because she worries that her husband might hear them, even under hypnosis, but later changes her mind after Hoffman has had Valdemar sign more paperwork. The film also suggests that Jessica's relationship with her lover is no less centered on wealth. During foreplay, Hoffman discusses how much money Jessica put in the safe, asserts that he hasn't "gotten anything out of this" and reminds her that his share of her husband's assets should be in cash so that there's "nothing to connect us," a reference to their scheming that takes on a clear double meaning.

Hoffman is a practitioner of hypnotism. Early in the film, he dictates the hypnotized Valdemar's responses to his lawyer over the phone and later has Valdemar sign papers in the same state. The lawyer has told Jessica that it will take several weeks for all of the assets to be transferred but, unfortunately for her and Hoffman, Valdemar flatlines and their attempts to resuscitate him fail. To preserve their scheme, they store Valdemar's corpse in a large freezer, unaware that his still being under hypnosis at the point of death will shortly present some unexpected complications: First, Valdemar communicates with them, and later, his corpse functions both as a doorway and a puppet for beings who seemingly occupy the same liminal space as his consciousness. Valdemar's now-ambulatory body kills Jessica. Hoffman wakes him, but the Others merely semi-materialize at Hoffman's apartment, kill him and occupy his corpse instead.

Williams, one of the only scholars to discuss "Valdemar," argues that its supernatural elements are unnecessary, and so focuses on the metaphor of how, as he says, "Jessica and Hoffman intend to feed off Valdemar's wealth in the same way as Romero's zombies desire human flesh" (T. Williams, *Cinema* 161). But he never examines the literally undead Valdemar and Hoffman themselves in the context of the zombie. While the undead Valdemar and Hoffman are not zombies in the post–*Night of the Living Dead* tradition, they do visually evoke them. This resemblance is no doubt aided by the fact that Tom Savini, who worked on 1978's *Dawn of the Dead* and 1985's *Day of the Dead*, acted as the film's special makeup effects supervisor. But whatever the practical causes, the result makes available an intertextual association, especially in Hoffman's case. The reanimated Valdemar moves slowly and his skin has a pale, bluish cast, which might recall Romero's zombies for audiences. But that echo of Romero's and other comparable film zombies is potentially stronger in the reanimated Hoffman who, not having been refrigerated after death, makes his appearance bloodied and rotting, with yellowish skin, prominent ribs, sunken eyes and drawn-back lips, moving one step at a time with his arms outstretched. He would, in other words, fit right in on any episode of *The Walking Dead*—minus, perhaps, the large metal metronome that protrudes from his torso, his own tool for hypnotism having been used to fatally impale him (see Fig. 10).

The film thus visually suggests a connection with a specific type of zombie that Romero is most commonly credited with popularizing. Lauro argues that lauding *Night of the Living Dead* "as the origin of the apocalyptic zombie narrative" constitutes an oversimplification, since Del Tenney's 1964 film *The Horror of Party Beach* features "[m]ost of the contemporary elements—the implication of the role of human science in the zombie's creation, the communicability of the zombie's state, and its appetite" (loc. 1943). The designation of "Romeran zombie," then, should be understood as used here advisedly, for convenience in differentiating a certain imagining of the zombie from its imagining in the Afro-Caribbean tradition, a term that itself performs a similar simplification. These Romeran zombies, with the exception of *Day of the Dead*'s minimally aware Bub, appear in the three *Dead* films that Romero made prior to "Valdemar" and in some of the films that they influenced as dead persons transformed by some unknown cause into animated corpses that seem to have little to no human subjectivity as we

Figure 10. Robert Hoffman (Ramy Zada) displays a strong resemblance to a typical cinematic zombie in *Two Evil Eyes* (1990, ADC Films and Gruppo Bema).

would recognize it. They act independently, but almost entirely as a consequence of a drive to consume human flesh—which Roger Luckhurst contends is actually a trace of the association of Haiti with cannibalism as "the index of savage otherness to Western civilization" (55)—and they can be killed by destroying their brains. This last characteristic is one that differentiates the undead Valdemar from a Romeran zombie: As Valdemar is warning of the Others and asking to be woken, Jessica shoots his freezer-bound body in the head twice to no effect; a third shot in the head as Valdemar's body advances on her also has no results. The significant distinction here rests in the location of consciousness and its relationship to the body.

Carl H. Sederholm posits in the concern with this relationship an affinity among "Valdemar," Poe and Romero's early zombie films. He argues that "Valdemar" "dwells on the same strange and uncanny divide between life and death that fascinated Poe, that space when the dead become the undead," and that movies such as *Night* and *Dawn* similarly "reflect Poe's own anxieties that some bodies exist without meaning, just mindless entities that shamble without purpose" (39, 41), a state that of course evokes the capitalist subject in his various forms, from plantation laborer to contemporary consumer.[14] In Romero's adaptation, after Valdemar's death, his consciousness remains intact, as, we can presume, does Hoffman's. Valdemar confirms, "I have been sleeping, and now I am dead," leading Hoffman, who insists, "There's a logical explanation for everything," to conclude, "There is consciousness after death." "It seems impossible," he admits earlier, "but there's no other explanation that makes any sense." Valdemar knows to whom he is speaking, asking Hoffman to wake him and addressing Jessica by name.

We get no confirmation of this sort of complete survival of consciousness after death in Romero's zombies to this point in his filmography, although something like it occurs in the *Return of the Living Dead* series, and, more importantly here, it is potentially more compatible with the Afro-Caribbean zombie tradition. Early on, Hoffman describes Valdemar as "still completely at my command," and while the subjectivity of the deceased remains under control of the hypnotist, it also remains in some way tied to yet separate from the body. The exact nature of this relationship between the consciousness and the body is unclear, but some bond is clearly present. This ambiguous relationship anticipates that between Thad Beaumont and his doppelgänger and alter ego George Stark in *The Dark Half*: George similarly appears to possess a consciousness and will of his own even as he represents a creation of and conduit for Thad's own repressed desires. Valdemar's ability to communicate audibly as he would in life provides one example of this kind of obscure bond: In Poe's story, the narrator describes observing for approximately a minute "a strong vibratory motion ... in the tongue," after which there "issued from the distended and motionless jaws a voice" ("M. Valdemar" 1070). In Romero's film, the voices of the undead similarly issue from motionless jaws, but Poe's motion of the tongue is removed, a change which divorces the production of the sound and, by extension, the expression of the subject, entirely from the body. Poe described Valdemar's voice as sounding as if it comes from a "vast distance, or from some deep cavern within the earth" (1070), and his and Hoffman's voices in the film are processed to give them an element of monstrousness or otherworldliness. More importantly, however, the undead speech in the film seems to come from nowhere and everywhere, similarly to how we hear non-diegetic music on a film's soundtrack, but also heard only when the body of the speaker, if that is the right word, is on camera. One exception occurs when Jessica hears Valdemar from a staircase before his corpse walks through an archway to appear at the bottom, but that still associates his voice with his body. Further, when questioned by Hoffman, the deceased Valdemar reports that he is comfortable and has no pain, as well as that he sees "Lights. Very bright. Very far in the distance. Can't reach them. Where I am, it is dark. Dark. Cold. Very cold." One could possibly attribute the reported feeling of cold to his corpse being in a freezer, but his visual impressions would require some other form of perception divorced from but replicating that of his physical body.

If the ambiguous mechanics of Valdemar and Hoffman's speech and perception imply that the subject is not solely a function of the body yet nevertheless in certain circumstances remains tethered to it postmortem, then, troublingly for common conceptions of the self, the subject's relationship to its body is not exclusive. Barbara Creed writes, "Fear of losing oneself and one's boundaries is made more acute in a society which values boundaries over continuity, and separateness over sameness," and that "death is represented in the horror film as a threat to the self's boundaries, symbolized by the threat of the monster" (*Monstrous-Feminine* 29). Chase Pielak and Alexander H. Cohen similarly argue, "[W]e are in a period during which there is a much less distinct means of distinguishing ourselves from others. ... This marks a fundamental identity crisis from which we have yet to emerge and which is the most disturbing aspect in these [zombie] films. The loss of a stable foundation for self is that of which we are really afraid" (50). Valdemar's predicament speaks directly to this contemporary anxiety, one exacerbated by capitalism's "transformation" of the subjects' bodies into "work machines" (Federici, *Witches* loc. 418). He says that where his consciousness is, he can perceive "[m]any, many others. Looking at me. Watching me. They want something." Later, he elaborates, "The Others are coming. I am part of both worlds. Theirs and yours. They want to use me to pass through. To pass through. They're coming." It is at this point that Jessica shoots him in the head as he is asking to be released from hypnosis, and the failure of Hoffman to wake him in time results in the Others assuming their own connection to Valdemar's corpse.

This connection exists along with rather than replacing his own, though it offers control that his own does not. "It isn't me, Jessica. It's the Others," Valdemar says in the scene in which his increasingly bullet-riddled corpse forces her to shoot herself; "It's the Others, Jessica. Using my body." Hoffman does subsequently wake Valdemar, but Valdemar informs him, his mouth now moving when he speaks, that it is too late: "The Others—without me, they can't return. They're with you now. They're with you." These Others, whose smooth, faceless, grayish forms we see briefly flickering in and out of embodiment, will murder Hoffman and take control over his reanimated body, and while this is not quite a zombie bite, it is almost as if Hoffman had been infected by his involvement with the undead Valdemar. This sequence of events aligns with Hills' discussion of what he calls possession horror, which "offers many instances of the interplay between object-directed emotion (experiences where the possessive force is 'housed' in one specific body) and object-less anxiety, where the possessive force exceeds any one body/object and hence potentially saturates a *mise-en-scène*" (27). He adds that zombie movies, which include "the question of who is 'infected' by the monstrosity," produce a similar set of anxieties (27). Romero's "Valdemar" participates in both the possession and zombie-infection strands of horror. However, it is not, or not only, the infectious, flesh-eating zombie that Romero's film primarily draws upon in developing its monsters but rather the Afro-Caribbean zombie.

Zombies in the Afro-Caribbean tradition focus on different fears about subjectivity than do their typical Romeran counterparts. Lauro defines the zombie as "a myth about the capture of souls and the reduction of the body to a machine" (loc. 2053) and asserts that the myth has simultaneously been appropriated by and infected American popular culture (loc. 320). Tracing the narrative to seventeenth-century West Central Africa (loc. 415), she says, "Zombies at first explained slavery as an act of sorcery that steals the person's soul" (loc. 418). These "fears of soul capture" (loc. 415) mean that earliest printed references to zombies are to spirits rather than animated corpses. The first printed occurrence, in the French-language novel *Le Zombi du Grand Perou*, which dates from no later than 1697, denotes "biting, pinching, hair-plucking spirits" that act as "accomplices" to a sorcerer or "spirits that walk around having left their bodies resting elsewhere" (loc. 765), a meaning that approaches Valdemar and Hoffman's situation.

While the idea of embodied zombies appears in a passage in an 1809 work referring to years-earlier anthropological research (loc. 910), it existed alongside rather than replaced the idea of a zombie as a spirit. An 1872 book titled *Americanisms: The English of the New World,* defines "Zombi" as "a phantom or a ghost, not unfrequently [*sic*] heard in the Southern states in nurseries and among the servants" (loc. 1580); and an 1889 article about Martinique in *Harper's Magazine* associates "the word zombi ... with a shape-shifting spirit" (loc. 866). According to Ann Kordas, by the 20th century, in Haiti, a zombie might be "a soul stolen from a living person by a magician," "a dead person who had willingly ... given his or her body to the Vodou gods to use as a receptacle" or "a reanimated, mindless, soulless corpse taken from its grave to serve the master who had awakened it" (loc. 278–82). She notes that, although late nineteenth- and early twentieth-century American fiction had represented zombis as "powerful spirits of African origin," it is this last version of the zombie that almost exclusively features in American pop culture following the 1929 publication of *The Magic Island,* the white author William Seabrook's account of his travels in Haiti.

Lauro makes the case that Romero explicitly points to this Afro-Caribbean zombie tradition in a *Day of the Dead* monologue "spoken by a black man from the Caribbean who wears a machete at his hip: this is a wink to the zombie's longer lineage, its relevance to the themes of enslavement and rebellion, and, I think, Romero's acknowledgement of his own complicated intervention in such a mythos" (loc. 2010). The enslavement in "Valdemar" is of the metaphorical sort, a domination by capitalist greed. This is a film in which Jessica awakens to a radio discussing retail and market trends, the camera focuses in on a vacuum cleaner logo reading "Commercial" when a maid service is working, and a detective comes right out and says, "The sick stuff always turns out to be rich people." The two protagonists are seemingly punished for using illicit means to secure the assets of a man who, as far as we know, is withholding Jessica's portion from her out of the concern which he expresses that "that bitch of a wife of mine" is out spending his money.

Between Valdemar's death and reanimation, Jessica worries that a lawyer's visit might ruin their plans, but Hoffman responds that this won't happen: "As long as he gets his fees, that's all he cares about. That's all anybody ever cares about in the end." Later, Jessica feels confident in her intention to bury Valdemar's body in the woods behind their home because people won't ask questions "as long as there's enough money" involved. Such elements lead Williams to see Hoffman as becoming "a *homo economicus* in death as he did so in life. He is little better than a programmed machine" (*Cinema* 163). In his association with capitalism and his being controlled bodily by others for their own purposes, he also, like Valdemar, recalls the soulless Afro-Caribbean zombies of films such as *White Zombie*, who labor for an individual master. Seen this way, Hoffman initially occupies a role akin to zombie master, though, again, he is mostly usurped in that role by the Others' occupation or puppeteering of Valdemar's body. Lauro observes that *White Zombie* demonstrates the beginnings of the zombie produced from the entanglement of "the mad scientist's living corpse and the Haitian zombie" and that films through the 1930s and '40s "often combined a doctor's passion for science and a Vaudou theme" (loc. 1971). Hoffman himself embodies this combination: He is a medical doctor and has created a kind of at-home critical care unit for Valdemar, yet he is simultaneously an expert hypnotist and asserts hypnotism's superiority to Western medicine in at least some circumstances, telling Jessica it is "better than any pill." He also retains sole power to wake someone he has hypnotized. He says of Valdemar, "Somewhere deep in his consciousness he knows exactly what we're doing to him. But when I wake him, it'll all disappear. Like the fragments of a dream," a description that inverts the idea that a zombie created by a sorcerer is unaware of his or her undead state unless he or she consumes salt or his or her master dies.

If the fact that Valdemar's consciousness loses control over a body that moves and acts under the control of others recalls zombie mythologies more than it does Poe's story, Romero's film also shares elements with the 1962 version of the story in the Roger Corman–directed, Richard Matheson–written anthology film *Tales of Terror*, which itself evokes films in the *White Zombie* lineage. In Corman's "The Case of M. Valdemar" as in Romero's version, Valdemar's (Vincent Price) voice issues from an unclear location with no visible movement of the mouth, and Valdemar similarly reports after death that he sees only darkness and multitudes of people. Corman also, like Romero, gives Valdemar a wife not present in the original in order to set up a love triangle and alter the motivation of the hypnotism from scientific research to manipulation. Similarly to Hoffman, Corman's hypnotist, Mr. Carmichael, plans to keep Valdemar under hypnosis until he gets what he wants from him, which in this case is not money and goods but Valdemar's wife Helene. Helene tells Carmichael, "I will marry you, on the stipulation that you set my husband free." He responds that she will do as he says or he will leave Valdemar as he is and never let him go. He threatens her in terms that are strongly reminiscent of Madeleine's zombification in *White Zombie*: "I shall take what I desire. Your body, and your soul if I demand it." Helene is also rescued by the corpse of a hypnotized Valdemar much as *White Zombie*'s Charles Beaumont, to help save Madeleine, manages to kill zombie master Murder while still under his hypnotic spell. When Helene screams for help, Valdemar opens his eyes and begins to rise, slowly advancing as she faints (for the second time in a very short film), his flesh melting as he does so. The segment ends with the hypnotist dead on the floor underneath Valdemar's decayed corpse.

The elements that Romero's "The Facts in the Case of Mr. Valdemar" shares with Corman's film, films such as *White Zombie*, Romero's own earlier *Dead* films, and Afro-Caribbean zombie mythology help to create undead beings that are as destabilized and destabilizing as the anxieties that they embody. Hoffman and Valdemar both are and are not zombies, as a zombie both is and is not living and does and does not have personhood, and as Hoffman and Valdemar's personhood, defined within capitalist relations, both is and is not tied to its embodiment in a way that leaves its boundaries permeable. In these liminalities, the film invites the "objectless anxiety" that Hills sees as especially common to possession and infection horror, as well as in what he calls the "monstrous indeterminacy" of "conclude[ing] on a note of uncertainty" (27). Hoffman is murdered after hypnotizing himself to sleep, leaving, as he says, no one to wake him. Thus, the film's ending with a policeman firing what we can assume from Valdemar's example are ineffective bullets leaves open the possibility that the Others will spread throughout our world, not unlike a zombie infection. Lauro describes the zombie figure as one that "was appropriated in an act of cultural piracy" but simultaneously "infect[ed] and inflect[ed] … American cinema and popular culture" (loc. 320). It is this ongoing multidirectional infection that we can see happening in the appearance in "The Facts in the Case of Mr. Valdemar" of elements of a zombie tradition that Romero is most often presented as having reinvented and moved beyond.

Lauren Berlant has argued that new aesthetic forms such as "the situation tragedy" and "cinema of precarity" emerged in the 1990s "to register a shift in how the older state-liberal-capitalist fantasies shape adjustments to the structural pressures of crisis and loss that are wearing out the power of the good life's traditional fantasy bribe without wearing out the need for a good life" (7). The films discussed here certainly engage with the costs of continuing to believe in the increasingly hollow and outdated promise of the capitalist "good life." However, rather than the rendering of the ordinary itself "into something that seems shocking and exceptional" in the "genre of crisis" (7) that Berlant explores, "Cat from Hell" and "The Facts in the Case of Mr. Valdemar," as horror films, instead insert the shocking into the ordinary as a means of registering anxieties about the natural and subjective precarities that are necessary consequences of capitalist relations. In doing so, they reanimate not only vengeful cats and husbands, but generic and narrative expectations, which, like zombies, acquire a new but changed life. If "Cat from Hell" and "Valdemar" refigure Poe, King and genre traditions in the service of anti-capitalist critique, *The Dark Half* similarly employs variations on the Jekyll and Hyde and doppelgänger traditions. However, while class considerations are present, its concerns center primarily on subjectivity and reproduction in relation to heteronormativity.

Queer Reproduction and the Family in *The Dark Half*

JOHN R. ZIEGLER

In George A. Romero's 1993 adaptation of Stephen King's novel *The Dark Half*, Liz Beaumont (Amy Madigan) accuses her husband Thad (Timothy Hutton) of having "become attached" to the pseudonym George Stark, under which he writes violent thrillers rather than the literary fiction for which he is known under his own name, for the behavioral license it affords him. When Thad says of one of "Stark"'s novels, "I hope you're not looking for any social significance ... because there ain't none to be found," one is tempted to view his admonition as a moment of metacommentary, one transgressive low-culture genre work comparing itself to another and distancing itself from examples of its genre with pretensions to high-culture prestige.

But it would be a mistake to take Thad at his word. Although Tom Fallows and Curtis Owen see *The Dark Half* as lacking "the socio-political core of Romero's work" (103), Tony Williams notes that the film "emphasises the critique of violent masculinity present in Romero's other films such as *Night of the Living Dead*, *The Crazies*, *Dawn of the Dead*, *Day of the Dead* and *Monkey Shines*" (*Cinema* 165).

The Dark Half begins in 1968, the same year that *Night of the Living Dead* was released, and it shares with that film a concern with threats to and from "the patriarchal family," although in a much more ambivalent manner than what Robin Wood characterizes as *Night*'s condemnation of the family and the social norms that it embodies ("Apocalypse" 163).[1] George Stark, who functions simultaneously as Thad's alter ego and doppelgänger, represents a threat to the heteronormative nuclear family that is both physical and ideological. Stark, as the villain, threatens to kill Beaumont's family. Stark also presents a more existential threat, much like the zombies of *Night*, not (only) to this actual, specific family but to the normative primacy of family itself.

A figure of unattached hyper-masculinity (as well as, perhaps, a manifestation of "willfulness" as theorized by Sara Ahmed in *Willful Subjects*), Stark literally cannot coexist with patriarch Beaumont: As one gets stronger, the other gets weaker. Additionally, Beaumont's success as a writer under Stark's name would seem to be tied up in the persona's rejection, even if imagined or incomplete, of domesticity and its reproductive orientation. The reproductive power of the patriarch is redirected instead into creating not only "low" art in Stark's name but also Stark himself as an embodied being. The generative force of Beaumont's writing works then as a type of asexual (and thus, by the measure of heteronormativity, queer) reproduction, with one man creating another. That Stark is in some way connected to Beaumont's parasitic twin, a second being that grew within Beaumont (significantly for the connection to creativity, within his head), reinforces the image of queer birth.

Both queer births result in deaths—the twin's, Stark's victims' and, ultimately, Stark's—outcomes that position the process as dangerously antithetical to future-oriented heterosexual reproduction. The sparrows who kill Stark in the climax are identified as psychopomps, guides to the world of the dead, but they can also be seen as helping to protect the reproductive heteronormativity that dominates the living world.[2] As psychopomps, they perform a supernatural function, but they can be interpreted simultaneously as avatars of the natural world, and so also as defending the natural, or more accurately, naturalized, heteronormative order by removing the unnaturally "born" Stark from Beaumont's domestic space via a deconstruction of Stark's body that constitutes an inverted echo of an organism's development. This containment of dangerous queerness, though, plays out in tension with the fact that the family and domestic life itself poses a threat to unfettered creativity and perhaps to masculinity of the type often valorized within heteronormative patriarchy, even as the existence of the hyper-masculine alter ego depends entirely on the seemingly compromised creativity of the family man.

Dualling Masculinities

When Liz is criticizing her husband's attachment to George Stark, she compares her husband to a Dr. Jekyll who becomes a Mr. Hyde when he is writing a Stark novel. However, in Robert Louis Stevenson's novella, both Jekyll and Hyde are conspicuously single men,[3] while in *The Dark Half*, participation in heterosexual family life acts as one of the primary distinctions between Thad and his own alter ego. The first shot that the audience sees when the film leaves 1968 for its present of 1991 focuses on two babies in footie pajamas, one each in the traditional colors of pink and blue, and then zooms out to include Thad's wife and their bedroom.[4] Adult Thad is thus introduced through an identification with the nuclear family and domestic space, and this identification extends throughout the film. Williams sees Liz's "gently persuading him to perform domestic duties" as "positively influencing Thad's gentle role as a father" (*Cinema* 166). As Mark Browning observes, "[W]e do see quite a lot of baby-related domesticity on-screen" (181). Williams also says, however, that this influence counters Thad's unconscious reaction against this role. If Thad's role in the patriarchal family is to preside over "anodyne scenes of domestic bliss" (M. Browning 181), then at least part of him "appears intuitively wishing for his worst side to emerge to escape from his mundane domestic world" (T. Williams, *Cinema* 166). If we admit liberatory potential to such escape, we might ask, following Leo Bersani, whether a "narcissistic discovery of the self" inaccurately "replicated outside the self," such as Thad's doppelgänger arguably provides, could "modify the dangerous property relations fostered by the generative model of relations—the couple, the family" ("A Conversation" loc. 2477). Imbued with such potential, the manifestation, figuratively and literally, in George Stark of Thad's resistance to the prescriptions of domestic(ated) heteronormative masculinity might radically undermine the oppressive prevailing modes of relationality exemplified in the nuclear family.[5]

Stark's threat to the traditional nuclear family is both to its physical embodiment and to its ideological underpinnings in reproductive futurism, which takes "the Child as the image of the future it intends" (Edelman loc. 76). This "narrative movement toward a viable political future" operates in conjunction with the "absolute privilege of heteronormativity" (loc. 91, 68). Queerness, in opposition, "names the side of those not 'fighting for the children,' the side outside the consensus by which all politics confirms the absolute value of reproductive futurism" (loc. 76). In Freudian terms, the double externally manifests "repressed drives," that which is "unacceptable" to the ego (Meehan loc. 100). Stark as a separate entity (along with the process of his becoming that separate entity) falls upon the side of unacceptable queerness, but even before Stark physically manifests as Beaumont's double, the part of Beaumont associated with the Stark persona violates the normative role of "gentle father." Reacting to a blackmail attempt by a man named

Fred Clawson (Robert Joy) that would expose Thad Beaumont as George Stark, Thad tells his female child, in a baby-talk voice, that Stark protagonist Alexis Machine would "cut off [the blackmailer's] pecker and shove it in his little rat mouth so when they found him they'd know he was a squealer." It is notable that this imagined violence focuses on attacking, symbolically, the target's masculinity and, literally, his means of reproduction. The attribution of the threat to Stark's protagonist further suggests the violent (sexual) threat that Stark will pose to Thad, a threat that Thad himself will create through the sort of queered self-reproduction anticipated by the implication of auto-fellatio in the image of the blackmailer with his own penis in his mouth. At the same time, the image hints at Stark's own failure to reproduce himself, and the use of "pecker" here also looks forward to sparrows as peckers at the climax, defending heteronormative reproduction by pecking into the lake house and pecking Stark into pieces (Fig. 11). But as a speech act, it also attacks the innocence of what Markus P.J. Bohlmann and Sean Moreland term "childness" as conceived and enforced by heteropatriarchal ideology. Bohlmann and Moreland prefer "childness" for its ability to point to itself as discursively constructed, to the extra-discursive elements of that construction, and to the conflation by terms such as "childhood" or "the child" of that construction with actual, living children (16).

Our culture defines childness as "largely a coordinate set of *have nots*"—"innocence, purity, emptiness" (Kincaid 10)—and this

Figure 11. The shadow of Fred Clawson (Robert Joy) with his "pecker" in his mouth adjoins a reference to those other peckers, the sparrows, in *The Dark Half* (1993, Orion Pictures).

"insistence on the blank innocence of childhood is also an insistence on a (future and legibly incipient) heterosexuality" (Ohi 84). Rather than preserving this blankness, the image, directed to a child, of the male blackmailer with a pecker in his mouth, a suggestion of auto-fellatio that does not sit far from the image of Thad as giving birth to himself, injects a disruptive queerness into the spaces of childness' prescribed emptiness. The reaction shot of the mother's disapproving expression is therefore not particularly surprising.[6] If *The Dark Half* is at least partly situated within the Gothic tradition—the doppelgänger, after all, first proliferated in literary form in the Gothic novel (Meehan loc. 388)—then we might see in such moments Thad as inheriting some of the characteristics of the "Gothic Hero," who, according to William Hughes, "is often queer in a metaphorical sense" even when he is depicted as unquestionably heterosexual (207).[7] Hughes further describes this hero as "often contemplating his own inability to meet cultural expectations or to control his allegedly antisocial desires" and thereby bringing into question "the definition of what it is to be normal in both the genre and its surrounding culture more generally" (207).[8] Thad's own antisocial impulses and friction with his cultural norms and expectations find outlets both in his own expressions of aggression and in their displacement onto and into George Stark.

Bersani finds in the work of Sigmund Freud a movement towards conceptualization of "nonerotic ... aggression (directed towards the world or towards the self) *as* intense erotic excitement" ("Can Sex" loc. 1823). Viewed in these terms, Thad's displaced aggression—both George Stark's destructive aggression towards "the world" and Thad and George's towards one another (and, as such, towards the self)—redirects erotic energy from what would be regarded as its proper place within (his) marriage. Thad's behavior implies that, on some level, he recognizes the troublesome nature of this dynamic for his roles as husband and father. Although he admits, "Half of me is a bastard," and expresses some admiration for Stark's simplicity and violence, he assures his wife, "I love you more than anything." And after talking about genital mutilation and murder to his child, he is shown feeding both babies (a nurturing contrast to feeding a man his own pecker) and asks them if it is time to say goodbye to "Uncle George." He interprets them as saying yes, which is significant not only for the obvious reason that it acknowledges that according to dominant sociocultural expectations, the gentle, innocence-preserving father must not also act as the violent, dirty uncle, but also because it invests in the children the authority of "the Child whose innocence solicits our defense," "a value so unquestioned, because so obviously unquestionable" under reproductive futurism

(Edelman loc. 61).[9] Defending the Beaumont children becomes the film's focus once Stark physically threatens them and then holds them hostage. Liz foregrounds that her "babies are in danger" in a call to the sheriff that partly takes place over close-ups of said babies in their play-pen, a bounded protective space set aside for the professedly innocent activity of childhood play. Thad realizes that Stark has "got my children" when Stark squeaks one of their toys, a marker of such play, over the phone. During the climax, Thad prevents one of his children from making Stark's straight razor a new toy, kicking it away as the child reaches for it and symbolically preventing the next generation of his family from taking up the Stark mantle.[10]

If Thad comes to successfully inhabit the role of protective father and husband, it is by banishing a particular type of hyper-masculinity embodied in Stark, one that remains detached from the heterosexually domestic and reproductive. Stark's hypermasculinity inheres in his physicality (he is described as stronger and more muscular than his double Thad) and in his preferences (he smokes, drinks hard liquor, and acquires a Toronado muscle car at the earliest opportunity). Stark is also specified to hail from Oxford, Mississippi. Postbellum Southerners often viewed themselves "in contrast" to what they viewed as "the effeminate nature" of Northern men (Friend xi). The "'effete characteristics' ascribed to Northerners included gentleness, interest in home life, [and] even finding friendship with one's wife rather than the guys" (xiii). The dichotomy between southerner George and Maine resident Thad might thus be seen to extend and map onto this historical perception, much as George might be seen as adhering to the twentieth-century emergence of a sense of Southern male honor typified in fictional role-model Rhett Butler and rooted in combativeness, competition and a reverence for drinking, hunting, swearing and fighting as "a powerful remedy for weakened southern masculinity" (xviii). Stark's violence itself is repeatedly couched in terms of masculinity. The blackmailer is in fact discovered dead with his phallus in his mouth. Stark's signature weapon, a straight razor, can itself be read as phallic (not to mention ideally suited for castration).

While *The Dark Half* is not, strictly speaking, a slasher, applicable here is Carol J. Clover's connection of wielding the slasher genre's cutting and penetrating weapons to the "assumption of the phallus" required for the adult subject, which is figured as a transition from femininity to masculinity (50). The razor's phallicizing power is showcased, for example, when Stark slashes the throat of Rick Cowley (Tom Mardirosian), one of Thad's literary agents, opening a deadly feminizing wound. Stark also beats Homer Gamache (Glenn Colerider) to death with his own wooden leg, a symbol of castration anxiety, and prefaces a deadly kick to another man's head with, "I guess I'd better punt," invoking masculine competition.[11] He tells Thad during a phone call that there is no need to get his panties in a bunch, assigning to him feminine-coded weakness; and, when George uses his psychic connection to Thad to make him stab himself in the hand with a pencil, the phallic instrument of his creation, George admonishes Thad to "[t]ake" this penetration—"I poked myself," he later describes it—"like a man."[12] During Stark and Beaumont's final confrontation, when the latter goes for the former's gun and is stopped, Stark targets both Beaumont's offspring ("I can do some real ugly shit to them," he warns) and his manhood, kicking Beaumont in the crotch—a favor that Beaumont, still on the floor, shortly returns, along with stabbing George in the neck with another pencil, reversing his earlier self-penetration to inflict an emasculating wound on George.[13] Notably, Stark's brand of hyper-masculinity does not extend to an assertion or exercise of (hyper) heterosexuality. He does not, for example, employ or threaten sexual violence against Liz when he holds her hostage, since taking Thad's place sexually would be tantamount to taking his place as husband and father and incompatible with George's role as antagonist to reproductive heteronormativity.[14] Even hints of self-reproduction, such as the Beaumont baby nearly taking up George's razor or George's beginning to write and thereby to replace Thad nonsexually, ultimately come to nothing.

Baring the Bird-Ends of Birth Without Women

While George Stark is consistently and sharply divided from heterosexual reproduction, Thad Beaumont participates in both reproductive futurism and the asexual, queer reproduction of which Stark is the result. This queer reproduction draws on Thad's will, his creativity and his body, the relationship of each to George's creation offering a different perspective on Thad's self-reproduction. Thad's academic colleague Reggie Delesseps (Julie Harris) focuses on the first of these. She declares to him that George Stark is "an entity created by the force of your will," which used Thad's parasitic twin, surgically removed when Thad was a child in 1968, as a vessel. She tells Thad that he wanted it to live "so badly, it actually came to be." Sara Ahmed sees willing as "splitting" the subject by making the self both subject and object (*Willful* 27). We might see Thad's generative willing as externalizing and concretizing this process.[15] Further, Ahmed points out that willing oneself to do something carries the possibility of not enacting what is willed; thus, via such "self-variation," willing can also act as a kind of "escape valve" (29). In Thad's case, his not carrying out his own commands (such as to act within the confines of the role of "good" husband and father) is displaced onto George, who acts as the escape valve for his disinclination to obey himself.

Browning complains that the creation of one character by the subconscious of another "not only lacks credibility, it is inconsistent. Stark is more decisive and violent, certainly, but he kills people with whom Beaumont has no argument; i.e., he is only acting out his wishes in the style, not the actuality of his actions" (M. Browning 79). However, if we view Stark as a literalization of the self-variation inherent in willing, then such inconsistency is lessened: Stark is not, as Browning says, carrying out Beaumont's wishes (or will) but rather his desire *not* to carry out his own will. Stark's actions and existence represent for Beaumont an instance of an experience of "'non-sovereignty,' ... the subject's constitutive division," which means that the subject can never completely know or control itself, its motivations or its desires (Berlant and Edelman loc. 156).[16] Relatedly, Stark may be seen as an aspect of Beaumont's willing in that the subject tends to imagine the will as a voice coming from outside the self, which may be given "existence" as "a certain character (as friend, as foe ... and so on)" (Ahmed, *Willful* 30).

The work of the will can also be to attempt to convincingly "close the gap" between how one does and "should" feel (52). The gap in the example that Ahmed references (a bride who "should" be happy on her wedding day) maps easily onto the gap for Thad, who "should" be happy as a married, financially successful father. Happiness itself can be seen as a "regulatory norm" that abjects that which "resists incorporation" (Berlant and Edelman 18). The act of "willing against oneself" in turn holds open the possibility of what conforming to happiness would foreclose (18). Stark emerges from and exists within these gaps of the "should" and of self-resistance.

In finding his agency within that gap, George acts as a willful subject, to use the term as explored by Ahmed, in relation to the wills both of Thad and of heteronormative society. Ahmed defines the willful subjects as those who "insist on their own way" and will "only what is agreeable, that is ... in accordance with their own desire" (Ahmed, *Willful* 85). To take one example, when George tells Thad in a phone call that he is getting revenge for Thad, something that is not among Thad's "wishes," as Browning says, because of the removal of Thad's self-variation via the displacement of his conflicting desires into another subject (George), those displaced desires accord with the new subject's desires, and

George actively insists on carrying them out in express defiance of Thad and the legal system. Something similar occurs in the earlier *Monkey Shines*, in which, Kendall R. Phillips observes, protagonist Allan's (Jason Beghe) "rage and anger become funneled into [helper monkey] Ella, who becomes the vessel for his intentions" (50).[17] As with Stark, though, Ella begins to act willfully, moving beyond the foundations of Allan's projected rage and desires for revenge against certain persons to threaten both Melanie (Kate McNeil), in whom Allan has a romantic interest, and—much as Stark attempts to destroy (and replace) Beaumont—Allan himself.

George's willfulness stands in contrast to Thad's (outward) will*ing*ness: willing "parts must be willing to do what they are assumed to be for" (Ahmed, *Willful* 101), such as to act as the patriarch of a nuclear family. The family, made up of such willing parts, represents a "fantasy of the 'whole social body'" (113), which perhaps in turn mirrors the image of the undivided subject. Even children must act as willing parts of the family and be willing to create a new family "body" (113). The willful subject, however, refuses the duty of reproduction, in both senses of the word (114), a refusal that aligns with the anti-reproductive futurist queerness linked to George. Queerness furnishes "the freedom not to participate" (194), a freedom that Thad at least partly desires and that George enacts.[18] That queerness is often seen as "self-regard" or "turning away from the straight path" and "towards oneself" (116) seems particularly applicable to the dynamic between George and Thad.

If George Stark is birthed by the force and operation of Thad Beaumont's will, both reflecting that will and acting willfully against it, Stark is equally birthed by Beaumont's creative faculties. While will and creativity doubtless overlap one another, enough distinction exists, especially in the film's formulation of them, to treat the relationship of the creative process to the asexual reproductive process separately here. In the opening sequences, young Thad's mother blames his headaches and his seizure on his literary endeavors: "I know it's your writin', Thad. This all started about the same time you started with your stories." While she is wrong in attributing his ailments to eyestrain, her blame of Thad's writing is not entirely misguided, as one could certainly discern an implication that it is in fact his writing that is fueling the growth of his parasitic twin—as if his creative energies were developing not only imaginative beings composed of words on a page but also a separate being composed of cells inside his body. Later, as an adult, Beaumont's creation of the Stark persona, subsequently to take on flesh, diverts a portion of his (pro)creative energies from their normative, acceptable outlets, literary fiction and the nuclear family. He channels these energies instead into the creation of "low" genre fiction, and they eventually result in the reproduction of himself, by himself, as an adult man rather than a child. If in patriarchal thought, men produce while women reproduce and the pregnant mind is masculine while the pregnant body is female (S. Friedman 52), then Beaumont's begetting of Stark both as idea and as body collapses, to a degree, these structuring binaries. The long-established image of the male author's creativity as a process of giving birth, an image that becomes more literal in *The Dark Half*, rests on a similar, and similarly anxiety-producing, blurring of categorical boundaries.

The metaphorical association between authorship and childbirth can be traced back, in the Western tradition, to Plato's *Symposium* and its comparison of a poet to a biological parent and his poem to his child, and this metaphor became "a conventional figure" for writers, often male, from the classical and medieval periods through to today (Castle 194). While Beaumont does not explicitly call Stark and Stark's books his children, he comes close to using a childbirth metaphor regarding his work under his own name when he says, "It's not comin' outta me easy."[19] Further, he does specify that the writing room in the family's lake house is where Stark "came into being." He, in other words, enacts rather than employs the metaphor.

The result can be viewed as playing out a fantasy of masculine asexual reproduction alongside a fetishized vision of the male creative who can "give birth" to works without thereby compromising his (version of) masculinity. The commercial success of Beaumont's offspring appears to stem at least partly from an embrace of violent, non-familial and non-reproductive masculinity in place of a domestic patriarchy that would best nurture reproductive futurism's children and their guarantee of social futurity. If "[d]isturbance can be creative" (Ahmed, *Willful* 204), then perhaps creativity can also be disturbing. Such disturbance applies not only to the rejection of reproductive futurism by Beaumont's progeny—both Stark and the novels in his name—but in the association created by that rejection of queerness with what might otherwise be seen as a normative hyper-masculinity. Thad asserts to his students that everyone is really two people: a timid, usually false outside presented to the world and an inner being that is "[p]assionate, uninhibited, even lustful." Leaving aside the accuracy of this rather questionable generalization, Thad's description of the inner being sounds very much like stereotypes about queer people, especially men, and their excessive sexuality.[20] Thad, rubbing a spot on his head, continues that while most people keep that inner being hidden, the fiction writer not only does not have to but in fact must not, for the sake of his work, keep that inner being locked away.

Willing brings what is background to the foreground or "brings forth" (Ahmed, *Willful* 37), and, as we have seen, Thad's willing does exactly that for his inner being. What Thad brings forth in and through Stark is referred to by Clawson as something that Thad would not want his mother to find out that he wrote, suggesting its incompatibility with the maternal and the familial. A police officer who remarks "Ask Mama if she believes this" upon finding the bloody truck that George drove after murdering Homer gestures towards a similar incompatibility. It is predictable, then, that the biggest supporters of Thad's work under his own name are women, who are associated under patriarchy with the pregnant body (and literal children) over the pregnant mind (and metaphorical children).[21] His wife, a mother, argues for Thad to kill off his pseudonym. In a deleted scene, Sheriff Pangborn's (Michael Rooker) wife Annie (Chelsea Field), another mother, reveals to her husband that she likes Thad's books but started a Stark book and could not finish it because it was "awful" and "nasty." Even in the case of Beaumont's agents, the woman, Miriam (Rutanya Alda), is more supportive of killing off the Stark persona than her male partner Rick, and characterizes Rick's avowal that he reads Stark for fun and Beaumont as work as support for their having divorced. It is noteworthy that the gendered reaction to Thad's creative output holds even though Miriam, as a childless woman in New York City who continues to work with her ex-husband, otherwise represents a kind of urban decadence antithetical to the traditional suburban family life that Thad ostensibly represents and "should" embrace. Stark's novels, about "tits and tough guys," as Clawson alliteratively puts it, are themselves counter to a traditional family-oriented masculinity, and Clawson dismisses Thad's work under his own name as a couple of "highbrow books about yuppies and faggots."[22] The assertion that the audience for Thad's work is "faggots" indirectly insults the type of insufficiently masculine domestic manhood that Thad represents, but it also points back in the direction of his reproduction without women. Even as in Judeo-Christian tradition, the "power of the Word became the paradigm of male creativity, indeed the foundation of Western patriarchal ideology" (S. Friedman 53), Beaumont's giving birth via words both to books and to another man remains, by heteronormative standards, stubbornly queer.

Stark is not born only by means of words or manifestations of psychological mechanisms, however; there are also physical aspects to the process. First, Stark is identified with the parasitic twin that Beaumont grew internally, gestating another inside his head, symbolic seat of his creativity, in a grotesque parody of female pregnancy. The doctor's comments that what is growing inside Thad's head once was a twin but "now, it's nothing" and that it was "[u]nborn, but absorbed into the system" seem somewhat contradicted by his admission that the twin had somehow "started to grow" again (we glimpse an eye, part of a nostril and a couple of teeth inside Thad's opened skull) and the fact that the twin's eye opens and moves around, almost as if it were aware.[23] The surgery that removes this developing, reactive (partial) being acquires intimations of a cesarean birth. (One might think here of a perverse echo of Athena, goddess of wisdom and war, being born from the head of Zeus with the help of an axe [Hard 77, 181].[24]) Reinforcing the image of queer birth, which is also here a death, a non-reproductive, non-futurist birth, we learn that Thad's mother and father insisted "that the excised tissue be treated as human remains and signed over to them." Later, Thad's nightmare vision of a pulsing, leaking stuffed turkey splitting its skin provides an echoing image that conflates pregnancy, birth and death, a conflation extended when Thad turns away from the turkey only to elicit a squeak from a baby toy by accidentally kicking a diaper bag shown in close-up as Stark walks by him.[25]

Thad's skull functions as a womb, but a womb that is simultaneously a grave. In considering this confluence, it will be useful to reformulate Bersani's famous linkage of the rectum and the grave. Bersani asserts that "if the rectum is the grave in which the masculine ideal (an ideal shared—differently—by men and women) of proud subjectivity is buried, then it should be celebrated for its very potential for death" ("Is the Rectum" loc. 414). Bersani makes this pronouncement in his discussion of queer sexual encounters, but it holds equally true for *The Dark Half*'s queer reproduction. The death that Bersani is talking about points both to biological death (death as a result of AIDS) and to the shattering of the self that occurs in sexual contact. In *The Dark Half*, the male womb, the skull, takes the place of the rectum as the point of contact with the Other, and it can be linked to the same types of death.[26] Further, when George Stark is "born" for a second time, a literal grave acts as his womb: Digger (Royal Dano) points out that it looks like someone dug his way out of his own grave, a sort of unnatural (re)birth from the family plot.

Having been birthed from this grave, Stark causes (and eventually suffers) both biological death and the self-shattering experience for Thad of subjective non-sovereignty. His experience of non-sovereignty can be seen as having similar effects to those that Bersani assigns to queer art's "impersonal narcissism" ("Is There" loc. 466). Bersani identifies in some examples of visual art "a rather uncanny invasion of the visual field by a relation of sameness or self-multiplication, a sameness that at once extends a figure and destroys its boundaries, its contained integrity" ("Is There" loc. 484), much as George does to Thad and which relation recurs in Thad's (George's?) written art, with Alexis Machine doubling George as George doubles Thad. These multiplied selves, their cohesion, are linked both to Thad's art and to his physical body. First, Stark appears to require a new Stark novel, a further multiplication of Alexis Machine, to continue to survive, to maintain his self-cohesion. Second, *The Dark Half* puts a spin on the consistent folkloric postulation that "it is dangerous, or even fatal, to be in the same place at the same time as one's double" (Meehan loc. 73) in that Stark physically cannot coexist with his double—and, as reproductive futurist patriarch, antithesis—Beaumont. The dynamic of one getting stronger as the other gets weaker works both ways: After Stark overcomes his fear of putting pencil to paper and starts to compose, Beaumont grows pale, leaks brown fluid from a wound in his head, and develops blisters on one side of his jawline. Again, Allan and Ella provide a parallel in *Monkey Shines*. During Allan's paralysis, Ella's is the powerful, mobile and "unconstrained body"; but after Allan kills Ella, ending her own willfulness, he undergoes a "physical restoration" not only through corrective surgery but also in his "romantic union" (Phillips 50, 57), which restores him as a heteronormative subject. As a result of Thad and George's similar relationship, in the end, Thad too reacquires physical and heteronormative soundness while George undergoes decomposition in multiple senses of the word.

When Pangborn is trying to figure out where Stark, this "man who never was," came from, he invokes queer reproduction, asking Thad, "Did you just sort of give birth to him one night?" He then adds, "Did he pop out of a damn sparrow's egg?" The sparrows, of course, are the physical instruments of Stark's final dissolution, taking apart his body in a kind of un-development. Although the sparrows are supernatural, their appearance evokes the natural world, and they excise Stark from that world and specifically from the domestic space of the Beaumonts' lake house, thereby preserving the natural(ized) hetero-reproductive order outside of which Stark was transgressively and destabilizingly created. The sparrows act as an important motif throughout the film, which opens with an enormous flock of birds taking flight from barren trees, and their intertextual resonance with the preternatural avian swarms of Alfred Hitchcock's 1963 *The Birds* can be illuminatingly read in juxtaposition with Edelman's arguments for the birds' queer function in the latter film. While in Romero's film, it is Thad's arguably gender non-conforming academic colleague Reggie, with her male name and her pipe and her association with the workplace rather than with maternity, who explains the sparrows' function as psychopomps to Thad,

The Dark Half inverts the queer negativity of the birds in Hitchcock's film and renders them defenders rather than disrupters of reproductive futurity.[27]

According to Edelman, Hitchcock's birds attack not only children but also what they represent, including "the ideology of reproductive necessity" (loc. 1867). They, like George Stark, do not mean homosexuality but are queer in their denial of reproductive futurism's fantasies of meaning and coherence (loc. 1979, 2206). These "ravaging birds" are also "too like the children" whom they assault, an equivalency absent in *The Dark Half,* except perhaps in the brief moment when the child reaches for Stark's razor, as Romero's film is interested in conserving the "sacralization of childhood" under siege from Hitchcock's birds, some of which are themselves sparrows (loc. 1875, 1867, 1987).[28]

Rather than Hitchcock's "future-negating force" (loc. 1917), Romero's birds are a reparative force, swooping in to save the reproductive nuclear family from the threat posed by Stark and the family's head from the subjective rupture and irruption of drives that Stark represents and engenders. Stark's references to "Endsville, where all rail service terminates" conjure an image of non-futurity that signals the manifestation of the queer force of *The Birds'* birds in Stark himself; and the sparrows' "flying again" marks Stark's presence only insofar as it entails its own impending absence. Whereas Hitchcock's birds, as the avatars of an arbitrary and unpredictable queer negativity, threaten the loss of individual cohesion and to dismantle "an ideologically naturalized reality" (loc. 2198, 1995, 2041), Romero's sparrows redirect and literalize that threat in physically dismantling Stark in order to repair both Beaumont's subjective cohesion and any damage to the fabric of his naturalized heteronormative reality.[29] The fantasy-made-flesh of self- and social defiance and dissolution embodied in Stark safely reverts to the fantasy of reproductive futurism.

The imagery in the climax of *The Dark Half* points to the successful containment of the queerness discussed to this point and (re)assertion of the heteropatriarchal reproductive order. The sparrows peck holes in the walls of Thad's writing room, literally breaking down the boundaries of a space previously dedicated to George Stark and not to the family (the room is windowless, with its door concealed as a sliding bookcase, self-contained and cut off from the domestic spaces of the lake house), as the Beaumont babies laugh and express amusement at the light playing through the holes made by the flock of birds. When Stark aims to shoot one of the children, Beaumont strikes Stark's arm with a typewriter, the tool with which Beaumont creates his high-culture literature, foiling Stark's will and affirming Beaumont's mastery. The sparrows peck Stark to pieces, uncreating him, and fly the fragments out of the home and into a hole or portal in the sky, a symbolic return to a womb that is also a tomb.[30] However, the containment and repair of the threats and ruptures connected to Stark may not be as successful as they appear.

For instance, Browning views the closure regarding Thad's post–George creative trajectory as incomplete: "The plot ends before we see the kinds of more worthy, literary work that Beaumont can now produce, but there is little sense that it will be more interesting" (181). One might see this observation as gesturing to lack of resolution of the tension in which Thad's role as patriarch seems to inhibit the full expression of his creativity and, more broadly, his will. A more significant lack of closure, however, may lie in the incomplete containment and repair effected by the sparrows, those "messenger[s] between life and death," the former of which is associated with the Beaumont family and their children and latter of which is associated with Stark and queer negativity (M. Browning 178). Williams posits a direct cause-and-effect relationship between Thad's loss of George-the-persona as an outlet for resentments stemming from his "commitment to the full-time role of devoted father" and the asexual birth of George from the grave (*Cinema* 168). Will George's second death, then, have the desired effect of Thad's unconditional acceptance of this role? Williams casts doubt on "any positive outcome," citing Thad's use of a pencil against George and the resemblance of Thad's "final threat" to "Stark's own speech" (170). Even if the film does not, as Williams says, explore this ambiguity, neither does it manage to entirely banish the possibility that Stark and what he represents have been temporarily repressed (again) rather than extinguished. A "healthy" subject might be imagined as in accordance with itself and its will, but at the same time, the will always preserves "wiggle room, ... the room to deviate" (Ahmed, *Willful* 81, 191). The sovereignty of the subject, or its fantasy, involves "normativity's will to social closure and coherence" (Berlant and Edelman loc. 269). There is always nevertheless room for deviation, as "the structuring incoherences that queer the self as the center of consciousness, and so of a pseudo-sovereignty, remain unavailable to the subject except in rare moments of traumatic encounter" (9). The traumatic encounter referenced by Edelman is unbearable (sexual) enjoyment, but encounter with (the product of) queer reproduction can serve the same function. If life entails "the repetitive working through" of what doesn't work or works only provisionally (11), including "happiness" and mastery of the incoherence of the subject, and if Stark acts as the instrument of that working through, then there seems in fact little chance that we have seen the end of George.[31]

Phillips groups *The Dark Half* with *Monkey Shines* and *Bruiser* as the middle work in a "'minor' trilogy" that pits norms against desires at the site of the body, including the doubled body (56). All three of these films also resonate with issues of white male privilege and its consequences (58), although *Bruiser* is the only one to take these issues as its primary focus. In doing so, it not only continues the concerns present in *The Dark Half* with selfhood and masculinity (and particularly, in *Bruiser*, masculinity in crisis), but it does so in a way that strongly invites narcissistic masculine spectatorship.

11

"The New (White) Face of Terror"

White Male Victimization in Bruiser

CAIN MILLER

Bruiser (2000), the last film that George A. Romero made that was not part of his *Dead* franchise, remains one of his more obscure titles due to it not receiving a theatrical release. Adapted from Romero's original screenplay, *Bruiser* tells the story of Henry Creedlow (Jason Flemyng), a disparaged employee for a fashion magazine company (aptly titled *Bruiser*) who one morning awakens to find that his face has transformed into a featureless white mask. What ensues is a violent revenge fantasy in which the "faceless" vigilante disposes of those who mistreated him, including his unfaithful wife, bullying boss and money-laundering best friend. Kendall Phillips argues that *Bruiser* is the third installment of Romero's unofficial "body-as-site-of-contest" trilogy, preceded by *Monkey Shines* (1988) and *The Dark Half* (1993), all of which feature white male protagonists who manifest their insidious desires into sentience (53).

As argued in the chapters on *Monkey Shines* (Chapter 8) and *The Dark Half* (Chapter 10), the protagonists' desires are projected into separate Othered beings with Ella and George Stark (Timothy Hutton), respectively. Yet the significance of *Bruiser* lies in how the protagonist's desires (specifically his feelings of emasculation) are not channeled into a detached body but into his own body. The focus of bodily contest in *Bruiser* is not projection, but transformation. By situating Henry and his repressed desires as one unit, *Bruiser* marks the white male as Other. This theme of white Otherness relates to the trend of white male oppression stressed in many media texts of that era. This chapter will analyze how *Bruiser* represents, and potentially critiques, the mode of

1990s white male victimization media, how this victimization relates to narcissistic spectatorship, and how whiteness is constructed as ideology in relation to masculinity.

The 1990s and White Male Victimization

The 1990s witnessed a continuation of the neo-conservative sentiments of the prior decade, as many reactionary pundits directed particular ire at the third-wave feminist movement. Unsurprisingly, third-wave feminism's attention to the intersection of social factors like race, class and sexuality was largely viewed as an attack on the white patriarch. Consequently, masculinity was (once again) believed to be in crisis. This rhetoric is perhaps best exemplified in Rush Limbaugh's infamous coining of the term "feminazi," an obviously derogatory expression that equates feminism with fascism in an effort to situate men as the *actual* oppressed ones. These themes were largely expressed in the decade's trend of "white male victimization" films. Latham Hunter provides insight into this trend, arguing that 1990s cinema frequently features "disempowered" white men who seemingly lose their individualism within larger corporate structures. This trend includes films like *Falling Down* (1993), *In the Company of Men* (1997), *American Beauty* (1999), *Office Space* (1999) and *Fight Club* (1999), all of which portray men as "victimized" and situate violence or misogyny as an adequate compensation for their emasculation (72).

Building on Yvonne Tasker's work on spectatorship and the male action hero, Hunter further notes how the protagonist's victimization invites the male viewer to identify with him in their shared feelings of impotence (75). Hunter additionally argues how the ambiguity of the protagonists' names, such as the unnamed narrator of *Fight Club*, encourages the male viewer to project himself into these on-screen victimized roles (77). Horror was no exception to this trend, as films like *Misery* (1990), *Jacob's Ladder* (1990), *Spontaneous Combustion* (1990), *Thinner* (1996), *The Dentist* (1996) and *American Psycho* (2000) all emphasize physical and/or mental male suffering, a contrast to the genre's expected punishment of women.[1] Furthermore, as demonstrated in *Misery*, *Thinner* and *The Dentist*, these men are often victims at the hands of women.

And yet these films are often read less as glorifications of toxic masculinity and more as satirical takedowns of white male oppression fantasies, specifically through their critiques of these supposedly victimized men. *American Psycho* provides a morbid skewering of patriarchal capitalism as investment banker Patrick Bateman's (Christian Bale) striving for hegemonic masculinity quite literally drives him insane. *Fight Club* depicts the violent consequences of escalating toxic masculine behavior. The "splatstick" film *The Dentist* is less a glamorized revenge fantasy and more a tongue-in-cheek look into the depravity of the bourgeoisie, a theme that director Brian Yuzna has tackled in his other films, particularly *Society* (1989). When dentist Alan Feinstone (Corbin Bernsen) discovers that his wife has cheated on him, he exercises his anger by torturing his innocent patients. As Jon Towlson argues, Feinstone is not heroic but instead "obsessive" in maintaining control of his hegemony, symbolized in his compulsion to perfect people's teeth (194). Similar to *American Psycho*, *The Dentist* portrays a neurotic figure who turns to violence when his hegemony is threatened, but for Feinstone, his actions ultimately result in his institutionalization.

Even *Falling Down*, one of the most cited examples of this white male victimization trend, is not without satirical layers. When white-collar worker William Foster (Michael Douglas)—often referred to as "D-FENS" in reference to the letters on his license plate—feels suffocated by society's hardships, he embarks on a violent vigilante streak, mainly targeting people of color and poor and working-class individuals. On the surface, *Falling Down* could easily be read as nothing more than an updated retelling of older "white man vs. the world" films like *Dirty Harry* (1971) and *Death Wish* (1974). Yet *Falling Down* occasionally points towards a more self-reflexive revision of the vigilante narrative. Firstly, director Joel Schumacher presents the story in an overly animated, at times almost comically theatrical fashion, something not unfamiliar in Schumacher's filmography. Examples range from Foster holding a fast-food cashier at gunpoint because the restaurant stopped serving breakfast, to Foster blowing up a construction site with a rocket launcher—actions that would come across as bombastic in even the most over-the-top vigilante film. In relation to this point, the *Falling Down* characters often read as caricatures rather than real people. They include an overly frugal Korean shop owner and impulsively violent Latinx gang members.

While potentially regressive in their own right, these characters are almost cartoonish in comparison to the more straightforward racial Others in a more conventional film like *Death Wish*. Moreover, the *Falling Down* narrative is clichéd and features numerous well-worn action cinema tropes. The most notable example of this is present in Police Sgt. Martin Prendergast (Robert Duvall), who must solve one last case before retirement. These stereotypes, clichés and exaggerated actions hint that *Falling Down* is not a simple rehash of the vigilante narrative but a critique of a reactionary formula that so heavily promotes these problematic images.

The most apparent satirical element of *Falling Down* is present in Foster, a far cry from the typical vigilante protagonist. Instead of an honest family man or hard-nosed police officer—character types associated with a Charles Bronson or Clint Eastwood role—Foster is an erratic divorcee whose ex-wife has a restraining order against him. These sentiments are further emphasized in the film's most-discussed scene, where Foster confronts a neo–Nazi (Frederic Forrest) who expresses admiration for Foster's killings of minorities. In response, Foster states, "I'm an American, you're an asshole" and kills the Nazi. Many argue that this dialogue distances Foster from reactionary ideology and invites viewers' identification with him. For example, Jude Davies argues that Foster

> defines Americanness as an openness to debate and respect for diversity, against the closedness of racism and fascism. He construes America as essentially multicultural, as composed of people with diverse ethnic and gendered identities and sexual orientations. The speech distances D-FENS from patriarchal exclusivity and "masculine" closedness, and establishes him as standing up for liberal American values [149].

Davies further notes how the film's attempts to liberalize Foster are immediately diminished by his continued toxic behavior following that scene. However, this scene also provides a sense of irony as Foster seemingly does not realize that he is ideologically the same as the Nazi, as demonstrated in his attempted distinction between "American" and "asshole." After killing the Nazi, Foster steals and brandishes an army jacket from the Nazi's military surplus store, further mirroring the two characters and drawing attention to the fine line between patriotism and nationalism. This scene also serves as a critique of the glorified vigilante character and the viewers who identify with him: One would have to be a literal white supremacist to support Foster's actions.

The ending of *Falling Down* is arguably the film's most thematically uneven component, as it seemingly undermines the film's satire. When Prendergast and Foster engage in a Western-style duel, Foster is shot and killed. But his death is revealed as a staged suicide because his life insurance can now provide for his young daughter. Foster's self-sacrifice then solidifies his paternity and hegemony. But even Foster's final masculine act is skewered. As Prendergast and Foster draw their weapons, Foster reveals that he only possesses a toy water pistol. Foster's sacrifice being paired with children's iconography indicates the juvenile nature of his actions—it took Foster a violent crime spree to become the patriarch instead of fulfilling this role through non-violent, traditional fatherhood.

For a similar addressal of the intersection of whiteness and vigilante violence, one can turn to *Bruiser*. Released at the tail end of the white male victimization trend, right before depictions of American masculinity became saturated by post–9/11 anxieties, *Bruiser* features a similar narrative to many of the aforementioned films. However, like *Falling Down*, *Bruiser*'s ideological implications are, at best, muddled, as the film almost simultaneously glorifies and critiques Henry's violent vigilantism. When assessing the complexity of *Bruiser*'s themes, one must first analyze how Henry and his actions are framed in narrative context, and then relate these characteristics to the film's broader, more theoretical portrayals of whiteness and white violence.

Bruiser *and White Male Victimization*

Returning to Phillips' rhetoric on the body-as-site-of-contest trilogy, *Bruiser* indeed boasts themes of emasculation but in an arguably more direct fashion than the previous two films. The opening draws particular comparisons to *Monkey Shines*, as both films begin with their protagonists engaging in morning exercise routines while their naked lovers lie in bed, indicating the men's bodily and sexual dominance. However, while Allan Mann (Jason Beghe) loses his hegemonic masculinity due to his paralysis, *Bruiser* quickly makes it clear that Henry's masculinity is already imbalanced, as he is belittled by his wife, his co-workers, his boss and even his dog. Henry's fractured masculinity is best symbolized by his house, which is still in the process of being built. In contrast to the stable home, a common sign of hegemony, Henry's house, and thus his masculinity, is in pieces. Henry's lack of hegemonic masculinity is also displayed in his declining mental stability, as he loses himself in violent hallucinations whenever his masculinity is threatened. These hallucinations include pushing a woman under a moving train immediately after learning that he lost money in his investments and killing his wife Janine (Nina Garbiras) with an ax after discovering her infidelity. This signifies that Henry is not in control of his own body, a sign of mental castration and another mark of emasculation.

What concretely separates *Bruiser* from the other two body-as-site-of-contest films is how Henry's emasculation is channeled. In contrast to the *Monkey Shines* and *Dark Half* protagonists, who manifest their masculine anxieties into separate bodies, Henry's emasculation is manifested through his own body, a process represented through his white mask (Fig. 12). Consequently, Henry, like Ella and George Stark, is the id—the primary bringer of violence. This distinction supports Phillips' argument that *Bruiser* is partly a comment on white privilege rather than a sheer championing of violence as a response to threatened hegemony. Phillips notes that while the white men in *Monkey Shines* and *The Dark Half* must defeat other beings to regain their masculinity, Henry instead must overcome himself. Phillips elaborates:

> Henry is unable to embrace his own power and privilege and is an almost comic exaggeration of the doormat—when his wife confronts him about his unwillingness to stand up for himself, even to her, he responds: "I try my best, you know. ... There are rules." This change in his appearance, however, releases within Henry a murderous version of his white male privilege, and it cannot be ignored that his first victims are a woman of color and his wife [54–55].

The latter point is particularly noteworthy when assessing how Henry's violence is framed in connection to his whiteness. Shortly after Henry first awakens with his white face, he encounters his Latinx housekeeper, Katie (Beatriz Pizano), who steals money from his wallet. As Katie takes Henry's belongings, she talks to herself in Spanish. Henry then approaches Katie and, to her surprise, speaks Spanish in response before killing her. This exchange demonstrates the often-contradictory relationship between language and race; the use of Spanish by Katie, a woman of color, labels her as a foreign Other invading a white space, while the use of Spanish by Henry, a white native English speaker, labels him as affluent and well-educated.

This scene's inspection of white privilege is furthered when Janine

Figure 12. Henry Creedlow (Jason Flemyng) manifests his emasculation through his white mask in *Bruiser* (Le Studio Canal+, 2000).

arrives home after a night spent with Milo (Peter Stormare), Henry's boss. As she undresses to only a white bra, a sign of both literal whiteness and high-end materialism, she calls Milo and states her plan to leave Henry. Henry overhears this, though he does not impulsively kill Janine like he did Katie, despite previously fantasizing about her murder. Janine has arguably emasculated Henry much more prodigiously than Katie, but her whiteness, represented by both her skin and clothing, does not label her as an Other who must be abolished; thus, white privilege works in her favor, just as it does for Henry.

These attentions to white privilege encourage the possibility that *Bruiser* is a deconstructive satire of toxic masculinity, similar to many of the previously mentioned films. Henry's violent hallucinations draw overt connections to Patrick Bateman, a figure whose own violent fantasies are almost second to the horrific nature of his real-life misogyny and classism.[2] Romero also directly references *Taxi Driver* (1976), one of the most cited cinematic deconstructions of toxic masculinity. After committing his first two murders, Henry stands shirtless in his living room, aims a pistol in various performative poses, and recites a monologue that proclaims his drive for revenge. This pays homage to *Taxi Driver*'s notorious "You talkin' to *me*?" scene, another example of a white male, Travis Bickle (Robert De Niro), seeking to combat his emasculation through a vigilante fantasy. Henry's monologue, however, concludes with him shooting a framed picture of Pupsie, Janine's toy poodle, who is one of Henry's main nuisances and a factor that led to his violent breakdown. The overlap of Henry's violent rhetoric with the benign image of a toy poodle provides the scene with a comedic tone, seemingly drawing attention to the juvenile irrationality of Henry's actions.[3]

Henry's privilege is also apparent in how he faces no consequences for his killing spree. Even after he admits to his killings on a public radio show, he is never apprehended. This is a stark contrast to Katie, one of the film's few people of color, who is immediately killed for a much lesser crime. When Henry is caught on camera during his murder of Janine, police still hesitate to prosecute him, as they instead suspect Rosemary (Leslie Hope), Milo's wife. Thus, Henry's privileged position as a white male conceals him—his white mask acts as a literal disguise that grants him anonymity and absolves him of repercussions.

This connection of whiteness and violence is evident in the film's poster. The right side of the artwork features an extreme close-up of Henry's white mask. The mask bears two red lacerations, indicating Henry's damaged hegemony. The artwork's left portion displays Henry's silhouette brandishing a knife as he approaches a cityscape while the red text above him reads "Meet the new face of terror." The pairing of these images frames Henry not as a masculine savior but a predatory figure—he mirrors the antagonistic Others of more conventional vigilante films who lurk outside of American domesticity with malicious intent.

However, this is not to say that *Bruiser*'s subtextual acknowledgment of Henry's white privilege inherently classifies it as a socially forward-thinking text, as its themes of race and gender can be complex and often contradictory. Firstly, Henry's placement as the id is undermined by the genuine sympathy his character exudes. Before he is taken over by the mask, Henry is the proverbial "nice guy." He shows affection for his wife, places too much trust in his friends, condemns Milo's chauvinism in the workplace, and is seemingly the only person to show empathy for Rosemary, who is in the process of divorcing Milo. Furthermore, Henry's niceness is paired with his underdog status (his peers constantly take advantage of him). Henry is ignored by his co-workers, belittled by Milo, dominated by his best friend Jimmy (Andrew Tarbet) who secretly embezzles money from Henry, and, as previously mentioned, is cheated on by Janine. Henry's status as an underdog makes him a possible locus of identification for the assumed white male viewer. Additionally, returning to Hunter's rhetoric, Henry's anonymous white mask serves as a blank canvas into which the male viewer can project himself, similar to the nameless characters of other white male victimization texts.

The framing of Henry as a relatable underdog also presents the film's most reactionary theme: Henry is unironically oppressed. Although the film acknowledges Henry's white privilege, his numerous hardships situate him as the primary victim, consequently justifying his killings. Moreover, the people whom Henry kills are given few, if any, redeeming qualities and are portrayed as deserving of their deaths. This distinction distances *Bruiser* from the more satirical white male victimization films. In contrast to *Falling Down*'s possible comment on white male fragility by framing Foster's violence as a response to trivial inconveniences, *Bruiser* situates Henry as a masculine savior who rightfully rids society of immoral persons. This final point is particularly noteworthy when assessing the film's relation to spectatorship and how it complicates the typical sadism expected of horror viewership.

Bruiser *and Dual Spectatorship*

When assessing how spectatorship relates to white male victimization, one might assume that this trend solely encourages narcissistic

projection, yet this is often not the case because these films rarely feature signifiers of narcissistic identification such as point-of-view shots
or glamorizations of the male physique. Some of the most popular white
male victimization films, such as *Taxi Driver*, *Fight Club* and *American Psycho*, even purposefully distort narcissistic pleasure by obscuring where the protagonist's reality ends and violent fantasies begin.[4]
With regard to the latter detail, *Bruiser* contrasts these films. While
Henry experiences violent fantasies, the film uses choppy editing and a
loud non-diegetic score to indicate when he snaps in and out of reality,
thus providing a more stable protagonist with whom viewers can identify. Although *Bruiser* detaches itself from the white male victimization
trend, its politics of spectatorship relate it to another violent subgenre:
the slasher.

At its core, *Bruiser* indeed boasts many slasher conventions. The
film's forementioned poster even alludes to this, as Henry's silhouette
brandishes a phallic knife despite his character never actually using one.
Consequently, *Bruiser* draws upon the masculine pleasures of slasher
spectatorship. Firstly, Henry presents a narcissistic model through both
his identification-inviting persona and his assertion of power through
violence. Secondly, Henry invites sadistic pleasure through his killings of those who emasculated him—a sentiment that likely resonated
with male viewers who shared Henry's feelings of victimization due to
real-life emasculating "threats" like third-wave feminism. However,
Henry's status as a victim also invites a layer of masochistic pleasure
for the male viewer. As discussed in Chapter 4, horror cinema often
does not offer clear-cut narcissistic identification for male viewers due
to its lack of stoic patriarchal figures. On one level, Henry indeed invites
traditional narcissistic identification because he kills those involved
in crime or sexual promiscuity—threats to his hegemony. Yet at the
same time, Henry does not represent the patriarch due to his diminished hegemonic masculinity. The only patriarchal character present is
Milo, the well-off corporate executive, though his evident position as
the boorish antagonist hardly invites narcissistic projection.[5]

Instead of patriarchal power, Henry's masculinity is asserted
through compensatory violence, as it is a response to his lack of hegemony. It is this distinct lack of hegemony that also presents masochistic pleasure because Henry's supposed oppression invites the male
viewer to share in his suffering. However, in contrast to more conventional masochistic pleasure in horror, which, as Barbara Creed argues,
features the male identifying with the feminized monster, Henry presents a duality in spectatorship in that he simultaneously provides masochistic and narcissistic pleasure ("Dark" 120–23). His whiteness is

contradictory—he must be simultaneously oppressed *and* superior. This dual whiteness is symbolized by Henry's face. On one layer, Henry possesses his human face, which is associated with his emasculation. On another layer, Henry possesses his white mask, which represents his violent authority. Furthermore, although Henry's mask signifies his power, it also makes his victimization apparent. Upon first realizing his facial transformation, Henry attempts to forcefully remove the mask and cuts his face in the process. Later, when Henry kills Janine, she scratches his face, leaving several red lesions. These mark Henry with the "wound," indicating that his white hegemony is damaged. Later, Henry even paints his mask with an assortment of non-white colors, symbolically marking himself as a person of color, and thus an oppressed figure. This dual spectatorship heightens *Bruiser*'s slasher classification. Slasher villains, while violently masculine, are often bullied outcasts whose ostracism serves as the reason for their killings. Moreover, like slasher villains, Henry's "doubling" of whiteness allows him to act as both the id and the superego. He is violent, yet characters like Milo, Janine and Katie (the non–American, the overly sexual woman and the person of color) are depicted as the actual Others who must be eradicated.

Of course, the slasher film also invites other forms of spectatorship. Carol J. Clover notably argues that the male spectator identifies not with the antagonist but with the "final girl" who ultimately prevails (35–41). *Bruiser* subtly invites this identification. Shortly after his murder of Katie, Henry travels to his office to catch Janine and Milo in their affair. Through a point-of-view shot, the camera dollies down a hallway before arriving at Milo and Janine having intercourse. However, the film then cuts to a reaction shot of Rosemary catching them in the act, indicating that the point-of-view shot was from her perspective. This subversion provides another sense of dual narcissistic and masochistic pleasure. The male viewer can narcissistically project himself into Rosemary because she is the final girl. Rosemary has short hair and dresses conservatively, common features in these masculinized characters. These characteristics also relate to Rosemary's role as the "virgin," as her sexual freedom is negated through Milo's infidelity. In this scene specifically, Rosemary's status as the virgin is stressed through her contrast to the "whore," Janine, who is first displayed through fetishistic scopophilia and then expectedly killed by Henry as punishment. Rosemary also brandishes a common icon of the final girl, a phallic symbol, represented by the camera that she uses to photograph Milo and Janine.[6] Outside of this scene, Rosemary's position as the final girl is stressed in the conclusion, as she is the only major character to survive Henry's onslaught, a gift granted to her as a result of her sexual suppression. Yet Rosemary also presents masochism for the viewer. Most evidently, Rosemary naturally possesses the wound which, similar to Henry's facial cuts, signifies her lack of power. Also similar to Henry, Rosemary is an oppressed figure. She is overlooked at work (even by her own husband, Milo), caught in a tumultuous marriage, and even briefly pursued by police due to her connection to Henry's murders. Even Rosemary's possession of the camera is only used to capture evidence to expedite her divorce, thus somewhat diluting the object's power, given that it only further progresses Rosemary's hardship.

The concept of dual spectatorship is not uncommon in Romero's work. Given his penchant for casting women and people of color in leading roles, viewers of his films often project themselves into characters who actively command the narrative yet are also tormented. Examples include the metaphorical racism Ben (Duane Jones) endures in *Night of the Living Dead* (1968) and the misogyny experienced by Joan (Jan White) and Sarah (Lori Cardille) in *Jack's Wife* (1973) and *Day of the Dead* (1985) respectively. Indeed, the supernatural horrors that terrorize these characters are practically secondary to the very real oppressions that they face. And it is this point that makes *Bruiser* and the other body-as-site-of-contest films appear obtrusive in Romero's filmography: They all tell stories of upper-class white men whose perils pale in comparison to those of the aforementioned marginalized characters. Henry's closest analogue in another Romero character is perhaps the titular Martin (John Amplas) who also provides both narcissistic and masochistic pleasure through his simultaneous role as the victim and victimizer. However, Martin's masochism is the result of far more egregious oppressions when compared to Henry, as Martin experiences extreme classism and coded homophobia. This comparison relates to the final question regarding *Bruiser*'s dual spectatorship: Why would its male viewer need both narcissism and masochism? In the context of Peter Hutchings' work, the male spectator enjoys masochistic horror because his masculinity will be reaffirmed once the film concludes and he returns to his patriarchal order (91–92). However, this concept seemingly does not apply to the spectators of *Bruiser* who returned to a reality in which, according to them, their masculinity was under attack. Consequently, while *Bruiser* provides sadistic pleasure through its revenge fantasy, the masochistic pleasure derived from Henry's oppression works to reaffirm the viewer's own feeling of victimization.

This sentiment is stressed in the film's conclusion. After Henry's face returns to normal following his killing of Milo, he leaves his corporate lifestyle and becomes an office mail clerk. Having abandoned his hegemony, Henry now bears tie-dye clothing and grown-out hair and is noticeably happier. However, when he is confronted by a belligerent corporate higher-up, he turns around to reveal that he has once again donned the white mask. As Henry stares into the camera, this freeze frame serves as the film's final image. In this conclusion, the male viewer receives masochistic pleasure in Henry's emasculation and sadistic pleasure knowing that he will once again resort to compensatory violence. For further analysis of *Bruiser*'s intersections of race, gender and violence, one must turn to the film's broader theoretical constructions of whiteness.

Constructions of Whiteness in Bruiser

Arguably the biggest thematic detractor in *Bruiser* is its essentialist portrayals of race and gender, as it often relies on well-worn stereotypes. But unlike the intentionally bombastic *Falling Down*, *Bruiser* does little to critique these caricatures and consequently operates on rudimentary understandings of race and gender, a notable differentiation from Romero's other work. This essentialism is apparent in the opening scene. As Henry enacts his morning routine, he listens to a distraught man call in to a radio show. The caller laments his inability to afford his inherited house due to taxes. The caller shows particular distress that he cannot leave the house to his son, signifying his inability to maintain the hegemonic head-of-the-household position. The caller then shoots himself on air.[7] Although the caller's race is never revealed, due to the natural invisibility of whiteness, he is assumed to be white. This monologue is paired with the image of Henry who, after staring at himself in the bathroom mirror, fantasizes shooting himself, connecting him to the caller. As Henry looks at his reflection, he sees himself in the anguished caller who also suffers from emasculation. Henry then, like the caller, believes himself to be better off dead than without hegemony.

The connection of these two characters establishes a sense of white male unity, a theme that proceeds to dominate the rest of the narrative.[8] This theme is immediately stressed when Henry discusses the caller's suicide first with Janine and then with his female co-workers, both of whom dryly respond with "It takes all kinds," a sentiment that outwardly disparages men's feelings of victimization. These interactions establish a dichotomy in which the women of *Bruiser* are callous while the men are degraded yet sympathetic. Henry eventually finds solace in Tom (Jeff Monahan), a fellow white male co-worker. Henry and Tom bond over their statuses as doormats. Their unity is further stressed in a later scene where Tom, after witnessing Janine's murder, states he cannot report Henry to the authorities because Henry might be the "best friend" he has ever had, despite the fact that the two barely know each other outside of work and only affiliate over their mutual meagerness.

The only inkling of satire is found in Milo, whose virility is exaggerated. Milo smokes oversized cigars, flashes his genitals to his co-workers, and engages in affairs with the magazine's potential models; he is perhaps a parody of toxic masculinity and is undeniably framed as the antagonist. The clear criticism of Milo's behavior is most apparent in his introductory scene, in which he chooses a model for the next cover of *Bruiser*. After looking through the photographs, Milo scoffs at the numerous white models and states, "We've seen this face a hundred times before, haven't we?" Milo's dialogue draws attention to the ambiguity associated with whiteness, the very same ambiguity that later allows Henry to succeed in his killings. Milo ultimately chooses the model identified as Number 9 (Marie V. Cruz), the only woman of color, because he believes she will stand out amongst the magazine's "white bread." Milo proceeds to fetishize the model by kissing her picture and calling her "perfect." When Milo asks if the model is a "chink or Jap," Rosemary and Tom retort that she is American and of Korean and Dominican descent, to which Milo responds by labeling the model a "spick-nip." Milo's excessively derogatory behaviors indeed point to satirical subtext, as he could easily be compared to a Patrick Bateman or William "D-FENS" Foster. This scene even specifically critiques the countless American entertainment industries that profit off of their appropriation of ethnic bodies.

However, *Bruiser* once again contradicts itself in that it abides by the very same racial objectification it supposedly critiques. When model Number 9 enters the narrative, she is first portrayed in a skimpy bikini at Milo's pool party, not given any dialogue, and instead placed in the gaze of Tom and Milo, who remark on her attractiveness. Here, Number 9 is only an objectified image, similar to the aforementioned scene in which she only appeared as a photograph.[9] Her only other significant scene appears later, in which she is fully naked and gives Tom oral sex in his hot tub, and is again placed in the gaze of two white men, Tom and Henry, the latter voyeuristically watching from afar. When model Number 9 is finally given dialogue, she comes across as stereotypically ditzy. This is an example of the hackneyed archetype where an attractive ethnic woman is portrayed as infantile in order to symbolize (and eroticize) her sexual inexperience.

On top of the film's sexual objectification of non-white bodies, *Bruiser* also incorporates brash generalizations of these identities. In the climax, which is set in an elaborate masquerade hosted by Milo, model Number 9 dresses as a geisha, an icon of Japanese culture. Despite the model's Korean heritage, *Bruiser* opts to compound all Asian identities into one category, and Number 9 is consequently reduced to a broad racial Other.[10] Even Milo is subjected to racial-ethnic generalization. Although he is recognized as white, he is not American. Milo is a former Communist refugee, though his country of origin is never clarified. Consequently, Milo is simply categorized as a person of vaguely Eastern European descent.[11] His skin might be white, but he is nonetheless a foreign Other—a contrast to the blond-haired, blue-eyed Henry. This is an example of the common double standard America has historically held in regard to the intersection of whiteness and nationality, as demonstrated in the prejudice displayed against Eastern European immigrants in the late 1800s and early 1900s, and the Irish immigrants before them.

The most unfortunate component of *Bruiser*'s reactionary depictions of race is just how sharply it goes against Romero's previous tacklings of the topic. In his landmark 1988 essay "White," Richard Dyer uses *Night of the Living Dead* as an example of a deconstructive text that subverts many racist ideologies expected of the horror genre. Dyer notes how *Night* situates whiteness and monstrosity as one and the same. This is best exemplified in an aerial shot showcasing what are first assumed to be zombies but are revealed to be white vigilantes ("White" 60). White monstrosity is also portrayed in the conclusion when the vigilantes murder the black protagonist Ben. This ending offers a bleak comment on the endless hardships that white supremacy thrusts upon people of color. It is not the masses of undead who kill Ben, but instead fellow (white) humans whose violence may or may not have been racially motivated. The film's closing images layered over the credits stress this point, as the vigilante mob's burning of the dead bodies exhibits an uncanny resemblance to lynching photographs, one of the most infamous examples of using visual media to purport the dominance of white masculinity. Dyer further notes how *Night*'s most transgressive element is perhaps its portrayal of bodily control. Not only are the white zombies not in control of their own bodies, but they are also not in control of Ben, the black body. This theme opposes America's history of white figures exploiting black bodies. Dyer notes that this "fear of not being able to control other bodies," specifically the exploitation of non-white bodies for capitalist purposes, is where the film's true horror lies (63). *Bruiser*, in contrast, uses whiteness to demonstrate a person being in greater control of their body, as it is Henry's obtaining of the white mask that leads to him regaining his masculinity.

Further building on Dyer's work, we see that *Bruiser* also displays the three theoretical concepts through which whiteness is constructed, those being Christianity, "race" and imperialism. Firstly, whiteness is embodied through Christ and Mary. They are models of whiteness; however, the divinity they represent can never be achieved. In Dyer's words, this presents a "dynamic of aspiration" where one strives for transcendence and this striving is displayed through "suffering, self-denial and self-control" (*White* 17). This process creates expectations for the "white ideal" (17). For men, they must mirror Christ, whose masculinity is defined by his bodily suffering, a feat that allows for his transcendence (28). For women, they must mirror Mary, whose whiteness is equated with beauty, and whose transcendence is defined by her virginity (74). Secondly, whiteness is defined by "race" as a social construct, as people of color are often reduced to their bodies. White people, however, do not experience this reduction because the invisibility of whiteness separates it from cultural expectations and assumptions connected to "race" (14–15). This creates a white–non-white dichotomy in which whiteness is unremarked upon. Lastly, whiteness can be defined by imperialism, specifically through the exploitation of non-white (or even, in some cases, white) bodies (15). In *Bruiser*, Henry demonstrates all three embodiments of whiteness.

Henry's Christ-like presence is best stressed through his symbolic death and rebirth. At first, Henry seemingly bears the burden of mankind through his victimization. This is visually signified when he paints a black cross on the forehead of his white mask, indicating that he literally carries the cross. He is even betrayed by a Judas-like companion in Jimmy. Henry then "dies" through his suicide fantasy only for him to be reborn with his white mask. As previously mentioned, Henry's suicide fantasy is mirrored with the real on-air suicide over the radio. This connection provides a sense of publicity to Henry's fantasy, similar to the theatrical, exposed nature of a crucifixion. Henry's transfiguration also situates Rosemary (as her name suggests) as Mary because she created the original mold for Henry's mask; thus, she births him without the need for sex. Lastly, Henry is juxtaposed with the sinful Milo who, in the masquerade climax, is fittingly dressed as Satan.

Milo is also significant in that his comparison to Henry highlights how the film constructs "race" and whiteness. *Bruiser* strictly abides by the white–non-white binary, as Henry's white mask firmly situates everyone else as Others who must be eradicated. This dichotomy is also stressed in the forementioned theme of white male unity, as it enforces a strict "Us vs. Them" narrative. Consequently, this dichotomy also demonstrates how *Bruiser* constructs whiteness through imperialism. In the climax, Henry subdues Milo, attaches him to a wiring system, displays his body in front of numerous partygoers, and uses a laser to castrate Milo before killing him. Henry's imperialist whiteness is showcased in his public destruction of Milo's foreign body. This scene draws comparisons to the concluding lynching imagery of *Night*, although *Bruiser* utilizes this iconography to reinforce white superiority, not critique it.

Through this framework, *Bruiser* draws comparisons to *Vanilla Sky* (2001), a film released one year later. But while Cameron Crowe's film situates the white mask as a signifier of suffering—protagonist David Aames (Tom Cruise) dons a mask to hide his scarred face, representative of his damaged hegemony—*Bruiser* never seeks to hide Henry's victimization because, as previously noted, the large red scars covering his mask make his feelings of oppression bluntly apparent to both characters and viewers; Henry is performing both his masculinity and his victimization. This notion of performing masculinity-victimization is best showcased during the masquerade climax, specifically due to the scene's direct homage to *The Phantom of the Opera* (1925) in having Henry wear a black cape, black hat and (significantly) another white mask covering his facial mask. This scene draws comparisons to the masculine performativity of Lon Chaney, a figure who consistently channeled America's post–World War I bodily emasculation anxieties through his deformed characters.[12] As Gaylyn Studlar notes, "Chaney's extraordinary, grotesque physicality came to represent a masculine difference that turned him into a suffering object. ... On-screen, Chaney starred in films whose plots were often lurid meditations on the disabled or pain-racked male bodies" (201). *Phantom* perhaps provides the most apt example of this given that the Phantom (Chaney) must compensate for his deformity and ostracization through theatrical displays of public violence. By channeling the Phantom, Henry also displays these violent compensatory masculinities in response to his oppression, as displayed through his execution of Milo. But Henry's emasculation is far from the severity of that experienced by the Phantom. While the Phantom wears his mask to conceal his disfigured face—the symbol of America's "wound" in the post-war era—Henry's mask only conceals his facial mask, which is scarred and painted, markings that were largely his own doing. Thus, the mask that Henry wears in the climax does not "mask" any genuine suffering, but rather only hides his own fabricated victimization.

With only a straight-to-video distribution, the release of *Bruiser* garnered little attention. What few critical reviews it received were only mildly positive, as some did appreciate its attempts at parody and black humor. Yet *Bruiser*'s narrative incoherence often muddles any potentially satirical qualities. At times it comes across as a cartoonish

mocking of white male fragility like many of the aforementioned cinematic examples. Henry's white mask could indeed be read as an exaggerated mode of white masculine performativity, as his mask allows
him to reap the benefits of his privilege without consequence. Will Dodson shares this reading in his comparison of the film to *Jack's Wife*, noting how both films revolve around oppressed characters and how said
characters' violent acts stem from their "[s]ocial entrapment" within
"traditional gender roles as conditioned by American capitalism and
the punishing echoes of Puritanism" (14). Dodson further notes how
both films point to larger systemic issues given that both characters
"find themselves back in the same cycle of anonymous conformity they
sought to escape" (15). This is indeed the case with *Bruiser's* ending
since Henry, despite his violent rages against the structures that oppress
him, is ultimately still confined to the corporate lifestyle.

However, *Bruiser* carries a tone of haughty nihilism that contrasts
the more general pessimism associated with Romero's other work. Tony
Williams provides further reasoning for this tonal shift: He posits that
Henry's feelings of inadequacy are perhaps representative of Romero's own struggles to find commercial success throughout the 1990s, as
Romero was widely viewed as a has-been whose radical films couldn't
translate to the corporate, blockbuster-driven American film industry
that replaced the New Hollywood (*Cinema* 172). In some ways *Bruiser*
feels like a manifestation of Romero's own feelings of victimization as
a result of working for an industry that had seemingly left him behind.
Indeed, whatever social commentary *Bruiser* attempts to make is largely
overshadowed by its derogatory stereotypes, outdated gender politics,
and uncomfortable racial subtext, consequently marking it as one of
the rare socially regressive films in Romero's catalogue. After *Bruiser*,
Romero returned to his more marketable zombie films, concluding his
career by making *Land of the Dead* (2005), *Diary of the Dead* (2007) and
Survival of the Dead (2009).

Conclusion

From Amusement *to* Evil

This volume concludes its examination of the non-zombie films written and/or directed by George A. Romero by looking at a pair of anomalous works in his oeuvre. The short work *The Amusement Park* (1973) had been seen by a negligible number of people until the George A. Romero Foundation oversaw its restoration and release 48 years after its creation. It provides an early example of Romero blending the concern with sociopolitical and socioeconomic commentary that is evident right from the opening minutes of *There's Always Vanilla* with elements of the horror genre through which much of that commentary would be delivered throughout his career.

A quarter of a century later, in 1998, Romero wrote a script for a film adaptation of the video game *Resident Evil*. His version was rejected in favor of one eventually written and directed by Paul W.S. Anderson and released in 2002. The available draft of Romero's script engages with themes that recur throughout his work, such as critiques of gender inequality and capitalist exploitation. In addition to alluding to genre films such as *Aliens*, Romero's *Resident Evil* occupies a unique place as a Romero-authored adaptation of a heavily Romero-influenced text, which it acknowledges with at least one direct reference to *Night of the Living Dead*.

The sometimes-caustic critiques of individual, domestic, and civic life—both separately and in conjunction with one another—that characterize, as we have seen, Romero's work and its telos can also make it uncomfortable to confront their thematics, which may grate on a population that currently appears consumed by partisanship over ethics. In a 2016 interview, Romero posited that the film industry had become less receptive to overtly sociopolitical zombie projects:

> I don't think you could make *Night of the Living Dead* now. You certainly can't pitch it. ... I thought *Dawn of the Dead* was a pie in the

203

face to consumers, but people say there's this underlying message of anti-consumerism in it. I think it's way upfront. The only way you could make a film like this is to hide the message—unless it's a message that is currently acceptable. You cannot pitch an idea the way I did. It would not get financed [Kohn].

The year before, Romero lamented in another interview that the zombie renaissance of the 2000s had abandoned social commentary for escapism, saying that his reason for making zombie films "was social satire of some kind, and I don't find any of that any more. *Walking Dead* is purely a soap opera and the rest is an entertainment, purely an entertainment" (Kiang). Whether one agrees with these analyses or not, they underscore key facets of Romero's overarching vision, one that seems incommensurate with the auto-consumerism of middlebrow cinematic adaptations of video games. He has a very different and very real definition of evil that is interpersonal, moral and ultimately resident within rather than external to humanity.

Keeping It Too Real: The Amusement Park

The conclusion that people are the real monsters is a commonplace of horror cinema, and in Romero's zombie films, it is both figuratively and literally true; his non-zombie horror films, from *The Crazies* to *Bruiser*, make use of it as well. The type of individual and social critiques (of greed, of capitalism, of gender normativity, of the patriarchal family, etc.) that appear in such films via threat and monstrosity appear as well in *The Amusement Park*, rendering it horror adjacent even if its monstrosity is figurative. *The Amusement Park*, which runs just under an hour, was commissioned by the Lutheran Service Society of Western Pennsylvania and the Pitcairn-Crabbe Foundation to promote better treatment of the elderly but was "never released, reportedly because the producers were horrified by the results" (McDonagh 22).

Whether or not it was actually shown at community centers as intended, the film was unavailable to the general public. Then, following a few showings for film festival and museum audiences, a restoration—made from the single scratched, faded and torn 16mm print given to the director's widow Suzanne Desrocher-Romero in 2017—debuted on the streaming service Shudder in June 2021 ("Reviving"). Romero's public-service film is not unique in "flirt[ing] with established tropes of the horror film" (Fryers 34; see also 41–42)—the public-service film is, after all, a genre that includes warning viewers of and sometimes dramatizing death and mutilation—but it does provide an example of

Romero employing strategies of critique common to horror outside of the genre in which he would come to work for most of his career. It is closest in this, perhaps, to *Jack's Wife*, released the previous year and with which it shares a prominent use of quick cuts. *Jack's Wife* similarly uses some of the tropes and tone of horror to critique the position and treatment of a marginalized population, women rather than the elderly, without itself being a horror film. Such hybridization helps to enact the type of defamiliarization advocated by Viktor Shklovskii: "The purpose of art is to impart the sensation of things as they are perceived and not as they are known. The technique of art is to make objects 'unfamiliar,' to make forms difficult, to increase the difficulty and length of perception because the process of perception is an aesthetic end in itself and must be prolonged" (72). In rendering the familiar strange, Romero puts this aesthetic perception in the service of moral perception.

The Amusement Park, written by Walton Cook, was shot in three days and stars a pre–*Martin* Lincoln Maazel ("Reviving"). It begins with a preface, delivered by the 70-year-old Maazel, about the marginalization of the elderly. As Maazel walks through a deserted amusement park on an overcast day, his prologue invokes "the many problems and frustrations of the world as it is today" and includes age with "levels of income, environmental deprivation [and] geographical accident" as reasons for individual rejection by and inability to participate meaningfully in society. Maazel also notes that the "supporting players" in the film are volunteers and that the older volunteers are people "living in institutions, in lower-income housing areas, or in city slums." From the start, then, the film contextualizes the lack of adequate support and compassion for the elderly within a larger network of social ills, especially those related to capitalism.[1] The prologue further observes that viewers have already been "preached" to and are familiar with the statistics regarding these struggles of old age, so the approach of *The Amusement Park* is to make the viewers "feel the problem, to experience it" in order to spur direct action. In other words, it renders textual what is subtextual in much of Romero's work.[2]

Horror conventions provide touches that work towards this goal of having the audience "feel the problem." The fictional part of the film is marked by an opening credits sequence that includes quick flashes of red, followed by a panning shot that reveals Maazel as an exhausted-looking, bloodied, bandaged man in a white suit, holding a cane and seated in an entirely white room with white folding chairs. A neatly groomed version of himself then enters, *sans* cane, and asks if the first man wants to talk, do something or go outside. The beaten version of the man asserts more than once that there is "nothing" outside, failing to prevent his double from leaving to see for himself even as his "nothing" imagines the space of American society as apocalyptic.[3]

Outside the void, an existential purgatory to which the protagonist will return in the end as the physically and mentally beaten version of himself to enact the other half of the same conversation from the opening scene, the crowds are often shot tight and from about hip level, creating a feeling of disorientation and claustrophobia. In wide shots from above, those teeming masses cannot help but recall a zombie horde. Quick, jarring cuts abound; at one point, a passenger on a miniature train suddenly wears a monster mask (or perhaps has become a monster), while at others we see a creepy sad clown with a bandaged head and catch brief glimpses of the Grim Reaper. One of these glimpses occurs during a sequence in which the crowds suddenly vanish, leaving the park disorientingly silent and empty except for a small clock in the middle of the thoroughfare. The protagonist is then beaten and robbed by a trio of bikers with weapons, who, having dismounted, approach him in a short series of jerky jump cuts, lending them an unnatural air.[4]

After the beating, the crowds instantaneously re-materialize to look in passing at but fail to help the protagonist. Subsequently, rows of canes, wheelchairs and medical supplies are panned across in a way that lends them an air of threatening overwhelmingness, similar to the crowd; and a physical therapy room (into which the protagonist is bodily pushed by people assuring him that it is "fun" and he will "like it") is presented with quick cuts among extreme close-ups and a whining buzz that increases in volume, investing the space with a panicky oppressiveness, if not suggesting a kind of torture chamber.

The uncanny experiences of the protagonist are tied throughout the film to a critique of the harsh conditions of old age under capitalism. The roller coaster requires a yearly minimum income and doesn't accept credit; a fender bender on the bumper cars (featuring a cameo by Romero as the driver who runs into an elderly couple) results in the older drivers involved unable to afford their motor vehicle insurance any longer (we later see the one leading the other atop a horse); and, in a segment that plays a bit like a silent comedy sketch, a rich man is served lobster and has his chair and table turned by waiters so that he does not have to see the protagonist, who can afford only French fries and some hard-to-identify chunks of meat in sauce.

Based on their incomes, the elderly are denied dignity and quality of life by means of an artificial Malthusian crisis manufactured in a place where there are plenty of resources to go around. However, the horrors produced are also notably intersectional. While the protagonist and, for instance, the young couple to whom a fortune teller reveals a bleak future of inadequately maintained rental housing and inadequate medical care in their old age are white, *The Amusement Park*, perhaps because it is peopled with volunteers reflecting the actual makeup of the community in which the film was made, features a large number of people of color as well. The three people in line before and the two after the protagonist to sell their possessions to the (white) ticket agent for less than they think that they are worth are all black. Black men, women and children appear throughout the park, including prominently in front of the roller coaster, and a black man takes the protagonist's seat at the "restaurant" table when he decides to share his food. At least one black and one white couple respond to the protagonist waving them over and the waiters try to shoo all of these undesirable low-income people away as they snatch at the unappealing food. The authority figures who fail or actively exploit the elderly include the ticket agent; the police officer responding to the bumper car collision; the priests who ignore a woman who needs help with a coffin-like crate to carry their own Bible as if it were a two-man job and who go on break from their "sanctuary" tent just when the protagonist arrives; various members of the medical profession who at best offer a literal Band-Aid; and a father-son duo who try to convince bystanders to sell their homes at a supposedly fair value while they are pickpocketed. These figures are white, reflecting white dominance of predominantly harmful social institutions.[5]

Maitland McDonagh's description of the film as "grimly entertaining and impressively on message" could serve to describe the way that many of Romero's non-zombie films function, even if the messages, as such, are less overt (22). That the film's elderly people are functionally "invisible" (except to the ticket seller, who exploits them for profit) is, for instance, reminiscent of the central conceit of *Bruiser*, with its relation of Henry's grievances to his literal facelessness (23). This dynamic also applies (at least) to Joan in *Jack's Wife* and to Allan in *Monkey Shines* following his accident. We might usefully apply Susan Sontag's evaluation of television news to these cinematic issues of visibility and invisibility. Sontag writes that the

> insistence on good taste in a culture saturated with the commercial incentives to lower standards of taste may be puzzling. But it makes sense if understood as obscuring a host of concerns and anxieties about public order and public morale that cannot be named, as well as pointing to the inability to otherwise formulate or defend traditional conventions of how to mourn. What can be shown, what should not be shown—few issues arouse more public clamor [68–69].

New Genre, Familiar Foes: Resident Evil

Decades after *The Amusement Park* used elements of horror to bring viewers into phantasmagoric confrontation with what they fail or refuse to see and, more importantly, act on, Romero's script for *Resident Evil* similarly hybridized horror tropes with a non-horror genre in the service of enacting social critique.

Resident Evil has long since become a sprawling transmedia franchise, but by the time of Romero's never-produced script, the video game series was releasing only its first sequel. While human zombies do play a role in these games, the monsters created by the Umbrella Corporation's experimentation with bio-weapons make *Resident Evil* more than a traditional zombie property, as demonstrated by the inclusion in Romero's initial draft not only of zombie sharks but also of a giant vampire plant and an enormous snake (see Romero 34, 61–62).[6] This project would have seen Romero working more in the sci-fi–action–horror vein of films such as *Aliens* (1986), which his draft recalls in places, while both returning to themes that had appeared throughout his body of work and playfully referencing his own contributions to a genre tradition that by this time had become much more mainstream.

Romero's first draft spends much of its time with a group of soldiers from S.T.A.R.S. (Special Tactics and Rescue Service, a police-affiliated special forces group in the *Resident Evil* universe) trying to fight their way out of the secret Umbrella facility concealed beneath Arkley Mansion. While one can posit an affinity in this situation with *Day of the Dead*'s military personnel in their underground bunker, there are also strong echoes of the non-zombie film *Aliens*. Romero's Alpha Team squad of 12 commandos, most of whom are killed off over the course of the script, strongly recall the Colonial Marines of James Cameron's film, including Rosie Rodriguez, "a tough, body-built" Latinx woman reminiscent of Private Vasquez (Jenette Goldstein), the tough, body-built Latinx woman of *Aliens*.[7] Meanwhile, Jill Valentine, one of the playable protagonists of the first *Resident Evil* game, evokes in at least one moment in Romero's script Sigourney Weaver's Ellen Ripley. Neither Valentine nor Ripley is a member of the military team beside whom she ends up fighting—Jill is with S.T.A.R.S.'s Bravo Team and Ripley is a sort of civilian advisor—and in *Aliens*, Ripley is kept in the dark as to the true purpose of the Marines' mission,[8] while Valentine excoriates the leader of Alpha Team, Albert Wesker, for keeping her similarly uninformed: "I lost three me[n]. ... Because I didn't know what to expect ... because you ... didn't tell me! ... I wasn't told anything!" (28, second and third ellipses in original). Finally, the xenomorphs in the *Alien* franchise famously have acid for blood, to the detriment of more than one Colonial Marine, and Romero's script contains a scene in which cylinders triggered by sensors fire vaporized acid. A number of commandos are "burned by liquid drops," and one zombie is melted. As more zombies trigger the acid, "Chris [Redfield, the other playable protagonist of the first *Resident Evil* game] and Jill are spattered. Burned" (55).

As they and the remaining commandos try to escape into the air ducts—a tactic used by characters in *Aliens* as well—an acid-splashed zombie (still alive because "the acid hasn't reached its brain yet") grabs Redfield: "Acid from the zombie's hands is burning his leg. ... He's able to hold the thing's head back, but he's stuck. ... Jill presses the barrel of her own weapon into the zombie's forehead" and fires (56). This close call resembles the *Aliens* moment when Corporal Hicks (Michael Biehn) is burned by acid when he shoots an alien that has held open the doors of an elevator as he and Ripley try to escape, and Ripley must then help the wounded soldier strip off his armor and physically support him. While these situations are similar, Valentine arguably has the heroic edge here over one of the archetypal strong female sci-fi–horror leads, as she rather than her male companion dispatches the pursuing monster. These intertextual echoes highlight how Romero's initial script uses elements of the zombie genre for which he is best known in order to create something outside of that tradition, much as he does in "The Facts in the Case of Mr. Valdemar," here hybridizing the zombie siege and sci-fi action horror traditions.

Just because Romero's *Resident Evil* would have marked a departure in genre for the filmmaker does not mean, however, that it would have departed as well from the common sociopolitical concerns in his work. As we see with Jill Valentine saving Chris Redfield, for instance, the script engages with gender normativity, a consistent feature of Romero's oeuvre beginning as far back as *Night of the Living Dead* and *There's Always Vanilla*. Jill may be the only woman on Bravo Team, but she also "ranks the highest" of its "tough Special-Forces types" (9). And Alpha Team medical officer Rebecca Chambers, a non-combatant, asserts her womanhood to a group of soldiers among whom "as worthless as a dame" functions as an insult (22). When Wesker says "Three men stay here," she objects, "I'm not a man," and Rosie Rodriguez follows up a line later with "I'm better than a man" (22).

In addition to depicting women navigating a patriarchal organization and masculine-coded spaces of combat, the first draft of the script specifies Chris Redfield as being "part Mohawk," reproducing some of the same dynamics of race, representation and colonialism as *Creepshow 2*'s "Old Chief Wood'nhead" (5). Redfield, whose name perhaps

takes on additional connotations with this characterization, is introduced feeding fish to eagles among hilltops "three-thousand feet above
the highest water" (2). "More than simply an outdoor type," the description tells us, Chris "seems perfectly in place, almost part of the environment" (2). However well-intentioned, such characterization participates
in "colonial cinematic discourse, which developed a tradition of stereotyped, objectified, romanticized, and homogenized representation of
Indigenous people" (Knopf 8). Chris also adheres to the Hollywood stereotype of the stoic Indian when he tells Jill, "Indians are never con-
fused. At least, they never let it show" (Romero 5). And, though we don't
know who would have played Chris Redfield had Romero's version of
Resident Evil been made, in the video game franchise, he is outwardly
white.

The script makes better use of indigeneity and America's settler
past in using them to critique the military-industrial complex. One
of the Bravo Team soldiers remarks of Arkley Mansion that the "area's
been 'secure' since the French and Indian War," linking Umbrella Corporation's bio-weapons experiments, which the military is aware of if
not a participant in, and the monstrosities that the experiments produce
with the (militarized) monstrosity of North America's colonial past (10).
Wesker, who turns out to be a villain and working for Umbrella, compli-
ments Redfield, "You must have been in the military, son." But Redfield
rejects this connection: "Native American. Exempted," putting the military and indigeneity into opposition and redirecting admiration from
the former to the latter (38).

The critique of the military-industrial complex appears on the very
first page of the script, with a group of unidentified individuals watching
a recording from the outbreak of monstrosity in the Umbrella research
laboratory: "We see NO FACES. But expensive WATCHES, sleeves with
high-ranking STRIPES, indicate wealth, power, and a military presence" (1). Wesker also specifically identifies Arkley Mansion as belonging to the "Feds" and eventually reveals one of the goals of research to
have been creating soldiers "who can't die" (21, 31). He also describes
Umbrella, which has been financing the experiments, as a multina-
tional "private corporation" that is "[s]o huge that they have ... connections ... in high places," clarifying, "That's why we're here" (30, ellipses
in original).

The destructive interpenetration of militarism and capitalism and
the resultant horrors serve, then, as one throughline in Romero's narrative. There are echoes of *The Crazies* in the excuse for cordoning off
Raccoon City and forcibly evacuating the residents, that a "military air-
craft, carrying live weapons, has crashed" in the nearby hills, as well as

in a soldier almost beating the local sheriff and firing on Chris Redfield in order to keep the truth secret, and in the T-virus causing all the problems having initially spread "in the water supply" of the lab (12–13, 31). The unethical animal experimentation for profit—the researcher who "developed the organism that caused all this ... did it for humanitarian purposes" and was unaware that "a separate team" was "corrupting" his research to create bio-weapons (70)—also recalls "Cat from Hell." Redfield summarizes that the true struggle is against the "kind of evil that ... resides in all of us. Makes us ... greedy, uncaring. The kind of evil that will ... wipe us out, in the end. Unless we stand up against it" and resist what another character terms "powers that have ... ruled the world since before we were born" (82, ellipses in original). Such a mission statement would be at home, as we have seen throughout this book, in the majority of Romero's works.

Romero's *Resident Evil* script also playfully alludes to that cinematic legacy. In addition to the close echo of *The Crazies* in the human-engineered virus accidentally spreading through the water supply, the fact that the virus kills the organism, "revives the brain" and then spreads through bites causes one character to exclaim, "Christ, this is like.... *Night of the Living Dead!*" (31, ellipses in original). A zombie scientist who is still writing "random, erratic marks" on a notepad displays the same dim memory of its living state as Bub in *Day of the Dead* and zombies in *Land of the Dead* and *Survival of the Dead* (33). And the realization that a "head-shot" (28) is needed to bring down the undead creatures created by the T-virus hearkens back to the sheriff's recommendation in *Night of the Living Dead*. These allusions function as acknowledgments, perhaps especially for knowledgeable horror fans, that Romero is employing to new ends the tropes that his adaptation of zombie mythology made standard in the first place. The script nods to this evolution in its description of the infected lab employees as having "turned into mindless ... ghouls" (71, ellipses in original), the term that Romero used for his version of zombies before they became known as zombies.

While Romero's *Resident Evil* was never realized, a (zombie) bite-sized piece of what might have been does exist in the form of a 1998 Romero-directed commercial for the *Resident Evil 2* video game that he filmed for the Japanese market.[9] The commercial is what led Sony Pictures to make Romero its first choice for a *Resident Evil* film (Chernov 116). In the ad, a helicopter's spotlight illuminates the front entrance of the Raccoon City Police Department as zombies spill up the front steps into the building. (We may be reminded here of *The Crazies'* final shots, in which a helicopter airlifts Colonel Peckem [Lloyd Hollar] from within a rectangle of lights, carrying him away from the failed containment of an outbreak by a symbol of the military's ostensible powers of surveillance and control.) Officer Leon Kennedy (Brad Renfro) looks down at the scene from a window and checks the remaining ammunition for his pistol. Fleeing from some zombies down a hallway lined on one side with jail cells, Kennedy comes across Claire Redfield (Adrienne Frantz), younger sister of the first *Resident Evil*'s Chris, coming through a door, and they briefly point their guns at each other. He tosses her a shotgun, and they assume defensive stances as zombies burst through a gate and encroach on them from both sides ("George").

Focusing as it does on slow-moving zombies (one of them a police officer) overrunning an enclosed space, the commercial is strongly reminiscent of Romero's *Dead* films, aside from Leon and Claire's game-accurate costumes. In this resemblance, the commercial lacks the more video game–style elements that Romero's *Resident Evil* script takes from the first game, such as colored key cards and more fantastical creatures, elements that help to move the script beyond the traditional zombie movie in the Romero tradition. In a making-of video, Romero says that the goal was for the commercial to feel like a movie, so it was produced like one. He adds that it's "great" that there is a game that is "like a flashback to that genre, and I can feel, maybe a little bit, like I had some influence on it, so I feel very flattered" ("George"). While not the full-scale genre hybrid of Romero's *Resident Evil* script, this mini-film provides a glimpse of Romero adapting an adaptation of a strain of generic tradition that he himself primarily originated and popularized.[10]

A Living Heart in a Dead World

Although the initial draft of Romero's *Resident Evil* script is, for obvious reasons, more in line with mainstream Hollywood films than some of his other work, it nevertheless failed to come to fruition. Most of the films discussed in this book did not find the same success, especially upon theatrical release, as his initial trilogy of *Dead* films. The juxtaposition of *The Amusement Park* and the script for *Resident Evil*, one relatively unseen and one unmade, separated by a quarter of a century, helps to further crystallize some of the continuities that run through Romero's work as an artist, including engagement with class, gender, greed and inequity. Romero's non-zombie films share these and related concerns with the *Dead* films for which the writer-director is more well-known and more often discussed, but perhaps, paradoxically, these themes are more palatable to wider audiences when wrapped in rotting flesh.

Approaching from a different angle, one might return to the moment of metacommentary in *The Dark Half* with which we began Chapter 10, when Thad warns, "I hope you're not looking for any social significance because there ain't none to be found." While films represent the collaborative product of a number of visions, it is nevertheless useful to note Romero's own seeming ambivalence about the social significance of his works, laying claim to certain subtexts and traces while disavowing others. In the same interview in which he calls *Dawn of the Dead* openly anti-consumerist, he asserts that *Night of the Living Dead* is not a political film, although he adds that he can see "why it seemed that way" to others: "Maybe it's because I can't erase the things that were in our minds when we were making the film. Forget race. It was all about people stuck in a situation where the world is changing outside" (Kohn). Mingled with his often-repeated denial that the film is in some way about race, however, Romero describes its engagement with what might easily be described as political issues: "It was the idea of the family unit. ... Back then, in 1968, everything was suspect—family, government, and obviously the family unit in *Night of the Living Dead* completely collapses. That's what we were focused on. I don't see the broader statements on race" (Kohn). Despite acknowledging a critique here of a domestic social institution in relation to the *polis*, the type of critique, intentional or otherwise, that recurs in his zombie and non-zombie films alike, Romero seeks to put this sociopolitical critique in terms of a coming together that is arguably less threatening than questioning the fundamental structures of American society: "The message is, '[Why] can't we just get along?' If they pulled together, they'd be OK. To that extent, that's exactly what's happening now in the United States. It's bisected. If you're a Republican, you can't vote this way, and if you're a Democratic you can't vote that way. It's garbage—just crap" (Kohn).

Additionally, Tony Williams notes Romero's "often-repeated disavowals concerning the psychoanalytic significance of his work" (*Cinema* 118). Perhaps such framing points to the difficulty in confronting the thematics of Romero's works, one which, again, grates on a population consumed by partisanship over ethics, but it also perhaps represents a simplification of the text that relates to its status as genre fiction. The majority of Romero's non-zombie films could be classified as horror, for example, and while horror fans, knowing the genre's "conventions and representations, ... actively 'read' aesthetically and thematically" (Hills 74), there also certainly exists a segment of popular film fandom vocally opposed to recognizing that art is inescapably political, an audience that champions the position "You're overthinking it; it's just a movie." Maybe we see then in Romero's accounts of his films' "significance" a reflection of the tension between a film declaring itself to be more than "just" horror or genre and avoiding what some in the audience would categorize as pretension, a tension which might map onto the conflict between commercial and independent filmmaking that marked so much of Romero's long and, yes, significant career.

Perhaps a career of challenging boundaries and social constructs and practices was not destined for mainstream commercial success, but the films that it produced leave much for scholars to investigate. In bringing fresh attention to Romero's non–*Dead* films, we hope to have provided a next step towards future scholarship not only on these films but also on his underexamined work in television, comics, prose and other media beyond film.[11] Such scholarship will doubtless be enriched by the establishment of the George A. Romero Archival Collection at the University of Pittsburgh. (Additionally, the George A. Romero Foundation supports filmmakers and artists inspired by his work.) Among its materials, the archive contains 114 unrealized projects at various stages, 80 of which were initiated or conceived by Romero; shooting scripts, including for *The Crazies* and *Martin*; commercials and industrial films made by Romero; and a 20-minutes-longer work print of *Knightriders*. One of the most notable items is a "lost," approximately 20-minute short film about a Florida cryptid called *Jacaranda Joe*. Incorporating a found-footage approach, Romero made it in 1995 with Valencia College students, faculty and area locals (Rubin and Hart). The ongoing work of the Romero Archive in processing materials highlights just how much is yet to be said about this endlessly compelling figure of American cinema.

Chapter Notes

Preface

1. The films are *Night of the Living Dead* (1968), *Dawn of the Dead* (1978), *Day of the Dead* (1985), *Land of the Dead* (2005), *Diary of the Dead* (2007), *Survival of the Dead* (2009) and the 1990 remake, also titled *Night of the Living Dead*.

2. Suzanne Desrocher-Romero has said of *The Amusement Park* that "shelved" is more accurate than "lost" ("Reviving").

Introduction

1. That Williams makes this claim while often (in his book on *The Cinema of George A. Romero*) disparaging or distancing Romero from the elements or trappings of genre film speaks to the special status accorded the early *Dead* films (see, for instance, 4–6).

2. This volume cites location numbers when page numbers are not provided in sources formatted for Kindle.

3. This is not, of course, to argue that all or even most such engagement is intentional (or ethical).

4. In addition to moral weakness, Drogan displays bodily weakness, which one might also read as emasculation, when the cat causes him to have a fatal heart attack.

5. At the same time, he condemns the concluding use of the trope of miraculous restoration of able-bodiedness, attributed not to the filmmakers but to studio interference.

6. Lee Schweninger observes that "no one term will suffice to include or identify" the millions of people belonging to tribal groups in North America and describes himself as "forced and resigned to being comfortable" using several terms "somewhat interchangeably" (19). This book follows Kerstin Knopf and Michelle H. Raheja in using "Indian" to refer to "constructed, stereotyped and objectified images of Indigenous people" (Knopf xxi), including those circulated by Hollywood (Raheja loc. 3556, note). Otherwise, it follows Knopf in using "indigenous" to refer to "the original inhabitants of North America and their descendants" (xxi). Knopf objects to what she sees as the primitive connotations of "Native American" (xxi).

7. See Steve T. Brown pp. 87–90 for a brief summary of manifestations of the doppelgänger across cultures.

Chapter 1

1. The scene in which the female protagonist goes through the steps to obtain an at-the-time illegal abortion is, unlike anything else in *There's Always Vanilla*, like something out of a horror movie, with dark alleys, heavy rain, mysterious figures, ominous statements, and, as the closed captions say, "foreboding music." It is legitimately a frightening scene, preparing the viewer for the character's death rather than for what actually happens. As *The Amusement Park* was intended to illuminate the plight of the elderly in America but did so by means of horror tropes, this scene is an argument in favor of legalized abortion as well as a tiny horror movie in the midst of a cynical relationship drama.

2. Both the synthetic nature of the scene and the leap into bed rather than a walk down a path holding hands seem to be poking fun at traditional, and traditional Hollywood representations of, courtship. That a boom microphone can be seen at one point adds to the artifice.

3. The decision to open the film with the shooting of a beer commercial could be a gesture to Latent Image's award-winning Duke Beer ad from the mid–1960s; several members of Latent Image play roles on the fake commercial's film crew as well, including Russell Streiner and John A. Russo, appearing, Fallows says (perhaps not intending to be uncomplimentary), "as themselves" (*George* 29, 31).

4. One entertaining but brief scene has Michael working with another actress on a commercial for "Nice-Nap Carpets"; the representative from Nice-Nap is unconvinced that "Wouldn't you really *love* to lay one on your floor?" falls on the right side of the (always in flux, particularly at the time) line between decent and "filthy." Michael assures him that anything less sexually suggestive would be old-fashioned.

5. Although there is no zoom in on a calendar showing that it was a spring day in 1969 that Lynn and Chris met, it is suggested by both the presence of *The Ultimate Machine* and Chris asking Lynn, "What do you think they'll find on the moon?"

6. I have not been able to confirm whether this was existing audio footage from or for a local television broadcast or something similar or if Romero scripted the viewer responses, but the video footage is almost certainly "found" footage rather than a simulation. (A television talk show clip late in the movie is scripted and staged, as are clips of Lynn's father's call-in radio show.)

For more on the 1969 Three Rivers Arts Festival and "The Ultimate Machine," see Geoffrey Tomb's "Heads Shake for Arts' Sake: Annual Arts Festival Opens Tomorrow," in the 5 June 1969 *Pittsburgh Post-Gazette*, the same author's "Arts Festival Exhibit Has Gravity Pains" from the 7 June 1969 edition of the newspaper, and Jacob Paul's article on alumni returning

to campus, notably including the student artists from the class of 1969, "Alumni, from Class of 1969 to 2018, Converge during Carnival" from the 15 April 2019 edition of the CMU student newspaper, *The Tartan*.

7. This gendered wrestling for control over a narrative is a technique that Romero revisited late in his career in *Diary of the Dead* (2007), where filmmaker Jason continues to record events over his girlfriend Debra's objections. Just as Chris is vying for dominance over a nearly complete narrative, Debra, who fought with Jason over his desire to continue gathering footage for his movie until he died, picks up Jason's camera and his mantle of documentarian: "I'm going to finish his movie," she says, making his student film/outbreak road trip documentary her own through arranging the primary and supplementary videos into a narrative—the film itself—that asks if humans are even worth saving.

Chapter 2

1. Filmed in 1972 under significant budget constraints and challenges during production and post-production, Romero's film was recut and released under the title of *Hungry Wives* and marketed by its distributor as soft-core porn; this decision may have been in part because Romero's previous film, *There's Always Vanilla*, as well as the subsequent *The Crazies*, was made in collaboration with Lee Hessel's Cambist Films as the sexploitation distributor sought to move toward an intersection of arthouse/independent and adult cinema. (For more on Cambist Films, see Tom Fallows' "'More than Rutting Bodies': Cambist Films, Quality Independents, and the 'Lost' Films of George A Romero.") While Romero was, at the time, exploring genres outside of horror and collaborating with Cambist, he wasn't trying to enter the porn market, and despite its consideration of female sexuality and some caftans and chest hair, it is not an erotic film, which likely contributed to the release not being successful. When, after *Dawn of the Dead*, the distributor retitled it *Season of the Witch*

and attempted to re-release it as a new Romero film, he was no more successful.

2. Williams identifies the actor as Bill Hinzman (*Cinema* 50), but that is incorrect; Peters is not credited for this role, but through comparison of these scenes and his (credited) role in *There's Always Vanilla*, this has been confirmed.

If indeed Romero double casted Neil Fisher as well as Ken Peters, this could be a budget issue—frequent collaborator Bill Hinzman plays Joan's nightmare intruder as well as being a crew member—but the fact that both doublings take place in consecutive scenes suggests both dream logic and symbolism.

3. The ankh became popular among Western countercultures in the 1960s; some new-age sources suggest that the shape, in a more organic rather than textual font form (see Figure 3), is an "Atlantean [or 'Atlantis'] cross," said to be a progenitor of the ankh from the lost continent of Atlantis that bears all of the protective strength attributed to an ankh without negative connotations relating to the ankh as a symbol of pharaonic power and control. Suffice to say that the symbol is intended to suggest magic, probably spelled with a K. (See, for example, the Alicja Centre of Well-Being, "where science and spirituality meet," www.intuitivedowsing.com/atlantis-cross-silver/.)

4. The edition cited uses location numbers in the preface and page numbers thereafter.

5. *The Stepford Wives* was published the year that *Jack's Wife* was made and so, while representative of the zeitgeist, was not itself an influence. However, it is worth remembering that Stepford had a women's club six or more years previous to the events of the novel and that Friedan spoke at a meeting where "[o]ver fifty women applauded Mrs. Friedan as she cited the inequities and frustrations besetting the modern-day housewife" (37), confirming that "it was indeed the rise of the women's movement in suburban Stepford that led to the activities of the Men's Association" (Beuka 174), that is, replacing their feminist wives with robots who "experience that mysterious orgiastic fulfillment [that] the commercials promised when waxing the kitchen floor" (Friedan 511) or doing other housework. Evidence of this event is one of Joanna's earliest hints that the perfect wives of Stepford are not natural.

6. To be clear, this was not a "witch hunt," a case of the academy repressing an uncomfortable truth: it was bad scholarship by a scholar working outside her field, using only sources that could be manipulated to support her ideas and drawing conclusions based on minimal evidence; Mimi Winick identifies this as "fantastic scholarship" (in the Todorovian sense, not as a value judgment) "engag[ing] in imagining new possibilities for women" (565) using the genre of "scholarship" popularized in Gothic and sensation fiction of the 18th and 19th centuries.

7. As an aside, Romero worked on this film on a summer break from school (Fallows, *George* 5)

8. Research suggests, although I cannot say with absolute certainty, that this is not a real book; the cover seems handmade, with no author's name, and includes the symbol from the extended release's opening credits; Sady Doyle claims that all rituals in the film are from Paul Huson's 1970 *Mastering Witchcraft* (230).

9. This is also the first scene where a small white ceramic bull, possibly Greco-Roman in design, is shown in flashes of lightning when the camera cuts away from Joan. Throughout the remainder of the film, this bull features prominently in scenes of sex, ritual and Joan's nightmares of home invasion by a horned figure, suggesting deliberate symbolism. Perhaps it is a demon (as the nightmare invader seems to be), a god like Pan, representing sex and chaos and integrated into the neopagan pantheon, or a representation of forbidden sexuality in the form of Pasiphae's bull: Pasiphae was herself a witch in a lineage of witches who was famously compelled to lust after and have sex with a white bull (and birth the Minotaur). Of course, horns can also represent the cuckolded husband, the man who has lost control over his wife and is emasculated by her infidelity.

10. The scenes with the police officers and with the cleaning woman are oddly comical interludes in an otherwise serious film.

11. Perhaps to make the community seem less affluent and more relatable, the theatrical release cuts other references to domestic help within the community as well as Gregg's dismissal of community outreach because "a guy in the ghetto doesn't want a bunch of ladies from Nob Hill coming in with their box lunches and their husbands' old paintbrushes to clean up their proud little neighborhood"; these details emphasize the social class of the women, anticipating and acknowledging critiques of the non-inclusivity of second-wave feminism and the development of intersectional third-wave feminism.

12. As many a meme reminds us, married women could not get credit cards of their own (and single women also had difficulties) until 1974, when the Equal Credit Opportunity Act was signed; however, the name on the credit card is neither Jack nor Joan Mitchell; it's George A. Romero. The entire scene of Joan driving, shopping, completing her first ritual and hiding her supplies is set to psychedelic folk-pop musician Donovan's "Season of the Witch"; the scenes run the exactly the length of the song, but as the lyrics briefly touch on feelings of surveillance and primarily repeat variations on "must be the season of the witch" and rhyming lines about knitting, rabbits, and beatniks, it would seem that Romero and his crew were just getting their money's worth out of rights to the song rather than using it to make a statement deeper than "she has decided to become a witch."

13. Which, again, may be a prop created specifically for the movie given the presence of typos in the few pages shown.

14. It may be a gesture toward Lent as the season of penance or just an issue of editing, but Jack apologizes to Joan for hitting her in a brief scene after this, although that action was, by the film's chronology, at least one business trip and several days ago.

Chapter 3

1. *The Crazies* (2010) was written by Scott Kosar and Ray Wright, directed by Breck Eisner. Romero's role was limited to Executive Producer.

2. This setting and aesthetic will be recalled in Michael Cimino's Vietnam war film *The Deer Hunter* (1978), inviting potentially productive avenues for comparison as rural, Rust Belt anti-military and anti-war films.

3. Tony Williams comments on the war crime and Nazi imagery of burning bodies: "We must also remember that during the time Romero filmed *The Crazies*[,] analogies between American soldiers in Vietnam and Nazis were very common. The film also appeared three years after The Winter Soldier investigations when veterans openly confessed to committing atrocities and several years after the My Lai Massacre" (*Cinema* 69).

4. Defined by Primo Levi: "*Muselmänner*, the drowned, form the backbone of the camp, an anonymous mass, continually renewed and always identical, of non-men who march and labour in silence, the divine spark dead within them, already too empty to really suffer. One hesitates to call them living: one hesitates to call their death death, in the face of which they have no fear, as they are too tired to understand" (96).

5. Derrida: "*Différance* is the systematic play of differences, of the traces of differences, of the spacing by means of which elements are related to each other. This spacing is the simultaneously active and passive (the a of *différance* indicates this indecision as concerns activity and passivity, that which cannot be governed by or distributed between the terms of this opposition) production of the intervals without which the "full" terms would not signify, would not function."

6. The "concentrationary universe," a concept of a universe defined and prescribed by the effects of the Holocaust as outlined by David Rousset.

7. Christopher Sharrett interprets *The Crazies* as a film more spiritually akin to Goldhagen's hypothesis: "Romero's focus not only on what we have done to various populations here and abroad, but to our enjoyment of all things military" ("Crazies" 17).

8. Langer calls this ethical misappropriation "preempting the Holocaust": "Using—and perhaps abusing—its grim details to fortify a prior commitment to an ideal of moral reality, community

responsibility, or religious belief that leaves us with space to retain faith in their pristine value in a post-Holocaust world" (1).

9. Langer explores Delbo and the concept of "deep memory" stemming from unresolved trauma in the first chapter of *Holocaust Testimonies*, titled "Deep Memory."

10. Robin Wood notes regarding the ambiguity of the symptomology between the infected and those who are victims of the military occupation (rather than virus): "The 'crazies,' in other words, represent merely an extension of 'normality,' not its opposite" ("Apocalypse" 164).

11. Robin Wood observes of this ambiguity: "Once . . . a doubt is implanted, it becomes uncertain what instigates the uncontrolled and violent behavior of virtually everyone in the film" ("Apocalypse" 165).

12. An important distinction is identified by Romero per an interview:

> **CFQ:** Do you think there is a similarity between *The Crazies* and *Night of the Living Dead*, and if so was this intentional due to the commercial success of your first film?
>
> **Romero:** No, it really wasn't. We had the basic story which was written by one of our commercial directors here, and the script came out of that. On my draft, my version of the script, I wasn't looking for any intentional similarities at all. I think that some people are gonna say that it has similarities. One of the commanding officers in the film is a black man, and it's the same thing, a band of people trying to survive against this onslaught, in this case, military personnel trying to button up a town. And it does, in that sense, have those similarities, but beyond that the similarity is gone. It's a different commentary altogether [30].

Chapter 4

1. The inclusion of a black protagonist who faces a racially coded conflict perhaps contributed to the film's success with black audiences in inner-city theaters. Kevin Heffernan provides more insight into the film's exhibition in his essay "Inner-City Exhibition and the Genre Film: Distributing *Night of the Living Dead* (1968)."

2. This scene is also comparable to the conclusion of *Night of the Living Dead*, as the police fail to eradicate the actual menace (Martin/the ghouls) and instead compulsively kill a black character whom they incorrectly viewed as a threat.

3. The theme of intersecting race and class is also present in *The Amusement Park* (1973), most notably early in the film when a group of black carnival-goers sell their belongings for access to the park, only to be scammed by the white ticket attendant.

4. In a departure from Romero's tendency to deconstruct hegemonic figures, one of the elderly figures on stage is a veteran dressed in full uniform. Unlike the anti-military sentiments displayed in *The Crazies* and *Day of the Dead*, the veteran here is meant to be sympathetic, a helpless figure being jeered for his age.

Chapter 5

1. *Knightriders* is a loose enough adaptation of Arthuriana that it includes several figures more typically aligned with Robin Hood, whose stories originated centuries after those of Arthur.

2. Medieval scholar and King Arthur expert Norris J. Lacy enjoyed and admired *Knightriders*, writing in his article about "the tyranny of tradition" as an obstacle to making a truly great work of Arthuriana that Romero is "exuberantly unrestrained" by "literary precedence" (80) and uses his sources "as inspiration, as a flourishing legend rather than an artifact" (81).

3. Ed Sikov delightfully elaborates: "Toward those outside the troupe, Romero hurls ... a torrent of sarcasm, bitterness, and contempt—and hurls it with such glee" (32). Sikov identifies this view of outsiders as that of "a director with profound reservations about his own complicity in the construction of his artist-image" and the expectations of his audience. Tony Williams says that the crowds are "the director's depiction of those elements who view his films merely for visceral excitement and nothing else" (*Cinema* 105).

4. Fully aware that a medieval reenactment group is not actually a monarchy, I will nonetheless be using the language of the movie when referring to the "king," "queen," "knights," the king's "subjects," and the "kingdom" itself; in addition to these terms, I identify the group as a "troupe" because there is no useful umbrella term provided by the movie: while some critics have called them "K/knightriders," that is notably the name given to Morgan's faction by the sleazy promoter, and another name put forth by some viewers, "Fight or Yield," seems to be based on the motto painted on the side of one of their transports.

5. This last phrase is uttered ironically within a movie that is a "dissipated vision of an America undone by consumerism" (Pugh and Weisl 96).

6. Notably, Steve, a lawyer, is not a member of the troupe and typically stays in hotels when he travels with them, although he rides a motorcycle; only the outsider is involved in the mundane and bureaucratic, their permits, bookings, finances, etc., keeping Camelot itself free from the taint of the modern world. Billy's response to Steve's reminder is "You can keep the money you make off this sick world, lawyer. I don't want any part of it," ignoring that motorcycle parts, gasoline, food, permits and medical supplies do not just appear at their campsites.

7. It is not possible to identify the speakers as this dialogue is part of a large group discussion.

8. Billy's knights are also not hobbyist historical reenactors (see above: motorcycles—the only history they're reenacting is their own). Renaissance Faires weren't corporate commercial entertainment at first, but instead started as a fundraiser for public radio. Now, though, they're almost exclusively corporate-owned.

9. According to one estimate, roughly 85 percent of the population of what is now England were peasants (serfs or freemen), working land belonging to a nobleman or an institution (Bovey). Unlike their medieval analogs, the characters whom Morgan identifies as "serfs"—and to be pedantic, the merchants and crew are more freedmen than serfs—have all of their needs met and all profits are shared equally.

Chapter 6

1. Tony Williams argues that the form of the horror genre itself "may attempt to repress revolutionary insights" (*Hearths* 15). This argument does depend, however, on the claim that the spectacle of special effects portraying violence or monsters distracts from thematic elements. Such a claim seems to assume that, rather than the viewer's relationship to a film (like and including spectatorial identification) being multiple and fluid, the viewer can only inhabit a single relationship to a film as a whole, not to mention at any given moment, or that if this were the case, a viewer could not watch the film again with a different focus.

2. See Williams, *Hearths* 11. With their intrafamilial threats, he argues, these films "contradict normal idealized family images in mainstream American film and television" (11). *Creepshow*, again, partakes in both this and the more conservative 1980s horror tradition.

3. Jackson links this relationship in part to film's status as a consumer product (20). While the book in which she makes these comments focuses on post–9/11 horror such contradictions are far from a new phenomenon in popular culture: the tension between upholding and subverting sociocultural norms appears throughout early modern English drama, for example.

4. For instance, we might add to hierarchies *of* gender hierarchies *within* gender, such as "the hierarchies of masculinity" that subordinate non-hegemonic masculinities (Connell and Messerschmidt 846).

5. EC began as Educational Comics before becoming Entertaining Comics (S. Brown 33). On the primary uses of comics-style visuals in *Creepshow*, see S. Brown 68.

6. This is true as well of the title character in "The Facts in the Case of Mr. Valdemar." See Chapter 9.

7. "Verrill" was originally published under the title "Weeds," and *Creepshow* as a whole was intended by Romero and

King to attract investor interest to an adaptation of *The Stand* that they hoped to make (S. Brown 12, 21).

8. The *Creepshow* television series episode "Model Kid" (2021) recycles a more elaborate version of this story, with an uncle who assumes custody and becomes a substitute father.

9. This dynamic provides one example of the collision between the post–World War II nuclear family as an emblem of democracy and social mobility in media such as *Life* magazine—in which "strategies of legitimation aligned national imperatives with domestic ideals" (Kozol 191)—with endemic inequality on both micro and macro scales.

10. Viewers of *Knightriders* might perceive an intertextual echo in this character, as the actress playing Billy's mother also plays that film's "battered wife and mother" (T. Williams, *Cinema* 116).

11. Two cuts during this sequence to the jack o' lantern in the front window of the family's home perhaps suggest the hypocrisy of Stan's condemnation of Billy's comics while participating in the more sanitized, acceptable horror of Halloween. The smiling pumpkin additionally figures as the happy outward face of the troubled suburban family. This outward face contrasts the "fearful nature" of the home suggested by periodic cuts to mounted animal heads (T. Williams, *Cinema* 116). We might also notice the proprietary undertone of Stan's "My boy."

12. Williams identifies Stan's hidden reading material as his own "retreat into fantasy," hypocritically paralleling Billy's comics (*Cinema* 116).

13. This presentation as rational and knowledgeable about rather than frightened by horror films exists in tension with a desire to experience that state of fear marked as childish (Hills 80).

14. The first garbage collector also contrasts Billy's bad, anti-horror father, and his association with Savini heightens that contrast.

15. See S. Brown pp. 39–40 on puns as subversive humor in EC comics.

16. Like Billy, Carrie originally arises from the pen of Stephen King. Gwen Hofmann sees Billy as the next, even more violent generation of white patriarchy.

17. Both Tony Williams and Simon Brown write that Bedelia says, "You screwed me up" here, but there is not, so far as I am able to tell, an "up" in the line as delivered in the film.

18. Elsewhere, Sylvia infantilizes Henry by calling him a "sweet boy" and Cass and Henry by scolding them like children about the volume of their music, another instance of the family replicating its own unhealthy dynamics. In contrast, one might see in Bedelia's statement about Yarbo, "Everything I wanted, he wanted for me," a healthier dynamic that resists the severing of relationship endemic to patriarchy.

19. Williams reads Nathan's possessiveness and the family's verbal aggression towards one another as "paralleling cannibalism" and a "reworking of ideas" in Romero's first three *Dead* films, *Night* in particular (*Cinema* 118).

20. See also S. Brown 44. Even the animated transition following the segment links the family with violence through an ad that invites *Creepshow* readers to sell "Bolt, the family newspaper that nobody knows about." It claims that three million people sell this paper to "friends, relatives, and neighbors" every week, and it promises in return prizes including bows, guns, tanks and nuclear warheads.

21. Nathan's attitude and situation here find strong echoes in the title character of "The Facts in the Case of Mr. Valdemar." See Chapter 9.

22. It is perhaps worth noting that Father's Day, the holiday—created at least in part in imitation of Mother's Day—on which Bedelia kills Nathan and on which she returns home every year, was patently unsuccessful until it was taken up as a capitalist venture almost two decades after it was established and was not made a national holiday until a 1972 proclamation by Richard Nixon ("Father's Day" 285–286). Until the 1938 establishment of a commercial council, the holiday was seen, revealingly, as sentimental, and thus incompatible with fathers.

23. Nathan's reanimated corpse is played by John Amplas, who also played the titular role in *Martin*. In an intertextual mirroring, Martin, linked to the reanimated figure of the vampire, is killed by the patriarchal Cuda, while

Nathan, of course, himself acts as the patriarchal killer.

24. The name Mrs. Danvers is a clear allusion to Daphne du Maurier's *Rebecca* (1938), filmed by Alfred Hitchcock in 1940. However, while the Mrs. Danvers of *Rebecca* is certainly haunted by the dead, she was dedicated to the deceased Rebecca herself and not her husband who murdered Rebecca. Here, Mrs. Danvers herself falls victim to the murderous husband instead.

25. Williams envisions Vickers' equipment as also part of a critique of "the television apparatus" that appears in other of Romero's films (*Cinema* 122).

26. Hofmann connects Becky with a different fish, writing that Vickers' undead wife resembles the poisonous fish in a split shot of his fish tank and represents the "venomous remnants" in his life. She adds that his death results from the actions of this "slutty" woman. While I do not disagree in principle with this second fishy parallel, I find it hard to see the film presenting Becky in quite this way. What little we see of her while she is alive positions her as her husband's victim, and he does not make for a very sympathetic wronged spouse. If we are meant to condemn Becky at all, I would argue that her transgression of her role is one part of a much more ambivalent presentation, similar to Billie's transgressions in "The Crate."

27. The abusive horror-film husband whose home is his panopticon has received a recent update in Leigh Whannell's *The Invisible Man* (Blumhouse, 2020).

28. The panoptic function of home movies here presents a variation on the surveillance by Billy's father of Billy's media consumption. In contrast to Billy's comics, however, personal screens and video are associated—somewhat paradoxically given the seemingly nostalgic incorporation of black-and-white TV and movie clips in both *Creepshow* and *Creepshow 2*—with the film's villains (Richard Vickers and, with his personal computer screen, perhaps also Upson Pratt) and with bodily harm (Jordy Verrill). The year after *Creepshow*, David Cronenberg's *Videodrome* (1983) would memorably and much more explicitly

locate menace in the television screen and the videotape.

29. Vickers pouring himself a drink to watch the drownings from his living room links him with male heads of household Stan, drinking in his wing chair, and Jordy Verrill, who also drinks in front of a TV.

30. While Becky does not watch any screens, as the subject of Vickers' camera, she is presented in a few black-and-white shots without the frame of the diegetic TV that they are playing on, a visual allusion, perhaps, to *Night of the Living Dead*, which traps its own women in a domestic space.

31. The reversal is partial because the revenge is not Becky's alone, although she and Harry seem to retain their connection beyond the grave, a victory of female desire over patriarchal control.

32. "Oh, just call me Billie" contrasts with another faculty wife's "Actually, it's Tabitha" when complimented on "Tabby," a refusal of casual intimacy which marks her as the more proper wife.

33. She later repeats these sentiments: "Oh, Henry, you are such a little kid. ... I mean, where would you be without me to take care of you?"

34. Williams writes that Henry tells Dexter to stop being "so damned hysterical" (*Cinema* 124). While this would fit nicely with portraying Dexter as womanly, Henry actually says to stop being "so goddamned elliptical."

35. Billie's relationship to the invented male-victimized woman remains ambivalent here: her reaction during this exchange is difficult to read but seems to teeter between empathy and morbid curiosity.

36. As he shakes Billie against the crate during these lines, one might see a secondary meaning that he is trying to "wake" Billie, to shake her from her behavioral patterns.

37. Fears of emasculation spill over into the animated transition following the segment. An ad in the comic, which evokes print ads from Charles Atlas, reads, "Get the complete Brad Benchpress Program" and features a drawing of a muscular man posing shirtless. He is identified as Brad Benchpress, "Mr. Big-Muscle U.S.A." Customers are

promised the "Complete Guide to Muscling Up," "Muscle-Up Equipment!," a "Muscle-Up Guide to Nutrition!," "And Brad Benchpress' Secret Ingredient X That Assures You of Muscle-Up **Success!**" A smaller drawing on the bottom left depicts a blond beach bully telling a skinnier young man, "Eat sand, wimp!" while a bikini-clad girl admires, "Wotta Man!" "Don't Let This Happen to You," advises the ad.

38. Similar anxieties about emasculation as those that manifest in this scene appear also in the image of Ella the monkey emerging from Allan's body in *Monkey Shines* (see Chapter 8). We might also extend the comparison to the dynamics of George Stark's "birth" in *The Dark Half* (see Chapter 10).

Chapter 7

1. On the choice to use "indigenous" in this context, see note 6 in the Introduction.

2. The dynamic here perhaps echoes the complicated centrality of male friendship, love and rivalries in the film Western (Raheja loc. 824). Martha, the only female character in this segment, represents the inverse of Ray's trusting, respectful attitude to and relationship with Ben.

3. Raheja notes a partial exception in the prominence of indigenous characters, plots and subplots in a number of silent films, which stands out sharply against the "virtual invisibility of Indigenous people in popular media today" (loc. 1019).

4. Notably, Ray is introduced singing "The Blue-Tail Fly" (also known as "Jimmy Crack Corn") to himself, which gained popularity in the 1840s via the blackface minstrel group the Virginia Minstrels and is commonly attributed to Daniel Decatur Emmett, one of the group's members (Perkins et al. 309).

5. The first written instance of "How!" in this sense dates to 1817.

6. Andy later appears with a black biker jacket as well.

7. See Bass for a discussion of an example from the Great Dismal Swamp in the southeastern United States.

8. In part because both color and black-and-white versions of the episodes were filmed, the series was in fact syndicated into the 1970s (McNeil 156). The 20 or more weekly prime-time Westerns that were running by the beginning of the 1960s testify to the genre's significance in American (screen) culture (Manchel 92) alluded to by *The Cisco Kid*'s presence in "Old Chief Wood'nhead."

9. Examples of this dysfluent speech are included in *Creepshow 2*, as with Pancho asking, "Don't you realize me?" instead of "Don't you recognize me?"

10. When the Chief murders Fatso, shots of his being pierced by arrows are intercut with posters and a figurine in Fatso's trailers, two of which depict topless women, arguably offering a connection with his symbolic penetration by the Chief. One of the posters, though, depicts popular model Samantha Fox with a motorcycle and another depicts artwork of the band Iron Maiden's monstrous mascot Eddie, linking Fatso with contemporary popular culture just as he is killed by an avatar of older forms of popular culture. One might extend this privileging of nostalgia to the film's relationship with the EC comics that inspired the series and that were published during the same period in which *The Cisco Kid* and other Westerns dominated television.

11. Sam's scalping can also be read as a castration, given his own coupling of his hair with his masculinity and his desired onscreen and offscreen reception in Hollywood. It is deeply ironic that this castration, the neutering of Sam's movie star and playboy aspirations, is carried out by a white Hollywood stereotype of stoic indigenous masculinity.

12. This representation is flattened further when the Chief appears only as a silhouette during Andy's murder.

13. The unmoving cigar store Indian might also be seen as related to the use by a large number of silent films of "the frontier as a metaphor for the doomed, static present of Native Americans set against the kinetic, animated future of the dominant culture" (Raheja loc. 810). We might note that Sam aspires to mobility in his desire to drive to Hollywood but dies without achieving it. In

a further opposition, the supernatural aspect of the Chief's temporary ability to move further assigns him "the mystical" aspect of the Hollywood Indian (Riley 70); meanwhile, the same figure's emblematization of "the downtrodden, the impoverished, and the vanquished" (70) manifests, in contrasting ways, in Sam and Ben.

14. Ray's good intentions and Ben's valorization of debt repayment contribute to obscuring that relations under capitalism, the point of contact, via Ben, between white and indigenous cultures, are necessarily violent and hegemonic. From a different angle, Ray and Martha's disagreement also reflects the way in which the Western, as Linnie Blake notes while linking it to Reagan's capitalization on his career in the genre, "simultaneously fetishised" both "radical individualism" and "cooperative virtues of hard working, frugal neighbourliness" (107).

15. Prominently visible on the shelf at the head of the escort's bed is a copy of Stephen King's novel *IT*, which not only displays its own strong sense of nostalgia but also, as Regina Hansen argues, marginalizes characters who are not straight, white males.

16. Annie's marital-economic situation bears some clear parallels to Jessica's in "The Facts in the Case of Mr. Valdemar": see Chapter 9 in this volume. Annie's economic dependence on her husband reminds us, in juxtaposition to the hitchhiker's own association with dependency, that a boundary, whether of race, class or monstrosity, functions as "both marker of separation and line of commonality" (Uebel loc. 5082).

17. One might also point out that perceiving oneself as "not racist" is not the same as being "antiracist," to borrow a term employed by Kendi and others.

18. We might recall here Jeffrey Jerome Cohen's discussion of the monster's resistance to "any classification built on hierarchy" (loc. 234) and the long tradition of rendering difference as monstrous in order to justify its spatial displacement (loc. 249–262).

19. The hitchhiker's undead state itself

performs a disruption of boundaries, albeit categorical rather than spatial.

20. Annie talks about herself here in the same way that she has talked about her Mercedes, imagining the person treating her concussion saying, "That'll cost ya 27,000 dollars. I know it sounds like a lot, but you're gonna look like you just drove yourself out of the showroom" and referring to herself as derisively as "Mrs. Lansing, the money machine." The objectifying language of restoring her "showroom"-quality appearance speaks critically to the patriarchal quality of capitalism.

21. It is hard not to read this sequence as Laverne being used and then immediately disposed of.

22. Andrew Scahill argues that, in transgressing "a cultural insistence on children's ignorance, innocence, and dependence," "the terrible child" in horror film elicits an ambivalent mix of horror and pleasure (2).

23. The lead bully's mix of spurs and black fingerless gloves and a black grommeted bracelet recall Sam and his gang's mix of Western and biker/rocker signifiers in "Old Chief Wood'nhead."

24. That Billy is both an avid reader of *Creepshow*, which stands in for both the films themselves and their EC inspiration, and featured on the cover of the comics (in an image of his use of a voodoo doll in the first *Creepshow*) positions him as the avatar of the *Creepshow* reader/audience member/filmmaker, implying that the default subject in all three cases is white and male. That the Creep distributes these *Creepshow* comics from the back of a military-style truck forges an odd connection with state power and violence.

Chapter 8

1. Indeed, Reagan was the masculine savior who could rescue the nation from the emasculation anxieties and identity crises outlined in Chapter 4.

2. Interpreting *The Thing* as an AIDS metaphor can be muddled given that it was released just as the epidemic received mainstream attention, though it can nonetheless be read as a

foreshadowing of the AIDS paranoia that would soon take over the decade due to the film's male-dominated cast and the characters' uncovering of infected blood.

3. *Scanners* notably emphasizes the male psyche rather than physical decay; thus, its fears of emasculation lie in the loss of mental well-being and psychological castration anxiety.

4. Travis Sutton, for example, argues that the film offers a more humanized portrayal of a character with quadriplegia and also notes that *Monkey Shines* is one of the few mainstream films to include a sex scene featuring a character with a disability (80).

5. This portrayal of Allan's body could of course be interpreted in many other ways beyond narcissistic identification, as there is certainly a queer sensibility to Allan's bodily objectification.

6. Specifically, Allan has regressed to the oral stage because the only pleasure he receives is through his consumption of food. He is not in the anal stage because he must rely on others to "clean" him; thus, he does not receive anal pleasure.

7. This image of Allan sucking on Melanie's breast further signifies how Allan remains in the oral stage, as he is symbolically being nurtured by a Madonna figure.

8. According to Tony Williams, Orion Pictures insisted on including this nightmare scene, which is why it noticeably contrasts Romero's typically subtle scares (141).

9. This further affirms the profuse homophobia in '80s media, particularly the numerous "killer queer" villains.

10. Geoffrey's physical reaction to entering the trance is also notably orgasmic, a detail that furthers his queer connotations since he enters the already queer psychological bond shared by Allan and Ella.

11. In his pivotal book *The Cinema of Isolation: A History of Physical Disability in the Movies* (1994), Martin F. Norden provides substantial insight into how a character's disability inherently marks them as the Other in the horror genre, specifically due to connections with Freud's concept of "The Uncanny" (6–13).

Chapter 9

1. Those that did not take aim at capitalism parodied Soviet communism (loc. 6763).

2. We might note as well that the capitalist "labor process becomes a ground of selfestrangement [*sic*]" (Federici, *Caliban* 256).

3. Maroš Buday makes a case for the influence of "The Black Cat" on *The Shining*, with its alcoholic protagonist and disintegrating familial relationship, as well (55–57).

4. This indefinite splotch grows into the shape of "the GALLOWS," pointing to both the narrator's having hanged Pluto and the legal punishment for murderers (842).

5. Federici attributes a new "differentiation" between humans and animals, which replaced the existing assumption of "continuity," to the rise of capitalism and its production of humans as disciplined workers (*Witches* loc. 340–347).

6. This is not King's only killer cat from beyond the grave. Church, the family cat in King's *Pet Sematary* (1983) also returns from the dead to provide a caution against man playing god and the white colonizer appropriating indigenous motifs and traditions. There is also the entirely beneficent protagonist of the horror anthology *Cat's Eye* (1985).

7. In the same year as *Tales*, *Two Evil Eyes* presented a more direct, though far from faithful, adaptation of Poe's "The Black Cat," directed by Dario Argento, alongside Romero's "Facts in the Case of Mr. Valdemar."

8. The connective tissue to Hogarth (animal torture as index to a depraved character) as well as to Poe (the revenge of a black and white cat on its abusive keeper) is apparent. The trajectory of Drogan is akin to that of Poe's protagonist (and Hogarth's, at that), moving from animal cruelty to murder and ultimately to the death of the perpetrator, although the inclusion of murder-for-hire in the case of Romero's and King's work (not general depravity as in Hogarth or the perverseness of human nature as in Poe) sharpens the explicit critique of capitalism.

9. Jason W. Moore argues that in the "story of Humanity and Nature ... capitalism was built on excluding most humans from Humanity," including indigenous people, enslaved people, most women, and certain categories of white men ("Rise" loc. 1697). See also Moore, "Rise" loc. 2336.

10. In making this point, Elmar Altvater specifically rejects the widespread belief that technology will provide solutions to mitigate such destruction (see, for ex., loc. 2881ff.). The research conducted by Drogan's pharmaceutical company echoes, again perversely, this sort of thinking.

11. According to Tom Fallows and Curtis Owen, Argento did consider Romero to have adapted Poe's "only zombie story" (88).

12. The story was published in the same year in two journals, one of which used the title "The Facts of M. Valdemar's Case."

13. Romero is not the first to make the connection between Poe's "Valdemar" and zombies. The protagonist of Robert Bloch's 1951 story "The Dead Don't Die!," which features a zombie master in the Afro-Caribbean tradition, dreams that he is in "the house of M. Valdemar" at the climax of Poe's story, with Poe himself attempting to awaken Valdemar (520). "Poe couldn't raise Valdemar," Bloch's narrator concludes, "But Varek [the zombie master] could. And he had" (521).

14. Sederholm notes as well Romero's stated debt to Lovecraft in creating "Valdemar's" Others.

Chapter 10

1. The first disruption to the Beaumont family comes from young, 1968 Thad's illness, which is associated with his creative writing, perhaps linking him to the writer of the disruptive 1968 *Night of the Living Dead* himself. Romero has said of *The Dark Half*, "What appealed to me as being a screenwriter, I can appreciate sort of the writer's problem, uh, which way should I go? Should I go commercial or should I try to stay true to my art, you know?" ("The Sparrows are Flying Again").

2. Celtic folklore features the double itself in the role of psychopomp (Meehan loc. 73). While *The Dark Half* divides the double and the psychopomp, it maintains the folkloric association of the double with death (and, by extension, with anti-futurity).

3. Mark De Cicco, for example, notes Elaine Showalter's argument that Jekyll conceals from society "distinctly non-heteronormative" activities and himself argues that Jekyll's "non-normative, anti-societal queer energy ... is unleashed in Hyde" (11, 12).

4. Meehan inaccurately refers to them as twin boys (loc. 3294), but they are credited as William and Wendy Beaumont.

5. The film's other male hero, Sheriff Alan Pangborn, is also a family man, married with a son, and Williams proposes that "perhaps George Stark is as much his dark half as Thad's" (*Cinema* 165).

6. The ambition of photographer Homer to publish a book depicting teddy bears in coffins as a commentary on the "American way of ... death" similarly conflicts with dominant ideas of childness' innocence, and Homer becomes Stark's first victim (though not, of course, because Stark himself is a defender of childness).

7. Hughes labels the Gothic genre itself a "without doubt 'queer,'" owing to an uneasy mixture of formal orthodoxy and typically "unpalatable ... subject matter" (207).

8. See Bersani, "Gay Betrayals" loc. 590ff for critiques of the practice of defining queerness more capaciously employed by Hughes and by this chapter. A detailed engagement with this important debate lies beyond the scope of this chapter.

9. The epithet "Uncle George" also conjures the stereotype of the "cool" uncle (or aunt) who encourages or facilitates transgressions of the rules by which the nuclear family attempts to maintain the "innocence" of childness.

10. One might see the threat in such taking up as rooted in the idea, risen to dominance in the Romantic period, of a child as "'seed' of the adult-to-be" (Bohlmann and Moreland 19), but one could

also read it, more disturbingly for the supposed innocence of childness, as signifying this child's/childness' monstrousness or corruption in itself (see Bohlmann and Moreland 19–21).

11. For Freud, "amputation of arms, legs, or head signal[s] castration" (S. Taylor 65).

12. The pencil enables both Thad's creation of Stark specifically and (a portion of) his literary creation in general, a type of generativity that has often been figured as producing metaphorical children if not as childbearing, as will be discussed later in this chapter.

13. The pencil here hovers ambiguously between reclamation by Thad for domestic hegemonic masculinity, thereby becoming a phallic opposite to George's razor, and its established association with George and his domestically incompatible brand of masculinity. See the conclusion of this chapter for further discussion of the residual ambiguity of the film's ending.

14. Intriguingly, a deleted scene depicting the kidnapping of Thad's wife and children from their home would have fashioned a different George had it remained. In it, after he removes one of the children from a playpen, he warns Liz not to fight back in sexually charged terms ("It turns me on to fight. I don't think you want me turned on. Or do you? Do you?") and briefly strokes her face. Later in the same scene, he muses, still holding the child, "you know, in a funny sort of way, I'm their daddy too." (All deleted scenes were accessed on the Shout! Factory Blu-ray release.)

15. By the end of the film, Thad believes that he can also will George into non-existence, saying that he thinks that Stark is finished no matter what happens because "I don't want him around anymore."

16. The edition cited uses location numbers in the preface and page numbers thereafter.

17. This connection is reflected in the orthographical echo of "Allan" in "Ella." (The spelling of "Allan" also gestures to Poe, whose work boasts its own murderous simian.)

18. It is important to note Ahmed's emphasis that willfulness is not only "againstness" or a "side" on which one can remain (*Willful* 149, 168).

19. Although the doppelgänger, the figure to which Thad gives birth, does not date back quite to Plato, it has its own lengthy tradition in the horror genre: the first ever feature-length horror movie, the German film *The Student of Prague* (1913, director Stellan Rye), which draws on stories by E.T.A. Hoffmann and Poe, centers on a doppelgänger (Meehan loc. 2186). *The Dark Half* itself presents a modified form of the relationship in Poe's story "William Wilson" (1839) of the title character to his doppelgänger, in which the latter manifests and serves as the former's conscience, thwarting Wilson's more iniquitous desires until killed by Wilson in a duel (loc. 563–579).

20. Pangborn's questioning why Homer's murderer didn't just "clip" him one and take the truck instead of committing homicide also points to a kind of excess in Stark; and the fact that the body of Stark, who comes into being via a queer process and indulges his desires, ends up sickening and coming apart could be seen as an oblique echo of the AIDS crisis.

21. As part of this association, Susan Stanford Friedman observes, in a patriarchal society, biological metaphors for writing marginalize women's creativity (50).

22. In the use of "yuppies," there is a class dimension to Clawson's insult: although the low-culture work of Stark is more profitable, or at least more commercial, it is also assumed that the fanbase itself is lower class, as opposed to the yuppies who read Thad's literary fiction. Clawson himself, interested in and familiar enough with Stark's work to figure out that the author is a pseudonym, appears dirty, his jacket sports holes, and he has taken the bus to New York.

23. At a stretch, one might hear in the "system" that the twin resists being fully absorbed into both Thad's body and the normative social body. Meehan notes that Romero's use in the film of Elvis Presley's music alludes to Elvis himself having had an unborn twin (loc. 3298).

24. Zeus arrogates the birth process to himself by swallowing Athena's pregnant

mother and, in one version of the story, does this as (nearly) in-kind revenge for his wife, Hera, bringing forth a male child without having heterosexual intercourse (Hard 77, 79).

25. The nightmare ends with Liz's skin shattering to reveal the skull underneath, which could itself be read as echoing George as and as within the hidden interior of Thad.

26. Here, contact with the Other is simultaneously contact with the self-as-Other. This simultaneity physicalizes Edelman's postulation, "To encounter another is to have to confront our otherness to ourselves" (Berlant and Edelman 68).

27. Reggie is in fact a man in the source novel.

28. Edelman discusses the liminal aggression of a wolf-whistling boy in *The Birds*, an admission into the film of childhood sexuality (which the "ideological labor of cuteness" works to misrecognize) firmly excluded from *The Dark Half* and its much younger children (loc 1882, 2056).

29. An initial staging of the film's ending has Stark attacked and then carried away mostly intact by the sparrows. This ending was changed at the request of the studio after it previewed the sequence with unfinished effects ("The Sparrows").

30. While Liz says to Thad of George, "He wants to take over your life," George's willingness to murder Thad's children suggests that he does not see them as a necessary component of such a takeover. The sparrows' removal of Stark to parts unknown possesses an affinity with the medieval confinement of monsters and/as Others at the edges of maps, attempting to contain them at the extreme cosmological periphery (see, for example, J. Friedman 45–48).

31. Alexis Machine too still survives, unless Thad plans on recalling and destroying all of his books written under Stark's name. Although there will be no further instances of Machine in new books, the existing ones will continue to circulate and, one might think, have new copies printed and sold to capitalize on a thriller author now linked with an investigation of multiple homicides.

Chapter 11

1. As discussed in Chapter 8, body horror also notably stressed male suffering, though with more emphasis on the male's physicality.

2. The film adaptation of *American Psycho* debuted at Sundance in January 2000, less than one month prior to the release of *Bruiser*.

3. This is also comparable to the climax of *Falling Down* and Foster's toy water pistol.

4. This is of course not to say that male viewers never derive narcissistic pleasure from these films. John Hinckley, Jr., for example, famously identified with Travis Bickle, which sparked his attempted assassination of Ronald Reagan.

5. Milo's hegemonic status is also somewhat fractured due to his imminent divorce from Rosemary.

6. The power granted to Rosemary's final girl status is also displayed through her point-of-view shot, as she quite literally takes control of the Gaze.

7. This scene draws comparisons to the *Creepshow* segment "The Lonesome Death of Jordy Verrill," as rural farmer Jordy (Stephen King) opts to shoot himself (while the radio gives agricultural market updates) after he and his crops are taken over by alien plant life—a possible metaphor for blue collar workers being consumed by big business.

8. The fact that this unity is connected through a radio program is representative of the growth of right-wing talk radio shows like *The Rush Limbaugh Show* during the neo-conservative era, a medium that often situated white males as victims.

9. Model Number 9's positioning as an object is perhaps best stressed by the film's credits, which, instead of giving her a name, simply label her as "Number 9."

10. Korean history has featured *kisaeng*, women comparable to geishas, though model Number 9's attire is a product of Japanese iconography.

11. This also contrasts actor Peter Stormare's national identity as a Swede.

12. See Skal pp. 66–68 on *Phantom* and war injuries.

Conclusion

1. The epilogue, delivered by Maazel in the same setting as the prologue, notes that whether "you" return without hope to the white room will "depend on a number of factors ... beyond your control."

2. The end of the film highlights that elder abuse is a cycle, and our inability to respond to the epilogue's request for intervention anticipates the cycle of cynical destruction which underscores *The Crazies*. In these films, the horror of a hell on earth is one that we ourselves create and perpetuate.

3. One might see an echo here of Samuel Beckett's existential absurdist drama *Waiting for Godot*, in which Estragon tells Vladimir that he was beaten when he left the play's sole setting, a featureless (except for a lone tree) area in which they wait. The roles of these two tramps are always cast as at least middle-aged and sometimes as elderly men. The structure of vignettes that move from one odd experience to the next, often presided over by capricious authority figures, also evokes *Alice in Wonderland*.

4. Maitland McDonagh notes that these bikers may anticipate those in *Dawn of the Dead*, which, with *Martin*, follows *The Amusement Park* chronologically.

5. It should be noted that the institution of the family also fails here, as symbolized when the protagonist finally finds a moment of connection and happiness by reading "The Three Little Pigs" to a young girl, who share her chicken with him, only to have her mother unceremoniously pack up her children and their picnic and depart partway through, leaving the protagonist in tears of despair.

6. The George A. Romero Archival Collection is in possession of copies of the screenplay, which we were unable to access prior to publication due to pandemic restrictions, dated September 29, October 5, and October 7, 1998, as well as one undated copy (George A. Romero Archival Collection).

7. Both films are also drawing on American war films, with their groups of soldiers composed of a selection of stock types. *Aliens* has been interpreted as an allegory of the Vietnam war, and Romero calls two characters in his *Resident Evil* "regular G.I. Joes, right out of every war movie" (17).

8. The goal of the Weyland-Yutani Corporation, owners of the colony destroyed by the aliens, of acquiring a xenomorph with an eye towards bioweaponry is unknown to the Marines as well.

9. The commercial thus refers to the game by its Japanese title, *Biohazard 2*.

10. One may of course discern some tension between the recurrence of anticapitalist critique in Romero's *Dead* films and filming a commercial for a game, a tension not dispelled by noting that Romero began his career in part with work shooting commercials.

11. Examples include, in television, *Tales from the Darkside* (1983–1988, writer) and the unaired pilot *Iron City Asskickers* (1998, director), a Pittsburgh-set WWE-style show heavy on profanity, improvisation and celebration of the "blue-collar," first made available to consumers in April 2021; in comics, *The Death of Death* (DC, 2004–2005) and *Empire of the Dead* (Marvel, 2014–2015); and the posthumous novel, completed by Daniel Kraus, *The Living Dead* (Tor Books, 2020).

Works Cited

Abbott, Stacey. *Celluloid Vampires: Life After Death in the Modern World.* U of Texas P, 2007.

Abbott. Stacey. "Taking Back the Night: Dracula's Daughter in New York." *Screening the Undead: Vampires and Zombies in Film and Television*, Kindle ed., edited by Leon Hunt, Sharon Lockyer, and Milly Williamson, I.B. Taurus, 2014, loc. 767–1032.

Agamben, Giorgio. *Remnants of Auschwitz: The Witness and the Archive.* Zone Books, 2002.

Ahmed, Sara. *The Promise of Happiness.* Kindle ed., Duke UP, 2010.

_____. *Willful Subjects.* Kindle ed., Duke UP, 2014.

al-Samarai, Nicola Lauré, and Peggy Piesche. "Whiteness." *Krisis: Journal for Contemporary Philosophy*, no. 2, 2018, krisis.eu/whiteness/.

Aliens. Directed by James Cameron, 20th Century Fox, 1986. DVD.

Altvater, Elmar. "The Capitalocene, or, Geoengineering against Capitalism's Planetary Boundaries." *Anthropocene or Capitalocene? Nature, History, and the Crisis of Capitalism*, edited by Jason W. Moore, Kindle ed., PM Press, 2016, loc. 2837–3107.

Améry, Jean. *At the Mind's Limits: Contemplations by a Survivor on Auschwitz and Its Realities.* Indiana UP, 1966.

The Amusement Park. Directed by George A. Romero, Laurel/Communicators Pittsburgh, 1973. Shudder.

Asher, Nina. "Race, Gender, and Sexuality." *The Routledge Companion to Race and Ethnicity*, edited by Stephen M. Caliendo and Charlton D. McIlwain, Routledge, 2011, pp. 64–72.

Bass, Nikki. "The Firebird Legend." *Descendants of the Great Dismal*, 2016–2020, descendantsofthegreat dismal.com/2020/03/23/the-firebird-legend/.

Benshoff, Harry M. *Monsters in the Closet: Homosexuality and the Horror Film.* Manchester UP, 1997.

Berenstein, Rhona J. "'It Will Thrill You, It May Shock You, It Might Even Horrify You': Gender, Reception, and Classical Horror Cinema." *The Dread of Difference: Gender and the Horror Film.* 2nd ed., edited by Barry Keith Grant, U of Texas P, 2015, pp. 145–170.

Berlant, Lauren. *Cruel Optimism.* Kindle ed., Duke UP, 2011.

Berlant, Lauren, and Lee Edelman. *Sex, or the Unbearable.* Kindle ed., Duke UP, 2013.

Bernardino, Craig. "Auteurdämmerung: David Cronenberg, George A. Romero, and the Twilight of the (North) American Horror Auteur." *American Horror Film: The Genre at the Turn of the Millennium*, edited by Steffen Hantke, UP of Mississippi, 2010, pp. 161–192.

Bersani, Leo. "Can Sex Make Us Happy?. *Is the Rectum a Grave? and Other Essays.* Kindle ed., U of Chicago P, 2010, loc. 1657–1839.

_____. "A Conversation with Leo Bersani with Tim Dean, Hal Foster, and Kaja Silverman." *Is the Rectum a Grave? and Other Essays.* Kindle ed., U of Chicago P, 2010, loc. 2337–2550.

_____. "Gay Betrayals." *Is the Rectum a Grave? and Other Essays.* Kindle ed., U of Chicago P, 2010, loc. 497–629.

_____. "Is the Rectum a Grave?" *Is the Rectum a Grave? and Other Essays.*

Kindle ed., U of Chicago P, 2010, loc. 34–419.

———. "Is There a Gay Art?" *Is the Rectum a Grave? and Other Essays.* Kindle ed., U of Chicago P, 2010, loc. 424–492.

Beuka, Robert. *SuburbiaNation: Reading Suburban Landscape in Twentieth-Century American Fiction and Film.* Palgrave Macmillan, 2004.

Bishop, Kyle William. *American Zombie Gothic: The Rise and Fall (and Rise) of the Walking Dead in Popular Culture.* Kindle ed., McFarland, 2010.

Blackford, James. Interview with George A. Romero. *Sight and Sound,* Feb. 2014.

Blake, Linnie. *The Wounds of Nations: Horror Cinema, Historical Trauma and National Identity.* Kindle ed., Manchester UP, 2008.

Blanch, Robert J. "George Romero's 'Knightriders': A Contemporary Arthurian Romance." *Quondam et Futurus,* vol. 1, no. 4, 1991, pp. 61–69. *JSTOR,* www.jstor.org/stable/27870156.

Bloc, Alex Ben. "Filming *Night of the Living Dead*: An Interview with Director George Romero." *George A. Romero: Interviews,* edited by Tony Williams, Kindle ed., UP of Mississippi, 2011, pp. 8–17.

Bloch, Robert. "The Dead Don't Die!" *Zombies! Tales of the Walking Dead,* edited by Stephen Jones, Kindle ed., Skyhorse Publishing, 2013, pp. 481–551.

Bohlmann, Markus P.J., and Sean Moreland. "Introduction: Holy Terrors and Other Musings on Monstrous-Childness." *Monstrous Children and Childish Monsters: Essays on Cinema's Holy Terrors.* McFarland, 2015, pp. 9–26.

Boon, Kevin Alexander. "Trailing the Zombie Through Modern and Contemporary Anglophone Literature." *The Written Dead: Essays on the Literary Zombie,* edited by Kyle William Bishop and Angela Tenga, McFarland, 2017, pp. 15–26.

Botting, Fred. *Gothic.* 1996. Routledge, 2007.

Bovey, Alixe. "Peasants and Their Role in Rural Life." *British Library: The Middle Ages,* 30 Apr. 2015, www.bl.uk/the-middle-ages/articles/peasants-and-their-role-in-rural-life.

Britton, Andrew. "Blissing Out: The Politics of Reaganite Entertainment." *Britton on Film: The Complete Film Criticism of Andrew Britton,* edited by Barry Keith Grant, Wayne State UP, 2008, pp. 97–154.

Brown, Simon. *Creepshow.* Auteur, 2019.

Brown, Steve T. *Japanese Horror and the Transnational Cinema of Sensations.* New York: Palgrave Macmillan, 2018.

Browning, Christopher. *Ordinary Men: Reserve Police Battalion 101 and the Final Solution in Poland.* Harper Perennial, 1993.

Browning, Mark. *Stephen King on the Big Screen.* Intellect Books, 2009.

Bruce, Barbara S. "Guess Who's Going to Be Dinner: Sidney Poitier, Black Militancy, and the Ambivalence of Race in Romero's *Night of the Living Dead.*" *Race, Oppression and the Zombie: essays on Cross-Cultural Appropriations of the Caribbean Tradition,* edited by Christopher J. Moreman and Cory James Rushton, McFarland, 2011, loc. 1170–1473.

Bruiser. Directed by George A. Romero, Le Studio Canal+, Barenholtz Productions, Romero-Grunwald Productions, 2000. DVD.

Buday, Maroš. "From One Master of Horror to Another: Tracing Poe's Influence in Stephen King's The Shining." *Prague Journal of English Studies,* vol. 4, no. 1, 2015, pp. 47–59, doi.org/10.1515/pjes-2015-0003.

Büken, Gülriz. "Construction of the Mythic Indian in Mainstream Media and the Demystification of the Stereotype by American Indian Artists." *American Studies International,* vol. 40, no. 3, 2002, pp. 46–56. *JSTOR,* www.jstor.org/stable/41279925.

Canby, Vincent. "Screen: Exurban Horror." Review of *The Crazies,* directed by George A. Romero. *The New York Times,* 24 Mar. 1973, p. 20.

Castle, Terry J. "Lab'ring Bards: Birth 'Topoi' and English Poetics 1660–1820." *The Journal of English and Germanic Philology,* vol. 78, no. 2, 1979, pp. 193–208. *JSTOR,* www.jstor.org/stable/27708466.

Chernov, Matthew. "The Film That Never Was: Why George Romero's 'Resident Evil' Failed to Launch." *Variety,* vol. 334, no. 10, 14 Dec. 2016, p. 116. *Gale Academic OneFile,* link.gale.com/apps/doc/A477085674/AONE?u=cuny_bronxcc&sid=AONE&xid=cec20cb0.

Clover, Carol J. *Men, Women, and Chainsaws: Gender in the Modern Horror Film.* 1992. Princeton UP, 2015.

Cohen, Jeffrey Jerome. "Monster Culture (Seven Theses)." *Monster Theory: Reading Culture,* edited by Jeffrey Jerome Cohen, Kindle ed., U of Minnesota P, 1996, loc. 164–608.

Coleman, Robin R. Means. *Horror Noire: Blacks in American Horror Films from the 1890s to Present.* Routledge, 2011.

Connell, Robert W., and James W. Messerschmidt. "Hegemonic Masculinity: Rethinking the Concept." *Gender & Society,* vol. 19, no. 6, 2005, pp. 829–859. *SAGE Journals,* https://doi.org/10.1177/0891243205278639.

Correia, David, and Tyler Wall. *Police: A Field Guide.* Kindle ed., Verso, 2018.

The Crazies. Directed by George A. Romero, Pittsburgh Films, 1973. Amazon Prime Video.

Creed, Barbara. "Dark Desires: Male Masochism in the Horror Film." *Screening the Male: Exploring Masculinities in Hollywood Cinema,* edited by Steven Cohan and Ina Rae Clark, Routledge, 1993, pp. 118–133.

_____. *The Monstrous-Feminine: Film, Feminism, Psychoanalysis.* Routledge, 1993.

Creepshow. Directed by George A. Romero, Warner Bros., 1982. Amazon Prime Video.

Creepshow 2. Directed by Michael Gornick, Laurel Entertainment Inc., 1987. Amazon Prime Video.

The Dark Half. Directed by George A. Romero, Orion Pictures, 1993. Blu-ray.

Davies, Jude. "'I'm the Bad Guy?' *Falling Down* and White Masculinity in 1990s Hollywood." *Journal of Gender Studies,* vol. 4, no. 2, 1995, pp. 145–152, https://doi.org/10.1080/09589236.1995.9960601.

De Cicco, Mark. "'More than Human': The Queer Occult Explorer of the Fin-De-Siècle." *Journal of the Fantastic in the Arts,* vol. 23, no. 1, 2012, pp. 4–24.

Delbo, Charlotte. *Days and Memory.* Translated by Rosette Lamont, Northwestern UP, 1990.

Derrida, Jacques. Interview with Julia Kristeva. *Positions,* U of Chicago P, 1981, p. 21.

Dodson, Will. "Bruiser" in "'The Death of Death': A Memorial Retrospective on George A. Romero (1940–2017)," edited by Kristopher Woofter. *Monstrum,* vol. 1, no. 1, 2018, pp. 3–57, www.monstrum-society.ca/uploads/4/1/7/5/41753139/romero_memorial_retrospective_-_monstrum_1.pdf.

Donaldson, Mike. "What is Hegemonic Masculinity?" *Theory and Society,* vol. 22, no. 5, 1993, pp. 643–657. *JSTOR,* www.jstor.org/stable/657988.

Doyle, Sady. *Dead Blonds and Bad Mothers: Monstrosity, Patriarchy, and the Fear of Female Power.* Kindle ed., Melville House Publishing, 2019.

Dumas, Raechel. *The Monstrous-Feminine in Contemporary Japanese Popular Culture.* Palgrave Macmillan, 2018.

Dyer, Richard. "White." *Screen,* vol. 29, no. 4, 1988, pp. 44–65, https://doi.org/10.1093/screen/29.4.44.

_____. *White.* 2nd Edition, Routledge, 2017.

Edelman, Lee. *No Future: Queer Theory and the Death Drive.* Kindle ed., Duke University Press, 2004.

Fallows, Tom. *George A. Romero's Independent Cinema: Horror, Industry, Economics.* Edinburgh University Press, 2022.

_____. "Independent Dreams, American Nightmare: Industrial Transgression and Critical Organization in the Work of George A. Romero." *Horror Studies,* vol. 12, no. 1, 2021, pp. 45–62, https://doi.org/10.1386/host_00028_1.

_____. "'More than Rutting Bodies': Cambist Films, Quality Independents, and the 'Lost' Films of George A Romero." *Journal of Popular Film & Television,* vol. 42, no. 2, 2018, pp. 82–94.

Fallows, Tom, and Curtis Owen. *The Pocket Essential George A. Romero.* Pocket Essentials, 2008.

"Father's Day." *Holiday Symbols and Customs,* Omnigraphics, 2015, pp. 285–88.

Federici, Silvia. *Caliban and the Witch: Women, the Body, and Primitive Accumulation.* 2004. EPUB, Anarchivists, 2014. *Internet Archive,* archive.org/details/CalibanAndTheWitchWomen-TheBodyAndPrimitiveAccumulation/mode/2up.

———. *Revolution at Point Zero: Housework, Reproduction, and Feminist Struggle.* Kindle ed., 2nd ed., PM Press, 2020.

———. *Witches, Witch-Hunting, and Women.* Kindle ed., PM Press, 2018.

Firth, Rhiannon. Afterword. *Journey Through Utopia: A Critical Examination of Imagined Worlds in Western Literature,* by Marie Louise Berneri. 1950. Ebook, PM Press, 2019, loc. 6672–7842.

Fisher, Mark. *The Weird and the Eerie.* Kindle ed., Repeater Books, 2016.

Fraser, Nancy, and Rahel Jaeggi. *Capitalism: A Conversation in Critical Theory,* edited by Brian Milstein. Kindle ed., Polity Press, 2018.

Friedan, Betty. *The Feminine Mystique (50th Anniversary Edition).* Kindle ed., W.W. Norton & Co., 2013.

Friedman, John Block. *The Monstrous Races in Medieval Art and Thought.* 1981. Syracuse UP, 2000.

Friedman, Susan Stanford. "Creativity and the Childbirth Metaphor: Gender Difference in Literary Discourse." *Feminist Studies,* vol. 13, no. 1, 1987, pp. 49–82. *JSTOR,* www.jstor.org/stable/3177835.

Friend, Craig Thompson. "From Southern Manhood to Southern Masculinities: An Introduction." *Southern Masculinity: Perspectives on Manhood in the South since Reconstruction,* edited by Craig Thompson Friend, U of Georgia P, 2009, pp. vii–xxvi.

Fryers, Mark. "Horrific 'In-betweenness': Spatial and Temporal Displacement and British Society in 1970s Children's Supernatural Television." *Supernatural Studies: An Interdisciplinary Journal of Art, Media, and Culture,* vol. 6, no. 2, 2020, pp. 30–58.

George A. Romero Archival Collection, 1962–2017, SC.2019.03, Archives & Special Collections, University of Pittsburgh Library System, digital.library.pitt.edu/islandora/object/pitt%3AUS-PPiU-SC201903/viewer#ref15.

"George A Romero's Resident Evil Commercial + Making Of (1998) Retro Horror." *YouTube,* uploaded by JoBlo Horror Trailers, 18 Sep. 2020, youtu.be/luKoDi6vr_c.

Ghodsee, Kristen R. *Why Women Have Better Sex Under Socialism: And Other Arguments for Economic Independence.* Kindle ed., Bold Type Press, 2018.

Gilens, Martin. "How the Poor Became Black: The Racialization of American Poverty in the Mass Media." *Race and the Politics of Welfare Reform,* edited by Sanford F. Schram, Joe Soss, and Richard C. Fording, U of Michigan P, 2003, pp. 101–130.

Gilligan, Carol, and Naomi Snider. *Why Does Patriarchy Persist?* Kindle ed., Polity Press, 2018.

Gleiberman, Owen. "Tales from the Darkside: The Movie." *Entertainment Weekly,* 18 May 1990, ew.com/article/1990/05/18/tales-darkside-movie/.

Goldhagen, Daniel. *Hitler's Willing Executioners.* Alfred A. Knopf, 1996.

Gomel, Elana. "Zombie: The Girl with All the Gifts." *Monsters: A Companion,* edited by Simon Bacon, Peter Lang, 2020, pp. 225–232.

Graebner, William. "The Living Dead of George Romero and Steven Spielberg: America, the Holocaust and the Figure of the Zombie." *Dapim: Studies on the Holocaust,* vol. 31, no. 1, pp. 1–26.

Grant, Barry Keith. "Introduction." *The Dread of Difference,* edited by Barry Keith Grant, 2nd ed., U of Texas P, 2015, pp. 1–13.

Grosz, Elizabeth. "Intolerable Ambiguity: Freaks as/at the Limit." *The Monster Theory Reader,* edited by Jeffrey Andrew Weinstock, U of Minnesota P, 2020, pp. 272–285.

Guerrero, Edward. "AIDS as Monster in Science Fiction and Horror Cinema." *Journal of Popular Film and Television,* vol. 18, no. 3, 1990, pp. 86–93, https://doi.org/10.1080/01956051.1990.10662021.

Hand, Richard J. "Disruptive Corpses: Tales of the Living Dead in Horror Comics of the 1950s and Beyond."

Vampires and Zombies: Transcultural Migrations and Transnational Interpretations, edited by Dorothea Fischer-Hornung and Monika Mueller, Kindle ed., UP of Mississippi, 2016, pp. 213–228.

Hanners, John, and Harry Kloman. "The McDonaldization of America: An Interview with George A. Romero." *George A. Romero: Interviews*, edited by Tony Williams, Kindle ed., UP of Mississippi, 2011, pp. 88–100.

Hansen, Regina. "Stephen King's IT and Dreamcatcher on Screen: Hegemonic White Masculinity and Nostalgia for Underdog Boyhood." *Science Fiction Film and Television*, vol. 10, no. 2, 2017, pp. 161–176, 299.

Hard, Robin. *The Routledge Handbook of Greek Mythology: Based on H.J. Rose's Handbook of Greek Mythology.* Taylor and Francis, 2003.

Harrington, Richard. "'Tales from the Darkside: The Movie' (R)." *Washington Post*, 5 May 1990, www.washingtonpost.com/wp-srv/style/longterm/movies/videos/talesfromthedarksidethemovierharrington_a0aae6.htm.

Heffernan, Kevin. "Inner-City Exhibition and the Genre Film: Distributing *Night of the Living Dead* (1968)." *Cinema Journal*, vol. 41, no. 3, 2002, pp. 59–77. *JSTOR*, www.jstor.org/stable/1225699.

Herman, Judith Lewis. *Trauma and Recovery.* Basic Books, 1992.

Hills, Matt. *The Pleasures of Horror.* Continuum, 2005.

Hofmann, Gwen. "Creepshow (1982) and 'Father's Day' Celebrate Patriarchy." *Horror Homeroom*, 21 June 2015, www.horrorhomeroom.com/creepshow/.

Hughes, William. *Historical Dictionary of Gothic Literature.* Scarecrow Press, 2012.

Hunter, Latham. "The Celluloid Cubicle: Regressive Constructions of Masculinity in 1990s Office Movies." *Journal of American Culture*, vol. 26, no. 1, 2003, pp. 71–86. *ProQuest*, https://doi.org/10.1111/1542-734X.00075.

Hutchings, Peter. "International Horror in the 1970s." *A Companion to the Horror Film*, edited by Harry M. Benshoff, Wiley-Blackwell, 2014, pp. 292–309.

———. "Masculinity in the Horror Film."

You Tarzan: Masculinity, Movies and Men, edited by Pat Kirkham and Janet Thumin, Lawrence & Wishart, 1993, pp. 84–94.

"There's Always Vanilla (1971)." *AFI Catalog*, catalog.afi.com/Catalog/moviedetails/54355.

Iron City Asskickers. Directed by George A. Romero, Cryptic Pictures, 2021. DVD.

Jack's Wife. Directed by George A. Romero. The Latent Image, 1973. Blu-ray.

Jackson, Kimberly. *Gender and the Nuclear Family in Twenty-First-Century Horror.* Palgrave Macmillan, 2016.

Jameson, Fredric. *Archaeologies of the Future: The Desire Called Utopia and Other Science Fictions.* Verso, 2005.

Jeffords, Susan. *Hard Bodies: Hollywood Masculinity in the Reagan Era.* Rutgers UP, 1994.

Jojola, Ted. "Absurd Reality II: Hollywood Goes to the Indians." *Hollywood's Indian: The Portrayal of the Native*, expanded edition, edited by Peter C. Rollins and John E. O'Connor, Kindle ed., UP of Kentucky, 2003, pp. 12–26.

Kendi, Ibram X. *Stamped from the Beginning: The Definitive History of Racist Ideas in America.* Kindle ed., Nation Books, 2016.

Kerman, Judith, and John Edgar Browning, eds. *The Fantastic in Holocaust Literature and Film: Critical Perspectives.* McFarland, 1997.

Kiang, Jessica. "Karlovy Vary Interview: George Romero Talks Modern Zombies, Ripping Off Orson Welles, and More." *IndieWire*, 15 July 2015, www.indiewire.com/2015/07/karlovy-vary-interview-george-romero-talks-modern-zombies-ripping-off-orson-welles-and-more-262008/.

Kincaid, James R. "Producing Erotic Children." *Curiouser: On the Queerness of Children*, edited by Steven Bruhm and Natasha Hurley, U of Minnesota P, 2004, pp. 3–16.

King, Stephen. "The Cat from Hell." *Just After Sunset: Stories.* Scribner's, 2008, pp. 352–74.

———. Introduction. *Just After Sunset: Stories.* Scribner's, 2008, pp. 1–6.

Knightriders. Directed by George A. Romero. Laurel Entertainment, 1981. Amazon Prime Video.

Knopf, Kerstin. *Decolonizing the Lens of Power: Indigenous Films in North America.* Rodopi, 2008.

Kohn, Eric. "George Romero Says Nobody Will Finance His Next Zombie Movie and 'Night of the Living Dead' Wouldn't Get Made Today." *IndieWire,* 27 Oct. 2016, www.indie wire.com/2016/10/george-romero-interview-night-of-the-living-dead-zombies-1201740739/#!.

Kordas, Ann. "New South, New Immigrants, New Women, New: The Historical Development of the Zombie in American Popular Culture." *Race, Oppression, and the Zombie: Essays on Cross-Cultural Appropriations of the Caribbean Tradition,* edited by Christopher M. Moreman and Cory James Rushton, Kindle ed., McFarland, 2011, loc. 263–573.

Kozol, Wendy. "'The Kind of People Who Make Good Americans': Nationalism and *Life*'s Family Ideal." *Looking for America,* edited by Ardis Cameron, Blackwell, 2005, pp. 174–211, https://doi.org/10.1002/9780470774885.ch7.

Kristeva, Julia. "Approaching Abjection." *The Monster Theory Reader,* edited by Jeffrey Andrew Weinstock, U of Minnesota P, 2020, pp. 95–107.

Lacy, Norris J. "Arthurian Film and the Tyranny of Tradition." *Arthurian Interpretations,* vol. 4, no. 1, 1989, pp. 75–85. *JSTOR,* www.jstor.org/stable/27868674.

Langer, Lawrence. *Preempting the Holocaust.* Yale UP, 1998.

Lauro, Sarah Juliet. *The Transatlantic Zombie: Slavery, Rebellion, and Living Death.* Kindle ed., Rutgers UP, 2015.

Lebowitz, Fran, Pat Hackett, and Ronnie Cutrone. "George Romero: From *Night of the Living Dead* to *The Crazies.*" *George A. Romero: Interviews,* edited by Tony Williams, Kindle ed., UP of Mississippi, 2011, pp. 36–46.

Levi, Primo. *The Drowned and the Saved.* Vintage International, 1988.

Levin, Ira. *The Stepford Wives.* 1972. HarperCollins, 2010.

Luckhurst, Roger. *Zombies: A Cultural History.* Kindle ed., Reaktion Books, 2015.

Magoulick, Mary. "Trickster Lives in Erdrich: Continuity, Innovation, and Eloquence of a Troubling, Beloved Character." *Journal of Folklore Research,* vol. 55 no. 3, 2018, p. 87–126. *Project MUSE,* muse.jhu.edu/article/706096.

Manchel, Frank. "Cultural Confusion: *Broken Arrow* (1950)." *Hollywood's Indian: The Portrayal of the Native,* expanded edition, edited by Peter C. Rollins and John E. O'Connor, Kindle ed., UP of Kentucky, 2003, pp. 91–105.

Martin. Directed by George A. Romero, Laurel Tape and Fim, Braddock Associates, 1978. DVD.

Masculin Fémenin. Directed by Jean-Luc Godard. Anouchka Films, Argos Films, Sandrews, and Svensk Filmindustri., 1966. Blu-ray.

McBrien, Justin. "Accumulating Extinction: Planetary Catastrophism in the Necrocene." *Anthropocene or Capitalocene? Nature, History, and the Crisis of Capitalism,* edited by Jason W. Moore, Kindle ed., PM Press, 2016, loc. 2418–2827.

McDonagh, Maitland. "Step Right Up!" *Film Comment,* Mar.-Apr. 2020, pp. 22–23.

McHale, Brian. *Postmodernist Fiction.* Routledge, 1987.

McNally, David. *Monsters of the Market: Zombies, Vampires, and Global Capitalism.* Brill, 2011.

McNeil, Alex. *Total Television: The Comprehensive Guide to Programming from 1948 to the Present.* 4th ed., Penguin, 1996.

Meehan, Paul. *The Ghost of One's Self: Doppelgangers in Mystery, Horror and Science Fiction Films.* Kindle ed., McFarland, 2017.

Meek, Barbra A. "And the Injun Goes 'How!': Representations of American Indian English in White Public Space." *Language in Society,* vol. 35, no. 1, 2006, pp, 93–128.

"Model Kid." *Creepshow,* season 2, episode 1, written by John Esposito, directed by Greg Nicotero, Warner Bros. Domestic Television Distribution, 1 Apr. 2021. *Shudder.*

Monkey Shines: An Experiment in Fear.

Directed by George A. Romero, Orion Pictures, 1988. DVD.

Monty Python and the Holy Grail. Directed by Terry Gilliam and Terry Jones. Python (Monty) Pictures, Michael White Productions, and the National Film Trustee Company, 1975. DVD.

Moore, Jason W. "Introduction: Anthropocene or Capitalocene? Nature, History, and the Crisis of Capitalism." *Anthropocene or Capitalocene?: Nature, History, and the Crisis of Capitalism,* edited by Jason W. Moore, Kindle ed., PM Press, 2016, loc. 111–323.

———. "The Rise of Cheap Nature." *Anthropocene or Capitalocene?: Nature, History, and the Crisis of Capitalism,* edited by Jason W. Moore, Kindle ed., PM Press, 2016, loc. 1682–2406.

Mulvey, Laura. "Visual Pleasure and Narrative Cinema." *Screen,* vol. 16, no. 3, 1975, pp. 6–18, https://doi.org/10.100 7/978-1-349-19798-9_3.

Murphy, Bernice M. *The Suburban Gothic in American Popular Culture.* Palgrave Macmillan, 2009.

Newitz, Annalee. "The Undead: A Haunted Whiteness." *The Monster Theory Reader,* edited by Jeffrey Andrew Weinstock, U of Minnesota P, 2020, pp. 241–271.

Nicotero, Sam. "Romero: An Interview with the Director of *Night of the Living Dead.*" *George A. Romero: Interviews,* edited by Tony Williams, Kindle ed., UP of Mississippi, 2011, pp. 18–35.

Night of the Living Dead HD (50th Anniversary). Directed by George A. Romero, Continental Distributing, 1968. Amazon Prime Video.

1990 Census of Population: General Population Characteristics: Maine. U.S. Department of Commerce, 17–22 Apr. 1992, www2.census.gov/library/publications/decennial/1990/cp-1/cp-1-21.pdf. Accessed 12 June 2020.

Norden, Martin F. *The Cinema of Isolation: A History of Physical Disability in the Movies.* Rutgers UP, 1994.

Ohi, Kevin. "Narrating the Child's Queerness in *What Maisie Knew.*" *Curiouser: On the Queerness of Children,* edited by Steven Bruhm and Natasha Hurley, U of Minnesota P, 2004, pp. 81–106.

Oliver, Kelly. "Witnessing, Recognition, and Response Ethics." *Philosophy & Rhetoric,* vol. 48, no. 4, 2015, pp. 473–93, https://doi.org/10.5325/philrhet.48.4.0473.

Ork, William Terry, and George Abagnalo. "*Night of the Living Dead*—Interview with George A. Romero." *George A. Romero: Interviews,* edited by Tony Williams, Kindle ed., UP of Mississippi, 2011, pp. 3–7.

Owens, Andrew J. *Desire After Dark: Contemporary Queer Cultures and Occultly Marvelous Media.* Indiana UP, 2021.

Parenti, Christian. "Environment-Making in the Capitalocene: Political Ecology of the State." *Anthropocene or Capitalocene?: Nature, History, and the Crisis of Capitalism,* edited by Jason W. Moore, Kindle ed., PM Press, 2016, loc. 3348-3696.

Patterson, Christina. "Me, Myself and I: How Easy Is It to Write Confessional Poetry?." *Independent,* 23 Jan. 2013, www.independent.co.uk/arts-entertainment/books/features/me-myself-and-i-how-easy-it-write-confessional-poetry-8463999.html.

Paul, Jacob. "Alumni, from Class of 1969 to 2018, Converge during Carnival." *The Tartan* [Pittsburgh, PA], 15 Apr. 2019, p.1, staging.thetartan.org/2019/4/15/news/carnival-theme.

Perkins, George B., Barbara Perkins, and Philip Leninger. "Emmett, Daniel Decatur (1815–1904)." *Benet's Reader's Encyclopedia of American Literature,* vol. 1, HarperCollins, 1991, p. 309. *Gale OneFile: Fine Arts,* link-gale-com.bcc.ezproxy.cuny.edu/apps/doc/A16848495/PPFA?u=cuny_bronxcc&sid=PPFA&xid=e28fbabf. Accessed 1 June 2020.

Phillips, Kendall R. *Dark Directions: Romero, Craven, Carpenter, and the Modern Horror Film.* Southern Illinois UP, 2012.

Pielak, Chase, and Alexander H. Cohen. *Living with Zombies: Society in Apocalypse in Film, Literature and Other Media.* Kindle ed., McFarland, 2017.

Pinedo, Isabel. "Recreational Terror: Postmodern Elements of the Contemporary Horror Film." *Journal of Film and Video,* vol. 28, no. 1/2, 1996, pp. 17–31. *JSTOR*, www.jstor.org/stable/20688091.

Poe, Edgar Allan. "The Black Cat." *The Unabridged Edgar Allan Poe*, edited by Tam Mossman, Running Press, 1983, pp. 837–845.

———. "The Facts of M. Valdemar's Case." *The Unabridged Edgar Allan Poe*, edited by Tam Mossman, Running Press, 1983, pp. 1064–1072.

Pollin, Burton R. "Stephen King's Fiction and the Heritage of Poe." *Journal of the Fantastic in the Arts*, vol. 5, no. 4 (20), 1993, pp. 2–25. *JSTOR*, www.jstor.org/stable/43308170.

Pugh, Tison, and Angela Jane Weisl. *Medievalisms: Making the Past in the Present*. Routledge, 2013.

Raheja, Michelle H. *Reservation Reelism: Redfacing, Visual Sovereignty, and Representations of Native Americans in Film*. Kindle ed., U of Nebraska P, 2010.

Redman, Peter. "Invasion of the Monstrous Others: Heterosexual Masculinities, the 'AIDS Carrier' and the Horror Genre." *Border Patrols: Policing the Boundaries of Heterosexuality*, edited by Deborah Lynn Steinberg, Debbie Epstein, and Richard Johnson, Cassell, 1997, pp. 98–117.

"Reviving Romero's The Amusement Park: A Panel Conversation." *YouTube*, uploaded by Shudder, 8 June 2021, www.youtube.com/watch?v=RFdVvCbX8cs.

Riley, Michael J. "Trapped in the History of Film: Racial Conflict and Allure in *The Vanishing American*." *Hollywood's Indian: The Portrayal of the Native*, expanded edition, edited by Peter C. Rollins and John E. O'Connor, Kindle ed., UP of Kentucky, 2003, pp. 58–72.

Robertson, David Brian. "Introduction: Loss of Confidence and Policy Change in the 1970s." *Loss of Confidence: Politics and Policy in the 1970s*. Pennsylvania State UP, 1998, pp. 1–18.

Robinson, Beth. "Sexuality, Racialized." *Encyclopedia of Race and Racism*, edited by Patrick L. Mason, Gale, 2nd edition, 2013. *Credo Reference*, bcc.ezproxy.cuny.edu:2048/login?url=search.credoreference.com/content/entry/galerace/sexuality_racialized/0?institutionId=307. Accessed 19 June 2020.

Robinson, Kim Stanley. Postscript: "Dystopia Now." *Journey Through Utopia: A Critical Examination of Imagined Worlds in Western Literature*, by Marie Louise Berneri. 1950. Ebook, PM Press, 2019, loc. 7747–7819.

Romero, George A. *Resident Evil Original Screenplay. Daily Script*, www.dailyscript.com/scripts/resident_evil_romero.html.

Roskies, David and Naomi Diamant. *Holocaust Literature: A History and Guide*. Brandeis UP, 2012.

Rothberg, Michael. *Multidirectional Memory: Remembering the Holocaust in the Age of Decolonization*. Stanford UP, 2009.

Rousset, David. *L'univers concentrationnaire*. Hachette Littérature, 1998.

Rubin, Ben, and Adam Hart. It Came from the Archives! Unearthed Treasures from the George A. Romero Archival Collection. University of Pittsburgh Library System, 9 Feb. 2021. Webinar.

Rubin, Rachel Lee. *Well Met: Renaissance Faires and the American Counterculture*. Kindle ed., New York UP, 2012.

Russell, Sharon. "The Witch in Film: Myth and Reality." *Planks of Reason: Essays on the Horror Film*, edited by Barry Keith Grant and Christopher Sharrett, rev. ed., Scarecrow Press, 2004, pp. 63–71.

Scahill, Andrew. *The Revolting Child in Horror Cinema: Youth Rebellion and Queer Spectatorship*. Palgrave Macmillan, 2015.

Schram, Sanford F. "Putting a Black Face on Welfare: The Good and the Bad." *Race and the Politics of Welfare Reform*, edited by Sanford F. Schram, Joe Soss, and Richard C. Fording, U of Michigan P, 2003, pp. 196–224.

Schweninger, Lee. *Imagic Moments: Indigenous North American Film*. Kindle ed., U of Georgia P, 2013.

Sederholm, Carl H. "Two Evil Eyes: 'The Facts in the Case of Mr. Valdemar'" in "'The Death of Death': A Memorial Retrospective on George A. Romero (1940–2017)," edited by Kristopher Woofter. *Monstrum*, vol. 1, no. 1, 2018, pp. 3–57, www.monstrum-society.ca/uploads/4/1/7/5/41753139/romero_memorial_retrospective_-_monstrum_1.pdf.

Seligson, Tom. "George Romero: Revealing the Monsters within Us." *George A. Romero: Interviews*, edited by Tony Williams, Kindle ed., UP of Mississippi, 2011, pp. 74–87.

Sharrett, Christopher. "The Crazies" in 'The Death of Death': A Memorial Retrospective on George A. Romero (1940–2017)," edited by Kristopher Woofter. *Monstrum*, vol. 1, no. 1, 2018, pp. 3–57, www.monstrum-society.ca/uploads/4/1/7/5/41753139/romero_memorial_retrospective_-_monstrum_1.pdf.

———. "The Horror Film in Neoconservative Culture." *The Dread of Difference: Gender and the Horror Film*. 2nd ed., edited by Barry Keith Grant, U of Texas P, 2015, pp. 281–304.

Shklovskii, Viktor. "Art as Technique." *From Symbolism to Socialist Realism: A Reader*, edited by Irene Masing-Delic, Academic Studies Press, 2012, pp. 64–81.

Sikov, Ed. "Knightriders." *Cineaste*, vol. 11, no. 3, Autumn 1981, pp. 31–33. *JSTOR*, www.jstor.org/stable/41692483.

Skal, David J. *The Monster Show: A Cultural History of Horror*. Revised edition, Faber & Faber, Inc., 2001.

Smiley, CalvinJohn, and David Fakunle. "From 'Brute' to 'Thug': The Demonization and Criminalization of Unarmed Black Male Victims in America." *Journal of Human Behavior in the Social Environment*, vol. 26, nos. 3–4, 2016, pp. 350–366, https://doi.org/10.1080/10911359.2015.1129256.

Sobchack, Vivian. "Bringing It All Back Home: Family Economy and Generic Exchange." *The Dread of Difference: Gender and the Horror Film*, 2nd ed., edited by Barry Keith Grant, U of Texas P, 2015, pp. 171–191.

Sontag, Susan. *Regarding the Pain of Others*. Picador, 2003.

"The Sparrows are Flying Again: The Making of 'The Dark Half.'" Produced by Michael Felsher, Scream Factory and Red Shirt Pictures, 2014. *The Dark Half*, Shout! Factory. Blu-ray.

Stewart, Michael, *Monkey Shines*. Freundlich Books, 1983.

Studlar, Gaylyn. *This Mad Masquerade: Stardom and Masculinity in the Jazz Age*. Columbia UP, 1996.

Sutton, Travis. "Avenging the Body: Disability in the Horror Film." *A Companion to the Horror Film*, edited by Harry M. Benshoff, Wiley-Blackwell, 2014, pp. 73–89.

Suvin, Darko. *Metamorphoses of Science Fiction*. Yale UP, 1979.

Tales of Terror. Directed by Roger Corman, American International Pictures, 1962. Amazon Prime Video.

Taylor, Charles. "Little Bites of Horror." *New York Times*, 21 Nov. 2008, www.nytimes.com/2008/11/23/books/review/Taylor-t.html.

Taylor, Sue. *Hans Bellmer: The Anatomy of Anxiety*. Massachusetts Institute of Technology, 2000.

There's Always Vanilla. Directed by George A. Romero, The Latent Image, 1971. Blu-ray.

Todorov, Tzvetan. *Facing the Extreme: Moral Life in the Concentration Camps*. Translated by Arthur Denner and Abigail Pollak, Henry Holt and Co., 1996.

Tomb, Geoffrey. "Arts Festival Exhibit Has Gravity Pains." *Pittsburgh Post-Gazette*, 7 June 1969, p. 13, archives.post-gazette.com/.

———. "Heads Shake for Arts' Sake: Annual Arts Festival Opens Tomorrow." *Pittsburgh Post-Gazette*, 5 June 1969, p. 27, archives.post-gazette.com/.

Towlson, Jon. *Subversive Horror Cinema: Countercultural Messages of Films from Frankenstein to the Present*. McFarland, 2014.

Two Evil Eyes. Directed by George A. Romero and Dario Argento, ADC Gruppo Bema, 1991. Amazon Prime Video.

Uebel, Michael. "Unthinking the Monster: Twelfth-Century Responses to Saracen Alterity." *Monster Theory: Reading Culture*, edited by Jeffrey Jerome Cohen, Kindle ed., U of Minnesota P, 1996, loc. 5059–5658.

Waldby, Catherine. *AIDS and the Body Politic: Biomedicine and Sexual Difference*. Routledge, 1996.

Wiater, Stanley. "George A. Romero." *George A. Romero: Interviews*, edited by Tony Williams, Kindle ed., UP of Mississippi, 2011, pp. 111–121.

Williams, Linda. "The Inside-Out of Masculinity: David Cronenberg's

Visceral Pleasures." *The Body's Perilous Pleasures: Dangerous Desires and Contemporary Culture,* edited by Michele Aaron, Edinburgh UP, 1999, pp. 30–48.

———. "When the Woman Looks." *The Dread of Difference: Gender and the Horror Film.* 2nd ed., edited by Barry Keith Grant, U of Texas P, 2015, pp. 17–36.

Williams, Tony. *The Cinema of George A. Romero: Knight of the Living Dead.* Kindle ed., Wallflower Press, 2003.

———. *Hearths of Darkness: The Family in the American Horror Film, Updated Edition,* University Press of Mississippi, 2014. ProQuest Ebook Central, ebookcentral.proquest.com/lib/bcc-ebooks/detail.action?docID=3039942.

———. "An Interview with George and Christine Romero." *George A. Romero: Interviews,* edited by Tony Williams, Kindle ed., UP of Mississippi, 2011, pp. 134–150.

———. "Trying to Survive on the Darker Side: 1980s Family Horror." *The Dread of Difference: Gender and the Horror Film.* 2nd ed., edited by Barry Keith Grant, U of Texas P, 2015, pp. 192–208.

Wilmington, Michael. "Movie Review: 'Darkside a Clever Cut Above Horror Fare." *Los Angeles Times,* 7 May 1990, www.latimes.com/archives/la-xpm-1990-05-07-ca-68-story.html.

Winick, Mimi. "Modernist Feminist Witchcraft: Margaret Murray's Fantastic Scholarship and Sylvia Townsend Warner's Realist Fantasy." *Modernism/modernity,* vol. 22, no. 3, 2015, pp. 565–592.

W.I.T.C.H. "W.I.T.C.H. Manifesto (1968)." *Burn It Down!: Feminist Manifestos for the Revolution,* edited by Breanne Fahs, Verso, 2020, pp. 465–466.

Wood, Robin. "Apocalypse Now: Notes on the Living Dead." *Robin Wood on the Horror Film: Collected Essays and Reviews,* edited by Barry Keith Grant, Wayne State UP, 2108, pp. 161–170.

———. *Hollywood from Vietnam to Reagan... and Beyond.* Kindle ed., Columbia University Press, 2003.

———. "An Introduction to the American Horror Film." *Robin Wood on the Horror Film: Collected Essays and Reviews,* edited by Barry Keith Grant, Wayne State UP, 2018, pp. 73–110.

———. "Neglected Nightmares." *Robin Wood on the Horror Film: Collected Essays and Reviews,* edited by Barry Keith Grant, Wayne State UP, 2018, pp. 181–200.

Worland, Rick. *The Horror Film: An Introduction.* Blackwell, 2007.

Yakir, Dan. "Morning Becomes Romero." *George A. Romero: Interviews,* edited by Tony Williams, Kindle ed., UP of Mississippi, 2011, pp. 47–58.

Yolen, Jane. Introduction. *The Fantastic in Holocaust Literature and Film: Critical Perspectives,* edited by Judith B. Kerman and John Edgar Browning. McFarland, 1997.

Young, Elizabeth. "Here Comes the Bride: Wedding Gender and Race in *Bride of Frankenstein.*" *The Dead of Difference: Gender and the Horror Film,* 2nd ed., edited by Barry Keith Grant, U of Texas P, 2015, pp. 359–387.

Index

Aames, David (character) 201
Abagnalo, George 17
Abbott, Stacey 6, 67–68
abjection 9–10, 68–69; fluids of 68–69
able-bodiedness 132–47, 215*n*5
ableism 10, 14
abortion 19, 27, 29, 133, 138, 215*ch*1*n*1
"Absurd Reality II: Hollywood Goes to the Indians" (Jojola) 113
"Accumulating Extinction: Planetary Catastrophism in the Necrocene" (McBrian) 154
action movies 3, 133–34; tropes of 188–89
Agamben, Giorgio 51
ageism 15, 32, 38, 40–41, 46, 71–72, 75
Ahmed, Sara 16, 87–88, 99, 105, 109–10, 171, 176–78, 180, 184, 227*n*18
AIDS 14, 132, 141–47, 187, 224–25*n*2, 227*n*20; and emasculation 141–47
AIDS and the Body Politic (Waldby) 141–42
"AIDS as Monster in Science Fiction and Horror Cinema" (Guerrero) 134
Aikman, Linda (character) 135, 137–40, 146
alcoholism 67, 225*ch*9*n*3
Alda, Rutanya 180
Alice in Wonderland (Carroll) 229*n*4
Alien (1979) 141
Aliens (1986) 203, 208–9, 229*n*7
al-Samarai, Nicola Lauré 128
alter ego 9, 14–15, 163, 170–72; *see also* doppelgänger; doubles
Altered States (1980) 134, 144
Altvater, Elmar 158, 226*n*10
"Alumni, from Class of 1969 to 2018, Converge During Carnival" (Paul) 23
American Beauty (1999) 187
American colonial expansion 119–21
American Psycho (2000) 187, 228*n*2

American settler culture 113, 119–20, 210
American Zombie Gothic: The Rise and Fall (and Rise) of the Walking Dead in Popular Culture (Bishop) 125, 158
Americanisms: The English of the New World (Schele de Vere) 166
Amerson, Albert 80
Améry, Jean 50–51
Amplas, John 65, 71*fig*5, 196, 221–22*n*23
The Amusement Park (1973) 1, 11, 15, 33, 46, 71–72, 203–8, 212, 215*n*2, 215*ch*1*n*1, 219*ch*4*n*3, 229*nn*1–5
"And the Injun Goes 'How!': Representations of American Indian English in White Public Space" (Meek) 116–18
Anderson, Paul W.S. 203
anger 7, 15, 23, 28, 40–41, 90–92, 104–5, 131, 178, 186–202; white male 7, 15, 23, 28, 87–105, 109–10; 138, 178, 186–202; women's 40–41
animal cruelty 152–53, 225*ch*9*n*8
animal experimentation 135, 139, 143–46, 150, 154–55, 211
ankh 34–35, 34*fig*2, 35*fig*3, 217*n*3
anthology films 2, 13–14, 87–131, 148–69
Anthropocene or Capitalocene? (Moore) 154, 156, 158, 160, 226*ch*10*n*9
anti-consumerism 204, 213, 220*ch*5*n*5
The Anti-Drug Abuse Act of 1986 124
anti-futurity 183, 226*n*2
anti-militarism 53–57, 218*n*2
"Apocalypse Now: Notes on the Living Dead" (Wood) 7, 170, 219*n*10, 219*n*11
"Approaching Abjection" (Kristeva) 9–10
Archaeologies of the Future (Jameson) 149–50, 159
Argento, Dario 2, 225*ch*9*n*7, 226*n*11
Arkley Mansion 208, 210

241

Aronstein, Susan 75
"Art as Technique" (Shklovskii) 205
"Arthurian Film and the Tyranny of Tra-
    dition" (Lacy) 219*ch*5*n*2
Arthurian legend 2, 5, 13
"Arts Festival Exhibit Has Gravity Pains"
    (Tomb) 23, 216*n*6
Asher, Nina 128
Asian characters 198–99
At the Mind's Limits (Améry) 50–51
Athena 181, 227–28*n*24
athleticism 14, 137–39
Atkins, Tom 90
Atlantean Cross 35*fig*3, 217*n*3
audience surrogate 13, 90, 92–93, 102
Aunt Bedelia (character) *see* Grantham,
    Aunt Bedelia (character)
Auschwitz 49–50, 52; deep memory of
    50
"Avenging the Body" (Sutton) 10,
    225*ch*8*n*4

Bale, Christian 188
Barbeau, Adrienne 98, 101–2, 160
Barbra (character) 125
Bass, Nikki 223*n*7
Bateman, Patrick (character) 188, 198
Báthory, Erzsébet 38
Beaumont, Charles (character) 168
Beaumont, Liz (character) 170–71, 175–
    77, 227*n*14, 228*n*25, 228*n*30
Beaumont, Thad (character) 8, 14–15,
    163, 170–85, 213, 226*n*1, 226*n*5,
    227*nn*12–15, 227*n*19, 227*n*23, 228*n*25,
    228*n*30, 228*n*31
Beckett, Samuel 229*n*3
Beecroft, David 122
Beer, Daniel 128, 135
Bell, Book and Candle (1958) 38
The Bell Jar (Plath) 30
Ben (character) 64, 125–27, 196, 199; as
    monster 125–26
Benshoff, Harry 61, 144–45
Berlant, Lauren 15, 105–6, 108, 168–69,
    177, 184, 228*n*26
Bernardini 74
Bersani, Leo 172, 174, 181, 226*n*8
Bernsen, Corbin 188
Bickle, Travis (character) 192, 228*n*4
Biehn, Michael 209
Big Daddy (character) 126
bikers 72, 206, 229*n*4; *see also*
    motorcycles
Billie (character) *see* Northrup,
    [Wilma] Billie (character)
Billy (character) 11, 14, 89–94, 100, 102,

128, 130–31, 221*n*16, 224*n*24; *see also*
    King Billy (character)
Billy's father (character) 89–94, 106
Billy's mother (character) 91–92, 95, 131
Biohazard 2 229*n*9
bio-weapons 47–57, 208–11, 229*n*8
birds 158, 171, 173, 173*fig*11, 182–84,
    228*n*29, 228*n*30; *see also* sparrows
The Birds (1963) 182, 228*n*28
birth 9, 176–85, 223*n*38, 227*n*12, 227*n*19,
    227–28*n*24; asexual 176–85, 223*n*38,
    227*n*19, 227–28*n*24; as metaphor for
    writing 179, 227*n*12; queer 9, 15, 109,
    154, 158, 171, 174, 176–85, 223*n*38,
    226*n*1, 227*n*19
Bishop, Kyle William 125, 158
"The Black Cat" (Poe) 148, 151–53,
    225*ch*9*n*3, 225*ch*9*n*4, 225*ch*9*n*5,
    225*ch*9*n*6, 225*ch*9*n*7, 225*ch*9*n*8
Black characters 10–11, 13–14, 58–59,
    64, 68–69, 110, 112, 121–28, 199,
    207, 219*n*12, 219*ch*4*n*1; 219*ch*4*n*2,
    219*ch*4*n*3; absence in horror and
    mainstream films 124; racist stereo-
    types 10–11, 112, 121–28
The Black Knight (character) *see* Sir
    Morgan, the Black Knight (character)
Black Sunday (1960) 38
Blackford, James 47
Blacula (1972) 62
Blaine, Cass (character) 94, 96–97,
    221*n*18
Blaine, Hank (character) 94, 96
Blair, Linda 68
Blake, Linnie 224*n*14
Blanch, Robert J. 75–76, 80, 83–86
Blaxploitation horror 62
Blessebois, Pierre-Corneille 165–66
"Blissing Out: The Politics of Reaganite
    Entertainment" (Britton) 132
Bloch, Robert 226*n*13
Block 6
Blodgett, Esther (character) 106
Blodgett, Grandmother Lettie (charac-
    ter) 106
"The Blue-Tail Fly" (Emmett) *see*
    "Jimmy Crack Corn" (Emmett)
bodily control, loss of 14, 132–47
bodily difference, visual representations
    of 9–10, 132–47
bodily transformation 186–202,
    191*fig*12
body-as-site-of-contest films 186, 190,
    196
body horror 8, 14, 132–47, 186–202,
    228*n*1

body politics 132–47, 186–202
Bogdanovich, Peter 62
Bohlmann, Markus P. J. 173, 226–27*n*10
Bond, Lilian 61
Bontempi, Joe 76, 84
Boon, Kevin Alexander 160
Boorman, John 74
Botting, Fred 152
boundaries: blurred distinctions
    between 9–10, 15, 47–73, 164, 168;
    threat to the integrity of 124–25,
    224*n*19
bourgeoise 66, 88–88, 94, 108, 129, 156;
    obsession with cleanliness 108; patri-
    archal norms 66, 88–88, 94; privi-
    lege 129
Bovey, Alixe 220.*n*9
Braddock, Pennsylvania 65, 72
Bradley, Chris (character) 9, 11, 18–29,
    28*fig*1, 216*n*5, 216*n*7
Bradley, Roger (character) 11
Brain Damage (1988) 134
Brecht, Bertolt 150
Bride of Frankenstein (character) 61
Bride of Frankenstein (1935) 61, 144
Bride of Re-Animator (1989) 134, 144
"Bringing It All Back Home" (Sobchack)
    88, 93–96
Britton, Andrew 132
Bronson, Charles 189
Brown, Simon 87, 89, 93, 98, 101, 110–13,
    118, 120, 122, 128–30, 220*ch*6*n*5, 220–
    21*n*7, 221*n*15, 221*n*17, 221*n*20
Brown, Steve T. 215*n*7
Browning, Christopher 49–50
Browning, John Edgar 51–52
Browning, Mark 88, 91–92, 108, 172,
    177–78, 184
Browning, Robert 25
Bruce, Barbara S. 125, 127
"Bruiser" (Dodson) 202
Bruiser (2000) 1, 11, 15, 119, 129, 131,
    185–202, 204, 207, 228–29*nn*1–11;
    critical reception of 201–2; straight-
    to-video distribution of 186, 201
Brundle, Seth (character) 134, 144
Bub (character) 162, 211
Buday, Maroš 225*ch*9*n*3
Büken, Gülri 118
bullying/bullies 14, 89–105, 130–31,
    186, 193, 224*n*23
Burbage, Harold (character) 146
Burke, Kathleen 145
Burns, Marilyn 63
Burtram, Tom (character) 197–98
Butler, Rhett (character) 175

Cagney, James 60
Caliban and the Witch (Federici) 8,
    225*n*2
Cambist Films 217*n*1
Camelot, recreation of 13, 75–86,
    220*ch*5*n*6
Cameron, James 208
"Can Sex Make Us Happy?" (Bersani) 174
Canby, Vincent 47
cannibalism 162, 165, 221*n*19
Capital (Marx) 150
capitalism 2, 6–8, 11–22, 66, 74–87,
    105–9, 122, 148–60, 167, 188, 202–7,
    120, 224*n*14, 224*n*20, 225*n*1, 225*n*2,
    225*n*5, 225*n*8, 226*ch*9*n*9; alterna-
    tives 7, 13, 20, 73–86, 149; consumer 7,
    18–22, 152; critiques 14, 73–86, 106–
    9, 148–69, 204, 225*ch*9*n*8, 229*n*10;
    destruction 157; exploitation of work-
    ers 153, 203; ideology 66, 108; mon-
    strousness 148–69; patriarchal quality
    224*n*20; violence 87–110, 149–57
*Capitalism: A Conversation in Critical
    Theory* (Fraser and Jaeggi) 20, 79
Cardille, Lori 196
Carmichael (character) 167–68
Carpenter, John 58
Carrie (1976) 93–94, 221*n*16
Carrillo, Leo 116
Carroll, Lane 56, 65
Carroll, Lewis 229*n*3
Carter, Jimmy 63
"The Case of M. Valdemar" (*Tales of Ter-
    ror*) 167, 226*ch*9*n*9; 226*ch*9*n*10
Castle, Terry J. 179
Castonmeyer, Lenore (character) 109
castration 63, 173–75, 190, 201; anxiety
    38, 57–73, 104–7, 131, 134, 140, 173–
    76, 190, 223*n*11, 225*ch*8*n*3, 227*n*11
"The Cat from Hell" (King) 148, 153–
    58, 169
"Cat from Hell" (1990) 5, 7, 10, 14, 111,
    148–69, 211, 215*n*4, 225*n*3, 225*n*4,
    225*n*5, 225*n*6, 225*n*7, 225*n*8
Catholicism 12, 32–35, 42–43, 68, 70;
    loss of faith in 68; repressive gender
    roles 35, 70; *see also* Christianity
cats 10, 14, 148–69, 225*ch*9*n*6
Cat's Eye (King) 225*ch*9*n*6
Cavanaugh, Andy 116–17, 117*fig*8,
    223*n*6, 223*n*12
"The Celluloid Cubicle: Regressive Con-
    structions of Masculinity in 1990s
    Office Movies" (Hunter) 187
*Celluloid Vampires: Life After Death in
    the Modern World* (Abbott) 67–68

Chambers, Rebecca (character) 209
Chaney, Lon 201
Cheap Nature 154, 156–57, 159,
    226ch9n9
Chernov, Matthew 211
child abuse 13, 90, 92, 94
childhood innocence 173–75, 224n2,
    226n6, 226–27n10; see also childness
childhood sexuality 228n28
childness 173–74, 226n6, 226ch9n10,
    226n6, 226–27n10
children 11–14, 89–102, 128, 130–31,
    221n16, 224n24
Chiles, Lois 121
The Chimes at Midnight (1965) 155
chivalric code 75–80, 85
Christianity 13, 40, 59, 200; see also
    Catholicism
Christina (character) 65, 69–70, 72–73
Church the cat (character) 225ch9n6
cigar store Indian 13, 118, 223n13
Cimino, Michael 218n2
The Cinema of George A. Romero: Knight
    of the Living Dead (Williams) 1, 3, 20,
    23, 25, 32, 40, 45, 70, 75, 77–78, 80,
    83, 93–98, 101–2, 104, 106–7, 111, 122,
    126, 155–56, 161, 167, 170, 172, 184,
    202, 213, 215n1, 217n2, 218n3, 219n3,
    221nn10–12, 221n19, 222n25, 222n34,
    225n11, 226n5
The Cinema of Isolation (Norden) 147,
    225n11
The Cisco Kid (character) 116–17, 128
The Cisco Kid (1950–1956) 116–17,
    223n8, 223n10; color and black-and-
    white versions of 223n8
Civil Rights era 123, 126
civilization, destruction of 47–57
Clank (character) 55–56
Clark, Bob 62
Clark, Eugene 126
Clarke, Mae 60
class 7–8, 11–15, 31, 39, 46, 49, 68,
    89–108, 112, 121–25, 128–36, 169, 187–
    88, 196, 212, 217n11, 218n18, 219n3,
    224n16, 224n20, 227n22; intersection
    with race 219ch4n3, 224n16
classical horror 59–62, 68, 70
classism 8, 101–2, 121–28, 192, 196
Clawson, Fred (character) 11, 173,
    173fig11, 180, 227n22
Clive, Colin 60, 144
Clover, Carol J. 175, 195
cockroaches 90, 105–9
cognitive dissonance 51–52
cognitive estrangement 149–51

Cohen, Alexander H. 164
Cohen, Jeffrey Jerome 224n18
Coleman, Robin R. Means 10, 124–25,
    128
Colerider, Glenn 175
Collingwood, Estelle (character) 63
Collingwood, John (character) 63
colonialism 159, 209
comics see horror comics
communal living 74–86
communication beyond death 149,
    159–68
concentration camps 49–52, 54
Confessions of an English Opium-Eater
    (De Quincey) 26
conformity 22–24, 29, 35–37, 88, 202;
    as necessary for happiness 88; resis-
    tance to 36
Connell, Robert W. 14, 59, 110, 220n4
consciousness 16, 48, 50, 159–61; 163–
    65, 167, 184; survival of after death 163
"Construction of the Mythic Indian in
    Mainstream Media and the Demystifi-
    cation of the Stereotype by American
    Indian Artists" (Büken) 118
consumerism 3, 21–22, 80, 86, 156, 204,
    220ch5n5; as emasculating 80; see
    also anti-consumerism; capitalism,
    consumer
"Conversation with Leo Bersani with
    Tim Dean, Hal Foster, and Kaja Silver-
    man" (Bersani) 172
Cooper, Harry (character) 64
Cooper, Karen (character) 64
Corman, Roger 167–68
Correia, David 126
counterculture 17–24, 31, 73–86, 133,
    197
Cowley, Miriam (character) 180
Cowley, Rick (character) 175, 180
Crampton, Barbara 144
"The Crate" (Creepshow) 9–10, 89–90,
    97–105, 129, 222n26
"The Crate" (King) 89
Craven, Wes 58, 63
The Crazies (1973) 12, 30, 47–57, 55fig4,
    65, 68, 156, 170, 204, 210–12, 214, 216–
    17n1, 218–19nn1–12, 229n2; critical
    reception of 47; similarity to Night of
    the Living Dead 219n12
creativity 15, 170–85, 226n1, 227n21;
    and birth 179; see also reproduction,
    asexual; reproduction, queer
"Creativity and the Childbirth Meta-
    phor" (Friedman) 17, 226n1, 227n21
Creed, Barbara 164, 195

Creedlow, Henry (character) 7, 10, 15, 186–202, 191*fig*12
Creedlow, Janine (character) 191–93, 195, 197
The Creep (character) 92, 224*n*24
Creepshow (1982) 1, 9, 11, 13–14, 87- 110, 107*fig*7, 112, 124, 126, 135, 155, 220–23*nn*1–38, 224*n*24, 228*n*7
Creepshow (2019–) 221*n*8
Creepshow (Brown) 87, 89, 93, 98, 101, 110–13, 118, 120, 122, 128–30, 215*n*7, 220*ch*6*n*5, 220–21*n*7, 221*n*15, 221*n*17, 221*n*20
Creepshow comics 91, 112, 130–31, 224*n*24
Creepshow 2 (1987) 2, 5, 7–8, 10–11, 13, 93, 110–31, 135, 209, 222*n*28, 223–24*nn*1–24; critical reception 111
Cronenberg, David 134, 222*n*28
Crowe, Cameron 201
Cruel Optimism (Berlant) 15, 105–6, 108, 168–69
Cruise, Tom 210
Cruz, Marie V. 198
cryptids 214
Cuda, Tateh (character) 13, 65–66, 69–73, 71*fig*5, 221–22*n*23
"Cultural Confusion: *Broken Arrow* (1950)" (Manchel) 223*n*8
Cutrone, Ronnie 17, 20

Dano, Royal 181
Danson, Ted 98
Danvers, Mrs. (character, *Creepshow*) 97, 222*n*24
Danvers, Mrs. (character, *Rebecca*) 222*n*24
"Dark Desires: Male Masochism in the Horror Film" (Creed) 195
Dark Directions (Phillips) 56, 65, 139, 178, 183, 185–86, 190–91
The Dark Half (King) 14, 158
The Dark Half (1993) 5–6, 8–9, 11, 14, 158, 163, 169, 170–86, 172*fig*11, 190–91, 213, 223*n*38, 226–28*nn*1–31; critical reception of 170; deleted scenes 227*n*14
David (character) 65
Davies, Jude 189
Dawn of the Dead (1978) 1–2, 5, 7, 17, 54, 58, 86, 112, 119, 156, 161, 163, 170, 203–4, 213, 215*n*1.Pref, 216–17*n*1, 221*n*19, 229*n*4
Day of the Dead (1985) 2, 5, 54, 58, 112, 135, 161, 166, 170, 196, 211, 215*n*1.Pref, 219*n*4, 221*n*19

Days and Memory (Delbo) 50, 219*n*9
Dead Blonds and Bad Mothers (Doyle) 30, 32, 37, 45, 46, 217*n*8
"The Dead Don't Die!" (Bloch) 226*n*13
Dead films (Romero) 1–3, 5, 7, 10–11, 16–17, 20, 47, 49, 54–55, 58–59, 64, 86, 90, 100, 112, 119, 125–27, 135, 149, 156, 159, 161–63, 166, 170, 196, 199, 202–4, 209, 211, 213, 215*n*1.Pref, 216*n*7, 216–17*n*1, 219*n*12, 219*n*1, 219*n*2, 221*n*19, 222*n*30, 226*n*1, 229*n*3, 229*n*10
The Death of Death (2004–2005) 299*n*11
Deathdream (1974) 62
De Cicco, Mark 226*n*3
Decolonizing the Lens of Power (Knopf) 114–15, 117, 210, 215*n*6
The Deer Hunter (1978) 218*n*2
dehumanization 47–57
Deke (character) 128–29, 131
Delbo, Charlotte 50, 219*n*9
Delesseps, Reggie (character) 176, 183, 228*n*27
DeMille, Cecil B. 115
De Niro, Robert 192
The Dentist (1932) 100
The Dentist (1996) 187–88
De Palma, Brian 62
Depression Era 59
De Quincey, Thomas 26
Derrida, Jacques 48, 218*n*5
Desire After Dark (Owens) 31
Desrocher-Romero, Suzanne 204
Diamant, Naomi 49, 52
Diary of the Dead (2007) 100, 202, 215*n*1.Pref, 216*n*7
différance 48, 218*n*5
direct-to-camera address 18, 24–29, 28*fig*1
disability 10, 131–47, 225*ch*8*n*4, 225*n*11; anxieties about 131; and masculinity 135
disabled bodies, representations of 10, 131–47, 225*ch*8*n*4, 225*n*11; as asexual 10; as sexual 225*ch*8*n*4; as site of fear 14
discrimination, racial 121–28
Disney World 108–9
divine right 76–78
Dodson, Will 202
domestic life as threat to creativity 15, 171, 178
domestic possessiveness motif 89–90, 98–99, 221*n*19
domestic violence 13, 41, 90–105, 152, 218*n*14, 221*nn*16–19, 221–22*n*23, 222*n*26, 222*n*27, 222*n*29, 222*n*35,

222n36; *see also* child abuse; spousal abuse
Donovan 218n12
doppelgänger 14–15, 163, 169–70, 172, 174, 186, 215n7, 227n19; *see also* alter ego
Dorian, Michael (character) 21, 29, 216n4
doubles 33, 50, 172–86, 206, 226n2; association with death 226n2; *see also* alter egos; doppelgängers
Douglas, Melvyn 61
Douglas, Michael 188
Doyle, Sady 30, 32, 37, 45, 46, 217n8
Dracula (1931) 59–61, 70
Dracula (character) 59–60, 67
The Dread of Difference (Grant) 9
dreams 22, 31–36, 42, 126, 139, 217n2; *see also* nightmares
Drogan (character) 7, 10, 14, 148, 154, 156–57, 215n4, 225n8, 226n10
The Drowned and the Saved (Levi) 12, 48, 50, 218n4
drug use 85, 141, 143, 146
duality 170–85
Dudgeon, Elspeth 62
Dugan, John 63
Duke Beer 216n3
Dumas, Raechel 100
du Maurier, Daphne 222n24
Duvall, Robert 188
Dyer, Richard 199–200
dysfluent speech 116–17, 223n9
dystopia/dystopian genre 98, 149–50, 159

Eastwood, Clint 189
EC Comics 13, 89, 100, 111, 128, 220ch6n5, 221n15, 223n10; moral codes 111
Edelman, Lee 94, 172, 177, 183–84, 228n26, 228n28
Eisner, Breck 218n1
elderly characters 59–65, 69–73, 204–7, 229n2, 229n3
elderly, marginalization of 204–7, 229n9
Elizabeth (character) 60
Ella (character) 9–10, 135–47, 178, 182, 186, 190, 223n38, 225n10, 227n17
emasculation 14, 58–73, 102–5, 132–34, 137–43, 175–76, 186–202, 191*fig*12, 215n4, 221n18, 222–23n37, 223n38, 224n1, 225ch8n3; bodily 132–24; economic 14, 59; national 67; *see also* castration anxiety
embodiment, destabilization of 149, 160, 164, 168

Emmett, Daniel Decatur 223n4
emotional detachment 26, 109; as a sign of maturity 109
empathy 56, 89, 109, 157, 193, 222n35; absence of 89, 109
Empire of the Dead (2014–2015) 229n11
epidemic 47, 54–57, 65, 141–47
epistemology 12, 49, 52, 55, 149–51
Erdrich, Louise 118
Excalibur (1971) 74
The Exorcist (1973) 68

facelessness 55, 128, 165, 186–202, 207
Facing the Extreme (Todorov) 50
"The Facts in the Case of Mr. Valdemar" (*Two Evil Eyes*) 7, 9–11, 14, 149–51, 158–69, 220ch6n6, 221n9, 224n15, 224n16, 225ch9n7, 226n13
"The Facts in the Case of Mr. Valdemar" (Poe) 14, 149–51, 158–69, 209, 226nn11–14; connection to zombies 226n11, 226n13
Fakunle, David 127
Falling Down (1993) 187–90, 197, 228n3; satirical elements in 189
Fallows, Tom 2, 6, 17, 20, 102, 170, 216n3, 216–17n1, 217n7, 226n11
Fantastic in Holocaust Literature and Film (Kerman) 51–52
father role/fatherhood 12, 19–20, 39, 41, 61–65, 89–99, 105–9, 132–38, 172–78, 184, 189, 221n8, 221n14, 222n28; absent 106–8, 137–38; abusive and controlling 12, 90–97, 135; "gentle father" 138, 172, 174–78, 184, 189; father figures 106–7, 132; substitute 221n8
"Father's Day" (*Creepshow*) 7, 9, 89–98, 121, 221n21
Federici, Sylvia 8, 87, 91, 108, 164, 225n2, 225ch9n5
Feinstone, Alan (character) 188
female sexuality 12, 40–42, 102, 140
"feminazi" 187
The Feminine Mystique (Friedan) 12, 30–46, 217n5
feminism 30–46, 62, 91, 103, 110, 187, 194, 217n5, 219n11; second wave 30–46, 62, 91, 103, 110, 217n5, 219n11; third wave 187, 194, 219n11
femininity, normative 21–22, 30–46, 66, 90, 95, 152, 220n4; hierarchies within 220n4; punishment for lack of adherence to 90, 99–105, 139–40, 222n26; rejection of 30–46, 90, 101–2

Femm, Horace (character) 62
Femm, Rebecca (character) 62
Femm, Roderick (character) 62–63
Femm, Saul (character) 62
Ferraro, Martin 76
feudal power structures 74–86
Field, Chelsea 180
Fields, W.C. 100
Fight Club (1999) 187–88, 194
"The Film That Never Was: Why George Romero's 'Resident Evil' Failed to Launch" (Chernov) 211
"final girl" character 195–96, 228*n*6
firebird (mythical creature) 116, 223*n*7
"The Firebird Legend" (Bass) 223*n*7
Firth, Rhiannon 149
Fisher, Geoffrey (character) 135, 137–40, 142, 144–46
Fisher, Mark 8
Fisher, Neil 32, 217*n*2
Flemyng, Jason 186, 191*fig*12
Ford, Gerald R. 63
Forrest, Christina 65, 103, 137
Forrest, Frederic 189
Foster, William "D-FENS" (character) 188–89, 198, 228*n*3
"The Four Stages of Cruelty" (Hogarth) 152
Fox, Samantha 223*n*10
Frankenstein (1931) 60–61, 144
Frankenstein, Baron (character) 61
Frankenstein, Henry (character) 60–62, 144
Frankenstein monster (character) 60–61, 67, 145
Frankl, Viktor 50
Frantz, Adrienne 212
Fraser, Nancy 20, 76
Freud, Sigmund 12, 30–47, 137, 174, 225*n*11, 227*n*11
Friday the 13th series 119
Friedan, Betty 12, 30–46, 217*n*5
Friedman, John Block 228*n*30
Friedman, Susan Stafford 179–80, 227*n*21
Friend, Craig Thompson 175
From Beyond (1986) 134, 144
"From 'Brute' to 'Thug': The Demonization and Criminalization of Unarmed Black Male Victims in America" (Smiley and Fakunle) 127
"From Southern Manhood to Southern Masculinities" (Friend) 175
Fry, Esther (character) 137
Frye, Dwight 60–61
Fryers, Mark 204

Fuller, John 33
futurity, reproductive 179, 183; *see also* anti-futurity

Gale, David 144
Gamache, Homer (character) 175, 180, 226*n*6, 227*n*20
Ganja & Hess (1973) 62
Garbiras, Nina 191–92
"Gay Betrayals" (Bersani) 226*n*8
Gaynor, Janet 106
gender 2–3, 6, 8–9, 12, 15, 21–22, 30–46, 58–73, 79, 85, 88–89, 94–110, 125, 132–47, 182, 187–204, 209, 212, 220*n*4; normativity 8, 30–110, 204; restrictive gender roles 21–22, 30–46, 94–110, 132; role reversal 101–5; transgressive representations of 30–46, 58–73, 97–105; 132–47; *see also* femininity, normative; masculinity
Gender and the Nuclear Family in Twenty-First-Century Horror (Jackson) 88, 220*n*3
gendered violence 97–105
"generic shock" 151–53, 159
genre film's ability to address serious concerns 6–7
"George A. Romero" (Wiater) 5–6
George A. Romero Archival Collection 214, 229*n*6
George A. Romero Foundation 203, 214
"George Romero: From *Night of the Living Dead* to *The Crazies*" (Lebowitz, et. al.) 17, 20
"George Romero: Revealing the Monsters within Us" (Seligson) 7
"George Romero Says Nobody Will Finance His Next Zombie Movie and 'Night of the Living Dead' Wouldn't Get Made Today" (Kohn) 204, 213
George A. Romero's Independent Cinema (Fallows) 2
"George Romero's 'Knightriders': A Contemporary Arthurian Romance" (Blanch) 75–76, 80, 83–86
Ghodsee, Kristen R. 160
The Ghost of One's Self (Meehan) 172, 174, 182, 226*n*2, 226*n*4, 227*n*19, 227*n*23
ghosts 105–8, 160–66; zombies as a form of 160–66
ghouls 1, 5, 58, 159, 211, 219*n*2
Gilens, Martin 123–24
Gilligan, Carol 8–9, 26, 88–90, 96–100, 102, 109–10
Glelberman, Owen 155

Godard, Jean-Luc 18
Goldblum, Jeff 134
Goldhagen, Daniel 49
Goldhagen's hypothesis 218*n*7
Goldstein, Jenette 208
Gomel, Elana 149
good-evil binary, erosion of 50, 52, 62, 65–66
Goodbye, Columbus (Peerce) 17
Gornick, Michael 112
Gothic (Botting) 152
Gothic genre 7, 36, 64, 152–56, 174, 217*n*6, 226*n*7; horror cinema, references to 68; as queer 226*n*7; suburban 36
government conspiracy 47–57
The Graduate (1967) 17, 42
Graebner, William 48, 54
Grant, Barry Keith 9
Grantham, Aunt Bedelia (character) 9, 94–97, 110, 121, 221*n*17, 221*n*22
Grantham, Nathan (character) 94–97, 106, 121, 221*n*19, 221*n*22, 221–22*n*23
Grantham, Richard (character) 94–97
Grantham, Sylvia (character) 94, 97, 221*n*18
gray zone 12, 48–50, 96
Great Dismal Swamp 223*n*7
The Great Migration 123
greed 7, 110, 112, 120–21, 150, 155, 166, 204, 210–12; capitalist 166, 210–12
Green, Jeremy 129
Greenwald, Virginia 32
Gribbens, Fatso (character) 116–17, 223*n*10
Grosz, Elizabeth 10
Guerrero, Edward 134
Guess Who's Going to Be Dinner: Sidney Poitier, Black Militancy, and the Ambivalence of Race in Romero's *Night of the Living Dead*" (Bruce) 125, 127
guilt 7, 27, 148, 152–53
Gunn, Bill 62

Hackett, Pat 17, 20
hair 114–15, 223*n*11
Haiti 162, 166–67; association with cannibalism 162
Halloween series 119
Halsey, Megan (character) 144
Halston (character) 14, 148, 153–54, 156–57
Hamilton, Marion (character) 32, 38–39, 42, 44
Hand, Richard J. 1
Hangsaman (Jackson) 30

Hannah, Page 129
Hans Bellmer: The Anatomy of Anxiety (Taylor) 227*n*11
Hansen, Regina 224*n*15
happiness 87–88, 99, 103, 105, 110, 177, 184; maintenance of other's happiness 103; as regulatory norm 177, 184
Hard, Robin 181, 227–28*n*24
Hard Bodies (Jeffords) 133
hard bodies/soft bodies dichotomy 132–47
Hardman, Karl 64
Harker, John (character) 60–61
Harrington, Richard 155
Harris, Ed 74, 82, 92, 94–95
Harris, Julie 176
Harris, Lynn (character) 11–12, 17–29, 216*n*5
Harrison, John 155
Hart, Adam 214
Harvey, Don 116
Hearths of Darkness: The Family in the American Horror Film, Updated Edition (Williams) 5, 87–89, 95, 220*n*1, 220*n*2
Heffernan, Kevin 219*ch*4*n*1
"Hegemonic Masculinity: Rethinking the Concept" (Connell and Messerschmidt) 14, 59, 110, 220*ch*6*n*4
Hellbound: Hellraiser II (1988) 134
Hellraiser (1987) 134
Hera 227–28*n*24
"Here Comes the Bride" (Young) 61
Herman, Judith Lewis 50
Hessel, Lee 217*n*1
heteronormativity 9–10, 13–14, 59–73, 87–110, 132, 169–85, 226*n*3; challenges to 9, 169–85
heterosexual-homosexual binaries 66, 142
Hickey, William 155–56
Hicks, Corporal (character) 209
Hill, Dr. Carl (character) 144
Hill, Joe 90–91, 94–95
Hills, Matt 91–92, 150–51, 165, 168, 213, 221*n*13
Hinckley, John, Jr. 228*n*4
Hinzman, Bill 217*n*2
Historical Dictionary of Gothic Literature (Hughes) 174, 228*n*7, 228*n*8
Hixon, Ken 76
Hitchcock, Alfred 58, 182, 222*n*24
Hitch-hiker (character) 121–28, 224*n*16, 224*n*19
"The Hitch-hiker" (*Creepshow* 2) 7, 11, 13, 112, 121–28, 224*nn*15–20

Hitler's Willing Executioners (Goldhagen) 49
Hoagie Man (character) 84
Hodges, Maryanne 137
Hoffman, Gwen 95, 97, 107, 221*n*16, 222*n*26
Hoffman, Dr. Robert (character) 9, 159–68, 162*fig*10
Hoffmann, E.T.A. 155, 227*n*19
Hogarth, William 152, 225*ch*9*n*8
Holbrook, David 116
Holbrook, Hal 98, 101
Hollar, Lloyd 211
Hollywood from Vietnam to Reagan (Wood) 87–88, 108
"Hollywood Injun English" 116
Holocaust 12, 48–57, 218*n*6, 218–19*n*8, 219*n*9; significance of in Romero's films 48
Holocaust Literature (Roskies and Diamant) 49, 52
Holt, Digger (character) 181
home invasion 42, 44, 67, 217*n*9
homophobia 67, 141–47, 179, 196, 225*ch*8*n*9
homosexuality 141–47; and homosociality 144
Hooper, Tobe 58, 63
Hope, Leslie 192
"Horrific 'In-betweenness': Spatial and Temporal Displacement and British Society in 1970s Children's Supernatural Television" (Fryers) 204
horror comics 1, 13–14, 89–93, 99–12, 128, 130–35, 220*n*5, 221*n*10, 221*n*11, 221*n*14, 223*n*10, 229*n*11; critique of 89–92, 99, 221*n*10, 221*n*11; defense of 89, 99, 222*n*28 128
The Horror Film (Worland) 66–67
horror genre 2–3, 6–15, 19, 30–73, 87–167, 203–5, 208–14, 2155*ch*1*n*1, 220*nn*1–3, 221*n*11, 221*n*13, 221*n*14, 224*n*22, 225*n*11, 227*n*19; conventions of 205–8; punishment of women 19, 187–194–95; tropes of 204, 215*ch*1*n*1
Horror Noire (Coleman) 10, 124–25, 128
housewife role, rejection of 12, 30–46, 67, 217*n*5; *see also* wife role
"How the Poor Became Black" (Gilens) 123–24
Howard, Father (character) 70
Hughes, William 174, 228*n*7, 228*n*8
humanism, critique of 47–57
Hungry Wives marketed as soft-core pornography 217*n*1; *see also Jack's Wife*

Hunter, Latham 187
husband role 13, 31–46, 65, 89–105, 170–77, 217*n*9, 222*n*27, 224
Huson, Paul 217*n*8
Hutchings, Peter 66, 196
Hutton, Timothy 170, 186
hybridization of genres 205, 209–12
Hyde, Mr. (character) 169, 171–72, 226*n*3
hypersexuality 134, 179; connected to AIDS and homosexuality 134
hypnotism *see* mesmerism

I Am Legend (Matheson) 5, 158
I Spit on Your Grave (1978) 62
id 139–40, 190, 193, 195
"'I'm the Bad Guy?' *Falling Down* and White Masculinity in 1990s Hollywood" (Davies) 189
Imagic Moments: Indigenous North American Film (Schweninger) 215*n*6
imperialism 159, 200
impotence 103–4, 137, 140; *see also* virility
In the Company of Men (1997) 187
The Indian (character) 80, 83
"indigenous" 223*n*1
indigenous actors 13, 113, 223*n*3; erasure from cinema 113
indigenous characters 10–11, 13–14, 112–21, 209–10, 215*n*6, 223*n*3; invisibility of 223*n*3; played by indigenous people 13, 113; played by non-indigenous people 112–19; *see also* vanishing Indian trope
indigenous peoples 13, 112–21, 210, 215*n*6; 223*n*1, 223*n*3, 223*n*11, 223–23*n*13, 224*n*14, 225*ch*9*n*6, 226*ch*9*n*9; displacement and dispossession of 119–21; representations of 10–11, 13–14, 113–21, 210, 215*n*6, 223*n*11; stereotypes of 113–21, 210, 215*n*6, 223*n*11, 223–24*n*13
indigenous speech, Hollywood representations of 116–17, 223*n*5
infected vs. uninfected binary 12, 48, 53, 55–56, 58, 64, 145, 165, 211, 219*n*10, 224–25*n*2
Ingersoll, Amy 75
"Inner-City Exhibition and the Genre Film: Distributing *Night of the Living Dead* (1968)" (Heffernan) 219*ch*4*n*1
"The Inside-Out of Masculinity: David Cronenberg's Visceral Pleasures" (Williams) 134
intersectionality 11, 121–28, 187, 206–7

intertextuality 151–52, 161, 182, 210–12, 221*n*10
"Intolerable Ambiguity" (Grosz) 10
"Introduction: Holy Terrors and Other Musings on Monstrous-Childness" (Bohlmann and Moreland) 173, 226–27*n*10
"Invasion of the Monstrous Others" (Redman) 143
invisibility 186–202, 206
The Invisible Man (2020) 222*n*27
Iron City Asskickers (1998) 229*n*11
"Is the Rectum a Grave?" (Bersani) 181
Island of Lost Souls (1933) 144–45
isolation 105–9
IT (King) 224*n*15
It Came from the Archives! (Rubin and Hart) 214

Jacaranda Joe 214
Jacklight (Erdrich) 118
Jack's Wife (1973) 1, 3, 7, 9, 12, 30–46, 34*fig*2, 48, 64, 156, 196, 202, 205, 207, 217–19*nn*1–14; parts cut from theatrical release 34–35, 40–41; theatrical release 34, 34*fig*2
Jackson, Kimberly 88, 220*n*3
Jackson, Shirley 30
Jacob's Ladder (1990) 187
Jaeggi, Rahel 20, 76
Jameson, Fredric 149–50, 159
Jampol, Noah Simon 47–57, 148–69
Japanese Horror and the Transnational Cinema of Sensations (Brown) 215*n*7
jealousy 10, 89–90, 95, 98–105, 110, 132–47
Jefferson, Thomas 127
Jeffords, Susan 133
Jekyll, Dr. (character) 169, 171–2, 226*n*3
Jesus Christ 200
"Jimmy Crack Corn" (Emmett) 223*n*4
Johansen, David 155–56
John, Domenick 130
Jojola, Ted 113
Jones, Duane 64, 125, 196
Jones, Jim 78
jousting 9, 13, 74–86, 135
Joy, Robert 173
Judas Iscariot figure 200
Judy (character) 56, 65
Just After Sunset (King) 153
justice 89–90, 94, 108, 119, 128, 148, 152–53, 157

Kamin, Dan 118
Karloff, Boris 60–61, 64, 145

"Karlovy Vary Interview: George Romero Talks Modern Zombies, Ripping Off Orson Welles, and More" (Kiang) 204
Karras, Father Damien (character) 68
Kendi, Ibram X. 123–24, 127, 224*n*17
Kennedy, George 112
Kennedy, Leon (character) 212
Kiang, Jessica 204
Kincaid, James R. 173
"'The Kind of People Who Make Good Americans': Nationalism and Life's Family Ideal" (Kozol) 221*n*9
King, Joe *see* Hill, Joe
King, Stephen 14, 84, 87–89, 105, 107*fig*7, 125, 148, 153–58, 169, 220–21*n*7, 221*n*16, 224*n*15, 225*5ch*9*n*3, 225*ch*9*n*6, 225*ch*9*n*8, 228*n*7; appearances in films 84, 105–9, 228*n*7; scripts written by 87
King Billy (character) 13, 74–86, 92, 94–95, 100, 102
King Kong (character) 77
Knightriders (1981) 5, 7, 9, 11, 13, 74–86, 81*fig*6, 92, 95, 102, 112, 118, 135, 214, 219–20*nn*1–9, 220*n*4, 221*n*10
"Knightriders" (Sikov) 75–77, 82–82, 219*ch*5*n*3
Knopf, Kerstin 114–15, 117, 210, 215*n*6
Kohn, Eric 204, 213
Kordas, Ann 166
Kosar, Scott 218*n*1
Kozol, Wendy 221*n*9
Kraus, Daniel 229*n*11
Kristeva, Julia 9–10

"Lab'ring Birds" (Castle) 179
Lacy, Norris J. 219*ch*5*n*2
Lahti, Gary 79
Laine, Ray 18, 28*fig*1, 40
Lamour, Dorothy 113, 117*fig*8
Lanchester, Elsa 61
Land of the Dead (2005) 2, 126, 202, 211, 215*n*1.Pref
Langer, Lawrence 50, 52, 218–19*n*8, 219*n*9
Lansing, Annie (character) 7–8, 121–28, 130, 224*n*16, 224*n*20
Lansing, George (character) 122, 127–28
Larson, James (Jimmy) (character) 193, 200
The Last House on the Left (1972) 63–64
latent Image 20, 28*fig*1, 34*fig*2, 216*n*3
Latinx characters 11, 191–92, 195, 208–9
Laughton, Charles 62, 144
Lauro, Sarah Juliet 159, 162, 165–68
Laverne (character) 129–30, 224*n*21

Leatherface (character) 134
Lebowitz, Fran 17, 20
Legendre, Murder (character) 168
Leninger, Philip 223n4
Lent 42–43, 218n14
Levi, Primo 12, 48, 50, 218n4
Levin, Ira 36–37, 217n5
Lewis, Herschell Gordon 58
life vs. death dichotomy 54, 163, 168
Limbaugh, Rush 187
Lindfors, Viveca 94
literary fiction 170, 178–80, 184, 227n22
The Living Dead (Romero and Kraus) 229n11
"The Living Dead of George Romero and Steven Spielberg" (Graebner) 48, 54–55
Living with Zombies: Society in Apocalypse in Film (Pielak and Cohen) 164
"The Lonesome Death of Jordy Verrill" (*Creepshow*) 89–90, 93, 105–10, 220–21n7, 221n8, 228n7
"The Lonesome Death of Jordy Verrill" (King) 89, 220–21n7
Lord Tennyson, Alfred 25
Lormer, Jon 94
Loss of Confidence (Robertson) 63
Lota the Panther Woman (character) 145
love, sacrifice of 8, 90–91, 97–101
Lovecraft, H.P. 226n14
"low" genre fiction 170–71, 179, 227n22
Lowell, Robert 27
lower-class 108, 141, 227n22; *see also* working class
Luckhurst, Roger 158, 163
Lugosi, Bela 59, 159
The Lutheran Service Society 1, 15, 204
lynching imagery 199, 201

Maazel, Lincoln 65, 71–72, 71fig5, 205, 229n1
Machine, Alexis (character) 173, 182, 228n31
MacNeil, Regan (character) 78
mad scientist archetype 144–46, 155
Madigan, Amy 170
"Madonna" figure 140, 225ch8n7
The Magic Island (Seabrook) 166
The Magnificent Ambersons (1942) 155
Magoulick, Mary 118
male bodies 14, 132–47, 136fig9, 201, 225ch8n5; objectification of 14, 132–47, 136fig9, 225ch8n5
male bonding 197–98

male gaze 11–12, 29, 59–60, 67, 112, 136, 198, 228n6
male inadequacy *see* emasculation
male privilege 185–202
male sexuality 98–105, 132–47
Manchel, Frank 223n8
Mann, Allan (character) 10, 14, 135–47, 136fig9, 178, 182, 190, 207, 223n38, 225ch8n5, 225ch8n6, 225ch8n7, 225n10, 227n17
Mann, Dorothy (character) 136–37, 140
Mann, Jock (character) 138
Manners, David 60
Manson, Charles 78
Manson family 62
Mardirosian, Tom 175
marital infidelity 9, 41, 67, 98–105, 160–61, 186, 188, 190–93, 195, 217n9
marketing 20–22
marriage 8, 30–46, 61, 67, 87–110, 122–23, 160–61, 166, 174, 196, 244n16; absence of as dangerous 105–10; as business transaction 122–23, 160–61, 166; hostility towards 105–9; as proprietary ownership 98–105, 161; rejection of 90, 105–9; as stifling 30–46, 87–105, 122; violence as inherent to 87–110; women's financial security linked to 122–23, 160–61, 224n16
Marshall, E.G. 105
Martin (character) 7, 58–73, 70fig5, 196
Martin (1978) 2, 7, 13, 58–73, 70fig5, 100, 112, 156, 196, 214, 219ch4n1, 219ch4n2, 219ch4n3, 219ch4n4, 221–22n3, 225n11, 229n4
Martinique 166
Marx, Karl 150
Masculin Féminin (Godard) 18
masking 186–202
masochistic pleasure 194–97
mass violence and death 49–57
masculine-feminine binaries 140, 142, 145; blurring of lines between 62, 66
masculinity, hegemonic 6, 8, 12, 14–15, 17–29, 58–73, 79–81, 88, 96, 102, 106, 110, 112, 131–48, 155–56, 158, 170–202, 217n9, 220ch6n3, 220ch6n4, 222–23n37, 223n11, 227n13; challenges to 58–73, 131, 135, 174; changing conceptions of 62–65, 88; family-oriented 178–84, 189; hyper-masculinity 9, 14–15, 106, 132, 171, 175–76, 179; lack of 190–202, 222–23n37; loss of 136–47; and monstrosity 58–110, 158; qualities antithetical to 59–62, 68, 87–109, 131–41; qualities of 26, 59, 68, 87–110,

222n37; stoic 109, 133–34, 139. 194, 210, 223n11; subordination of women 59, 69–70, 89–105, 132, 135, 139–41, 146, 190, 217n9; and violence 59–60, 131, 135, 170, 173–202; *see also* emasculation; toxic masculinity
Mastering Witchcraft (Huson) 217n8
materialism 75–78, 192; equated with financial stability 77
Matheson, Richard 5, 158–59, 167–15, 26, 58–73, 80–81, 88, 96, 102, 106, 110, 112, 131–47, 155, 158, 167, 170–72, 175–76, 179–80, 185, 187–202, 223n11, 227n13
McBrien, Justin 154
McCallany, Holt 113, 117fig8
McClain, Joedda 35
McDonagh, Maitland 204, 229n4
McHale, Brian 53
McMillan, Will 65
McNally, David 150–51
McNeil, Alex 223n8
McNeil, Kate 140
"Me, Myself and I" (Patterson) 27
medical experimentation 48, 54, 65, 143–46, 160, 208–11; *see also* animal experimentation
Medievalisms (Pugh and Weisl) 75–76, 78, 80–82, 85, 220n5
Meehan, Paul 172, 174, 182, 226n2, 226n4, 227n19, 227n23
Meek, Barbra A. 116–18
Men, Women, and Chainsaws (Clover) 175, 195
Merlin (character) 82
mesmerism 60, 148, 159, 160–61, 165, 167
Messer, Peter 95
Messerschmidt, James W. 14, 59, 110, 220n4
Metamorphoses of Science Fiction (Suvin) 148–49
middle class 30–46, 49, 95, 217n11
military 47, 53–57, 63, 65, 68, 208–10, 218n7, 218n12; as a male-driven organ of hegemony 56–57, 65, 209
militias 55, 65
Miller, Cain 58–73, 132–47, 186–202
Miller, Jason 68
Mina (character) 60
Minotaur 217n9
minstrelsy 113, 223n4
Misery (1990) 187
misogyny 186–202
Mississippi 175
Mitchell, Jack (character) 31, 33–34, 36, 41–46, 216–17n12, 216–17n14, 218n12

Mitchell, Joan (character) 7–8, 12, 30–46, 65, 196, 207, 217n9, 218n12, 218n14
Mitchell, Nikki (character) 32, 35, 41–42
mob violence 61, 68, 199
"Model Kid" (*Creepshow* 2021) 221n9
Monahan, Jeff 197
monarchy 74–86
Monkey Shines (1988) 9–10, 14, 131–47, 136fig9, 155, 170, 178, 182, 185–86, 190–91, 207, 223n38, 224–251–11
Monkey Shines (Stewart) 135, 137, 146
monkeys 2, 9–10, 132–47, 155, 223n38
monogamy 66, 98; enforcement of 98
monologue 18, 25–29, 166, 192, 197; dramatic 18, 25–26; in poetry vs. drama 25–26
"Monster Culture (Seven Theses)" (Cohen) 224n18
The Monstrous-Feminine: Film, Feminism, Psychoanalysis (Creed) 164
The Monstrous Races in Medieval Art and Thought (Friedman) 228n30
The Monster Show (Skal) 19, 145–46, 228n12
monsters 6–7, 10, 14, 37, 60–67, 87, 90–98, 103–5, 125–26, 128, 120–31, 135, 143–45, 155, 164, 194, 206, 209, 228n30; AIDS carriers as monsters 143–45; definition of 128–29; identification with 90, 126; in plain sight 130; sympathetic 66–67
Monsters in the Closet (Benshoff) 61, 144–45
Monsters of the Market (McNally) 150–51
The Monstrous-Feminine in Contemporary Japanese Popular Culture (Dumas) 100
Monty Python and the Holy Grail (1975) 76
Moore, Eva 62
Moore, Jason W. 154, 156, 158, 160, 226ch9n9
Moral Majority values 132
"'More Than Human': The Queer Occult Explorer of the Fin-De-Siècle" (De Cicco) 226n3
Moreau, Dr. (character) 144
Moreland, Sean 173, 226–27n10
Morgan le Fay 75
"Morning Becomes Romero" (Yakir) 53, 158–59
Le Morte d'Arthur 74
mother role/motherhood 27–28, 30, 35, 175, 180

motorcycles 9, 13, 74, 76, 79, 84, 114, 138, 223*n*10; accidents 138; gangs 114; *see also* bikers
Moynihan, Daniel P. 123
Muffly, Ann 39, 109
Multidirectional Memory (Rothberg) 56
Mulvey, Laura 59, 136
murder 12, 64, 73, 90, 94–105, 111–31, 139, 146, 150, 152, 155–56, 161, 165, 174–80, 195, 198–99, 223*n*12, 225*ch*9*n*8, 228*n*30
murdered pet trope 152–54
Murphy, Bernice M. 36–37, 45
Murray, Margaret 37
Muselmänner 48, 54, 218*n*4
My Lai Massacre 218*n*3
"My Last Duchess" (Browning) 25
Myers, Michael (character) 119, 134
myths 38, 77, 83, 159, 165

Nadeau, Elayne 67
Nadja (1994) 6
narcissism 24–26, 112, 181, 185–202, 228*n*4
narcissistic pleasure 193–97, 228*n*4
"Narrating the Child's Queerness in *What Maisie Knew*" (Ohi) 174
narrative control 11–12, 17–86, 216*n*7
nature/natural world 171, 182, 154, 156–59, 210, 226*ch*9*n*9, 226*ch*9*n*10; and capital 154, 156, 226*ch*9*n*9, 226*ch*9*n*10; degradation of 154, 156–59, 226*n*10; and the feminine 142; and indigenous peoples 114, 210; *see also* Cheap Nature
Nazis 47–52, 218*n*3; imagery 218*n*3; *see also* neo–Nazis
"Neglected Nightmares" (Wood) 156
The Negro Family (Moynihan) 123–24
neoconservatism 73, 132–47, 187
neo-Nazis 189
neopagan practices and beliefs 37, 39, 217*n*9
Nero, Tom (character) 152
Neville, Robert (character) 158
"New South, New Immigrants, New Women, New" (Kordas) 166
Newgate Calendars 26
Newitz, Annalee 10
Newley, Rosemary (character) 192–93, 195–96, 198, 200, 228*n*5, 228*n*6
Nicotero, Sam 17
Nielsen, Leslie 98
Night of the Living Dead (1968) 1–3, 5, 10–11, 16, 20, 47, 49, 54–55, 58–59, 64, 90, 125, 127, 149, 156, 159, 162–63, 170, 196, 199, 203, 209, 211, 213, 215*Pref. n*1, 219*n*12, 219*n*1, 219*n*2, 221*n*19, 222*n*30, 226*n*1; commercial success of 58; critical reception of 47; racial subtext of 58–59; similarities to *The Crazies* 219*n*12
Night of the Living Dead (1990) 1, 215*n*1. Pref
"*Night of the Living Dead*—Interview with George A. Romero" (Ork and Abagnolo) 17
nightmares 42–45, 141, 181, 217*n*2, 217*n*9, 224*n*8, 225*n*8, 228*n*25; *see also* dreams
1960s horror 30–31, 36–37, 62, 146
1970s horror 1, 13, 30–73, 62–63, 89, 93, 146
1980s 73–75, 87–147, 155, 220*n*2, 225*n*9; excesses of 155; Hollywood cinema 132; horror 14, 87–147, 220*n*2; media 225*n*9
1990s 187–192
Nixon, Richard 63, 124, 221*n*22
No Future: Queer Theory and the Death Drive (Edelman) 94, 172, 183–84, 228*n*28
non-sovereignty 177, 181
non-white characters 8, 10–11, 13–14, 58–59, 64, 68–69, 110, 112, 121–28, 188, 191–92, 195, 198–201, 207–9, 219*n*12, 219*ch*4*n*1, 219*ch*4*n*2, 219*ch*4*n*3
Norden, Martin F. 147, 225*n*11
Northrup, [Wilma] Billie (character). 9, 101–5, 110, 222*n*26, 222*n*32, 222*n*36
Northrup, Henry (character) 101–5, 221*n*18, 222*n*34
nostalgia 13, 74–86, 116–18, 122, 131, 133, 223*n*10, 224*n*15
Notes on the State of Virginia (Jefferson) 127
novum 148–49, 159
nuclear family 6, 8–9, 13–15, 61, 64–66, 72, 75, 87–110, 123–24, 134–35, 137, 143, 170–85, 204, 213, 220*n*2, 221*n*9, 221*n*11, 221*n*18, 221*n*19, 221*n*20, 226*n*5, 226*ch*10*n*9, 229*n*5; hierarchies generated and reinforced by 8, 89–110; patriarchal 8, 59–62, 87–110, 170; psychopathology of 87–110; queering of 60–62; reproductive 90, 108–9; as site of horror 87–110; violence in 87–110, 204, 221*n*9, 221*n*11, 221*n*12, 221*n*14, 221*nn*16–20, 221*n*22, 222*nn*27–31

Number 9 (character) 198–99, 228*n*9, 228*n*10
Nye, Carrie 94

objectification of women 18–22, 97, 198
Odawa tribe 116
O'Dea, Judith 125
Office Space (1999) 187
Ohi, Kevin 174
O'Kelly, Tim 64
"Old Chief Wood'nhead" 13, 112–20, 128, 209, 223–24*nn*2–14, 224*n*23
Old Chief Wood'nhead (character) 113, 223*n*10, 223*n*12, 223–23*n*13
The Old Dark House (1932) 61–62
Oliver, Kelly 157
O'Malley, Bingo 106, 159
The Once and Future King (White) 74
ontological shock 151–52, 155, 159
ontology 12, 53, 55
Ordinary Men (Browning) 49–50
Orion Studios 136*fig*9, 146, 173*fig*11, 225*ch*8*n*8
Ork, William Terry 17
Orlok, Byron (character) 64, 70
Others 9–11, 58–73, 87–105, 113–30, 132, 144–45, 159–62, 165, 181, 186–202, 225*n*11, 228*n*26, 228*n*30; disabled 225*n*11; female 9–10, 87–105, 144–45, 195; non–American 199; non-heteronormative 59–60, 66–73, 132; non-human 10, 144–45; non-white 10–11, 58–69, 113–30, 188, 191, 195; racialized 61, 68–69, 113–28, 199; urban 124–25; white males 186–202; working class 68–69, 125
Owen, Curtis 102, 170, 226*n*11
Owens, Andrew J. 31

Pan 217*n*8
Pancho (character) 116–17, 128, 223*n*9
Pangborn, Sheriff Alan (character) 180, 182, 226*n*5, 227*n*20
Pangborn, Annie (character) 180
Pankow, John 135
panopticon, home as 222*n*27, 222*n*28; *see also* surveillance
Parenti, Christian 154
parents/parenting 89–97
Parker, Melanie (character) 10, 140–41, 146, 178
Parks, Richard 122
Pasiphae 217*n*9
patriarchy 6, 8–9, 11–13, 17, 26, 30–110, 122, 132, 171, 179–80, 221*n*16, 221*n*18; critique of 12, 17, 30–110, 221*n*16;

hierarchies generated and reinforced by 8, 73–89; violence perpetuated by 87–110, 186–202, 221*n*16
Patterson, Christina 27
Paul, Jacob 23, 216*n*6
peasants 59, 220*n*9; *see also* serfs
"Peasants and Their Role in Rural Life" (Bovey) 220*n*9
Peckem, Colonel 56, 211–12
"pecker" 173–74, 173*fig*11
Penderel, Roger (character) 61–62
Penthouse Forum letters 26
Perkins, Barbara 223*n*4
Perkins, George B. 223*n*4
Perkins, Gladys (character) 61–62
perpetrator vs. victim distinction 12, 48–49, 66–67, 94
personhood 50, 110, 128, 168
the perverse 14, 148, 152–54, 158
Pet Sematary (King) 225*ch*9*n*6
Peters, Ken 33, 217*n*2
phallic power 134–36
phallic weapons 174–76, 194
phallocentrism 132–47
The Phantom of the Opera (1925) 201, 228*n*12
pharmaceuticals 150, 154–56, 226*n*10
Phillips, Kendall R. 56, 65, 139, 178, 182, 185–86, 190–91
Pielak, Chase 164
Piesche, Peggy 128
Pinedo, Isabel 62
Pitcairn-Crabbe Foundation 204
Pippin (character) 9, 76, 82
Pittsburgh, Pennsylvania 3, 18–20, 23, 28, 42, 47, 137, 160, 214
Pizano, Beatriz 191
Plains Indians 113–14
Plath, Sylvia 26, 30
Plato 179, 227*n*19
"playing Indian" 112–20, 128
The Pleasures of Horror (Hills) 91–92, 150–51, 165, 168, 213, 221*n*13
Pluto the cat (character) 153, 225*ch*9*n*4
The Pocket Essential George A. Romero (Fallows and Owen) 102, 170, 226*n*11
Poe, Edgar Allan 14, 148, 152, 154–55, 159, 163–64, 169, 225*ch*9*n*8, 226*n*12, 226*n*13, 227*n*17, 227*n*19
Police: A Field Guide (Correia and Wall) 126
police brutality 62, 64–65, 68
Pollin, Burton R. 153
Pontiac Firebird 116–17, 117*fig*8
"Porphyria's Lover" (Browning) 25–26
Porterhouse, William (character) 62

possession 160–61, 165, 167
posthumanism 3, 6, 49–50, 54, 157
postmodern horror 12, 18, 49, 52–53, 59–64, 66
Postmodernist Fiction (McHale) 53
post–World War I era 201
Potchikoo stories 118
poverty/the poor 7–9, 65–66, 105–10, 114, 121–28, 188, 205–7, 224*n*16; racialized images of 114, 122–26, 188, 206; rural 105–10
Powell, Michael 58
Pratt, Upson (character) 7, 90, 105, 108–10, 222*n*28
Preempting the Holocaust (Langer) 50, 52, 218–19*n*8, 219*n*9
pregnancy 17, 19–20, 29, 35, 65, 138, 179–80; as metaphor for writing 179; parody of 180–82, 227–28*n*24
Prendergast, Martin (character) 188–89
Presley, Elvis 227*n*23
Pretorius, Dr. (character) 61
Price, Vincent 167
"problem with no name" 12, 30–46
"Producing Erotic Children" (Kincaid) 173
The Promise of Happiness (Ahmed) 16, 87–88, 99, 105, 109–10
pseudo-vampires 58–73, 145–46, 221–22*n*23
Psycho (1960) 88
psychopomps 171, 182–84, 226*n*2
psychosexual stages of development 137–39
Pugh, Tison 75–76, 78, 80–82, 85, 220*ch*5*n*5
Punch (character) 9
punishment 90, 101, 109, 134, 152–53, 158, 187, 197, 225*ch*9*n*4

quadriplegia 10, 132, 135, 137, 141, 225*ch*8*n*4
Queen Linet (character) 75, 77–78, 83
queer-coded characters 59–62, 65–73, 132–47
queerness 9, 14–15, 60–62, 132–47, 170–85, 225*ch*8*n*5, 225*n*10, 226*n*3, 226*n*8

Raccoon City 210–11
race 2–3, 6, 8, 10, 13, 88, 110–31, 138, 187–202, 209–10; 213, 219*ch*4*n*3, 224*n*16; essentialist notions of 197; intersection with class 219*ch*84*n*3, 224*n*16; relationship to language 191
Rachel (character) 129

racism 8, 10–11, 13–14, 49–50, 62, 64, 75, 110–202, 219*ch*4*n*2, 224*n*17
"The Raft" (*Creepshow* 2) 14, 112, 128–31, 135, 224*n*21, 224*n*22
Raheja, Michelle H. 113–14, 116, 119–20, 215*n*6, 223*n*2, 223*n*3, 223–24*n*13
Randolph, Shirley (character) 39–41
Randy (character) 128–31, 135
rape *see* sexual assault
Raymond, Tabitha (character) 103, 222*n*32
Reagan, Ronald 13, 85, 112, 124, 133, 224*n*14, 224*n*1, 228*n*4
Reagan-era 75, 85, 132
realism 48, 58, 150–51
reanimated corpses 9–10, 14, 54, 94, 101, 148–49, 159, 161–62, 165–66, 221–22*n*23; *see also* zombies
Re-Animator (1985) 134, 144
Rebecca (du Maurier) 222*n*24
Rebecca (1940) 222*n*24
Recreational Terror (Pinedo) 62
redfacing 113–14
Redfield, Chris (character) 209–12
Redfield, Claire 212
Redman, Peter 143
Regan, Elizabeth 94
Regarding the Pain of Others (Sontag) 207
relationship (experience of connecting) 89–90, 96–99, 107–9
relationships (appearance of connection) 89, 99, 109
Remnants of Auschwitz (Agamben) 51
Renaissance Faire culture 2, 84–85, 220*n*8
Renaldo, Duncan 116
Renfield (character) 60
Renfro, Brad 212
Renn, Max (character) 134
repetition, pleasures of 151–52
representation, impossibilities of 50–51
repressed desires: return of 90 94–95, 125, 150, 162, 172, 184, 186–202
reproduction 6, 8–9, 14–15, 60–61, 88, 90, 95, 105–10, 141, 144–45, 154, 169–85, 200, 227*n*20, 227*n*28*n*24; asexual 9, 15, 154, 171, 179–80, 184, 200, 227–28*n*24; heterosexual 176; non-heteronormative 9, 15, 60–61, 69–85, 90, 105–9, 141, 144–45; queer 15, 144–45, 171–85, 227*n*20; writing as 171, 178–82; *see also* birth; family, nuclear
Resident Evil (never-produced video game script) 1, 11, 15, 203, 208–12, 229*n*7

Resident Evil 2 211
responsibility, avoidance of 121–28
Return of the Living Dead series 163
revenge 1, 14, 38, 45, 63, 89–90, 93–95,
98–100, 112–13, 119, 121, 126, 128–131,
139–40, 148, 152–57, 161, 177–78, 186–
202, 222*n*31, 225*ch*9*n*8, 227–28*n*24
The Revolting Child in Horror Cinema
(Scahill) 95, 224*n*22
Revolution at Point Zero (Federici) 91,
108
Reynolds, Carl (character) 108
Ricci, Richard 21
Richards, Leah 17–29, 30–46, 74–86
Riley, Michael J. 223–24*n*13
Ripley, Ellen (character) 208–9
roaches *see* cockroaches
Robertson, David Brain 63
Robin Hood stories 219*ch*5*n*1
Robinson, Beth 124
Robinson, Kim Stanley 150
Robinson, Mrs. (character) 42
Robson, May 106
Rodriguez, Rosie (character) 208–9
Romero, George A.: adaptations of Ste-
phen King's work 87–110, 155–58,
170–85; appearances in his own films
70; commercials made by 20, 214,
216*n*3, 219*n*10; screenplays written by
47, 148, 156, 186, 203, 208; struggles
to find commercial success 202, 212;
unrealized projects of 214
"Romero: An Interview with the Direc-
tor of *Night of the Living Dead*" (Nic-
otero) 17
Rooker, Michael 226*n*5
Root, Stephen 146
Rosemary's Baby (1968) 42
Rosenthal, Mack 27
Roskies, David 49, 52
Ross, Gaylen 98
Rossetti, Christina 25
Rothberg, Michael 56
Rousset, David 218*n*6
Routledge Handbook of Greek Mythology
(Hard) 181, 227–28*n*24
Rubin, Ben 85
Rubin, Rachel Lee 84–85
Rush, Benjamin 127
The Rush Limbaugh Show 228*n*8
Russell, Sharon 30, 38, 45
Russo, John A. 216*n*3
Rye, Stellan 227*n*19

sadism 97–105, 193–97
Saldano, Katie (character) 191–92, 195

Sally (character) 63
Salsedo, Frank 113
Samson and Delilah (1949) 115
Santini, Mrs. (character) 67, 69–70
Saraceni, Ivy Jean 91
Sarah (character) 196
Satan figure 30, 200
Satterfield, Paul 128
Savini, Tom 75, 81*fig*6, 92, 161, 221*n*14
Sawyer, Grandpa (character) 63–64
Scahill, Andrew 95, 224*n*22
scalping 114, 118, 223*n*11
Scanners (1981) 225*ch*8*n*3
Schele de Vere, M. 166
Schiff, Marty 92
Schon, Kyra 64
Schumacher, Joel 188
Schweninger, Lee 215*n*6
science fiction 47, 52–53, 148–49;
hybridization with horror 144
Seabrook, William 166
Season of the Witch see *Jack' Wife*
"Season of the Witch" (Donovan)
218*n*12
Sederholm, Carl H. 163, 226*n*14
selfishness 121–28, 130
Seligson, Tom 7
serfs 220*n*9
Sex, or the Unbearable (Berlant and
Edelman) 177, 184, 228*n*26
sexism 8, 17–29, 75, 129, 135, 186–202,
209; *see also* misogyny
sexual assault 42, 65, 112, 129–30, 135,
144, 173–74, 173*fig*11
sexual objectification 18–22, 132–47
sexual penetration 60, 125, 137, 140–43,
146; men's fears of 143
sexual revolution 19, 31, 35, 41–42, 85
sexuality 6, 9–10, 12, 19, 66, 85, 89–110,
133–47, 170–85, 187, 216–17*n*1, 217*n*9,
228*n*28; alternative models of 85; devi-
ant 140–42; as reproductive 66, 90
Sharrett, Christopher 218*n*7
The Shining (King) 225*ch*9*n*3
Shklovskii, Victor 205
Shook, Warner 76, 94
Short Parker, Madeline (character) 168
Showalter, Elaine 226*n*3
Shudder 204
sidekick characters 116–17, 128, 144–45
Sikov, Ed 75–77, 82–82, 219*ch*5*n*3
silencing of women 89–105
silent film era 18, 223*n*3, 223–14*n*13
Sir Alan (character) 79–80
Sir Morgan, the Black Knight (character)
75, 77, 79–84, 81*fig*6, 220*ch*5*n*4, 220*n*9

Skal, David J. 19, 145–46, 228*n*12
slasher (characters) 119, 133–34, 139–40, 195
slasher genre 133–34, 175, 187, 194–95; conventions of 194; punishment of women in 187, 194–95
Smiley, CalvinJohn 127
Sobchack, Vivian 88, 93–96
Society (1989) 134, 188
socially regressive films 186–202
sociopolitical commentary 15, 128–68, 203–4, 209, 213
soldiers 48, 54–55, 55*fig*4, 63, 133, 135, 208–10, 218*n*3, 229*n*7; *see also* military
"Something to Tide You Over" (*Creepshow*) 7, 89–90, 93, 95, 97–105
Sontag, Susan 207
sparrows 158, 171, 173, 173*fig*11, 182–84, 228*n*29, 228*n*30
spectatorship 6, 11, 15, 59, 112, 139–40, 185, 187, 193–98, 220*n*1; dual 193–97; male 15, 59, 136, 139–40, 185, 193–98; narcissistic 187, 194
Spontaneous Combustion (1990) 134, 187
spousal abuse 13, 97–98
Spruce, Martha 113–14, 119–21, 117*fig*8, 223*n*2
Spruce, Ray 112–21, 223*n*2, 223*n*4, 224*n*14
Stamped from the Beginning (Kendi) 123–24, 127, 224*n*17
Stan (character) 90–91, 93, 221*n*11, 222*n*29
The Stand (King) 220–21*n*7
Stanley, Dexter (character) 101–5, 222*n*34
A Star Is Born (1937) 105–6
Stark, George (character) 9, 11, 14–15, 158, 163, 170–86, 190, 223*n*38, 226*n*5, 226*n*6, 227*nn*12–15, 227*n*20, 227*n*22, 228*n*25, 228*nn*29–31
"Step Right Up!" (McDonagh) 204, 229*n*4
The Stepford Wives (Levin) 36–37, 217*n*5
Stephen King on the Big Screen (Browning) 88, 91–92, 108, 172, 177–78, 184
"Stephen King's Fiction and the Heritage of Poe" (Pollin) 153
"Stephen King's *IT* and *Dreamcatcher* on Screen: Hegemonic White Masculinity and Nostalgia for Underdog Boyhood" (King) 224*n*15
Steve (character) 78, 220*ch*5*n*6
Stevenson, Robert Louis 171–72
Stewart, Michael 135, 137, 146

Stormare, Peter 192, 228*n*11
The Strange Case of Dr. Jekyll and Mr. Hyde (Stevenson) 171–72
Streiner, Judith 18
Streiner, Russell 216*n*3
The Student of Prague (1913) 227*n*19
Studlar, Gaylyn 201
Styles, Miles (Milo) (character) 192–96, 198–200, 228*n*5
The Suburban Gothic in American Popular Culture (Murphy) 36–37, 45
suburban horror 36–37, 45, 121–31, 221*n*11
suburbia 12, 14, 18, 30–33, 36–37, 39–41, 45, 51, 84, 91, 112, 122, 124–26, 129–31, 135, 156, 180, 217*n*5, 221*n*11
Subversive Horror Cinema (Towlson) 188
suicide 67, 73, 108–9, 138, 158, 197, 200, 228*n*7; fantasies of 197, 200; staged 189
superego 139–40, 195
surveillance 67, 89–90, 98–100, 212, 218*n*12, 222*n*27, 222*n*28; and horrific spectacle 99–100
Survival of the Dead (2009) 202, 211, 215*n*1.Pref
Sutton, Travis 10, 225*ch*8*n*4
Suvin, Darko 148–49
Symposium (Plato) 179

"Taking Back the Night: Dracula's Daughter in New York" (Abbott) 6, 89, 93
Tales from the Darkside (1983–1988) 228*n*11
Tales from the Darkside: The Movie (1990) 111, 148, 155–56, 225*ch*9*n*7; critical reception of 155
Tales of Terror (1962) 167
Tarbet, Andrew 193
Targets (1968) 62, 64, 70
Tasker, Yvonne 187
Taxi Driver (1976) 192, 194
Taylor, Charles 153
Taylor, Linda 124
Taylor, Sue 227*n*11
Tenney, Del 162
The Texas Chain Saw Massacre (1974) 63
There's Always Vanilla (1971) 1–2, 5, 7, 9, 11, 17–29, 28*fig*1, 74, 150, 203, 209, 215*ch*1*n*1–216*n*7, 216–17*n*1, 217*n*1; release on home media 17
Thesiger, Ernest 61
"They're Creeping Up on You" 89–90, 95, 105–9

The Thing (1982) 134, 224–25n2
Thinner (1996) 187
This Mad Masquerade: Stardom and Masculinity in the Jazz Age (Studlar) 201
Thompson, Bobby (character) 64
Three Rivers Arts Festival 23, 216n6
Thunhurst, Bill 31
The Time Machine (Wells) 52
Todorov, Tzvetan 50
Tomb, Geoffrey 23, 216n6
torture 50–51, 188, 225n8
Total Television (McNeil) 223n8
Towers, Richard 63
Towlson, Jon 188
toxic masculinity 80–81, 187–202; *see also* masculinity, hegemonic
"Trailing the Zombie Through Modern and Contemporary Anglophone Literature" (Boon) 160
The Transatlantic Zombie (Lauro) 159, 162, 165–68
"Trapped in the History of Film: Racial Conflict and Allure in *The Vanishing American*" (Riley) 223–24n13
trash culture, pleasures of 91–92
Trauma and Recovery (Herman) 50
"Trickster Lives in Erdrich" (Magoulick) 118
Trixie virus 47, 54–57, 65
Tucci, Stanley 136
Turner, Janine 135
Twilight Zone: The Movie (1983) 111
twins 15, 171, 176–77, 180–81, 226n4, 227n23
Two Evil Eyes (1990) 2, 148, 162fig10, 225ch9n7
"Two Evil Eyes: 'The Facts in the Case of Mr. Valdemar'" (Sederholm) 163, 226n14
tyrants 76–83, 91–93

Uebel, Michael 224n16
The Ultimate Machine (ΣAE) 18, 22–25, 29, 216n5, 216n6
the uncanny 151, 181–82, 225n11
unconscious mind 31–34
"The Undead: A Haunted Whiteness" (Newitz) 10
United States Senate Subcommittee on Juvenile Delinquency 93
"Unthinking the Monster: Twelfth-Century Responses to Saracen Alterity" (Uebel) 224n16
upper class 59, 121, 136–37, 166, 192, 196

Valdemar, Ernest (character) 9, 149, 159–68, 220ch6n6, 221n9, 226n13
Valdemar, Helene (character) 167–68
Valdemar, Jessica (character) 160–61–68, 224n16
Valentine, Jill (character) 208–9
vampire narratives 6, 12–13, 59–73; *see also* pseudo-vampire narratives
vampires 65–73, 145; men with AIDS compared to 145
Van Helsing, Professor (character) 12–13, 59–62, 65; deconstruction of 12–13; masculinity of 60
Vanilla Sky (2001) 201
The Vanishing Family: Crisis in Black America (CBS) 124
vanishing Indian trope 120, 223n3
Van Patten, Joyce 137
Van Sloan, Edward 59
Vasquez, Private (character) 208
Verrill, Jordy (character) 7, 89, 93, 103, 105–10, 107fig7, 222n28, 222n29, 228n7
Vickers, Becky (character) 98–101, 110, 222n26
Vickers, Richard (character) 98–105, 222n28
victim vs. perpetrator distinction *see* perpetrator vs. victim distinction
video games 1, 14, 203–4, 208–12
Videodrome (1983) 134, 222n28
Vietnam War 53–55, 62–63, 65, 218n2, 218n3, 229n7; protestors 65; veterans of 65
vigilantes 65, 68, 186–202; and whiteness 190–93
Virgin Mary 200
virginity 35, 41, 195, 200
virility 144, 146, 198; *see also* impotence
"Visual Pleasure and Narrative Cinema" (Mulvey) 59, 136
voodoo doll 93, 224n24
Voorhees, Jason (character) 119, 133–34

Waiting for Godot (Beckett) 229n3
Waldby, Catherine 141–42
The Walking Dead (2010–2022) 162, 204
Wall, Tyler 126
Watergate scandal 63
Wayne, John 60
wealth 7–8, 25, 60, 99, 107, 113, 120, 137, 154, 156–57, 160–61, 166, 210, 224n20
Weaver, Fritz 101–2
Weaver, Sigourney 208
"Weeds" (King) 220–21n7
The Weird and the Eerie (Fisher) 8

Weisl, Jane 75–76, 78, 80–82, 85, 220*ch5n*5
welfare/public assistance, dependance on 112, 122–24
"welfare queen" 112, 123
Well Met: Renaissance Faires and the American Counterculture (Rubin) 84–85
Wells, H.G. 52
Wentworth, Harry (character) 98–101
Wesker, Albert (character) 208–10
Western genre 3, 113–20, 131, 189, 223*n*2, 223*n*8, 223*n*10, 224*n*14, 224*n*23
Weyland-Yutani Corporation 229*n*8
Whale, James 60
Whanell, Leigh 222*n*26
"White" (Dyer) 199–200
White, Carrie (character) 93–94, 221*n*16
White, Jan 30
White, Mr. (character) 110
White, T.H. 74
white male feelings of victimization 15, 186–202, 228*n*8
white male fragility 193
white male victimization media 186–202 186–202, 228*n*8
white male unity 197–98, 201
white privilege 9, 13, 110–31, 172, 185–202
White Zombie (1932) 159, 167–68
Whitemoon, Ben (character) 113–15, 118–21, 223*n*2, 224*n*14, 224*n*24
Whitemoon, Sam (character) 113–21, 117*fig*8, 130, 223*n*11, 223–24*n*13, 223–24*n*13, 224*n*23
whiteness 10–11, 105, 124–29, 186–202; and imperialism 200–1; and monstrosity 199; as default racial subject 10–11, 128–29, 197, 200; construction of 124–25, 186–202;
"whore" figure 140, 195
Why Does Patriarchy Persist? (Gilligan and Snider) 9, 88–90, 96–100, 102, 109–10
Why Women Have Better Sex Under Socialism: And Other Arguments for Economic Independence (Ghodsee) 160
Wiater, Stanley 5–6
wife role 8, 20–46, 87–105, 109, 180, 224*n*16; *see also* housewife role
Wiggins, Tudi 137
willful subjects 171, 177–78
Willful Subjects (Ahmed) 171, 176–78, 180, 184, 227*n*18
"William Wilson" (Poe) 227*n*19

Williams, Linda 134
Williams, Tony 1, 3, 5, 12, 17, 20, 23–25, 32, 40, 45, 70, 75, 77–78, 80, 83, 87–89, 93–96, 98, 101, 104, 106–7, 111, 122, 126, 155–56, 161, 167–70, 172, 184, 202, 213, 215*n*1, 217*n*2, 218*n*3, 219*n*3, 220*n*1, 220*n*2, 221*nn*10–12, 221*n*17, 221*n*19, 222*n*25, 222*n*34, 225*n*8, 225*n*5
Williamson, Gregg (character) 9, 40–42, 44–45, 218*n*11
Willis, Brember 62
Wilmington, Michael 155
Winick, Mimi 217*n*6
The Winter Soldier investigation 218*n*3
Wiseman, Dr. John (character) 136–37, 139, 146
"The Witch in Film: Myth and Reality" (Russell) 30, 38, 45
witchcraft 12, 30–46, 217*n*8, 217*n*9, 218*n*12; feminist potential of 38–41; as a retreat for non-conforming women 39–40
witches 12, 30–46, 216*n*9, 218*n*12; cinematic 38–39
Witches, Witch-Hunting, and Women (Federici) 87, 164, 225*ch9n*5
women as property 87–110
women's agency 12, 14, 30–46, 91
Women's International Terrorist Conspiracy from Hell (W.I.T.C.H.) Manifesto 30, 40
women's liberation *see* feminism
women's subordination 8, 11–12, 30–46, 59, 70, 87–105, 135, 140; resistance to 70, 140
Wood, Robin 7, 12, 66, 87–88, 108, 156, 159, 170, 219*n*10, 219*n*11
Woods, James 134
working class 49, 105–9, 121–28, 188, 228*n*7, 229*n*11
Worland, Rick 66–67
The Wounds of Nations: Horror Cinema, Historical Trauma, and National Identity (Blake) 224*n*14
Wright, Ray 218*n*1
Wright, Tom 121
writer/writing 170–85

Yakir, Dan 53, 158–59
Yarbro, Peter (character) 95, 221*n*18
Young, Elizabeth 61
Yunza, Brian 188
yuppies 180, 227*n*22

Zada, Ramy 159, 162*fig*10
Zeus 181, 227–28*n*24

Ziegler, John 87–110, 111–31, 148–69,
170–85
Le Zombi du Grand Perou (Blessebois)
165–66
"zombie" 166
zombie masters 168, 226*n*13
zombies/zombie genre 1–3, 5–9, 14–16,
48, 54, 58, 86, 97–98, 121–22, 125–26,
135, 148–49, 150–52, 158–63, 165–70,
199, 202--13, 224*n*19, 226*n*11, 226*n*13;
anti-capitalist 8, 14, 148–49, 159; and
colonialism 159; as ghosts 160–66;
humans behavior as similar to 64;
Romero's Rules 14–15, 149, 155, 162,
168, 211; rooted in Afro-Caribbean
mythologies 5, 14, 149, 159–63, 165–
68, 226*n*13; as soulless 160–67; *see
also* reanimated corpses
Zombies: A Cultural History (Luckhurst)
158, 163
"Zombie: *The Girl with All the Gifts*"
(Gomel) 149